ISBN 978-1-331-98042-1
PIBN 10007305

LADY GRISELL BAILLIE,

AGED 69.

(*From a Portrait at Mellerstain, probably by Maria Verelst.*)

THE

EHOLD BOOK OF
GRISELL BAILLIE

1692-1733

, with Notes and Introduction, by

RT SCOTT-MONCRIEFF, W.S.

EDINBURGH

University Press by T. and A. Constable

the Scottish History Society

1911

HOUSEHOLD BOOK OF LADY GRISELL BAILLIE

1692-1733

Edited, with Notes and Introduction, by

ROBERT SCOTT-MONCRIEFF, W.S.

EDINBURGH

Printed at the University Press by T. and A. Constable

for the Scottish History Society

1911

CONTENTS

LIST OF ILLUSTRATIONS

INTRODUCTION

This volume forms one of a series of publications issued by the Scottish History Society dealing with household expenditure during the seventeenth and eighteenth centuries, and goes far to fill the hiatus in years between the Foulis Book [1] and the Ochtertyre Book.[2] For this reason alone it would serve a useful purpose, but considerably more than this is claimed for it. In the first place, it deals with a much wider range of subject-matter than is usually included in what are termed 'House Books,' taking these words in their ordinary acceptation. To a certain extent, therefore, its title is inadequate. In the second place, owing to the various changes of residence of the family with which it deals, it affords an opportunity of contrasting the expenses of living in the country with those of living in a close in the High Street of Edinburgh, and again of comparing these with the expenses of living in London, in Bath, and on the Continent. In the third place, it gives us memoranda as to the duties of servants, as to the arrangement of the dinner-table, as to travelling, and as to many other matters of interest. And lastly, it brings us indirectly into touch with a remarkably interesting group of people, whether viewed socially, politically, or intellectually, who were well known in their day and generation, and whose history it is a pleasure to study.

The Baillies of Jerviswood were cadets of the Baillies

---

[1] *The Acc^o^unt B^oo^k of Sir John Foulis of Ravelston*, 1671-1707.

[2] *Ochtertyre House Booke of Accomps*, 1737-1739.

of St. John's Kirk, who in their turn were cadets of the Baillies of Lamington, 'the original Balliols,' according to Lord Fountainhall. The first Baillie of Jerviswood was George Baillie, second son of Baillie of St. John's Kirk,[1] and grandfather of Lady Grisell's husband. As was then common, he entered into trade, duly compeared before Thomas Inglis, Dean of Guild of the City of Edinburgh, and others, on 8th September 1613, 'sufficientlie armit with ane furnisht hagbut,' and was sworn in as a 'Merchant Burgess' of the city. What he traded in it is impossible to say, but he at least owned a share in a ship to which he had succeeded through his first wife Christian Vorie.[2] This lady, who was the illegitimate[3] daughter of John Vorie in Balbaird, died without issue on 7th October 1628. George Baillie throve, became a town councillor[4] in 1631, purchased in 1636 the lands of Jerviswood in Lanarkshire from the family of Livingston, and in 1643 the estate of Mellerstain in Berwickshire from Andrew Edmonston of Ednem. The titles to these properties, along with his 'best clothes' and his 'silver and goldsmyth work,' were 'all totallie burnt' in August 1645, 'the tyme of that Lamentable fyre that was then in Edinburgh,' they being contained in 'ane trunk and ane kist' in the house of James Baillie, Merchant Burgess of Edinburgh, which was 'totallie burnt' (Act of Parliament, 1647).

It was probably before 1636 that he had made his second marriage—that with Margaret Johnston, daughter of James Johnston, Merchant Burgess of Edinburgh,

---

[1] *Reg. Mag. Sig.*, 14th June 1647.

[2] *Edinburgh Commissariot Testaments*, 24th December 1623.

[3] Letters of legitimisation granted to Christian Vorie, natural daughter of the late John Vorie in Balbaird, spouse of George Baillie, Merchant Burgess of Edinburgh.—*Reg. Mag. Sig.*, 7th July 1625.

[4] *Reg. Mag. Sig.*, 25th March 1631.

ROBERT BAILLIE OF JERVISWOOD.

and sister of Sir Archibald Johnston, Lord Wariston, by whom he had several children, namelv :—

1. John Baillie, who predeceased him.
2. Robert Baillie, who succeeded him.
3. Archibald Baillie.
4. Captain George Baillie of Mannerhall.
5. Captain James Baillie of the City Guard of Edinburgh.
6. Christian Baillie.
7. Elizabeth Baillie,[1] was married to Mr. James Kirkton, at one time minister of Merton, afterwards of the Tolbooth, Edinburgh, 31st December 1657 (*Edinburgh Register of Marriages*).
8. Rachel Baillie, was married first to Mr. Andrew Gray, one of the ministers of Glasgow; second, to Mr. George Hutcheson, at one time minister in Edinburgh, afterwards in Irvine.

George Baillie probably died early in 1646, for the 'Account of the Annual Rents belonging to the Children of George Baillie' begins in March of that year. He was succeeded by his eldest surviving son Robert. A sketch of the life of this remarkable man will be found on p. 269. The original is not in the handwriting of Lady Grisell, but it is endorsed by her 'My father-in-law.' As will be seen from this sketch, Robert Baillie first came into the clutches of the law in 1676, through rescuing his brother-in-law, the Rev. James Kirkton, from the hands of Captain Carstairs. The story is a curious one, and will be found fully set forth in volume forty-four of the *Proceedings of the Society of Antiquaries of Scotland.* The result of the trial was that Baillie was fined £500 sterling,[2]

[1] This lady's name is erroneously given in Scott's *Fasti Ecclesiæ* as 'Grisell.' Both Kirkton and Hutcheson suffered for their principles, the latter on one occasion being fined half a year's stipend for not keeping the Anniversary of the Restoration.

[2] This fine, or at least a considerable part of it, was subsequently remitted by the Earl of Lauderdale.

and incarcerated in the Edinburgh Tolbooth. It was during his confinement at this time that his son George Baillie first made the acquaintance of his future wife, then Grisell Hume, aged twelve, the eldest daughter of Sir Patrick Hume, afterwards Earl of Marchmont. Sir Patrick was anxious to communicate with Jerviswood, to whom he was deeply attached, and in order to avoid suspicion sent his little daughter from Redbraes, his country seat, to execute this dangerous and delicate commission. She succeeded so well 'that from that time her hardships began, from the confidence was put in her and the activity she naturally had far beyond her age in executing whatever she was intrusted with.'

When Robert Baillie was arrested in 1683 for high treason, he was residing in London, and was accordingly first confined in the Tower. As his condemnation by an English court would only have entailed forfeiture of his movable estate, it was resolved to send him and his fellow-countrymen in misfortune to Scotland, where their heritable estates could also be confiscated. The prisoners were accordingly shipped north, and we have the following pathetic note as to her husband's arrest and journey to Scotland in the handwriting of Mrs. Baillie. It is contained in a small commonplace-book of her husband's, and has for convenience been divided into sentences.

We war Led in presen by en order from his Majest, writer of it Sr Lyen Jenkins, detted 27 of Joun 1683.

*Last Oct^r^* 1683.

We cam from London by the Kings yach called the Kettchen yach, on Capten Croo our skiper and on sergen histinns, 12 sogers, all of the Kings owen foot gard. We was sheped opon the Last of Octr and had a very dengerowes Jarny, and cam to Leth opon 14 day of Novb^r^, when 11 gentellmen was garded w^t^ horse and foott, the preseners being in coshs ontill they cam to the Netherbow ell, and then Mager Whett cam from the Chansler and traserer and commanded them to go on foot

RACHEL JOHNSTON

WIFE OF ROBERT BAILLIE OF JERVISWOOD

(From a Portrait by John Scougall at Mellerstain.)

and so they did, garded w^t hors and foot, to the Tollboth, where thay ar keeped geloss. The end of Des^r we got in twes wt Sr Will petterson and pettrick Menzies, Clark to the Counsell. Then in Jan^r I got in tow days wt a keeper, then being stoped agen in feb^r I got in ones a day or more wt on of the good men. We got opon dors preson dors upon 18 Aprell 1684. Thay war med clos presoner in Jully 24 opon a thursday, and w^tin 8 dayes my husband fell very sik and was put clos in a rume alone and keeped ther un'ell he was allmost ded and opon the 14 Agust my sister was Let in to him and 3 dayes after I myself was Lett in and stayed 18 dayes w^t him, and we was taken from him when non wold have toght he could heve Lived en houre and he stayed Loked op tell the six of novbir all a Lone.

The trial and its result are too well known to require more than a passing notice here. Jerviswood, who had been desperately ill in prison, was carried to court in his 'night gown,' [1] and driven to execution a few hours after sentence had been pronounced. Wodrow reports that he said to his son George, who had been recalled from his studies abroad, 'If ye have a strong heart ye may go and see me nagled; but if ye have not a heart for it ye may stay away.' From what Lady Murray says in her *Memoirs* he appears to have gone, but whether he remained with his aunt Mrs. Graden to see the body 'cut in coupons and oyled and tarred' is nowhere mentioned. Lady Murray, however, states that his mother and aunts said 'that it ever after gave that grave, silent, thoughtful turn to his temper which before that time was not natural to him.' It also gave him what was by no means so common at that period, namely, feelings of compassion towards his political opponents when the wheel of fortune placed some of them in the same position in which his father had been. After the ''15,' when he was a Lord of the Treasury, and at a time when to speak his mind might easily have damaged his position, he publicly 'declared himself for

[1] See p. lxxi.

mercy to the poor unhappy sufferers by the rebellion,' and began a long Parliamentary speech 'by saying that he had been bred in the School of affliction which had instructed him in both the reasonableness and necessity of showing mercy to others in the like circumstances.' As his accounts show, he did more than talk, for there are several entries of payments made to the unfortunate prisoners taken at Preston 'To the Laird of Wedderburn when in Prison, £5' · 'To James Hume of Aiton My Ld Humes brother, £1, 1s. 6d'; 'To Mrs. Hume Whitefield, £1, 1s. 6d.,' wife of Hume of Whitefield, and to others—thus confirming Lady Murray's statement as to his helping 'the wives, sisters, and other relations and friends of the poor prisoners.' That Lord Kenmore's body was handed to his relatives instead of to the surgeons for dissection was entirely owing to his intervention and foresight.

His conduct to these unfortunates is made even more remarkable by the fact 'that they plundered several gentlemen's country seats (particularly the houses of Sir John Pringle of Stitchell and Mr. Baillie of Jerviswood) carry'd away what peuther they could get to melt down for Bullets, destroyed their corn, etc.' [1]

Robert Baillie cannot have been much over fifty,[2] if so old, at the time of his death. Lord Fountainhall in his *Chronological Notes* describes him as being a 'huffy proud man' who 'huffed a little that he should be esteemed guilty of any design against the life of the King or his brother whereof he purged himself as he hoped for mercy.' He was survived by his widow and by the following

---

[1] *The History of the Rebellion raised against King George*, etc. (1715), by Peter Rae, 1718.

[2] His father's first wife died on 7th October 1628, and as he was the second son of his father's second marriage, he cannot have been older than fifty-three, and was probably a little younger.

children, who were all born at Jerviswood Tower, which he made his residence :—

George, who succeeded him, born 16th March 1664.

Archibald, born 15th April 1665.

Robert, born 4th July 1666.

William, born 24th January 1669.

Rachel, born 3rd April 1671, married Dundas of Breastmilne, Linlithgowshire.

James, born 9th June 1673.

John, born 14th March 1675, died 1717. His funeral cost £11, 16s. 6d. (see p. 59).

Helen, born July 1676, married John Hay, Writer in Edinburgh, died in 1717.

Elizabeth, born 25th September 1677, married Mr. Robert Weems of Graingemuir, made Collector at Alloa March 1717.

Robert Baillie's execution took place on 24th December 1684, and while his head was exhibited on the Netherbow Port of the city of Edinburgh, his quarters were exposed on the Tolbooths of Jedburgh, Lanark, Ayr, and Glasgow. The quarter which was sent to Lanark Tolbooth, not a mile from his own house of Jerviswood, remained but a short time in its position, for 'a band of young men, headed by a certain yeoman named William Leishman, came and stole it away for burial.' [1] This Leishman's son and namesake was afterwards sent to college by the Jerviswood family out of gratitude for this service, and eventually became Principal Leishman of Glasgow University.

The execution of Robert Baillie made it evident to his old friend Sir Patrick Hume that if he wished to preserve his life he had better get out of Scotland as soon as possible. The story of Sir Patrick's concealment and subsequent

---

[1] *A Son of Knox, and other Studies*, by J. F. Leishman, 1909.

escape to Holland, and of the heroic part therein played by his daughter Grisell, is too well known to need repetition here. Suffice it to say he lay hid first for a month in the family vault under Polwarth Church, where 'he had only for light an open slit at one end through which nobody could see,' and where 'his great comfort and constant entertainment [for he had no light to read by] was repeating Buchanan's Psalms, which he had by heart from beginning to end, and retained them to his dying day.' When this place of concealment could be endured no longer, he was brought to the house and shut up in a room of the ground floor, of which his daughter kept the key. Under the floor of this room his wife, daughter, and Jamie Winter, a carpenter who used to work in the house and who alone shared the secret, 'scratched' a hole in the earth, fitting into it a box with bed and bedclothes, whither Sir Patrick could retreat in the event of an alarm, then the flooring having been screwed down and the bed placed over the top it was hoped he would escape detection. 'After being at home a week or two, the bed daily examined as usual, one day, in lifting the boards, the bed bounced to the top, the box being full of water.' This and the news of Jerviswood's execution convinced him and his wife and daughter that safety must be sought elsewhere. Disguised and passing as a surgeon, he made his way through London to Bordeaux and from thence to Utrecht in Holland, where, settling under the name of 'Dr. Wallace,' his family soon joined him. Thither also fled George Baillie, a circumstance which does not surprise us with our knowledge of after events.

The estates of both exiles had been forfeited, that of Baillie having been given to the Duke of Gordon, while that of Sir Patrick Hume passed to the Earl of Seaforth, thus leaving both in nearly destitute circumstances.

'Dr. Wallace' made a living by practising medicine, of which he had some slight knowledge, while young Baillie and Sir Patrick's eldest son [1] entered the Prince of Orange's Horse Guards, where they served 'till they were better provided for in the army, which they were before the Revolution.' It was when in the Guards that the two friends, standing sentry at the gate, while the Prince dined in public, took toll of a kiss before letting any pretty girl pass in. Apparently the morose Baillie could relax at times!

When in 1689 the Prince of Orange sailed for England, Sir Patrick Hume, his son, and George Baillie sailed with him. The first attempt to cross the Channel proved a failure, the fleet being dispersed by a gale, and the ship in which were the Humes and Baillie being nearly lost. Baillie was so affected by his narrow escape that 'all his life after he kept a rigorous fast once every week, spending the whole day in meditation, prayer, and praises to his Deliverer.' [2]

Strangely enough, on his voyage to Holland he had also an experience which had a marked effect on his after life. Some of his companions in like condition to himself 'proposed playing at dice to divert themselves. He had the luck to strip the whole company, which left them in a most destitute condition. He returned every man his money with his advice not again to risk their all: and this occasioned his making such reflections on the frailty of human nature and the bewitchingness of play as made him resolve against it and hate it in all shapes ever after through out his whole life.' His hatred of play does not seem to have prevented his wife and daughters from frequently enjoying

---

[1] Patrick Hume predeceased his father on 25th November 1709.

[2] *An Historical Character of the Hon. George Baillie, Esq.*, by G. Cheyne, appended to Lady Murray's *Memoirs*.

a mild gamble, as the numerous entries in the London accounts show.

On his return to Scotland Baillie found himself in a very different position from that in which he had been when he fled the country. The Whigs and Presbyterians were all-powerful. His father and his grandfather—Lord Wariston—were regarded as martyrs for the cause; his uncle James Johnston had been appointed Secretary of State for Scotland; and his first cousin once removed, Mr. Gilbert Burnet, afterwards Bishop of Salisbury, was now King William's chaplain. It is not surprising, therefore, that he was at once elected one of the four members returned by the county of Berwick to the Convention of Estates; that he was appointed a Commissioner of Supply for that county and also for Lanarkshire; that his estates were restored to him; and that he was made Receiver-General of Scotland, a post which brought him in £300 a year, a good salary for those days. His prospects were now such as to entitle him to ask for the hand of Grisell Hume from her father, who in December 1690 had been created Lord Polwarth. The young people had always been deeply attached, and they were married at Redbraes, the seat of the Humes, on 17th September 1691. It was an ideal union. 'They never had the shadow of a quarrel or misunderstanding or dryness betwixt them, not for a moment.' 'He never went abroad but she went to the window to look after him; and so she did that very day he fell ill the last time he was abroad, never taking her eyes from him as long as he was in sight.'

It is from about a year after the date of the marriage that the accounts begin to be kept, but before referring to them it is necessary for their proper appreciation to say a few words regarding George Baillie's position, political and social.

It has been already stated, that Baillie sat in Parliament

GEORGE BAILLIE OF JERVISWOOD AND HIS DAUGHTER GRISELL.

(*From a Portrait at Mellerstain.*)

as one of the members for Berwickshire, of course as a Whig; but he was by no means the sort of man to vote blindlv for the 'Court Party,' however much that might be to his ınterest. When, therefore, questions arose in Parliament regarding the affairs of the unfortunate 'Company trading to Africa and the Indies,' better known as the Darien Company, in which he held £1000 of stock, and of which he was a director, he was one of those who, deeply resenting the interference of England, joined the new 'Country Party' which was then formed.[1] Of this party Baillie was one of the leaders, and 'gained a great reputation bv standing so stiffly by the interests of his country.'[2] So much so, that when in 1703, a year after the accession of Anne, a new Parliament was called, Baillie was returned as member for the shires of both Berwick and Lanark. Electing to sit for the latter, he continued to represent this constituency until his retirement in 1725. The Sessions that followed were most momentous ones, embracing the long struggle that preceded the passing of the Treaty of Union, but it is unnecessary here to trace the prominent parts played by the 'Country Party' and subsequently by the 'Squadrone Volante' in that fight, as they are well known. Baillie was in the forefront of the battle. He was one of the three representatives sent by the 'Country Party' to set their views before Queen Anne, was made Lord Treasurer Depute in the short-lived Tweeddale Administration and a member of the Privy Council, and, in short, was 'by far the most significant man' of the 'Squadrone Volante,' 'to whom he was a kind of dictator.'[3] The position occupied by Baillie at this time is well shown in the Jerviswood Correspondence, where we read the private views of the three leaders of

[1] George Ridpath's *Account of the Proceedings of the Parliament of Scotland*, 1703.

[2] *Lockhart Papers*. [3] *Ibid.*

the 'Squadrone Volante,' viz. of Secretary Johnston, that 'shrewd cunning fellow'; of the Earl of Roxburgh, 'the best accomplished young man of quality in Europe'; and of Baillie of Jerviswood, 'the morose, proud and severe, but of a profound solid judgment.'[1] We see how, step by step, they were driven to the conclusion that the only way to ensure the Hanoverian Succession, the Presbyterian form of worship, and equal trading rights with England was by an absolute union with her; they had no love for union in itself, seeing clearly what it entailed; but it seemed to them to be the least of the many evils that hovered over Scotland. The 'Squadrone Volante' has been accused of venalitv; but these letters make it clear that, while in the manner of the time the leaders had a keen eye to their own interests, and hoped to be eventually rewarded for the course they adopted, still in making up their minds to that course they conscientiously considered, in the first instance, the interests of their country.

That the Treaty of Union could not have been passed without the help of the 'Squadrone Volante' was fully recognised; and it was therefore not unnatural that Baillie should be one of the selected members who sat for Scotland in the first Union Parliament, and that he should be rewarded for his services by being appointed one of the Commissioners of Trade with a salary of £1000 per annum. The duties of this post he was eminently capable of discharging, as he had been a member of the important Council of Trade, which before the Union had reported on the exports and imports of Scotland.

The first elected United Parliament met in November 1708, and in this Baillie sat, as formerly, for the county of Lanark. Then followed the Queen's quarrel with the

[1] *Lockhart Papers.*

Marlboroughs, the ousting of Her Majesty's Whig advisers, the election of 1710, with the return to Parliament of a large Tory majority. Baillie, however, retained his seat, and in connection with his so doing his daughter writes : 'As he never liked making court to any minister when there was anything he thought proper for him to represent he always had a private audience of the Queen, who shewed so great a personal favour for him, that, on the change of her ministry in the end of her reign, she kept him in office a year after the rest of his party were turned out, and when they prevailed to have him removed, they pressed her to give some orders they thought necessary to hinder him of his election, which she absolutely refused.'

If Scotland had good reason to object to the treatment it had received at the hands of a Whig Government, it had still more reason to resent what was meted out to it by the now victorious Tory party. Both parties in Scotland were exasperated by one or more of the measures passed by Parliament, and even amongst the staunchest Whigs there was a feeling that the Union had been a failure and should be repealed. Indeed there was made by the Scottish members a movement in this direction, in which Baillie to a qualified extent joined.[1] The question even got the length of being raised in the Lords, but it was unsuccessful and, as it was not thought advisable to bring it forward in the Commons, it accordingly fizzled out. This result was in no ways due to the want of Parliamentary sympathy for the Scottish Jacobite party, who had always been opposed to the Union, for the Tories made little or no concealment of their intention to attempt the restoration of the Stuarts upon Anne's death. So fully was this recognised by the Whigs, that, resolving to resist to the

---

[1] *Lockhart Papers.*

death, they prepared themselves for civil war. Societies were formed of those favouring the Hanoverian Succession, and meetings were held to arrange for organised resistance and for the purchase of arms. That Baillie took his share in these warlike preparations is shown by the following entries in his accounts :—

1714. 15 May	For a gun and 30 swords £4 and for packing 4s. 6d. .	£4	4	6
18 Sept.	For 29 guns and Bagginets	18	4	$1\frac{4}{12}$
	For a barrill powder weighe $7\frac{1}{2}$ stone	3	6	8

One cannot help wondering if these arms fell into the hands of the Highlanders when they looted Mellerstain in the ''15.'

Mercifully for the peace of the country, Queen Anne's sudden death on 1st August 1714 threw out the calculations of the Jacobites, and before they had time to rally George had been proclaimed king and had landed in England

On his arrival there naturally ensued a complete change in Government, the Whigs once again being all-powerful.[1] Of Baillie's position at this period Lady Murray writes: 'Upon the accession of King George the First he was made one of the Lords of the Admiralty,[2] and soon after one of the Lords of the Treasury,[3] without his ever soliciting or asking for either of them; and had no thought nor expectation of being in the Treasury when the Earl of Stanhope, then at the head of it, sent him orders to come and take his place at the Board. There he continued till at his own earnest desire he laid down in the year 1725 against the opinion and

[1] 'The chief men in place are the Speaker, Sir Richard Onslow, Mr. Boscawen, Mr. Aislaby, Mr. Smith, Mr. Lechmere, Mr. Bayley, Mr. Putteney, Mr. Stanhope.'—*On the State of Party at the Accession of George I.*, by Mr. Wortley.

[2] Salary £1000 per annum. [3] Salary £1600 per annum.

entreaties of all his friends, and even the King desired him to continue and was a year before he accepted his demission.' [1] If Lady Murray is correct in the latter part of this statement, Baillie was more fortunate than the other members of his party, who in 1725 were all turned out of their posts by Walpole for not being sufficiently subservient to the English view of Scottish policy. Be that as it may, he ceased after the year 1725 to take a part in public affairs, and devoted himself to the education of his grandchildren, and to 'constant meditation, contemplation and prayer.' He died at Oxford on 6th August 1738, at the age of seventy-five, and was buried at Mellerstain in the private burial-ground prepared by himself. 'At one and the same time he was a most zealous patriot, a very able statesman, and a most perfect Christian.

. . . .

His courage was undaunted and his patience immovable; his piety unfeigned and his truth exact to the greatest precision.' [2]

In addition to his political work, Baillie, as was but natural, took a deep interest in the affairs of the Church of Scotland. He was chosen as representative elder to the General Assembly for the parish of Earlston, in which Mellerstain lies, and this position he held for many years, attending the Assembly with characteristic regularity. When resident in Edinburgh he had a loft in that part of St. Giles known as the Tolbooth, for which he paid £1, 10s. a year, and when in England he 'continued steadily in his own Church and principles,' having a pew in King's Street Chapel, London,

[1] He retired on a pension of £1600 per annum. In regard to this, Lady Mary Wortley Montagu, writing to her sister the Countess of Mar in 1726, says, 'Mr. Baily you know is dismissed the Treasury and consoled with a pension of equal value.'

[2] *An Historical Character of the Hon. George Baillie*, by C. Cheyne M.D., F.R.S., appended to Lady Murray's *Memoirs*.

for which he paid 9s. a quarter. He also contributed generously to the building funds of Presbyterian Churches both in England and Ireland. Not that he adhered to his own Church with 'rigidness and narrowness of soul,' for his Accounts show that when abroad his charities extended to priests and nuns and monks; and Lady Murray narrates how 'two of the poor Episcopal Clergy in Scotland came to ask charity for themselves and their brethren without the expectation of seeing him. He received them kindly, kept them to dinner with him, contributed to their necessities, and shewed great displeasure at his servants for not having taken proper care of their horses, nor bringing them so readily as they would have done to those from whom they expected a reward.'

It must not, however, be imagined that Baillie was entirely taken up with politics and religion. He had his 'hunting mares,' which we learn from the Accounts were specially fed with beans, and he went on hawking expeditions. He evidently could also take a hand in a carouse, for on 4th June 1706, the Earl of Haddington writing to the Earl of Mar says: 'Drinking indeed succeeds pretty well, thanks to my Lord Roths, Hindfoord, Anster, George Baillie, James Bruce and myself, who as long as the Assembly lasted lived as discreet a life as you could wish.'[1] When the family went to stay in London in 1715, Lady Grisell and he took part with their daughters in the 'ball, masquerades, parties by water and such like,' 'neither choosing to deprive us of them nor let us go alone . . . and they generally were calculated at times most convenient for my father.' Many are the references in the Accounts to these parties.

There is no doubt, however, that such diversions were 'not quite suitable to his own temper,' and that his chief

---

[1] Fraser's *Memorials of the Earls of Haddington.* 2 vols. 1889. 4to.

pleasure lay in his books and in retirement with them. The Accounts show that Baillie constantly bought books. He purchased from Mosman in the Luckenbooths, from Johnston, Knox and Vallance; he bought at auctions, and had heavy accounts with Andrew Bell, Bookseller, London. One of the earliest entries after his marriage is for the erection in his first house in Warriston Close of five double presses for books at a cost of £72 Scots or £6 sterling; and when he finally left Edinburgh for Mellerstain in 1708 he took with him four cartloads of books. He was not contented with reading himself, but must needs encourage reading amongst his dependants. He saw to it that they all had Bibles; and on one occasion we find him spending £3, 10s. sterling 'for books for the tenants and servants,' and on another, 2s. for a 'Thomas a Kempis to the servants.' It is to be regretted that the Accounts only give the names of a few of the volumes purchased, such as: 'Jaillots Maps,'[1] £12, 10s. stg.; 'Mazerays History,'[2] 3 vols., £6, 13s. 4d. stg.; 'Foster's Book,' 6s. 8d. stg.; 'Defoe's Book in defence of the Union,' 2s. 6d. (this of course purchased in 1707); 'Naphtali,' covenanting Records, by Sir James Stewart of Goodtrees; 'Johnston, Engraver, for his book of Maps, £2, 2s.'; 'a little Divinity Book,' 1s. 8d.; 'Atalantis' by Mrs. Manley, which was one of the scandalous works lent out by Allan Ramsay in 1726 from the first circulating library in the kingdom.

Even when travelling on the Continent books were purchased, and a box was sent home containing, along with several books of prints, maps and music, such works as Telimon's History, Don Quixote, Bocaccio, Le Fortunato Neapolinano (in two volumes), Delices de la Holland,

---

[1] Bernard Antoine Jaillot, a well-known map-maker in the early eighteenth century.

[2] Probably *Histoire de France*, published 1643 to 1651. Folio.

Delices d'Italy, History of the Painters, Salvini's Works, Monsign[r] della Casa's Works, Cato in Italian (unbound), Terense's Plays in Italian, Recueil de Pensees (in five volumes), Retratto di Venezzia, Confession of Augsburg, Dieu present par tout, etc.

The Mellerstain library contains to this day many hundreds of books with his bookplate carefully pasted in.

Baillie was also a patron of the Arts. He had 'wax pictures' done of his son and mother, presumably after their deaths, for which he pays £1, 14s. 4d. stg. and £3, 4s. stg. respectively. Then he purchased many pictures from John Scugald, whose name is associated with the first picture gallery in Europe, this artist having added an upper story to his house in Advocates' Close, Edinburgh, and fitted it up for the purpose of an exhibition.[1]

The prices paid strike one as small, even bearing in mind the remuneration of services at that time. For instance: 'To Scugald for 2 pictures and frames, £74 8s.' Scots (£6, 4s. stg.). 'Scuglad for pictures, £48' Scots (£4). 'Scugald balance, £96' Scots (£8 stg.). '1705 Decr. To John Scugald painter in full of all accounts, £84 Scots' (£7 stg.). The most curious entry, however, in connection with this artist is the following in 1706: 'For drawing Grisies peticoat by Skugald,' 5s. stg. Does this mean that he turned his artistic talents to designing clothes or grounding patterns for embroidery?

In 1710 Sir John Medina painted Baillie, his wife, and the 'two bairens's pictures' for £20 stg.,[2] and in 1711

---

[1] *Old and New Edinburgh*, by James Grant. 'For some years after the Revolution he was the only painter in Scotland, and had a very great run of business. This brought him into a hasty and incorrect manner.'—Pinkerton.

[2] Induced by the promise of customers to venture from London, the Spaniard Juan Bautista Medina had come to the unknown North, bringing with him in a smack to Leith an ample supply of canvases containing bodies and postures, male and female, ready painted, to which the heads of his future clients were to be affixed.—Graham's *Social Life of Scotland in the Eighteenth Century*. He was knighted in 1707, before the Union, by the Duke of Queensberry.

BOOK PLATE OF GEORGE BAILLIE
OF JERVISWOOD.

Hay did several pictures of Jerviswood as presents for various friends at the rate of £1, 10s. stg. each, and 10s. for the frame.

The most expensive work got is a portrait from William Aikman,[1] but of which member of the family is not stated.

1717	Mr. Aickman in pairt for picturs .	£21	0	0
	In full payd for the picturs at 5 guinys sitting and 5£ coppys	31	0	0
		£52 stg.		

When at Florence in 1733, Lady Grisell has portraits of her husband, her daughter Grisie, and her two grand-daughters, Grisie and Helen, painted by Mr. Martin at a cost of eleven guineas, and in Bologne a 'pictor of the Autom' is purchased for £2. Cases are bought for these works of art, the conveyance of which must have added considerably to the trouble of their homeward journey.

George Baillie died on 6th August 1738 and was survived by his widow and by two daughters—Grisell, born at Redbraes on 26th October 1692, and Rachel, born in Warriston's Land on 23rd February 1696. He was predeceased by his only son Robert, who was born on 23rd February 1694 and died on 28th February 1696. His daughter Grisell was married on 16th August 1710 to 'Mr. Alexander Murray, the son and heir of Sir David Murray of Stanhope, Baronet, by the Lady Anne Bruce, daughter of Alexander, Earl of Kincardine.'[2] Grisell's father, who 'was the most just and sagacious observer of mankind that was possible,' was opposed to the marriage, but overcome by his daughter's

[1] 'William Aikman (laird of Cairney) had been at his easel since 1712 in his High Street Close, a laird by rank, a good painter by craft, . . . but ten years were enough to weary Aikman of a poor business, and customers that grudged to be immortalised at £10 for a painted yard of canvas, "forbye a frame," and he quitted Edinburgh . . . and went to London.'—Graham's *Social Life of Scotland in the Eighteenth Century.*

[2] Appendix V. to Lady Murray's *Memoirs.*

tears, reluctantly gave his consent. The union turned out a most unfortunate one, for Mr. Murray 'under a pleasing exterior' possessed 'a dark, moody and ferocious temper' amounting almost to insanity, which 'made him the helpless victim of the most groundless suspicions.' This curious temper showed itself on the very first day after their marriage, and although he appears to have lived with his wife in his father-in-law's house for some five months, it was at length found necessary to obtain from the Court a Decree of Separation, which was pronounced on 5th March 1714. With all his unreasoning jealousy, which made life with him impossible and dangerous, Mr. Murray seems to have been really attached to his wife, for it is told that at the time when she was having her portrait painted in London, a gentleman, who afterwards was discovered to be her husband, came frequently to the artist's studio, where he 'would stand for an hour with his arms folded gazing at her likeness.'

Mrs. Murray, afterwards Lady Murray, was for many years a great friend of Lady Mary Wortley Montagu, until the latter 'thought fit to exercise her wicked wit in an infamous ballad; which of course she loudly disclaimed all knowledge of, but of which her own letters to her sister Lady Mar plainly enough betray her to have been the writer.'[1]

Lady Murray was famous both in London and Edinburgh for her singing. Gay refers to her in his lines to Pope as 'the sweet-tongued Murray,' and afterwards in her flat in the Parliament Square of Edinburgh 'she was still accustomed to sing the native airs and ballads of her own country with a delicacy and pathos quite peculiar to herself,'[2] and to draw tears from the eyes of her audience.

[1] Appendix V., Lady Murray's *Memoirs*.
[2] Appendix to Lady Murray's *Memoirs*.

LADY MURRAY,

AGED 33.

(*From a Portrait at Mellerstain by Maria Verelst.*)

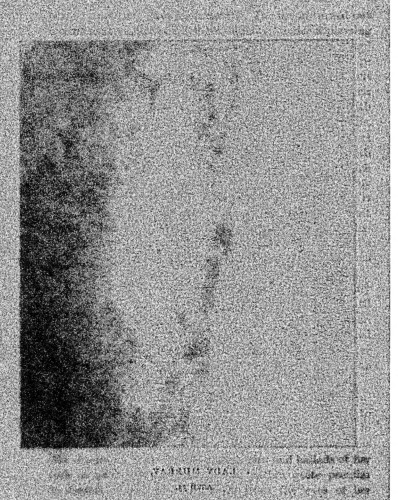

Lady Murray's younger sister Rachel was married at Edinburgh, on 3rd September 1717, to Charles, Lord Binning, the eldest son of the Earl of Haddington. This marriage was as happy as Lady Murray's was the reverse. Lord Binning [1] seems in very truth to have become one of the family, and his early death from consumption, at Naples, on 27th December 1732, was deeply felt both by Lady Grisell and her husband. 'His heart, etc., was buried in St. Corrolas Church Yeard and his corps sent home to Tiningham.' [2] It was to his father-in-law that Lord Binning on his deathbed confided the education of his children. Lord Binning was survived by :—

Grisell Hamilton, born 6th April 1719.

Thomas Hamilton, born 23rd October 1720, who succeeded his grandfather Lord Haddington.

George Hamilton, born 24th June 1723, who assumed the surname of Baillie and succeeded to the Baillie estates. His descendants eventually succeeded to the Earldom of Haddington.

Charles James Hamilton, born 8th October 1727.

Rachel Hamilton, born 3rd January 1729.

He was predeceased by Helen, born 8th October 1724; Charles, born 6th October 1725; and John, born 22nd October 1726.[3]

On Mr. Baillie's death his estate passed by destination to his widow in liferent, then to his elder daughter and her issue, whom failing, to his younger daughter and her second son. Thus, as Lady Murray had no children, Lady Binning's second son, George, succeeded to the

[1] Lord Binning, like his father, was a versifier of considerable skill. One of his songs, 'Ungrateful Nanny,' was published in the *Gentleman's Magazine*.

[2] Note by Lady Grisell.

[3] The above names and dates are taken from a Memorandum in Lady Grisell's handwriting, but judging from the Accounts there must have been another child of the marriage born in 1718, for in that year Lady Grisell spends a considerable sum of money for 'my Rachels cloaths to her child.'

properties of Jerviswood, Mellerstain, etc., assuming the name of Baillie. Through the failure of the male line of Thomas, Lady Binning's eldest son, the succession to the Earldom of Haddington opened to the descendants of her second son George. The Haddington and Baillie estates are thus now merged in the same proprietor, and Mellerstain is still the residence of George Baillie's descendants. Nothing now remains of the 'Old melancholick hous that had had great buildings about it,' [1] purchased by the first George Baillie of Jerviswood in 1643, and of the Mellerstain known to Lady Grisell only the wings are left. Although the old tower which she used to have repaired so regularly has been replaced by the present Adam's buildings, her own voluminous Memoranda and Account Books have been carefully preserved, and it is to her descendant, Lord Binning, the present occupant of Mellerstain, that the thanks of the Scottish History Society are due for his kindness in placing at its disposal these most interesting and valuable records of a bygone age and of an exceptional personality.

So many sketches of Lady Grisell's life have been published, dealing with her romantic history, her poetic talents, and her charming personality that nothing further need be said here upon these points. Her extraordinary business capacity has also been the subject of much comment, but as it is the side of her character which is most prominently brought into notice in this volume, a few words in regard to it may be pardoned.

From the time Lady Grisell, as a mere child, had proved her capacity through her skill in gaining communication

---

[1] 'Nov. 10, 1659. . . . We cam be Eccles and Stichell, and at lenth cam to Mellerstane, wher we met with Jerviswood, who took us in and we took a drink with him. It is ane old melancholick bous that had had great buildings about it. He cam with us to Lauder at night.'—*Diary of Andrew Hay of Craignethan.*

with Mr. Robert Baillie, she became the mainstay of her father's house. She went with her mother to London after her father's estates were forfeited in order to solicit an allowance for the support of the family; she came back from Holland by herself and brought over her younger sister Julian to Utrecht—and a wretched journey it was; at Utrecht she sat up two nights a week 'to do the business that was necessary for the household'; after her marriage she returned to her father's house, on one occasion for manv weeks, and worked day and night at putting his accounts in order; when her brother was abroad she managed his affairs, and seems also to have helped many of her friends as well. It is, therefore, little to be wondered at that her husband trusted her with the entire administration of his finances 'without scarce asking a question about them, except sometimes to say to her, "Is my debt paid yet?" though often did she apply to him for dircetion and advice.' 'In her family her attention and economy reached to the smallest things; and though this was her practice from her youth there never appeared in her the least air of narrowness; and so far was she from avarice, the common vice of the age, that often has my father said to her "I never saw the like of you, goodwife, the older you grow, you grow the more extravagant; but do as you please provided I be in no debt.' So writes Lady Murray, and an examination of the Accounts fully bears out her statement, showing as it does the most careful supervision, and also at times what must have struck her husband as dangerous extravagance. For instance, when the family went to London and the expenditure suddenly rises from £733, 16s. 11d. in 1714 to £1872, 18s. 10d. in 1715, the 'clothes' bills alone increasing from an average of about £60 to £346, 13s. 4d., one can quite undertsand Mr. Baillie being somewhat horrified.

As an example of the careful way Lady Grisell went

into all matters of expenditure, note the following little statement. The unusual circumstance—namely, that Lady Grisell makes a mistake in it and thus arrives at a wrong result—rather adds to its interest. It is merely a jotting on a scrap of paper in Lady Grisell's handwriting, and was drawn up while abroad in 1732 to enable her to judge whether it was cheaper to take a house or to go into lodgings.

				D.	C.	G.[1]
By wood in chamber	(£10	16	0)	54	0	0
Flamboys	(1	2	0)	5	5	0
Chocalet	(6	2	9)	30	7	0
Canary	(8	16	0)	44	0	0
Cyder and Ale . . .	(5	0	9)	25	2	0
Wax Candle	(2	5	7)	11	4	0
Tee	(1	4	0)	6	0	0
Sugar	(4	3	8)	20	9	0
Drinkmoney	(1	0	10)	5	2	2
Sundry smalls	(0	12	0)	3	0	0
Coffie	(0	4	11)	1	3	3
House Book in 13 weeks after taking what is above out of it .	(76	12	2)	383	0	5
				[2] 593	3	0

							383	0	5
House Rent	(24	0	0)				120	0	0
Saverio									
Maid . . .	(0	18	0)	4	5	0			
Cook . . .	(4	4	0)	21	0	0			
Cook's Boy	(0	18	0)	4	5	0	30	0	0
							533	0	5

this is 41 Ducat a week for 13 weeks and is in Sterling money £8 4 sh. pr week which is in 13 weeks st. 108. 12.

In Madam Petits we was 12 guinys pr week, which in 13 weeks is £163 14 0

---

[1] Ducats, carlins, and grains. See Appendix IV, p. 424.

[2] Lady Grisell turns the page here and carries forward 383.0.5 instead of 593.3.0.

I also reckon for goats milk Ice and sundry other things	10 0 0	this £10 either
	£173 14 0	taken of mine or aded to Madam Petits makes it the same thing.

with a much better dyit
2 more at table and very often strangers and many more candles.[1]

Madam Petits	£173 14 0
Naples	105 12 0
	£65 2 0

It is in 13 weeks more by the above sum of £65, 2sh. at Madam Petits than our own housekeeping which is just £5 a week more.

Somehow these odd jottings on margins and scraps of paper intensify the human interest of the Accounts. Here are two or three more of a like nature.

'Salvato Guarino near the Vice Roys Palice sells all Grossery wair.'
'remember to take out the velvet for Mr. Baillie's Night gown.'
'Francisco entered to Ld. Bn. the 15 of November at 5 Ducats a moneth without meat and gets livera.'
'The price of washing at Naples 1st January 1733.

a shirt and cravat	5	grains—2½d.
shifts	4	2
Table cloths fine	4	2
Ditt cours	3	1½
Shiets fine	4	2
Shits cours	3	1½
Aprons and wast coats	1	½
table napkins fine	1	½
Ditt cours	½	¼
all small pieces	½	¼'

We see from the Accounts that Lady Grisell shortly after her marriage took a course of cooking lessons from

[1] This evidently refers to her own housekeeping.

Mrs. Addison, for which she paid £1, 6s. stg., and also a course of dancing lessons for which £8 stg. was to be paid to 'perfite her.' Although no mention is made of her having taken lessons in book-keeping, one cannot help feeling that she must also have had careful instruction in this branch of education. Lessons in this could apparently be had easily, for in 1701 £2 stg. is paid for James Baillie—Lady Grisell's brother-in-law—'lairning book-keeping in pairt,' and in 1714 either she or one of her daughters received lessons from Mr. M'Gie at a cost of £3, 2s. stg. If she did not receive lessons, she must have been a born book-keeper, for her accounts are remarkably able productions.

Her principal account-book was what she termed her 'Day Book,' but what would nowadays be termed a 'Cash Ledger,' for in it she did not enter her expenditure as it occurred from day to day, but her expenditure as specialised under separate headings. These headings vary from time to time, some of the less important being occasionally merged in others. The following mav be taken as those of a fixed nature :

I. Household Expenditure. This included all expenses in connection with food, drink, lighting, firing, washing and feeding of animals destined for table use.

II. Sundries, which included Education.

III. Servants' wages.

IV. Men-servants' Clothing.

V. Clothing for herself, husband, and children.

VI. Furniture and Furnishings.

The minor headings which occur in some years but which are merged under Sundries in other years are :—

I. Expenses of Horses.

II. Doctors and Surgeons.

III. Business Charges.

IV. Estate Expenditure.

V. Cess.

VI. Pocket-monev.

It will thus be seen that Lady Grisell's 'Day Book' nominally embraces the whole of the family expenditure. Full details, however, are not given under the headings 'Household Expenditure' and 'Pocket Money.' The reason for this omission in the first case is that for small ordinary house expenditure Lady Grisell kept separate books, the monthly totals of which she alone posted to her 'Day Book'; in the second, the reason was probably that her husband, to whom the 'Pocket Monev' was paid, kept no account thereof.

Lady Grisell left three 'Day Books' folio size, the first running from 1692 to 1718 inclusive, and containing 442 pages; the second from 1719 to 1742 inclusive, and containing 354 pages, and the third from 1742 to the date of her death (6th December 1746), continued by her daughter, Lady Murray. She also left books containing the accounts of expenses in connection with their journeys to Bath and to the Continent; Books containing Inventories of Bottles, etc.; a Book of Receipts; a Book of Bills of Fare; Books relating to estate management during the years 1742, 1743 and 1744, and many other Account and Memoranda Books. All are written in her own clear handwriting, the character of which was so well known that in 1706, when the leaders of the 'Squadrone Volante' were corresponding in cypher, Secretary Johnston writes to Baillie, 'Write bv an unknown hand; your wife's is as well known as your own.'

It will be easily understood that with such a wealth of material in these papers, the difficulty of selection has been great. After careful consideration, the Editor has resolved to deal mainly with Lady Grisell's first 'Day Book,' adding one or two selections from the other books. The reasons that have led to this choice are, first, that Day

Book No. 1 deals with that intensely interesting period of Scottish history immediately preceding and succeeding the Union of the Parliaments; second, that it gives the expenses of living in Edinburgh, in the country, and in London; and third, that it gives the accounts for old Mrs. Baillie's funeral and for the marriages of Lady Grisell's two daughters. Even this selected volume can only be dealt with by means of extracts, and much interesting matter has thus to be left out. An attempt has been made to remedy this by the formation of appendices drawn from the whole volume and by the notes which follow; but such a method is at best unsatisfactory, taking as it were the flavour from the meat, and the Editor is only too conscious of its inadequacy.

Then as to the extracts themselves and their arrangement, it has been thought best not to select individual entries, which would have still further destroyed the character of the Accounts, nor yet to select individual years, which would have led in some cases to needless repetition, but to take as the unit of selection individual branches, choosing the most interesting of each respectively, and arranging these not chronologically as a whole, but, in order to facilitate reference, chronologically in their respective groups. Thus all entries dealing with any one subject, such as, say, 'Expenses of Horses,' will be found together.

As already stated, the Accounts begin about a year after the marriage of Mr. Baillie and Lady Grisell, that is, in the autumn of 1692, and are peculiarly rich in all sorts of information which can be most suitably referred to under separate headings.

I. Rents of Houses and of Lodgings and Expenses of Travelling

We learn from the Accounts that the young couple took up their quarters in a house in Warriston Close,[1] perhaps the same house which had belonged to Baillie's grandfather, Lord Warriston, and to which his father had turned on his way to execution with the remark to his sister-in-law, 'Many a sweet day and night with God had your now glorified father in that lodging or chamber.'[2] The rent paid for it was £200 Scots, or £16, 13s. 4d. stg., and the whole expenditure of their establishment, including upkeep of property, expenses of horses, journeys to London, etc., for the next three years averaged £430 per annum, which does not seem overmuch, according to our modern ideas, for a 'Baron,' as the county Members of Parliament were called. It must, however, be borne in mind that at this time the salary of a Judge of the Court of Session was only £300 (raised in 1707 to £500), while a Peer with an income of £500 a year could not plead poverty as an excuse for changing his politics.[3]

In 1697 old Mrs. Baillie died, leaving to her daughters, Helen Baillie or Hav and Elizabeth Baillie or Weems, her property, which consisted of household furniture and £50 stg. invested in the Darien Scheme.[4] Her death set free her jointure of £102, 13s. 8d., and George Baillie and his family accordingly moved into a more expensive house belonging to Bailie Hamilton, at a rent of £38, 6s. Their flitting cost them 18s. 4d. Here they remained but a short time, moving in 1700 to a house belonging to Sir James Foulis of Colinton (generally known as Lord Colinton),

[1] Warriston Close is still extant, running north from the High Street at a point nearly opposite to St. Giles.

[2] Wodrow's *Analecta*.

[3] *Lockhart Papers*.

[4] *Edinburgh Testaments*, 17th September 1707.

which was probably situated in Foulis Close, and for which the rent was £33, 6s. 8d. This house they occupied until 1707, when they gave up living in Edinburgh and retired to Mellerstain. Mr. Baillie, however, came regularly to Edinburgh for the Assembly of the Church of Scotland, lodging either at Mrs. Room's [1] (an excellent name for a lodging-house keeper) or Mrs. Marshall's, paying as a rule 5s. stg. per night :—'A chamber in Mrs. Marshalls 2s., candle, 2s., maid 1s., 5s.'

What added very considerably to Mr. Baillie's expenditure was the necessity of frequent journeys to London on political business. We find such entries as :—

1694. Augt. 1. Taken with me to England £948, 16s. (£79, 1s. 4d. stg.).

English road when I last came from London with the Secretary £80, 10s. (£6, 14s. 2d. stg.).[2]

1707. April 1. to London journey in his pocket 50 Gunys.

For to answer bills to London £103 stg. more.

To Mr. Watson for a bill sent to London to Jeris £2100, 4s. (£175, 0s. 4d. stg.).

There can be little doubt that when Baillie travelled by himself he rode, as there are constant references to the purchase, conveyance, and repair of 'Clog bags.' On one occasion, at least (1714), he returned by sea to Newcastle, which cost him £3, 7s., whence he proceeded to Mellerstain by horse, the hire of these (three) costing him £2, 5s.

Then in addition to these business journeys there were constant journeys for health. In 1696 an expedition was made to Bath at a cost of £84, 0s. 9d. stg.[3] The October

[1] George Hume of Kimmerghame, an uncle of the Earl of Marchmont, when he came to Edinburgh in January 1695 lodged 'in Mrs. Romes, up Blair's stair, the fourth story upon the street.'—*George Hume's Diary*, quoted in Miss Warrender's *Marchmont and the Humes of Polwarth.*

[2] Mr. Secretary Johnston, Baillie's uncle.

[3] This may have been a political journey, as the Court was often at Bath.

of the following year they were at Prestonpans [1] at a cost of £18 stg., where they spent a considerable sum on 'Scots tartan muslin.' In 1701 they went to Scarborough from 9th July to 12th September, during which time meat and lodgings cost them £33, 6s. 8d. stg. From thence they brought back 'Two barrils of souns and gullits,'[2] which cost 11s. (stg.) and 8s. 4d. (stg.) for carriage. It is curious to find Prestonpans a more expensive place of residence than Scarborough.

After the Union Baillie must have been more and more in London, for his daughter writes that 'he strictly observed his attendance in Parliament and blamed those who made a bustle to get in and then absented themselves upon any pretence.' Unfortunately we have no note of his expenses nor of the presents he always brought back to his children, unless the following are some of them :—

bought by my dear at London	For a goun to Rach	£9	12	0
	For a black gown to Grisie	7	0	0
	For three night gouns to me and the bairens	6	1	0
	For making the gouns by Madmosel Odinat	2	10	0

On the accession of George I., when Baillie became a Lord of the Admiralty, he moved all his family to London. Two servants, Tam Youll and Katie Hearts, were sent by sea, 'fraught to London victuals furnished by the skipper £1, 10s.,' and the heavy baggage, including four and a half barrels of herrings, was also sent by sea in three different ships at a cost of £3, 8s. The family went by stage-coach,[3]

[1] A small town on the Firth of Forth, eight or nine miles east of Edinburgh.

[2] When the Baillies dined with Lady Essex in London, on 21st December 1722, the second course consisted of 'a sadle mutton, a dish cod souns with hard eg and half yolks of egs and some poatched egs on it.'

[3] This must be a very early reference to stage-coaches in Scotland. There was no coach between Edinburgh and Glasgow until 1749.

five seats costing £22, 10s. and 2s. 6d. for booking money. A sum of £2, 7s. was paid for excess luggage, each person being allowed 20 lbs. free. The coach was apparently joined at Dunglass,[1] the Baillies taking with them 'little Robie Pringle,'[2] and the expenses of the six during the thirteen days which it took them to reach London were only £10. They arrived in London on 18th December 1714, and at first hired a furnished house at a rent of £14 per month. This they left at the end of June 1715, paying in addition to their rent 'To Mr. Brown for spoiling his furniture 10s. 2d.,' and took an unfurnished house, apparently at Chelsea, at a rent of £45 per annum. They must have taken the house as it stood, for the repairing of the roof, glazing of windows, painting and sundry 'reparations' were all paid for by them.

In August 1716 they paid one of their many visits to Bath. They travelled by coach *via* Oxford, the journey there and back to London costing £20, the servants and luggage going separately. Their lodgings there, four rooms and garrets, were at the rate of £2, 5s. 9d. per week. In addition to the entries relating to taking the waters, amusements, etc., there occurs the following :—'For cleaning all our teeth at Bath £1, 14s.'

As already stated, Rachel Baillie was married in 1717 to Lord Binning. As the marriage was to take place in Edinburgh, the family, five in number, left London on 5th August in a coach with six horses, which was to carry them to Scotland in nine days[3] for £32, 15s. The expenses on the road on this occasion amounted to £14, 13s. 9d.

[1] A property on the east coast of Berwickshire belonging to Sir John Hall. See p. 27.

[2] Probably the son of Mr. Robert Pringle, Under-Secretary of State, who was the third son of Sir Robert Pringle of Stitchell.

[3] This must have been very fast travelling for those days. In 1725 the hire of 'a close bodyed carriage and six horses' cost £30, and the journey took fourteen days. In 1717 the commissioners on the forfeited estates were each allowed £50 for their expenses on the road to Scotland.

[illegible] £[illegible], 10s. and 2s. 6d. for booking money. [illegible] was paid for excess luggage, each person [illegible] lbs. free. The coach was apparently [illegible] at [illegible],[1] the Baillies taking with them 'little [illegible] Pringle,'[2] and the expenses of the six during the [illegible] days which it took them to reach London were [illegible]. They arrived in London on 18th December 1714, and at first hired a furnished house at a rent of [illegible] per month. This they left at the end of June 1715, paying in addition to their rent 'To Mr. Brown for spoiling his furniture 10s. 2d.,' and took an unfurnished house, apparently at Chelsea, at a rent of £45 per annum. They must have taken the house as it stood, for the repairing of the roof, glazing of windows, painting and sundry 'reparations' were all paid for by them.

In August 1716 they paid one of their many visits to Bath. They travelled by coach *via* Oxford, the journey there and back to London costing £20, the servants and luggage going separately. Their lodgings there, four rooms and garrets, were at the rate of £2, 5s. 9d. per week. In addition to the entries relating to taking the waters, amusements, etc., there occurs the following:—'For cleaning all our teeth at Bath £1, 14s.'

As already stated, Rachel Baillie was married in 1717 to Lord Binning. As the marriage was to take place in Edinburgh, the family, five in number, left London on [illegible] August in a coach with six horses, which was to carry them to Scotland in nine days[3] for £32, 15s. The expenses on the road on this occasion amounted to £14, 18s. 9d.

[1] A property on the east coast of Berwickshire belonging to Sir John Hall. [illegible]

[2] Probably the son of Mr. Robert Pringle, Under-Secretary of State, who was the third son of Sir Robert Pringle of Stitchell.

[3] This must have been very fast travelling for those days. In 1725 the hire of 'a [illegible] coach and six horses' cost £[illegible], and the journey took [illegible] days. In [illegible] the commissioners on the forfeited estates were each allowed [illegible] for their expenses on the road to Scotland.

LADY BINNING,

AGED 29.

(From a Portrait at Mellerstain by Maria Verelst.)

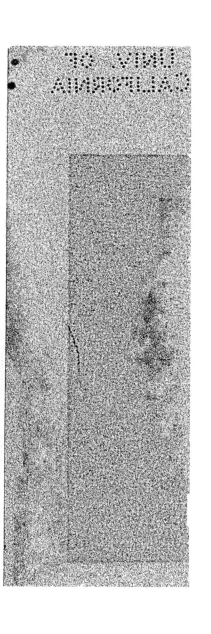

In 1729 the household were again resident at Mellerstain, and consequently the visit to Bath in that year was a much greater undertaking. The expedition consisted of a coach and six horses and eight riding horses, the journey from Berwick to Bath taking sixteen days. There were six of the family in the coach and two maids; and the cost of their provisions on the road amounted to £23, 18s. 6d. The board and lodging of seven men for the same period came to £5, 12s., or at the rate of 1s. per diem per head. while the cost of feeding the horses during the same period amounted to £30, 1s. 9½d. The horses got five days' rest at Bath, after which nine of them were sent back to Scotland under charge of 'Tam,' who got £14, 14s. for his expenses on the journey.

But by far the most important of their journeys was undertaken in 1731, when Lord Binning was ordered abroad for his health. Jerviswood, who was getting on in life, was by no means anxious to undertake the fatigues of a long foreign sojourn, but he yielded to the solicitations of his son-in-law, and on the 9th of June 1731 he and Lady Grisell, their daughters Grisie and Rachel, their son-in-law Lord Binning, and their granddaughter 'little Gris' landed at Rotterdam. They were accompanied by at least four servants, two women and two men, but it is a little difficult to gather the total number of the party, as friends seem to join and leave them. The accounts show clearly the course of their journey. They travelled by schuit or public canal boat, by diligence, by private carriage, and by chair. As was but natural, they made first for Utrecht, where Lady Grisell had lived in exile with her father, and where, in spite of poverty and anxiety, they had been a merry household. 'She had the greatest pleasure in shewing us every corner of the town, which seemed fresh in her memory; particularly the house she had lived in, which she had a great desire to see; but when she came there they would not let her in, by no arguments either of words or money, for no reason but for fear of dirtying it. She offered to put off her shoes, but nothing could prevail, and she came away much mortified at her disappointment.' [1]

The first long stay was made at Spa, where they took lodgings at the 'Loup,' engaging their own cook. They must have found this house comfortable, for the party makes a still longer stay in it on their return journey. Here they took the waters, and here also they gave a ball and supper to '70 persons.' The expense of this latter amounted to £13, 4s. 5d., including £1, 11s. 6d. for the 'fidels' and 12s. for the 'Buckie' (bouquet). Then they moved on through Liége, Namur, Arlon (where we find the suggestive note 'imposed on'), and other places on the road south. Each little town provided its custom-house worries and 'searchers' to be squared, sometimes not altogether satisfactorily, as witness Champagne, where 'we was searched overly,' and Châlons, where 'we was stopd 3 days by the impertinence of the Bourro.' They reached Lyons on 11th October, and contracted to be conveyed to Turin partly by chaises and partly by chairs 'over the Alps cald Munt Sines.' (It will be noted that the sums entered for conveying the party from place to place generally include meals, sometimes two and sometimes three a day.) Then they passed through Milan, Parma, Reggio, Modena, Bologna (where it is refreshing to see the first entry of 11s. 9d. for 'sasageses'), Loretto, and so to Rome, where they arrived on 'the 23 Novr. at one o'clock of the day 1731.' On this occasion but a short stay was made in the Eternal City, the party pushing on to Naples, which was their objective, and which they reached on 5th December.

---

[1] Lady Murray's *Memoirs*.

LORD BINNING.

(*From a Portrait at Mellerstain.*)

At Naples they took a house at £8 per month, for which they had to supply china, glass, cutlery, napery, etc. They also hired a coach and horses at £8 per month, and engaged a cook and cook-boy, a maid, and M. Saverio and a 'Vanditor.' Here Lady Grisell at once set to work to learn Italian, her master being paid the munificent sum of 13s. 7d. per month! In regard to this her daughter writes: 'At Naples she shewed what would have been a singular quickness of capacity and apprehension at any age much more at hers. She knew not one word of Italian, and had servants of the country that as little understood one word she said; so that at first she was forced to call me to interpret betwixt them; but in a very little while, with only the help of a grammar and dictionary, she did the whole business of her family with her Italian servants, went to shops, bought everything she had occasion for, and did it so well that our acquaintances who had lived many years there begged the favour of her to buy for them when she provided herself; thinking and often saying she did it to much better purpose than they could themselves.'

As well as studying Italian, the Baillies at this time also studied music, and had much music copied, amongst which the music of Corelli is specially mentioned.

They remained in Naples until the beginning of May 1732, when they went for the summer to Portiche, again taking a house and having to provide a good many furnishings. On the 14th November they returned to Naples, where apparently they were joined by two of Lord Binning's sons and a second daughter, and where Lord Binning died on 27th December. The Accounts show the expense of the mourning, including a velvet nightgown for 'my D.,' which sounds strange to ears accustomed to the modern meaning of the word 'nightgown.' After this sad event chaises and saddlery were repaired, boxes purchased and

At Naples thev took a house at £8 per month, for which they had to supply china, glass, cutlery, napery, etc. They also hired a coach and horses at £8 per month, and engaged a cook and cook-boy, a maid, and M. Saverio and a 'Vanditor.' Here Lady Grisell at once set to work to learn Italian, her master being paid the munificent sum of 13s. 7d. per month! In regard to this her daughter writes: 'At Naples she shewed what would have been a singular quickness of capacity and apprehension at any age much more at hers. She knew not one word of Italian, and had servants of the country that as little understood one word she said; so that at first she was forced to call me to interpret betwixt them; but in a very little while, with only the help of a grammar and dictionary, she did the whole business of her family with her Italian servants, went to shops, bought everything she had occasion for, and did it so well that our acquaintances who had lived many years there begged the favour of her to buy for them when she provided herself; thinking and often saying she did it to much better purpose than they could themselves.'

As well as studying Italian, the Baillies at this time also studied music, and had much music copied, amongst which the music of Corelli is specially mentioned.

They remained in Naples until the beginning of May 1732, when they went for the summer to Portiche, again taking a house and having to provide a good many furnishings. On the 14th November they returned to Naples, where apparently they were joined by two of Lord Binning's sons and a second daughter, and where Lord Binning died on 27th December. The Accounts show the expense of the mourning, including a velvet nightgown for 'my D.,' which sounds strange to ears accustomed to the modern meaning of the word 'nightgown.' After this sad event chaises and saddlery were repaired, boxes purchased and got ready, accounts settled, and a start made on the homeward journey. Before leaving Naples, however, they sent home by ship a supply of hams, parmesan cheese, and macaroni. They also shipped home marble slabs to the value of £646, 16s. sterling.[1]

They reached Rome on 29th March 1733, and remained there until 22nd April. Thence they proceeded to Florence, where Lady Grisell had the pictures already referred to of her husband, her daughter Grisie, and her two grand-daughters Gris and Helen painted by Mr. Martin for £11, 11s., and where she saw the ostrich in reference to which she afterwards notes for her grandsons, 'If you have any brass money in your pocket it will be very good for the ostrich.'[2] At Bologna they took a box in the Opera House, which they provided with a cushion and cloth; and at Venice they bought books and treacle! and attended amongst other things a 'Gundaliers' wedding, subscribing a shilling to the fiddlers. Thence through Verona, Trent, Innsbruck, Frankfort, Cologne, they worked their way back to Spa, where they again made a long stay, and then passing through Liége and Brussels to Paris they finally crossed over from Calais to Dover, carrying with them silver, lace, and clothes of all sorts.

Looking through these Accounts, one cannot but note the constant repairing required by the chaises, or 'cheases,' as Lady Grisell frequently writes it, the furbishing up of pistols and purchasing of sword belts, etc., indicative of

---

[1] Boxes containing all sorts of things, clothing, books, honey, treacle, pins, needles, lamps, etc., were sent home in various ways: 'by the Dut. of Newcastle to be left at Dr. Mowbrays,' 'in the trunk that goes to Leghorn to be sent in a man of war,' to be sent by John Gordon Banker in Rotterdam 'in a Scots ship to Robert Foulerton at the Custome House in Leath,' etc. Careful lists were kept of what each box contained, and at the top of one of these is a deleted note in Lady Grisell's hand, '43 Marbel Tables in the coach house, 2 tables in the galarie.'

[2] See p. 396.

GRISIE' AND 'RACHIE' BAILLIE,

AGED 6 AND 2 RESPECTIVELY.

(*From a Picture at Mellerstain by John Scougall.*)

the bad [1] and dangerous state of the roads. It will also be noticed that even at that early stage in the history of tea the British matron refused to do without it, and seemed to have had little or no difficulty in obtaining it.

Amongst the purchases, 'beavor' skin stockings strike one as peculiar; and the number of pairs of spectacles purchased is also remarkable. It looks as if a pair must have been left behind by mistake at every stopping-place.

Amongst the books purchased abroad there are three cookery-books added to Lady Grisell's household library.

II. Education and Amusements

As is but natural, entries relating to 'Grisie' and 'Rachie' bulk largely in the Accounts. We cannot trace the career of 'Grisie' from her birth, as that event took place shortly before the Accounts begin, but we can follow the life of Rachie from its very dawn, when £2, 18s. stg. is paid to Mrs Scott the midwife, 9s. 8d. to Mr. Livingston for christening her, 3s. 8d. to the 'bathel of the Church,' and 4s. 10d. in charity, up to the date of her marriage in 1717, when £4, 6s. is paid 'To my Rachys Proclamation etc.,' and £1, 1s. 6d. 'For the garland that is brock over the Brid's head,' 'For Bryds favours £3,' and 'To the Brids Garter £1, 3s.'[2] We can watch the two sisters grow-

---

[1] 'I bought a chaise at Rome, which cost me twenty five pounds, good English pounds, and had the pleasure of being laid low in it the very second day after I set out. I had the marvellous good luck to escape with life and limbs; but my delightful chaise broke all to pieces, and I was forced to stay a whole day in a hovel while it was tacked together in such a way as would serve to drag me hither.' So writes Lady Mary Wortley Montagu from Naples on 25th November 1739.

[2] 'At the marriages of persons of the upper class favours were sewn upon the bride's dress. When the ceremony was concluded all the members of the company ran towards her, each endeavouring to seize a favour. When the

ing up by watching their petticoats growing down. '1708. For lining Rachys gown and letting down her peticoats' 2s. stg. Then there are all the payments in connection with their education, and with Miss May Menzies who came 'at Lambis 1705 to wate on mv children,' and who remained as a friend of the family presumably until her death.

Miss Menzies was the daughter of William Menzies of Raw, W.S., and her nominal salary was £8 stg. per annum, but 'I have always paid her £100 Scots' (£8, 6s. 8d. stg.). She was a devoted friend to her charges, for in 1709 Lady Grisell enters, 'To her over and above her fie for her care of the bairens when they had the fever' £27, 12s. 2d. stg., and there are also many entries of presents given to her, such as dresses, etc. Talking of her girlhood, Lady Murray writes as follows: 'We were always with her [Lady Grisell] at home and abroad, but when it was necessary we should learn what was fit for us; and for that end she got Mrs. May Menzies, a daughter of Mr. Menzies of Raws, Writer to the Signet, to be our governess, who was well qualified in all respects for it, and whose faithful care and capacity my mother depended so much upon, that she was easy when we were with her. She was always with us when our masters came and had no other thought or business but the care and instruction of us; which I must here acknowledge with gratitude, having been an indulgent though exact mistress to us when young; and to this time, it being now forty-five years that she has lived with us, a faithful, disinterested friend, with good

---

confusion had ceased the bridegroom's man proceeded to pull off the bride's garter, which she modestly dropped. This was cut into small portions, which were presented to each member of the company.'—Roger's *Scotland, Social and Domestic.* We also learn from the same source that it was the custom when a bride of a more humble station entered her new home to break a cake of shortbread over her head, the fragments of which were gathered up by the young people and dreamed on. Perhaps the bride's garland here mentioned was a prettier form of the same custom.

SAMPLER AT MELLERSTAIN, WORKED UNDER THE DIRECTIONS OF MISS MENZIES.

(*The animals are copied from a book which belonged to Miss Menzies, and still Mellerstain.*)

sense, good temper, entirely in our interest, and that with so much honesty that she always spoke her mind sincerely without the least sycophantry.'

The following letter of instructions by Lady Grisell to Miss Menzies gives us some idea of her duties :—

Edinburgh, August 16, 1705.

Directions for Grisie given May Menzies

To rise by seven a clock and goe about her duty of reading, etc. etc., and be drest to come to Breckfast at nine, to play on the spinnet till eleven, from eleven till twelve to write and read French. At two a clock sow her seam till four, at four learn arithmetic, after that dance and play on the spinet again till six and play herself till supper and to bed at nine.

But the education of Grisie, poor mite, had begun long before this, and had been conducted partly at school and partly by special masters. On 10th November 1696, when she is just four years old, her reading master receives 4s. 10d. for the quarter, and her education in this branch is completed in 1701, when a payment of £1, 10s. is made 'to Porterfield to perfect Grisie in reading.' Mr. Thomson receives 9s. 8d. per quarter for teaching writing, Mr. Brown £1 for teaching arithmetic, and Mr. M'Gie £1, 1s. 6d. for teaching geography. We also read of 5s. 5d. as the quarter's fee for the reading school ; of 2s. 3d. for 'Rachies quarter at the School,' and of 4s. 10d. paid for 'the Bairens milk going to the School.' There is no mention of French lessons—except those given by Miss Menzies—until the family are in London in 1715, when 'Mistress Faucour' receives 10s. for a month's tuition and Mr. Dumbar £1, 1s. 6d. for the same.

Then there were dancing lessons, both for the children and, as already mentioned, for Lady Grisell herself. The children's lessons 'with the Frenchman' cost about £1, 3s. 8d. a month, just about half what was paid in London to 'Mr. Isaach for a months dancing to Rachie £3, 4s. 6d.'

Then of course they go to the balls given by their dancing masters, and we read :—

1702. May.	To Rachys Ball and Grisies .	£0	4	11
	For a straw hat to Grisies Ball	0	10	0
	Gloves to them . . .	2	6	0
	Cheries at the Ball . . .	0	10	0

We also find the rather suggestive entry: 'To Grisies master for coals' 1s. 2½d stg.

In addition to going out to dances they sometimes had the fiddlers in, for 4s. 10d. was paid 'To Thomson the violer for playing to the bairens a day,' and 9s. 8d. was paid 'For the Kelso fiddlers 2 days at Mellerstains.'

Of course the fiddlers may have been employed for the pleasure of their music alone, for music was one of George Baillie's delights, and one which was shared in by his wife and children. The musical education of the latter was certainly varied. 'Grisie' was taught to play the spinet, virginal, viol and harp. She was also taught singing and 'through bass,' while 'Rachie' learns the spinet, virginal, and flute. 'Grisie' continued her musical studies long after her marriage, and we find her taking advantage of her stay in Naples, then one of the principal schools of music in the world, to prosecute them there. By the way, there was apparently no one in Edinburgh competent to mend a virginal, although there were tuners there, for in 1714 the 'fine virginal' has to be sent from Mellerstain to Leith and shipped to London to be repaired. The repairs cost £12, 10s. and the expenses of getting it there and back came to £2, 3s. 8d. How devoted the family were to music is shown from their Accounts while in London, which show constant entries for tickets for operas and concerts. They evidently belonged to the Handel faction, and not to that of his rival, Bononcini, for they patronise the concert of Castruchi, the leader of Handel's Opera band, who was famous as a performer on the 'Violetta Marina,' an instrument of his own invention; and they go to hear Bernachi, 'Il Re dei cantatori,' take the part of Goffredo in Handel's 'Rinaldo,' and Berenstadt sing the bass part of Arganti. Evidently Bernachi, whose singing particularly appealed to the musically educated, was a special favourite of theirs. He presented them with a dog called 'Senorina,' and they presented him with a gold watch costing £25 and a gold chain costing £4, 10s. When her grandsons Lord Haddington and his brother went abroad in 1740, Lady Grisell specially directed them when at Bologna to 'ask also for Sig^{re} Barnachi the famous singer and Sig^{re} Sandoni the husband of the Cuzone,[1] they will be pleased to be of service to any of our family.'

Then they bought tickets from the famous singer Mrs. Anastasia Robinson, afterwards Countess of Peterborough, and they no doubt attended her weekly concerts in Golden Square, where were to be found 'all such as had any pretensions to politeness and good taste.'[2]

Concert tickets in London cost about 10s. each; while in Edinburgh we read of 'a concert to Grissie,' at various times costing 1s. 2½d. stg., 2s. 2d., 2s. 6d., etc.

Money was easily spent in London on less intellectual pleasures than music. Masquerades, a form of entertainment to which the king was partial, were naturally fashionable, and to many of these the Baillies went as 'Caposhins,' 'Pilgrims,' etc. Rachel was present as a 'Country Girl' at the famous masquerade at Montagu House, tickets for

---

[1] Cuzzoni, one of the most famous singers of the day. She appeared first in London on 12th January 1722 as Teophane in Handel's 'Otto.' It was while rehearsing for this opera that Handel in a rage seized her round the waist and threatened to throw her out of the window. On one occasion a gentleman in the gallery poetically exclaimed, 'Damn her, she has a nest of nightingales in her belly.' She married Sigr. Sandoni, a harpsichord master and composer of some eminence. She was a foolish and extravagant woman, and eventually died in great poverty.—Grove's *Dictionary of Music*.

[2] Burney's *History*.

which were much sought after, and where 'there was a drawing-room for the King who was not there,' and 'where everything was in great order and magnificence,' and 'could not have cost less than five or six hundred pounds.'[1] Then they lost money at cards at the Dukes of Roxburgh and Montrose, at the Earls of Stair and Rothes, at Ladies Loudoun, Strafford, Mar, Dupplin, etc. They dined with the Prince and Princess of Wales, with the Dukes of Chandos and Hamilton, Sir Robert Walpole, Mr. Speaker Onslow, Mr. Doddington, and scores of other interesting people,[2] 'and were as usual in the first circles, Mr. Baillie's house being the resort of the best company and the rendezvous of many of the wits of that day.'[3]

We have mentioned how the Baillies accepted a present of a dog from Signor Bernachi, but we read in Lady Murray's *Memoirs* of another present which was not so well received. She writes: 'He had an infinite pleasure in giving even little trifling presents to his friends, but did not like receiving. If it was from any he thought had a view to his interest for them he would not suffer it though never so trifling. He made us return a parrot given us when he was in the Admiralty by a gentleman who was soliciting something there.' As to this Mr. Harry Graham writes:[4] 'To be given a parrot at any time is annoying, but when such a gift partakes of the nature of a bribe it becomes doubly offensive.' Mr. Graham, however, forgot when writing this that Mr. Baillie's fondness for animals was well known. An examination of Lady Grisell's accounts shows that the gentleman who presented the parrot was not such a simpleton as Mr. Graham not

---

[1] *Diary of Mary, Countess of Cowper.*

[2] See 'Bills of Fair,' p. 281, in which Lady Grisell not only states with whom they dined, but what they had for dinner, and how the dishes were arranged on the table.

[3] Appendix to Lady Murray's *Memoirs.*

[4] *A Group of Scottish Women*, by Harry Graham.

unnaturally concludes, for Mr. Baillie had a sufficient liking for parrots to pay 4s. 10d. for having one brought from Glasgow in 1703, and a reward of 2s. 'for finding the parrit,' when it escaped in 1704. Besides this parrot there were purchased in 1705 a mavis for 2s. 6d., 2 lint whites for 1s. 8d., and in 1713 the then large sum of £1, 10s. is paid for a 'mavis cage.' 'The dog Lyon' is purchased in 1718 for 2s. 6d., and in the same year 10s. 6d. is paid 'To teach Jessie the dog tricks.'

III. Servants

The question of servants seems to have bulked as largely then as now. One is accustomed to talk of the good old-fashioned servant who came as a girl and died as a nuisance at an advanced age, but although there are occasional traces of this class of domestic to be met with in the Baillie Accounts, one is more struck by the constant changes in the household. In fact, those changes are so frequent that it is very difficult to judge of the size of the establishment,[1] and one is reluctantly driven to the conclusion that Lady Grisell was in some ways just too good a manager. For instance, there are eighteen different servants mentioned in the first three years of their married life, and that in an establishment consisting apparently of four women servants and a manservant. During the next ten years there are sixty different servants mentioned, of whom thirty-one do not remain a year and seventeen do not remain two years. When, after the accession of George I., the family took up its quarters in London, the same ill luck as to domestics followed them there. In 1715 there were no fewer than eight cooks: one remained a day, one a night, and one made out two months,

[1] In 1697 cess is paid for eight servants, and in London there were eight servants.

but was then carried away by the constables. The same misfortune overtook Hellen Williams the housemaid, who is charged with 8s. 2d. 'For constables and cariing befor a Justice of Peace.' No hint is given of their crimes, nor do we learn anything of their fate, unless this item in the following year's Accounts has reference to them :—'July 31. To the servants at Newgate Prison 2s. 6d.' In 1717 there were four cooks, one of whom stayed a night and one a fortnight and was paid for a month, which meant a good deal under Lady Grisell's careful sway. No wonder Lady Grisell when an old woman wrote to her daughter, Lady Murray: 'My dear, Stay till Saturday if Lady S. desires you, and tell her not to be uneasie at the disappointments in servants, for being a thing she will always meet, it would be a plague indeed if one laid it to heart. If she can lift her house to St. Giles's we should all live together and everyone serve another, but I would keep the purse and make them eat their meat in order. Our housemaid is so long that your sister has made two of her, for we have only her and the cook and I'm in no hope for a laundrimaid. You'll think I have said enough with a vomite on my stomach which is only by way of prevention.'[1]

There are, as has been hinted, several notable exceptions to this short service system. May Menzies, the governess, to whom reference has already been made, remained all her life, and Tam Youll, the coachman, seems also to have been more or less of a fixture. Tam entered the Baillies' service in 1706 as groom, at a money wage of £1, 10s. stg. and his clothes, excepting linen. He eventually became

[1] This is written by Lady Grisell in an old and shaky hand in the middle of an undated letter from Lady Binning to Lady Murray describing a seizure Lady Grisell had had the previous night, diagnosed by Dr. Carlton as the result of wind caused by too long fasts. He advises 'she should eat little at a time, and often, fasting long is very bad for her.'

coachman, and went with the family to London, where his wages were raised to £3. His career exemplifies another point in connection with Lady Grisell's household service, viz. the custom of fining the domestics for faults and charging them with any loss sustained through their carelessness or misconduct. Thus there is an entry in Tam Youll's account as follows: 1709. 'To him for George Dods loss of work when drunk and lam'd his leg £7, 4s. Scots.'[1] And George Dods's account for the same year contains this entry: 'March 25. For a velvet cap he spoilt £2, 8s. Scots.' In 1712 Tam is again in disgrace for having got drunk at Makerstoun, for which he is fined 10s. stg., the entry being, 'April 20. To him for excessive drinking.' In 1714 he meets with still severer punishment in connection with a mare which had apparently come by an accident through his carelessness, for he has not only to pay £1, 10s. stg. 'To the ferriers account,' but also 10s. stg. for the hire of a horse 'to the coch when the mare was spoilt'—£2 out of a money wage of £2, 10s. When his wife is ill a doctor and drugs are provided for her, but they are charged against him in his account—£1, 16s. 6d. It is the same with the accounts of all the other servants. They are carefully charged with anything provided or done for them or their families beyond the bargain of their service. They are fined for misbehaviour,[2] and have to pay for 'breakages' unless reported the same day.[3]

As this subject of servants is one of considerable interest, Lady Grisell's 'Memorandums and Directions to Servants'

---

[1] It was Youll who was drunk, and not Dods, as is shown by another entry. By the way there were not fewer than three 'Tam Youlls' in the establishment at the same time, which must have made things a trifle confusing.

[2] '1706. To James Carrin for wilful absence from his service, £3 Scots.' His wage was £30 Scots.

[3] See p. 275, rule 22.

has been included in this volume. It is rendered still more interesting by there being given a table of their weekly diet—diet which would certainly not suit the servant of to-day. It will be observed that there is no such thing as butter allowed with their 'oat loaf, broun bread or Ry.'

As already stated, it is difficult to gather from the earlier accounts how many servants were kept, but when the family were in London there appear to have been eight, and latterly at Mellerstain there must have been about seventeen, as is shown by a list of the servants as at Whitsunday 1740 :—

Ann Turnbull, Housekeeper	£5	0	0
Margaret Rutherd, Gentlewoman	[illegible]	0	[illegible]
Betty ogle, Landry maid		0	
Janet, Housemaid		0	
Ann Castles, Cook		0	
Margaret Hardy, Washer		0	
Hellen Youl, Dary Maid		0	
Pegie, Kitchen Maid		0	
Hendry de Pallie, Butler	1	0	
George Deans, Gardner	1	0	
Robert Taylor, Cochman		0	
William Hull, Footman		0	
Tam Youll, his land coachman about		0	
Andrew Youl, Postilion		0	
George Carter, Groom		10	
Tam Youll, Carter		0	
John, Under cook		0	
George Howison, herd without meat		0	
George Dods, officer without meat		5	0
	£94	15	0

In Appendix II. will be found a note of the money wages paid to servants prior to 1718 as shown in the Accounts. In judging of the figures there given as applicable to Scotland, it is necessary to add to the money wage the value of two pairs of shoes supplied annually to each maidservant, and the value of all clothes except linen supplied to most of the menservants. The former may be taken as having been worth about 4s. stg. per annum and the latter about £2 stg. per annum.

'Drink money' or tips to servants of course figures largely, and there seems little doubt that this burden was even more oppressive then than now. As far as can be judged, 'drink money' per annum averaged about one-fifth of the annual wage-bill of the servants. The entry which gives the largest amount of drink money is in 1717, and is as follows: 'For all drink money while at Edinburgh and travelling about the 6 moneths I was in Scotland £29, 10s. stg.' This would represent something like £200 of the money of to-day, and strikes one as a large sum even for people in such a position as the Baillies, who were no doubt accompanied by two or three servants.

It is not only the amount of the drink money that is surprising; it is also the servants to whom drink money is paid. The recipients are nearly always nurses.[1] Of course one can understand that at a christening the nurse would be the natural person to tip, but the occasions cannot always have been christenings, even admitting how fashionable large families then were.

As already stated, the menservants received clothing, but it is a little difficult to give details of what was supplied, as in most cases material is purchased and made up by the tailor at a wage of 4d. a day and his food. Still it is possible to glean a certain amount of information. Duncan Bisset, whose wage was £2 per annum, received in 1702 shoes 4s., linen running drawers 1s. 3d., running shoes 3s. 2d., twil drawers 1s. 2⅔d., string 3½d., hat 4s. 6d., shirts

---

[1] See vol. xxxix. of the *Proceedings of the Society of Antiquaries of Scotland*, p. 121, where Mr. A. O. Curle refers to this.

4s. 8d., cap 3s., drawers and gloves 2s. 8d., stockings 1s. 10d., a bonnet 1d., blue cloth for a coat £1, 14s. 3½d., for furnishing and making the same 4s. 8d. Duncan had to supply at his own expense 'linen to his neck,' which cost him 2s. 10d. In 1715 a suit of livery seems to have cost £4, 10s., and a big lined coat £2, 10s., while a suit of ordinary clothes for the barnman cost only £1.

We get another instance of Lady Grisell's careful management from such entries as the following: '1716. Nov. 16. For turning two coats into two waistcoats to George and Tam 10s.'

Board wages in Scotland were at that time 1s. a day, but this no doubt included lodging, as the cost of feeding a servant according to the dietary given by Lady Grisell on p. 277 works out at about 3d. a day. In 1716 the cost of feeding servants in England is given as follows:—

For meat to 4 servants when I was nine weeks at Bath from 8 Augt. till 8 Oct. from Betson	£0	15	2
For bread in that time	1	2	2
For candle, cheese roots, etc. in that time	0	6	6
For Bear	0	18	0
	£3	1	10

or nearly 1s. 9d. per head per week. Either the servants must have starved themselves in 1716 or they must have 'done' themselves uncommonly well in 1718, for under 8th October of that year we find the following corresponding entries:—

For meat to 4 servants for 6 weeks wt Mrs. Dundas [while] I was at Bath from Clements Butcher	£1	8	
bread	0	9	1
drink 2½ barrill	1	2	6
sundry other provisions	2	12	3
	£5	11	10

This works out at 4s. 8d. per head per week.

IV. Household Expenses

Under this heading, as already mentioned, Lady Grisell entered all expenditure in connection with provisioning, firing, lighting, and washing. Not only did she enter sums actually spent, but she also charged herself with the prices of all supplies drawn from the estate. These would no doubt be credited in some ‘ home farm ’ Account Book, but that has not been found. During the first years of her married life the details given under this heading are rather meagre, but they increase year by year, and are eventually very voluminous. It is, of course, quite impossible to refer to all the articles mentioned, and as the extracts from the Accounts may not give some of these, an attempt has been made by means of an appendix to keep a note of the most important of them and of their prices, though the Editor is aware that a tabulated state of this sort is apt to be misleading as it gives no indication of what was in common or only in occasional use. An attempt has also been made in the same Appendix to contrast, where data make it possible, the prices ruling in Scotland and in England in the early eighteenth century with those of the present day.

A careful examination of this part of the expenditure shows that on an average nearly a fourth of it was spent on alcoholic drinks, and that exclusive of the beer brewed at home. In Scotland, French wine (this may be another name for claret, although Lady Grisell seems to draw a distinction between the two), claret, canary, sack, mum, brandy, ale, and beer are the principal drinks and are bought in large quantities, while other wines and spirits, such as burgundy, aquavitæ, arrac, etc., are only rarely mentioned. In England, on the other hand, arrac and burgundy frequently figure, and champagne makes its appearance. These two latter wines are generally bought together and in the same number of bottles, rather indicating that they were got for special occasions.

Turning to temperance drinks, the first mention of tea in Lady Grisell's Accounts is in 1702, when a shilling is paid for a 'tee pot.' There is, however, a still earlier reference to tea in the Inventory of the furnishings of her mother-in-law's house in Edinburgh, which is dated 5th June 1696, and where we find mention of 'a whet (white) ern (iron) tee stop (stoup).' Little tea-cups to drink out of are also purchased in 1702, and a little 'yetlen [1] kettle' and spirits of wine for boiling the same.[2] In 1705 we have '2 dozen china plats, 2 dusin tee and jacolite dishes and a tee pot and basone bought by Greenknowe in Holland' £8, 2s. 6d. stg., and in 1706 1s. 4d. is paid for 'a pot for milk to tee.' We have thus the tea-table fairly complete. The first entry narrating the purchase of tea itself does not occur until 1708, when half a pound Bohea is purchased for £1. That is at the rate of £1, 9s. 1d. per pound avoirdupois. Probably prior to that date any tea got was purchased by Mr. Baillie when in London. With tea at such a price Lady Grisell naturally buys but seldom, and at first in half or quarter pound quantities, generally purchasing at the same time with Bohea an equal quantity of green tea, which cost about half as much. As the fortunes of the family improved and the price fell, tea was used more and more, and latterly figures pretty often in the Accounts. Coffee is mentioned in 1703, and a 'coper pott' for Coffee is entered in old Mrs. Baillie's Inventory of 1696. Chocolate is referred to as early as 1695. Fruits and confections are frequently bought, and occasionally 'taiblet for the bairens.'

---

[1] Cast-iron.

[2] Spirit lamps are mentioned in old Mrs. Baillie's Inventory already referred to, where we find 'two coper things for holding of cotten to burn with wein.'

As to food supplies, not much need be said. With the exception of anchovies, which are only once purchased, the other items mentioned in the Appendix occur with more or less frequency. Herrings of course bulk largely, and many barrels of them are sent as presents to Mr. Secretary Johnston in London. It is curious to note that when in London Lady Grisell finds it cheaper to have barley, starch, washing blue, butter, shelled peas, indigo, etc., sent from Edinburgh.

Cows, oxen, calves, sheep, lambs, and pigs are also largely used for food, as well as fowls, domesticated and wild, the latter being purchased at all seasons. Unfortunately there are no data to enable us to contrast the prices of butcher meat in Scotland and England, but it will be noted that in England mutton is dearer per pound than beef, and the relative prices of cattle and sheep indicate that this also was the case in Scotland. Lady Murray gives us a carefully drawn up statement of the quantities of supplies consumed by the establishment for several years after Lady Grisell's death, two of which are given as specimens,[1] but when considering these, it must be borne in mind that Mellerstain was at that time the residence of ladies only.

Perhaps it is not inappropriate under this head to refer to the question of menus. Lady Grisell left a book of these 'Bills of Fair' as she calls them. They are peculiarly interesting from the fact that they give not only her own dinners, but the dinners of the friends by whom she was entertained, and further, the lists are made so as to show the position of the dishes on the table. A few of these are printed,[2] and it will be seen from them that two courses, a relief and dessert, constituted a formal dinner. All the dishes of each course were set down on the

---

1 Pp. 304-306.

2 Pp. 281-304.

table, and a relief consisted of one or two dishes substituted for some of those of the first course. Sometimes Lady Grisell draws circles round the name of each dish to represent the plate. From these 'Bills' we see what was the dinner when the Baillies dined with the Prince and Princess of Wales at Richmond, with the Duke of Montrose, the Duke of Roxburgh, Bishop of Sarum, Duke of Chandos, Lord Stair, Lord Oxford, Lady Mary Wortley Montagu, etc., and what the Baillies gave these great people when they in turn dined with them. It will be noted that in these menus there is only one mention of potatoes, and that in one of the foreign menus in 1733.

The House Accounts contain many other odd items of information. For instance, we find that Lady Grisell made her own ink, and excellent ink it was, out of copperas and galls, and her blacking for boots out of lamp black and beeswax. We learn that a barrel containing thirty salted cod cost £1, and a barrel of pickled oysters 2s.; that out of thirty dozen oranges and twenty dozen lemons Lady Grisell had '8 gallons orange wine and large 12 gallons of panch and 2 doz. oranges besides to preserve'; that a flambeau cost from 1s. 2d. to 1s. 6d; that the salmon bill for the year amounted to £1, 7s.; that tobacco cost 2s. and snuff 4s. a lb., also that the ladies used the latter. We find that in London, as coals were expensive, a cinder sieve was purchased, and charcoal and billets of wood were burned, and brushwood and roots used. In fact, the information is inexhaustible.

V. Buildings, Gardens, and Estate Management

The picturesque old tower of Jerviswood had been the residence of George Baillie's father. There all his children had been born, and there his widow took up her residence when the estates were restored to the family. There is extant in the old lady's handwriting an Inventory of the furniture and plenishings at Jerviswood as at November 1694. It is an interesting and marvellously spelt document, and we learn from it how the various rooms were furnished, or rather unfurnished: witness the purple chamber, which contained only 'a very old bed all brok,' and 'My study,' which belied its title by containing nothing but water stoops, cups, coggies, spits, girdels, raxes, quiechs, etc. There was no drawing-room, 'My Chamber' having no doubt contrived a double debt to pay, and the dining-room held nought but 'en beg ern chemly [grate] with a bake' and 'a bege wenscott tebell and two fur tember one lesser.' Some of the windows would also appear to have been only half glazed, the lower half being a hinged wooden shutter, as indicated by there being 'In a beg pres' '4 pr of wendow bands' or hinges. Jerviswood and its furnishings, its 'three win glasses two of them wanting the foot,' was as typical of the Scotland that was passing as Mellerstain Tower, the Baillies' other residence, became typical of the Scotland that was coming.

As his mother was occupying the old family residence of Jerviswood, George Baillie had perforce to adopt Mellerstain Tower as his country residence. Unfortunately, there are no traces left of the latter place. It probably occupied the site of the buildings erected towards the end of the eighteenth century from the designs of R. and J. Adam, and united as these do now the two wings built by George Baillie. In spite of the beautiful roofs and exquisite woodcarvings of its successor, one cannot help regretting the disappearance of the old Tower, the top of which we learn from the Accounts was so carefully repaired every year.

Probably during old Mrs. Baillie's lifetime this old Tower was even less comfortable than Jerviswood, but she had not long been dead, and the estates freed of her jointure, before extensive repairs and additions began to be made to it. During the years 1701, 1702, and 1703 £217, 12s. 4d. was spent on repairing the Tower and offices. Each following year something was added. In 1706 there is paid 6s. for measuring off '33 acres, 3 ruds, 17 f. 8 ells for a park,' and in 1708 the park dykes are built at a cost of £54, 9s. 5d. In 1709, looking to the times, this most extraordinary entry occurs: 'Expense of building the Bath house £65, 4s. 4d.' In 1711 a new kitchen is built which apparently had a thatched roof. And so the additions go on.

Nor is the garden or planting neglected. In 1701 young trees are bought for 3s. 4d. from 'Hundalie,' and fir seed is frequently got—sometimes from London. The price of the latter seems to have varied considerably, from 2s. per lb. in 1704, to 15s. in 1711. There is a nursery formed at Jerviswood, and large numbers of young trees purchased for there and Mellerstain—limes, yews, thorns, planes, elms, geans, firs, chestnuts, walnuts, and fruit trees. Acorns are also got. In 1712 we have one of Lady Grisell's characteristic entries: 'For young trees bought by John Hope which was a perfit cheat £2, 10s.' and in 1715 we read of 1s. 8d. being paid 'For nailing up the vine tree.'

There were evidently a few well-grown trees still left in Scotland at this date, in spite of the general belief to the contrary, as shown by such entries as: 1703. 'Repairing tenants house in part,' 'all timber being cut in the wood,' and again in 1709, 'To James Blakie 2 days at Langshaw cutting timber.'

Unfortunately, little or no detail is given of seeds purchased for the garden. Of vegetables, spinach, peas, and parsley are mentioned, and of flowers anemones, ranunculuses, jonquils, and tulips.

A bowling-green is laid out in 1710 and 1711, at a cost

of £7, 3s. 1d., on which the peacock purchased in 1704 no doubt displayed itself.

The entries in regard to the enclosing of land are of interest, the first occurring in 1699, when £4 is paid for putting up one of the park dykes, and later on there are entries of abatements granted to tenants for 'dykes, eaten corns and cart roads.' The cost of building a dry stone dyke was 1s. per rood,[1] as compared with about 1s. per yard nowadays, and Lady Grisell took care to see that she got a good job, as witness the following document:—

> Be it known that whereas I George Cairncross Mason in Selikrete being imployed by the Right Hon. Lady Grisell Baillie on building these dry dykes at the strype being southward from the towne [?] hill at Mellerstain but there being thirty roods of the said dyke that are builded with small stones and thereby is not [*sic*] found not to be good and sufficient I therefore do hereby bind and oblige myself to hold good and sufficient the said thirty roods of dykes during the space of twentie years under the paneltie of five pounds Sterling given at Mellerstane this twentie-ninth day of Novemr 17 hundred and forty-three years before these witnesses Wm. Lamb and George Carter servants to the said Lady Grisell Baillie.
>
> (Sgd) George Cairncross.
>
> William Lamb, Witness.
> George Carter, Witness.

The most startling figures, however, in those Accounts are those relating to the building of cot-houses. Even assuming them to have been no better than the dwellings described by John Ray, 'pitiful cots built of stone and covered with turfs having in them but one room, many of them no chimneys, the windows very small holes and not glazed'—even at this the prices paid for the erection of some of them strike one as ridiculously small. In 1696

[1] A rood here probably meant 6 ells Scots, or 6 yards 6 inches Imperial.

a cot-house is built for 'Liddas the Marchant' at a cost of £1, but it must have been a building of a superior class, for in 1702 James Ormiston's cot house is built for 4s., and we find mention of others costing 11s. 1d., 5s., and 14s. 4d. In 1714 many of the details of building the 'new house' are given, the cost of which amounted to £4, 12s. 3d. This house was of a superior order, and was glazed with 'ches losens'—presumably small square panes of glass instead of diamond-shaped ones.[1] There can be little doubt that the low price at which cot-houses were erected is accounted for by the fact that the building material consisted largely of tuft divots, the supply of which is so often referred to. Divots, no doubt, also formed the roofing of these miserable dwellings, although the larger houses were either slated or thatched. In 1709 there is an entry dealing with the slating of Langshaw House, and in the same year we read of straw being supplied for the thatching of Mellerstain, 'For 85 threve oat stra crop 1707 @ 6s. to sting the house,' £2, 2s. 6d. stg., and of heather being got for the thatching of the Church of Earlston, 'For hather and thicking of the church,' 7s. stg.

VI. Furniture and Furnishings

The purchases of furniture and furnishings for the Baillies' Edinburgh house, for Mellerstain, and for their house in London, are given in great detail, and show a good supply of most of our modern requirements. Mr. Henry Grey Graham, in his *Social Life of Scotland in the Eighteenth Century*, refers to the lack of drinking glasses, and, as already mentioned, there would appear to have been a lack of these at Jerviswood. But

[1] The farm-houses in Dumbartonshire in the beginning of the nineteenth century are described as small buildings 'of dry stone, or at best cemented with clay, a roof of heavy timber covered with sod and rotten straw, or ferns.' —*General View of the Agriculture of Dumbartonshire.*

in George Baillie's establishment there were plenty of single wine-glasses purchased at 5d. each, double wine-glasses at 8d., ale-glasses at 1s., water-glasses at 1s., and decanters at 4s. each. There was also a glass churn which cost 1s. 8d., and which strikes one as a curious thing. Then there are scarlet carpets (1696), and in London oil-cloth for the dining-room floor; window curtains of crape, calico, muslin, and damask; arras hangings of plush, etc., which in 1712 began to give place to wallpaper, for we read of three 'pices of stamped paper' being purchased at 2s. 6d. each, and five 'pice varnished paper' at 13s., and in the following year twenty-five 'pices of stamped paper' for £4, 6s. This must be an early use of wallpaper, but the two following entries dealing with bells are still more interesting: 1696. 'For a bell and cord to the door' 2s. 5d. stg., 1705. 'For a bell to the low room' 2s. stg. The first of these clearly indicates a hanging front door bell instead of a tirling pin or knocker, while the second seems to indicate a bell communicating with the servants' quarters. As hanging bells in houses are said to have been unknown in France until the beginning of the eighteenth century, and were not introduced into England until the reign of Queen Anne, these two entries are distinctly worthy of note.

The decoration of rooms with mirrors was evidently much in fashion, and there seems to have been tradesmen in Edinburgh capable of making these, for in 1704 we read of £3, 1s. 6d. paid for a 'Chimney glass and silvering'; and again in 1709, 14s. paid for 'silvering the chimney glass.' Still the Edinburgh mirrors cannot have been equal to the London ones, for 'Chimney and pannel glass' to the value of £10, 17s. 10d. was shipped to Leith in that same year, and when the Baillies furnished their London house wall mirrors played a most conspicuous part in its decoration.

VII. Lawyers and Doctors

We get from these Accounts a considerable amount of information as to the fees paid to counsel and to agents. In December 1694, the King's Advocate, Sir Gilbert Elliot, gets £8, 8s. for four consultations; in April 1696 he is paid a fee of £1, 6s. 2d. for a consultation; in January 1696 he is paid a fee of £5, 5s.; and in November of the same year he is paid £3, 3s. for drawing two Deeds of Entail of Mr. Baillie's estates. Lawyers will note that the client consults counsel and pays his fees without the intervention of an agent, and that the Lord Advocate did not require, as he does now, to have a junior conjoined with him in a consultation. It is a little difficult to compare the charges of Mr. Baillie's solicitor, Mr. Chiesly, with those prevalent nowadays, as documents and business were of such a different nature. We do, however, learn that in 1705 2s. 5d. is paid for drawing a Bond and two Back Bonds, and 4s. 10d. for writing a Bond in the following year. In 1707 John Wood is paid 4s. 1d. 'for writing 2 mens tacks and a Court at Langshaw,' so we may safely assume that solicitors were no more overpaid than were the Judges of the Court of Session. It is interesting to note that Jerviswood was granting tacks of his land, a custom which did so much to improve agriculture in Scotland, but which was at that time only just coming into practice.

The fees paid to doctors and surgeons compare favourably with those paid to lawyers. Fees of 11s., £2, 2s., and £3, 3s. are common, and the practice of bleeding must have yielded to the surgeons a regular and remunerative return. The ordinary charge in Scotland for bleeding a member of the family was 9s. 8d., and for one of the servants, 4s. 10d. If the luxury of being bled from the 'Jouglar vain' was indulged in, it was more expensive, costing £1, 1s. 6d. In England the bleeding was done at the Bagnio or Baths, such entries as 'For cupping Rachy in the Banyo 5s.' being of frequent occurrence. The Bagnio in Edinburgh, situated in the Canongate and kept by one Rees, which is mentioned two or three times, did not apparently undertake surgery, but, curiously enough, it was possible to get accommodation there for the night, for in 1707 we read: 'For lodging 2 nights in the Bainio and 4 times bathing' £1, 4s. stg. Head baths could also be obtained, for £1 is paid to Mr. Knox for 'head baths.' These Bagnios or Baths were no doubt of the nature of Turkish Baths, and those in Edinburgh are referred to also in the *Account Book of Sir John Foulis.*[1]

The frequency with which the Baillies took these baths and went to watering-places, and the large quantities of mineral waters that appear so frequently in the accounts. 'Spa Water,' 'Scarbrough Water,' 'Queen of Hungry Water,' etc., indicate that either Lady Grisell or her husband or both were troubled with rheumatism or gout.

It is also to be noted that in 1705, when 'Rachy' is ill, a special nurse is got for her at a fee of 5s.

Two or three entries occur relating to the syringing of ears, which are explained by the fact that Mr. Baillie gradually became very deaf. Indeed, his increasing deafness was the reason given for his retirement from the Treasury.

It is impossible to leave this subject without a reference to dentistry. Throughout the Accounts no mention is made of the purchase of a tooth-brush, although the family go occasionally to a dentist to have their teeth 'cleaned,'

[1] The College of Physicians had a bath in the Cowgate about this time, for which 1/- stg. was charged, and $\frac{1}{12}$d. stg. as fee to the servant. This bath was let in 1714 to Alex. Murray, W.S., and John Russel of Bradshaw, W.S. Looking to the fees prevailing in the W.S. profession, one is not surprised to find two of the members trying to eke out their incomes by running a bath.

at which times powder is mentioned as being purchased. Thus in 1709: 'To teeth cleaning each half a crown and puders' 14s. '1717. To cleaning all our teeth at Bath £1, 14s.' Visits are also paid to the dentist for still more unpleasant purposes, as witness the entry in 1705: 'For stopping teeth with lead and something to clean 'em 10s.'; and the entry in 1717: 'July. to Vilponta for drawing Grisie's tooth 10s. 9d.'

VIII. Horses and Carriages

The Baillie expenses in connection with the keep of horses and upkeep of carriages and harness in Scotland averaged for the years 1692 to 1714 about £35 per annum, exclusive of the wages of coachmen and grooms. As there were certainly four coach mares, besides hunting mares and a cart horse, it may be taken that this figure covered the keep of at least seven horses, and that consequently the keep of a horse for a vear was under £5. As the Baillies bred their own horses, there are not so many entries dealing with their purchase as one might otherwise have expected. The highest price given for a horse is £22, 4s. 5d., paid in 1696 for a gelding. A pony for Grisie cost £3, 6s. 8d.; horses £10, £9, 14s. 8d., and £7; a mare £4, 8s. 11d. Colts are gelded at 2s., although, as Lady Grisell explains, the usual price is 1s., rumping costs 1s., and bleeding, which is of frequent occurrence, 10d.; while stallions for the mares cost £2, 2s. (Bath). Coach harness for a pair of horses cost in 1705 £4, 16s., in 1702 a leather side saddle is bought for 12s., while in 1712 'a fine sadle to Grisie yellow velvite trim'd with silver' costs £13; a pad saddle and furniture in 1701 costs £2, 2s., and a 'clog bag[1] saddle' and all its furniture costs, in 1704, 17s. 4d.

When the Baillies were first married, the carriage they

[1] Saddle bag.

owned was a 'berlyn,' a light carriage capable of containing two persons, said to have been invented about forty years before by 'Philip de Chiese, a native of Piedmont in the service of Frederick William, Elector of Bradenburg.'[1] In 1699, however, a chariot is purchased in London, whence it is brought to Edinburgh, at a cost of £5, 8s. The price of the chariot unfortunately is not given. Some idea of the state of the roads is obtained from the constant mention of purchases of glass for the chariot, and the frequency with which new wheels have to be got. These latter cost £5 a set, and on one occasion are bought at St. Andrews, and on another are made by the local workmen at Mellerstain.

The coach itself does not last long, for in 1704 it gets such a complete overhaul that, after reading the details, one wonders how much of the original coach was left.[2]

In spite of having had 'her' so thoroughly repaired, a new chariot is purchased and brought from London next year. This new chariot seems to have been not altogether a success, and must have been the subject of some complaint, for Mr. Secretary Johnston writes in regard to it: 'There could be no knavery in your Chariot considering the price of it, and since you saw it before it was covered, the wood, as it often happens, may not have been seasoned enough; none but workmen can judge of that.' Although the Baillies imported their carriages from London, it is evident that coaches of a sort could be procured in Scotland, for in 1707 we read: 'To King Coachmaker for helping

---

[1] *A Book about Travelling, Past and Present*, by Thomas A. Croal. It was in the Berline of Baroness de Korff that Louis XVI. and his queen attempted to escape from France.

[2] 1704 Oct. 26. For helping and dighting the coch £1 8/, nails to the coch 10/, Axe tree £5 8/.
For a hind axe tree £4 6/, a pair fitchers £4 10/.
For a transem £3, lining the bottom £2, 2 rollers 6/, mending £1 12/.
For 2 skins £1 8/, nails to her 14/2, drink 2/ (Scots money).

the Chariot, the money sent to Edinburgh by Francis Newton'[1] 15s.

When the family went to London, towards the close of the year 1714, they did not take their own carriage, but travelled by the stage-coach. It was thus necessary for them, on their arrival in London, to purchase a coach, which they did from one 'Mr. Baldwine,' at the price of £55, which was paid by instalments. Instead of horsing this themselves, they hired a coachman and two horses at £25 per quarter. Judging from the amount of chariot glass appearing in the London Accounts the streets of that city were not much better than those of the northern capital.

It will be noticed in Ladv Grisell's 'Memorandum' as to travelling on the Continent, that when the chaises[2] arrive at Trent, 'you must put an avan train to vour Chaise,' 'you cannot travel without these fore carriages, they not been used to drive as in Italy.'

It is evident from the directions which Lady Grisell gives her grandsons as to the careful adjustment of the 'avan train' that the chaises proceeded through Germany with six wheels each. These 'avan trains' were necessary in order to provide a seat for the driver, the chaises until Trent was reached having been driven by postillions, and Lady Grisell gave directions that they are to be got rid of at Cologne or Frankfort.

It will also be noted from the same 'Memorandums' that it was considered hardly worth while to bring these travelling chaises across the Channel, they being 'but unwildy and troublesome in our country,' therefore 'sell them for what you can get.'

---

[1] In 1693 the Scottish Parliament granted a monopoly to Wm. Scott, cabinetmaker, to build coaches, chariots, sedan-chairs, and calashes, coach 'Harnish and grinding of glasses.' Before that all coaches, etc., were imported.

[2] A chaise could be bought for £25.

One word as to carts! Mr. Henry Grey Graham, in his *Social Life of Scotland in the Eighteenth Century*, gives a description of tumbrils, which he said were regarded as 'a triumph of mechanism when the century was young.' He goes on to say: 'Carts were a later institution; and when in 1723 one carried a tinv load of coals from East Kilbride to Cambuslang, crowds of people, it is recorded, went out to see the wonderful machine; they looked with surprise and returned with astonishment.' 'Yet in many parts of the Lowlands they did not come into use until 1760.' This may have been so in certain districts, but in Edinburgh carts capable of carrying half a ton of coal seem to have been common enough. In 1696 ten carts of coal are brought from Carberry; coals are constantly being carted from Leith; in 1701 a 'cart and all that belongs to it' is purchased for £4; and in 1704 a new axle-tree is got for the cart. Both the price paid and the last entry show clearly that the Baillies' cart was not a tumbril, but had wheels revolving independently of the axle-tree, and there is no reason for assuming that it was in any way superior to the other carts mentioned.

IX. Clothing

It is a little difficult for a mere man to form an opinion in regard to matters of feminine clothing, and it is dangerous to express it when formed. The first thing that strikes one in looking through the Clothing Accounts is the change that has taken place in the meaning of the word 'night gown.' We find nightgowns of damask, of stained satin, of yellow satin, of striped satin, of calico, of velvet, etc., all lined with various materials, and costing anything from £1 to £5. They are frequently given as presents. George Baillie brings back 'night gowns' from London for his wife and daughter, and 'night gowns' are given to his wife's sister 'Jeanie,' and to his sister Mrs. Weems, costing respectively £3 and £2, 15s. From the number that are bought they are evidently more than dressing-gowns, and from the fact that elaborate ones are also purchased for Mr. Baillie himself, the term can hardly be synonymous with 'an evening gown.' In the case of ladies, it was probably a sort of tea-gown; and in the case of men, a dressing-gown for more or less public wear. It was no doubt in this sort of 'night gown' that Robert Baillie was tried and hanged, and not in the garment we now understand by the words.[1]

What would be now termed 'nightgowns' are called in the Accounts 'night clothes,' and were made of muslin or cambric.

In the matter of underclothing, the Accounts show but cold comfort, and it is with a sense of relief that one reads of the occasional purchase of flannel. No doubt the material for woollen underwear was woven at home, as we find frequent references to the purchase of wool, sometimes bought specifically to be 'made into flanell.'

Stockings of cotton, wool, and silk are purchased at prices ranging from 1s. 1d. to 14s. per pair, the finer kind being worn over woollen understockings. When abroad, specially thick stockings for travelling are bought, as are also stockings of beaver skin, which cost three florins (7s.) the pair. One would be inclined to doubt the meaning of the word, but a few entries further on 'baver skin gloves' are purchased, and 'baver' for a 'peticoat and clock,' the former costing 1s. 10d. per pair, and the latter £2, 19s. 3d. It will also be noted from the snuff-

[1] Lady Mary Wortley Montagu writes in 1716: 'I met the lover yesterday going to the ale house in his dirty night gown, with a book under his arm to entertain the club; and as Mrs. D. [the gentleman's fiancée] was with me at the time, I pointed out to her the charming creature; she blushed and looked prim; but quoted a passage out of Herodotus in which it is said that the Persians wore long night gowns.'

boxes and handkerchiefs purchased for the ladies that snuff was used by them as well as by the men.

On p. 203 and p. 213 will be found the trousseau accounts of Lady Murray and Lady Binning respectively, the bridal dress of the one, 'a sute clothes trim'd with silver,' costing, along with her sister's dress and some other items, £112, 8s. 6d., and of the other, 'For 25 yards silver stuff for gown and coat,' costing £41, 5s.

A plain suit of clothes for a gentleman cost between £4, 10s. and £7, but of course if expensive materials were used the cost might be anything. The accessories to the suit, such as the lace for cravats and ruffles, often cost more than the suit itself, on one occasion, in London, as much as £20, 5s. being spent on a cravat and two pairs of ruffles. A muff with its case was also a necessary part of a gentleman's equipment.

Wigs naturally figure frequently. We have campaign wigs at about £1, 5s., long wigs at £2, 5s., and undesigned wigs at £3, 5s. Then there are the concomitant nightcaps of wool or double holland for keeping warm shaved heads. Here also we notice Lady Grisell's careful hand. Nothing is thrown away that can be repaired: 'Helping the fore-head of a wig' 5s.; 'Helping a wig and shaving 8s. 7d. stg.'; 'Turning my poplin gown'; 'Dying red gown green'; 'Making up the old floord night gown,' etc.

X. Jerviswood's Brothers and Sisters

When George Baillie was restored to his family estates he became responsible for the payment of his mother's jointure of £102, 13s. 8d., and of the provisions made by his father for his younger children, amounting to 43,000 merks or £2388, 17s. 9d. stg. Along with her other accounts Lady Grisell kept an account of how this money was paid away to, or for the benefit of, the beneficiaries, and these Accounts give us some information on a different and not so pleasant side of eighteenth century life. It is evident from them that Jerviswood's immediately younger brother Archibald was not altogether a satisfactory character. At one time or another he was reduced to pawning his coat, his Bible, and, still more reprehensible, his brother's watch, which various articles were redeemed at the cost of 10s., 8s. 4d., and 12s. 6d. respectively. He eventually lands in the Tolbooth, presumably for debt, when we find the following entry: 'To him by Plumer when he was in ye Tolbooth £54, 8s. Scots' (£4, 10s. 8d.). If this sum was paid for his maintenance, and it looks as if such were the case, and if the expense of his board 'inside' was in any way commensurate with his board outside, he must have been in durance vile for some time, as his board, lodging, and pocket-money for six months when at liberty only cost about £10.

Evidently some sort of special arrangement had to be made about Archibald, as a separate account is kept for him long after his brothers and sisters have been paid off and their names have disappeared from the Accounts.

Just as the Accounts for Archibald cease, that is, about 1708, Lady Grisell opens an account in her ledger for 'Rachell Dundas.' No clue is given as to who this was, but she was probably a daughter of George Baillie's sister Rachel, who married Patrick (?) Dundas of Breistmilne. This child apparently possessed a little money, which Lady Grisell administered for her, and her name figures through the Accounts for several years. She went with the family to London, and she and Miss Menzies are occasionally sent to the theatre together: '1715. Ap. 6. For a play to Rachel Dundas and May Menzies gallarie 4s.'; 'Two gallerie tickets to ane opera 3s.'; 'To Rachel Dundas for going to a play 4s.,' etc. Looking to the small amount spent on her and on her amusements in comparison with her cousins, one is afraid she must have felt somewhat of a Cinderella.

XI. General Remarks

Having dealt with Lady Grisell's Accounts more or less in detail, it may not be out of place to add a word or two upon them as a whole. In Appendix v. will be found a statement showing the yearly expenditure under its various heads from 1693 to 1718 inclusive, and as far as possible giving the yearly income for the same period. The note of expenditure has been made up from Lady Grisell's Accounts, and may be taken as accurate, except in regard to the figures under headings 'Pocket Money' and 'London Expenses.' The former one feels can hardly give the whole of the pocket-money spent by Jerviswood, and the latter is certainly incorrect, for Baillie was in London every year after the Union attending to his parliamentary duties, and there is no mention of the expenses of these visits in the Accounts. With these exceptions, the figures give a fair idea of the expenditure of a country gentleman immediately preceding and succeeding the Union.

The figures setting forth Baillie's income are derived partly from balance-sheets, which were prepared periodically every few years either by Lady Grisell or her husband, and which give the rental of his estates together with a note of his investments and debts, and partly from the Records, which mention the salaries attaching to the various posts held by him.

In considering any of the branches of the expenditure it is always necessary to take a few years together, as wages and accounts are often left unpaid for several years, probably from the scarcity of coin. For instance, in 1707 'May Menzies' receives two years' wages; in 1717 'John Hume Garner at Mellerstaine' is paid his wages for three years; in 1709 Torwoodlee is paid £8 for a horse 'got 10 years since,' and there are many similar entries, although in the last case the length of delay is exceptional. Whether it was this want of ready money, or whether it was a legacy from his days of adversity, it is impossible to say, but certain it is that George Baillie had in December 1695 to redeem a gun from pawn at the small sum of 2s. 10d.[1]

The average expenditure in Scotland for the years from 1693 to 1714, exclusive of sums spent on estate management and expeditions to London, works out at rather under £550 sterling per annum, and it is strange to think of this sum being able to finance an establishment in which the number of servants must have averaged at least ten, and which boasted a carriage and four, besides hunters.

This naturally raises the question as to the relative value of money then and now, a difficult question, the answer to which alone can enable us to compare the prices of two hundred years ago with those of to-day, and to say that such and such an article was dearer or cheaper then than now. It is a problem that can be attacked in various ways, but for the purposes of this book it is perhaps sufficient to examine it from the charge side of the account, that is, from a study of what a man or woman was able to earn for labour, whether manual or mental: approached from this side an article may be said to be dear or cheap as its price varies to the earning capacity of the individual. If, therefore, we can find any fairly common ratio existing between salaries and wages of the various

[1] Truthful accounts not only at times give away the writer, but also are occasionally hard on others, as the following entry in 1717 bears out:—'To my Lady Lockhart, lent and never pay'd £1, 1s. 6d.' It is hard to think of such acts of omission rising up in judgment after so many years have elapsed.

trades and professions then and now, we shall at least be enabled to judge by it whether any special commodity has increased or decreased in value from a purchaser's point of view. Now it will be seen from Appendix IV., which has been prepared from the Accounts of Lady Grisell and from other sources, and which the Editor is well aware is far from exhaustive, that the salaries and wages therein referred to have increased from six- to ten-fold. It will also be seen that the increase in the wages of domestic servants, taking into account the cost of the clothes supplied and the cost of their maintenance, both relatively greater then than now, lies somewhere between the same two figures.

Let us therefore take eight, the mean of these two figures, as representing the decrease in the power of money to buy the services of men and women, and let us multiply by eight the price of any article in 1707 before comparing it with the price of to-day. The result should enable us to judge fairly accurately whether it has increased or decreased in value.

As long as income was spent on the employment of labour, such as servants, tradesmen, doctors, lawyers, etc., our ancestors were just as well off as we are to-day. The same may also be said in regard to one or two items, such as farmyard produce, keep of horses, etc., but, as will be seen from Appendix I., the cost of nearly every other commodity was relatively much dearer then than now. Even the staff of life, oatmeal, which costs now about 17s. the boll, cost then about 10s., that is, it was then relatively nearly five times dearer. This merely brings us to what we know already, namely, that our incomes go much further now than then, and that we are consequently much better off.

Mention has been made of the periodical balance-sheets

made out by George Baillie. In these Baillie valued his landed estates at so many years' purchase, gave a list of his investments, and a note of the debts due by him.

In 1693, Jerviswood and Mellerstain were both valued at twenty years' purchase, but the value of the latter was raised in subsequent statements to twenty-two years' purchase. In 1736 the Barony of Earlston was bought from Lord Haddington at twenty-five years' purchase, and in the same year the superiority of some subjects in Earlston was acquired at twenty-one and a half years' purchase. The following is rather a curious entry in relation to land purchase. Baillie, who had bought the estate of West-fauns for £2000, afterwards acquired the 'Snyp Rights upon it,' for £432, 4s. 7d., seeming thus to indicate that they were separable possessions.

These balance-sheets show that it was not until after the Union that Baillie began to save money, and that these savings he generally laid out in the purchase of land. His first balance-sheet in 1693 shows that he was worth £8037; his last in 1736 that he was worth £37,724.

Although it does not fall within the scope of this paper to treat of the effects which the Union of the Parliaments had upon Scotland, it is a subject which naturally bulks largely in the study of the career of George Baillie. In his own correspondence we learn that he foresaw much of what happened, but he probably did not see one effect, that is, the injury inflicted upon Scotland through the practical removal from her capital of such men as Baillie of Jerviswood and his father-in-law, the Earl of Marchmont. They saw no sin in the innocent enjoyment of music, singing, and dancing. We have already noted how George Baillie got in the fiddlers to play to his bairns, and Lady Murray gives the following delightful picture of her grandfather: 'As mirth and good humour, and particularly dancing, had always been one characteristic of the family when so

THE RIGHT HON. PATRICK HUME, EARL OF MARCHMONT.

(*From a Portrait at Mellerstain.*)

many of us were met, being no fewer than fourteen of his children and grandchildren, we had a dance. He was then very weak in his limbs and could not walk downstairs, but desired to be carried down to the room where we were to see us; which he did, with great cheerfulness, saying, "Though he could not dance with us, he could yet beat time with his foot," which he did, and bid us dance as long as we could; that it was the best medicine he knew, for at the same time that it gave exercise to the body, it cheered the mind. At his usual time of going to bed he was carried upstairs and we ceased dancing for fear of disturbing him; but he soon sent to bid us go on, for the noise and music, so far from disturbing, that it would lull him to sleep. He had no notion of interrupting the innocent pleasures of others, though his age hindered him to partake of it. His exemplary piety and goodness was no bar to his mirth; and he often used to say none had so good a reason to be merry and pleased as those that loved God and obeyed his commandments.'[1]

Both of these men were prominent Presbyterians, who had suffered for the cause, and whose principles were beyond suspicion. They were powerful socially, they were powerful politically, and their example, and the example of others like them, might have done at least a little to counteract the bigotry and despotism of the Presbyterian ministers, whose influence for so many years cast a shadow over Scotland.

The Editor begs to acknowledge his indebtedness to some notes left by the late Mr. Fitzroy Bell, into whose experienced hands the editing of Lady Grisell's papers had been entrusted, but whose untimely death prevented him from making more than a beginning of what would

---

[1] Lady Murray's *Memoirs*, pp. 77, 78.

have been to him a most congenial task. The Editor's thanks are also due to Dr. Maitland Thomson, Mr. A. O. Curle, Mr. Mill of the Signet Library, and many other friends, for much valuable help.

He also feels that he owes an apology to Lady Grisell for prying into books which were never meant to be seen. If Lady Grisell is cognisant of what goes on here, she is no doubt amazed, amused, and annoyed at the many wrong deductions which have been drawn from the Accounts, over which she must have spent so much time and trouble, and which she must have thought so clear.

THE HOUSEHOLD BOOK OF LADY GRISELL BAILLIE

Sundry debursments, 1692 [Scots]

		£	s.	d.
Novr. 1st	To David Robison vintner as acount and pr recept	122	0	0
1693	For sevarall things from Novr. 92 to Aprill 1693	112	13	0
Novr. 25	To Coptain Baillie [1] his interist from Lam. 91 to Lam. 92 . . .	136	0	0
	To said Coptain in full of all acct. betwixt him and me ather by bill or otherwise except what he has my bond for	1143	14	0
	To a glas to a chariot . .	60	0	0
	To payment of the cess for the year 1693 . . .	398	12	2
	To James Gordon, agent for the linin [2] manufactory and that in full payment of my entry for ten shars being 19s. st. per share .	114	0	0
1693	To James Drumond per tiket	120	0	0
Aprill 20	To Robert Baillie [3] of Manerhall			
	To Alexr Magill in full payment of a horss bought from him	116	16	0
ditt.	To Pockock, barber .	24	0	0
May 2d	To the drums . .	4	16	0
	To drink mony to nurses	11	12	0

[1] James Baillie, captain of the City Guard, uncle of George Baillie.

[2] For an account of this company, see 'Scottish Industrial Undertakings before the Union,' *Scottish Historical Review*, vol. ii. p. 53.

[3] George Baillie's cousin, son of his uncle, George Baillie of Manorhall, Peeblesshire.

	[Sundries]	[Scots] £	s.	d.
Dito 16	For cariadges to Edinburgh	8	18	0
	For taking horses out of Edinburgh	2	16	0
Ditto 20	To Chamber rent in Mrs. Hervies	86	2	0
	For pistols bought by my brother Will	36	0	
	To the colection for the poor	3	0	
	To James Baillie given out by him for me Sept. 25, 1691			
	To Georg Clark as p^r bill w^t the interest therof for 26 monethes being 64 lb. 14s. . .	904	14	0
	To anuity of my howss from Whitsunday 92 to Whit. 1693 .	12	0	0
	To John Hunter the cess for the terms of Whitsunday, Lambis and Mertimas 1693, and descharg'd for all precidings	85	0	0
1694	To McKuloch for linning a room in the top of Waristons Land	40	0	0
Febr. 4	To Mr. Will Liviston[1] at my childs christining	9	0	0
March 18	To Mr. Will. Vetch minister at Peebles per rect. from the collector of the vacant stipends of Meller-stens stipen 1693 . .	400	0	0
Jun. 18	To drinkmony to Mr. Ch. nurs .	2	18	0
August 1st	Taken with me to England .	948	16	0
Dito 15	For streat mony and poors mony per recept	11	4	0
	To a barber . .	1	16	0
	To a sclater for helping the howss	7	0	0
	Taken to the country and given out ther	–12	0	0
Oct. 9	For thirling to Mellarsteans .	3	14	0

[1] A writer in Edinburgh, who appears to have collected the fees for various Edinburgh churches. Sir John Foulis paid his fees to him 'when I gave up our names to be proclaimed.'

	[Sundries]	[Scots] £	s.	d.
1695				
	For helping glas windows 17s.	0	17	0
	To anuity for the howss per recept .	12	0	0
	For a coch from Barty Gibson to Walstons [1] buriall, Mrt. 94	30	0	0
	To my ant Huchison at sevarell times	30	0	0
	For baithing in Rees bathing hows	4	16	0
	For frawsht of 2 trunks and 2 boxes from London	16	12	0
	For survayanc mony and to watters	1	16	0
Jun.	To ant Hutchison 7 lb. To the Bainio in the Canigate 9 lb.	16	0	0
	To Mr. John Vass . . .	29	0	0
	For helping the watch .	8	14	0
	To Sornbegs man 10 merks .	6	13	4
	To Georg Mosman for books :	50	2	0
	To bringing goods from Lieth	3	6	0
Decr. 30	To John Smith for my expences on the English rood, when I cam last from London with the Secretar [2]	80	10	0
	To Mr. Watson for a bill sent to London to Jeris	2100	4	0
1695	To Georg Clark for the linin manufactory	120	0	0
Deer.	To the poll of my famely	30	0	0
	To expences at tinding for the years 1691, 1692, 1693, and 1694	73	17	0
	To the minister of Ersiltons for his stipon 1694	146	13	0
	To Will. Trotter, scoolmaster in Mellersteans	5	0	0
	To James Massie scolmaster in Mellerstains	10	0	0

[1] Frequently mentioned by Sir John Foulis as one of his companions.

[2] Mr. Secretary Johnston. See p. 286.

	[Sundries]	[Scots] £	s.	d.
	To David Hume colecter for the cess 1694 and 1695	572	19	8
1695	To Roger Hoburn by receat	200	0	0
Deer.	To expences at fair and other outgivins for years allowed to John Wight	186	3	0
	To 3 years rent allowed to Will. Brounlies, etc.	62	8	0
	To mending the cross .	5	12	0
	For lousing a gun was panded	1	14	0
	To the Linin manufactuary for Smallits recept . . .	180	0	0
	To cloath for Robert Baillie at Kelso	40	0	0
	For a coch howss to the Berlyn .	12	18	0
	To Mosman for books	40	0	0
G.P.	To John Hay for a sword to Cap. Baillie	36	0	0
		9040	12	0

	£	s.	d.		£	s.	d.
Take out of the third pag and this, Cap. Baillies, mony paid to him to be taken of this	2184	8	0				
It. More the linin manufactory	414	0	0				
It. More mony payd to the minister	546	13	0	sume	6193	0	0
It. More London jornay .	3048	0	0				

	£	s.	d.
There remains besid	2847	12	0
To Holland to my brothers .	120	0	0
Caried to page 13th S.	2967	12	0

Sundry debursments. 1696.

		[Scots] £	s.	d.
January 1st	To the poor per recept	4	0	0
	To the bathell of the church	1	9	0
	For a ring w^t the Quins hair	9	0	0
	For glasing the forroom window	2	8	0
	To Johnston barber .	8	8	0
Febr. 10	To Ridpath [1] at London .	24	0	0
23	To Mr. Liviston at Rachis christining	5	16	0
	To the bathell of the church	2	4	0
	To charity	4	18	0
	To Ms. Scot midwife . . .	29	0	0
	To Ms. Hutchison . . .	11	12	0
March	For munting 3 swords	6	0	0
	To John Hunter my cess preceeding Whitt. 96 .	73	0	0
	To John Hunter for polmony by act of parliment, 1695 for my whole famaly	32	7	0
	To charity . . .	3	14	0
	To Ms. Scot midwife . . .	5	16	0
Aprill	To lairn cookry from Mr. Addison	15	12	0
	To Will Johnston for books	36	0	0
	To Captain Baillie in balance of ane acount	217	0	0
	To a man in Gray Frirs for keeping up my childs grave	1	9	0
May 10th	For payment of the sess of the year 1696	93	1	6
	To my Ant Hutchison .	12	0	0
	For the expence of fliting	11	0	0
	To Ms. Guttary	3	0	0
	To Hew Brown a doller	2	18	0

[1] George Ridpath, Whig journalist, published a system of shorthand, wrote many party pamphlets and books, was obliged to fly the country in 1713 for a series of articles in the *Flying Post* and *Observator*. Lord Grange writing of him after his death states that 'his memory is not savoury here. I'm sorry he was so vile for he once did good service.' Frequent payments are made to him through these accounts, and he is often mentioned in the *Jarviswood Correspondence*.

[Sundries]		[Scots] £	s.	d.
	For drawing the blewhowse 2lb. 8, 4½ ounce silk and twisting	8	16	0
July	To the Wast Church .	20	3	0
	To the loss of mony by crying doun	5	12	0
	For 8 monethes sess per recept	286	18	10
July 19	To my jurnay to the Bath .	1008	9	0
	To Scugald,[1] painter 10 dollers	29	0	0
	To expences at the fairs July 96	4	4	0
Agust 12	To Grisies dancing master for 3 monthes	20	12	0
	To Scugald painter .	68	8	0
	To paper, pen and ink 10s.	0	10	0
	To the poor at Greenlaw Church	4	10	0
	To severall litle things in the country	3	4	0
	To Robert Young clark to the court	12	0	0
	To the scolmaster . . .	10	0	0
Octr. 1st	To Scugald for 2 pictors and frames	74	8	0
	To James Borthick for the poor per recept	4	2	0
Novr. 10th	To Grises reading master for a quarter	2	18	0
	To 5 monethes cess per recept Lamb and Merts. 96 .	162	17	8
	To the contrabusion for the fire in the Caningate . .	11	8	0
	For expence at the fair Oct. 96, 4lb. 8, expence at tinding 96, 11lb. 8s.	15	16	0
	To acount of expences in going to head courts and wt cess etc.	2	4	0
	To the linin manufactary	120	0	0
	For repairing of Mellerstean mill kill and howses	556	12	2
	To James Drumond by Ms. Hutchison 8 doll	23	4	0

S. 490 £.

[1] See p. xxvi.

Edenburgh, 1701. Sundry expences. Deb. to Cash.

		£	s.	d.
	For a big Bible and velvit pock .	18	0	0
	For drinkmony 2 ti. 18. more 3 ti.	5	16[*sic*]	
	For writing a paper, 14	0	14	0
	For poket	1	0	0
	For bearing rains to the coch and helphing her . .	2	10	0
	For 7 ounce white threed 3 ti 10 .	3	10	0
	To the church bathel . .	2	18	0
	For pins 19s. for a horn comb 6s. .	1	4	0
Feb. 5	For pictors in full of all I owed Scugald to this day .	96	0	0
	To poket	1	0	0
	For Grisies dancing a mounth with the Franch man . .	14	4	0
	For Robert Youngs sallary this year	[illegible]	[illegible]	0
	For a bridle and 2 curpils .		1	
	For a cariadge to Mellersteans			
	For blooding given Georg Kirton		1	
	For poket . .	11	12	0
	For pamphlits 4s. Grisies ball mony 1 ti. 9 s	1	13	0
	For cuping given Georg Kirton .	5	16	0
	For a thresher 21 day without meat	12	6	0
	For yron to the horss 1 ti. helping the barndoors 2 ti. . . .	3	0	0
	For hansels in January	23	0	0
	To Mr. Knox for head bathes .	12	0	0
	To Georg Kirton which pays him his account in full till January 1700.	76	0	0
June 10	For the rent of our loft in Tolbuth Church from Whitsunday 1700 to Whitsunday 1701 year .	18	0	0
	To nurses 5 ti 16s. to a barber to a nurses 3 ti. 4s.	9	14	6
	To the poor Aprill last	36	0	0

	[Sundries]	[Scots] £	s.	d.
	For sweet powder £2, coch hires 18s. 6d., and mending the coch 1ti 4s.	4	2	6
	To Porterfield to perfite Rachy in reading	18	0	0
	For Grisies quarter with Crumbin	19	7	0
	For ane express to Dunglas 2 ti 8s. nails 6s. rubarb 9s. . . .	3	13	0
	For 12 clouts to the cock 1 ti 4s. booking the mairs 6s.	1	10	0
	For the bairenes milks going to with [*sic*] ther scooll	2	18	0
	For shoes to a horss 8s. to sevarall outgiving by James Carrin 3 ti 8	3	16	0
	To poket 14s. 6d. more 6s. .	1	1	0
	For puting up the park dicks of Jerriswood in full of all .	9	3	4
	For lime to the dick barn .	2	0	0
	For a ledger book 5 ti 10 s. for sherping the milne 3ti. . .	8	10	0
	To the clarks for the rights of Ballan crief	4	7	0
	For books	23	0	0
July 8	For dreg staf eluting and grising the coach	1	16	0
	For wire and rings to the coch, 16s. for lokes to doors, 1 ti 9s. .	2	5	0
	For tows, 10 fadour, 10s. a smith for work 1 ti. 11s.	2	1	0
	For a horss to Ballancrieff 1 ti 16s.	1	16	0
	For a book 2 ti a book 1 ti letters in England 7 ti 4s.	10	4	0
	For snuf boxes 3 ti 12s. For pins and knitins 1 ti 10 .	5	2	0
	For a horss cumb and brush	1	8	0
	For horss hires to Edinburgh	300	0	0
Octob. 1st	For lead to the doors . .	0	6	0
	For tows to the stair of Mellersteans	0	16	0

	[Sundries]	[Scots] £	s.	d.
	For wax and wafers	0	15	2
	For a comb and spung	0	[illegible]	0
	For a colt helter .		1	
	For 3 bridles to water the horss			
	For helping the coach at Lidgertwood			
	For a blade and 2 scaburts to a sword . . .	4	16	0
	For severall little things at the fair	7	0	0
Ditto 2	For a sett of new coch whiles G.P. 60£			
	For 4 cariadges from Edenburgh .	6	0	0
	For caring clogbags and other things from Thorontonbridge and Newcastle to Mallersteans	13	4	0
	For cariadges by Munga Brounlies all cleard	9	19	0
	For expences at the 2 fairs with drumers, etc.	7	7	0
	For 2 sives and 2 ridles 1 ti 10s. suples 8s.	1	18	0
	For expence of selling 20 bolls oats	1	6	0
	To James Massie his salarie for this year	10	0	0
	For a carte bought at Mellersteans with all that belonges to it	48	0	0
	For Brounlies howse rent 6 ti 13s. 4d. ane emty hows 6 ti 13s. 4d.	13	6	8
	To Ms. Hume of Bogend	11	2	0
	For suples 12s. .	0	12	0
	For the head court at Kelso	0	10	0
	For young trees from Hundalie	2	0	0
	To the poor at Mellersteans 2 bols 4 f[irlots] 2 p[ecks] oats at 5£ per boll . .	14	10	0
	For biging Thomas Leadhowse's stable	82	0	0

[Sundries]	[Scots] £	s.	d.
For John Wights sallary the year 1700	40	0	0
To Androw Lamb .	0	14	6
To the contrabusion for the burning[1]	13	0	0
To Crombin for a quarter to Grisie	17	8	0
To my Ant Effie[2] . . .	5	16	0
For hering to Mr. Johnston	31	12	0
For painting the chariot .	3	12	0
For the cochmans seat 4 ti helping harnis 2 ti 2s	6	2	0
For plush to J. Rainalds	11	0	0
To Androw Lamb . . .	0	14	0
To Stewarts nurs . . .	2	18	0
For repairing Mallersten tower given out this year as by particular accumpts .	767	18	4
For 2 poks to bibles 10s. .	0	10	0
For a pad sadle and furnitur 25 ti. 4s. 2 huntin stoks 20 ti.	45	4	0
For feu duty at Jeriswood to account of bygans	15	13	0
	S. 1700	11	6

Edenburgh, January 1702. Sundry Expences, Deb. to Cash.

To the bathell in the church	2	18	0
To Adam Marchell .	2	14	6
To my brother Archibald .	1	9	0
For a window in the little closit	0	10	0
For Grisies ball mony . .	1	9	0
To Grisies singing master Krenberg	14	4	0
For helping the coach .	0	10	0
For Shaws to Dina Ridpath .	1	9	0
To Mr. Mitchell	0	14	6

[1] Fire in Lawnmarket, 28 October 1701.—*Foulis Accounts.*

[2] Youngest daughter of Lord Wariston. Died unmarried in 1715.

	[Sundries]	[Scots] £	s.	d.
23	To Georg Kirton to accumpt upon his letter . .	21	6	0
	To Grisies Candlesmas mony	2	18	0
	For lace to shirt hand	2	12	6
	For siringing the ears	3	0	0
	To Docter Sincklair for Rachy	28	8	0
	To Breastmills mans weding	2	18	0
	To a horss hire payd for James Baillie	1	16	0
	For caring our clogbag to Newcastle payd by Breastmille	2	18	0
Febr.	For books bought by Mr. Knox	34	0	0
28	For the Acts of the Assembly got from Mosman . . .	6	6	0
	For Grisies singing to Mr. Krenberg	7	8	0
	For Grisies singing book .	1	9	0
	For James Latie the measons coming to town . . .	0	14	6
March 8	For a diamond ring . .	63	5	0
	To 2 nurses Cavers[1] and Mrs. Watherburns[2]	5	16	0
	To Charly Hume . . .	7	4	0
	To Grisies nurs for lint sead	0	18	0
	To Doct[or] S. Christining £2 18s. to his nurs 2£ 18s. . . .	5	16	0
	To P.[3] Sabath 12 Aprill	6	0	0
	For puting one a new plate on the coch and new clouts .	6	0	0
	To Robert Young clark his salary for this year	6	0	0
	To James Massie schoollmaster his salarie for this year . . .	10	0	0
May	For letters from London	10	0	0
	To Docter Sincklair .	17	8	0
	To Hellin Garner . . .	4	7	0

[1] Cavers, the seat of the Kers. Lady Grisell's mother was a Ker of Cavers.
[2] Mrs. Hume of Wedderburn.
[3] To pocket.

	[Sundries]	[Scots] £	s.	d.
	To drink mony at Polwart[1] .	2	18	0
	To Marth Black lost of rent .	13	12	6
	To Munga Brunlies fathers howse and ane emty howse . .	13	6	8
	For a pair new Wings and helping all the coch	5	8	0
	For a new poll £3 mending the ax-tree 10s.	3	10	0
	To Thomas Bell . . .	29	0	0
20	For a siging book to Grisie	1	9	0
	To Thomas Bell	2	0	0
	To Will Simson in Lanark bate of his rent	12	10	0
1 day	To Mr. Kramberg, Grisells singing master for the mounth past .	7	8	0
ditto	To Mr. Crumbin Grisies playing master for a quarter past 6 dollers and a doller for tuning .	20	6	0
9	To Docter Sincklair .	18	0	0
	For letters 15s. more 5s. more £1 13s. more £1 16 10	4	9	0
	To the bairnes to goe to a bridle	5	0	0
	To Rachys ball and Grisies	2	19	0
	To Rachys dancing master .	8	14	0
	For a stra hat to Grisies ball 10s. gloves to them £1 12	2	2	0
	To Sutherlands man £1 9s. cheries at the ball 10s.	1	19	0
	For new tops to the coach	4	16	0
	To St. Andras Colledg given Mr. Pringle	14	4	0
	To Grisie to goe to a consert .	0	14	6
	To Stewarts nurs and christining	10	0	0
June 30	To Mr. Crumbin for a month to Grisie	7	8	0

[1] Polwarth, the village adjoining Redbraes, the seat of the Earl of Marchmont, frequently used as denoting Redbraes in these accounts.

[Sundries]		[Scots] £	s.	d.
	To Crumbin for a book .	1	4	0
	To my Lord Collinton [1] for his rent at Whitsunday 1702 and all precidings clear'd	366	13	4
	To Rachys dancing master .	8	14	0
August 6	To the rent of the loft in the church	18	0	0
	To Lith contrabution .	11	2	0
	To a consurt fro Grisie	1	9	0
	To a coller to Grisie .	1	6	0
	To brotherAndrow's[2] childs christining	5	16	0
	To Captain Burck the yrish man .	2	0	0
Ditto 26	For repairing John Wights dwelling howse .	21	10	0
	To puting up James Ormistons cott howse	2	8	0
	For mending the pinits at Mellersteans	1	10	0
	For a bible to Gris £1 7s. mending coch bridles 6s.	1	13	0
	For a little Galaway . .	26	0	0
	For letters £1 6s. 2 nurses £5 16., letters £1 16s. 14s. wath helping £2	11	12	0
	For letters £1 6s. 5 £1 15s. 6s. 5 .	3	17	0
	For sevarell things spent at the fair	10	0	0
Octo 29	For yron bought at Fairs .	3	14	0
	To a garner for seeds £1 9s. For mending a coat house	3	5	0
	To Androw Lamb given him for service	22	0	0
	To the pip and drum £2 16s. Drinkmony Green	5	14	0

[1] Sir James Foulis of Colinton, raised to the Bench as Lord Colinton. It was he who offered to prove the authenticity of the petitions to Parliament against the Union by bringing the Petitioners themselves, which was the last thing the Government wanted.

[2] See p. 27.

[Sundries]	[Scots] £	s.	d.
To pip and drum £2 16s. for mending my watches £2 8.	5	4	0
To drink mony £2 18s. letters £1 more 10s.	4	8	0
To a raffil £14 4s. Haburn 14s. 6d. Ms. Muir £1 9s.	16	7	6
To the domany in Mellersteans 3 bolls oats	13	10	0
Novr. 20 To Grisis singing master Cremberg £7 8 Brun for arthmetick £12	19	8	0
To Franch dancing master for Gris: and Rach.	17	12	0
For a flute £6 a quarter with Crumbin 6½ doll.	25	1	0
Decr. 30 To Mr. Knox for books	26	0	0
To James Massi this year	15	0	0
	S.1148	17	6

Edenburgh, January 1707. Sundry Accounts.
Deb. to Cash.

For mounthes at the violl to Grisie with Sinckolum	12	0	0
For mending her violl	2	0	0
To Mr. G. B. nurse	2	18	0
For letters £2 10s., 6s., 7s., £4 4s., £2 11s., 11s., 5s., 7s.	11	1	0
To Thomson writting master for Rachy one mounth	2	18	0
For chair heir 14s. 6d., £3 1s., £1 12s., 7s.	5	14	0
To Montroses nurs £3 5s., Marrs £2 18, Marrs £2 18s.	9	1	0
For Defos book[1] £1 10s. gune powder 14s.	2	4	0

[1] Defoe's book in support of the Union.

	[Sundries]	[Scots] £	s.	d.
	To Docter St. Clair for Grisie .	28	8	0
	To drinkmony in a shipe by Grisie . .	1	9	0
	For servants drinkmony at Lesly [1]	14	14	0
	To John Steall singing master, for 2 mounthes to Grisie . . .	24	0	0
	To a raffile for herpsicords by Grisie	14	4	0
	For gunn puder . . .	0	6	0
	For shoeing horses by Tam Youll .	2	0	0
	To drinkmony at Kinross [2] £2 18, 4 horses 3 servants 2 nights .	6	18	0
	To drinkmony at Dupplin [3] a fourtnight	9	0	0
	To drinkmony at Lesly £3 18, 4 hors, 3 servants 2 nights £3 12 .	7	10	0
	For crosing Quensferry £1 4s. crosing from Kingoren £2 12s. .	3	16	0
	For vizicater plasters 14s. .	0	14	0
	To Thomas Bellsson £1 9s. .	1	9	0
	To a man to goe to Rickerton [4] twise 16s.	0	16	0
May	For paper 9s. 9s. was [*sic*] 8s. gilt paper 9s. wax 6s. .	2	1	0
	For mending sadle graith £2 7s. .	2	7	0
	To hoboys £1 9s. drinkmony 6s. Ms. Carr £2 18s.	4	13	0
	To the bairens po: £3 3s. 1s. 8d.	3	4	8
	For drinkmony at the Reath [5]	3	12	6
	To May Minzies to buy gloves .	1	16	0
	For $\frac{1}{4}$ whit satin for the bairenses satin pice	1	2	6

[1] Seat of the Earl of Rothes.
[2] The residence of the Earl of Morton or of John Bruce of Kinross.
[3] Seat of Earl of Kinnoull.
[4] Probably Riccarton near Edinburgh, the seat of Robert Craig, advocate.
[5] Seat of the Earl of Melville.

[Sundries]	[Scots] £	s.	d.
For silks to it 6s. nails threed to the tent 1s.	0	7	0
For silk to make a purs and strings, 13s.	0	13	0
To La: Marrs footman 10s. .	0	10	0
For drinkmony twise at Cather House and groom .	7	5	0
For Londan journay in his poket April 1st 50 guinys . .	710	0	0
For to answer bills to London £103 str. more	897	0	0
To the Docters Pitcarin,[1] Dundas,[2] St. Clair,[3] Bailie . .	170	8	0
To Baillie for 3s. blooding and to his man	21	15	0
To Ms. Haliwall £1 12s. 6d. lamb 10s. Monros lad 10s.	1	12	6
For tickets to Steals consurt	7	2	0
For nails to the coch £1 17s. oyl to chair 14s. 6	2	11	6
To new traces and other things to the traveling coach got from Brutherstons last year .	30	0	0
For a new male pillion 12s. girthes and mendnig the sadles when I went to Dupplin .	2	2	6
To poket May 18th . .	10	10	0
For a handcurcher to May Minzies	1	9	0
To Crumbin for a quarter throwgh bass to Grisie 2 guinys . .	25	16	0
To the Marques of Tweddels groome for the coch mares .	5	16	0
For letters 10s. 10s. 10s. 5s. paper 18s.	2	13	0

[1] The famous Dr. Archibald Pitcarne, physician and poet.

[2] Dr. Alexander Dundas, Fellow of the Royal College of Physicians, Edinburgh.

[3] See p. 256.

	[Sundries]	[Scots] £	s.	d.
May	To chair man £1 10s., 16s., 14s. 6d.	2	0	6
	For mending window in pairt of Collintons rent . . .	3	11	0
June 6	For 3 mounthes writting Rachy with Thomson and 12s. for pens	9	6	0
	For letters 10s.	0	10	0
	For dresing the garden, to Wear in Hariots work .	6	0	0
	For 2 mounth to Grisie with St. Culume on the vyoll, etc. .	15	3	0
	For a Bible to John Harla £1 10	1	10	0
	For covers to books 15s. wafers 2s. 4d. poket 6s. .	1	3	4
Mellerst.	For mending Grisies watch . .	3	0	0
June 10	For a lock to the childrens room .	0	8	0
	For ane express from Edinburgh, £2 8s.	2	8	0
	For Androw Lams expences at Langsha, etc.	1	0	0
July 2	To Tam Youls weding . . .	3	14	6
	To drinkmony at Boughtrige, etc.	3	7	0
	For letters pay'd by Ms. Monro .	8	8	0
July 22d	For ane express to Mellerstaines sent by Kersland [1]	2	4	0
	To P. at Earleston, July	3[illegible]	[illegible]	[illegible]
	To poket £1 10s.		1	
	To the fair 18s.		1	
	For John Brouns house			
	To Widow Yellas .			
	To John Boe for puting us [? up] his house . .	2	0	0
	For Androw Brownlies house rent	6	13	4

[1] John Ker of Kersland, Ayrshire. The head of the Cameronian party. He intrigued with both Whigs and Jacobites, and was no better than a government spy. At this time he was willing to sell his influence either for or against the Union as might best pay him.

	[Sundries]	[Scots] £	s.	d.
	For puting up Androw Brownlies's house in pairt	0	6	8
	For mending the coch harnis by Androw Dods . .	0	10	0
	For ane express to Grange Muir [1] to Rob: Baillie . .	1	16	0
	To a Councell post .	0	14	6
Aug. 26	For letters payd by Ms. Monro	2	2	0
	To Grisie Monro . . .	1	10	0

Lady G. Baillie.

		£	s.	d.
	For lodging 2 nights in the Banio and 4 times bathing .	14	8	0
	For drinkmony £3 4s. drink, etc.	2	8	0
	For chairs	1	9	0
	To Mr. Knox apothicars account	46	0	0
	For silks for the childrens satine pice Ms. Miller .	3	12	0
	For helping the nurses house payd a wright in Fanns . . .	3	0	0
	To Ann Faa 12s. . . .	0	12	0
	To Docter Pitcarn 3 guinys	38	14	0
	To Docter Dundas 3 guinys	38	14	0
	To John Baillie one guiny	12	18	0
	To Francy Easton for blooding	2	18	0
	To a coach to Edinburgh 12sh. 6d.	7	10	0
	To Docter Dundas's man .	[illegible]	[illegible]	0
	To drinkmony at Cather .		1	
	For a horse to Cather . . .			
Sepr. 12	To Do. Abernathy 2 guinys at 21s. 6d.	25	16	0
14	To Doc. Abernathy a guiny	12	18	0
	To Telfoord, cherurgione, 2 guinys	25	16	0
	For 3 snuf milnes £4 . . .	4	8	0

[1] Seat of George Baillie's brother-in-law.

	[Sundries]	[Scots] £ s. d.
	To Rob. Hope £3, docters man £1 10	4 10 0
Sep. 27	To Docter Abernathy a jacobos and a guiny	28 10 0
	To all expences of puting up the loft in Erilston Church . . .	166 0 0
	For puting up the uter cattle rack etc. in the house by James Blakie	6 0 0
	For shoeing the horss at Mellersteans by Pate Newton from Sep. 23, 1706, to Sep. 29, 1707	13 4 0
	To James Duncon in Kelso payd by Pat Newton 14 years agoe	2 0 0
Sep. 29	To Troter in Kelso for mending sadles	3 14 0
Ditto	To Pringle in Kelso cherurgion his account .	23 0 0
	For a good strong bridle £1 2s. for head steels, etc. £1 12s. . .	2 14 0
	For letters payd Ms. Monro when I went away . .	1 10 0
Sep. 30	For yron to shoe the horses since Sep. 30, 1706 . . .	6 14 0
	For paper 10s. tows for the box with plate, etc.	0 17 6
	For cariing 2 cariages and a clogbag to Newcastle	12 0 0
	For Coltcrooks vicarage 1706 paid Mr. Gowdy	10 0 0
	For repairing Androw Brounlies house 4000 divids £2 8s. .	2 8 0
	To expence last winter by Androw Lamb	9 14 6
	For hay rakes 18 : suples 9s. mending stable door .	1 18 0
	To pip and drum, July fair	2 18 0
	To Androw Brounlies house puting up	6 13 4

	[Sundries]	[Scots] £	s.	d.
	For Rob. Dods house . .	3	0	0
	To Androw Lam 3 akers land	40	0	0
	To loss on Georg Trumbles house 3 years rent	24	0	0
	To the nurss house rent .	3	13	4
Sep. 31	For puting up the Hall House pay'd out for Widow Wight	8	12	0
	To James Massy scoolmaster in Mellerstains his sallary payable at Martimas 1707 . . .	10	0	0
	To James Miller, glazer, for a years at Mellerstains	4	18	0
	To Ms. Mean .	1	9	0
	For a pair sods to Docter St. Clairs lady	1	16	0
	To John Frazar he gave out at London	6	0	
Oct. 2	To Pegie M'Kinzie £6 14s.	6	14	
	To Isabell Dippo .	2	0	0
	To King, coachmaker, for helping the chariot the money sent to Edinburgh by Francis Newton	8	0	
	For letters £1 10s. £2 10 paid Francy Newton in full .	4	0	0
	To Tam Robisone in a year keeping up the Park 2 fous bea[n]s .	2	0	0
Oct. 3 [1]	For binding books to the ministers	3	14	0
	For Acks of Parliment	2	0	0
	For the news £1 paper £1 14s. more 17s.	3	11	
	For rubans to Peggy M'Kinzv .	5	15	0
	For binding the operas 14s.	0	14	0
	For shoeing the horse chariot rent etc. payd to Barty Gibson in full of all accounts . . .	54	0	0

[1] The last Scots Parliament met on this day.

	[Sundries]	[Scots]		
		£	s.	d.
	To John Baillie, cherurgion, for drogs from to October 3d, 1707 . .	158	0	0
	To Docter Trotter	12	18	0
Oct. 4	To drinkmony at Polwarth [1] .	2	18	0
	To the pip and drum at this moneths fair . .	2	18	0
	To Mr. Gowdy the vicarage of Coltcrooks this year .	10	0	0
	For repairing Mellerstaine Tour and other work there . .	241	19	2
		3386	6	8
	Take out the London journey .	1607	0	0
	S.	1779	6	8

Mellerstaines, January 1710. Sundry Accounts.
Deb. to Cash.

[Sterling]			
To Ms. Rume [2] for 9 weeks and 5 nights chamber rent at 3sh. 4d. per night and drinkmony	11	17	2
For coch and chaire hire at Edinburgh in abovesaid time . .	1	2	0
For drinkmony at severall places and to nurses	2	6	8
For compases to Grisie	0	2	6
To Mr. Crombine half a moneth . .	0	10	0
To Mr. M'Gie for teaching Grisie geographie		1	6
For tickets to consorts 7s. raffles £1 10s. . .	1	17	0
For writting paper and letters .	0	11	0

[1] See p. 12.

[2] See p. xxxviii.

	[Sundries]	[Sterling] £	s.	d.
	To Robert Morton and Ms. Riddle	0	5	0
	To the Lady Mannerhall [1] when her son died	1	0	0
Febr.	To John Baillie surgeon in full of all accounts . .	2	2	3
	To a man from Edinburgh to tune the spinits and virginells .	0	15	6
	For boat fraught at Rutherfoord [2]	0	2	0
	To Doet. Abernathys man	0	1	0
	To Piter Brown for measuring of land 2 days	0	5	0
	For letters . . .	0	2	6
May 24	For drinkmony at the Hirsill [3] nurs 10s. 9d. house 6s.	0	16	9
	For powder and lied . . .	[illegible]	[illegible]	[illegible]
	For drinkmony		1	
	For Spaw watter . . .		1	
	For letters			
	To Docter Gibson .			
	For drinkmony at sundry times		1	
	To Docter Abernathys nurs			
	For yron for uses in the house			
	To the Marques of Tweddels groom half a guiny . .	0	10	9
	To the two servants caried over the 4 mares 4 days . . .	0	4	0
May 29	For the cariages of two boxes from London	l	6	2
	For bringing my letters from Berwick . .	0	8	0
	For letters 5d. 10d. . . .	0	1	3

[1] George Baillie's aunt by marriage.

A ferry across Tweed at the old village of Rutherford, still in use.

[3] Seat of the Earl of Home. Lady Grisell's eldest and favourite brother, Lord Polwarth, married for the second time Lady Jane Home, daughter of the Earl of Home, 'Bonnie Jean o' the Hirsel.'

	[Sundries]	[Sterling] £	s.	d.
June 8	For drinkmony at Calder[1]	1	1	0
	To Rutherfoords cochman and Newtons[2]	0	5	0
	To my sister Julian[3] at Calder	0	5	0
	To Adam Mershall for the filly bringing	0	5	0
July 6	To Docter Abernathy when Rachell had a fever	7	10	6
	To the Docters man . . .	0	5	0
Aug. 30	To musick	0	5	0
	For letters 2 sh. 6d. an express 2s. 6d	0	5	0
	For ane express from Edinburgh	0	3	6
	For expresses to Edinburgh three times . . .	0	3	0
Sepr. 30	To Docter Gibson for blooding in the jouglar vain .	1	1	6
	For capris and gass for ink	0	1	2
	For cariing letters 1s., 2s. 6d., 1s 3sh. 8 . . .	0	8	2
	For drinkmony at Boughtrige and Ridbreas[4] . . .	0	10	0
	For cariages by Alexander Wood of books . .	0	2	6
	For sundry things to the house given out myself . . .	0	6	0
	To the ho boys	0	2	6
	For 2 nights lodging in Seatons house	0	5	0
	To John Carrs nurse 5s. other drinkmony 2s.	0	7	0

[1] Seat of Lord Torphichen.

[2] Lady Grisell's aunt, Julian Hume, married Richard Newton of that Ilk.

[3] Julian Hume, Lady Grisell's sister, eloped in 1698 with Charles Bellingham, a man of no means or position. She was no doubt staying at this time with her sister Jean, who married James, seventh Lord Torphichen, in 1703.

[4] The seat of the Earl of Marchmont.

[Sundries]	[Sterling]		
	£	s.	d.
For teath cleaning each half a crown and puders	0	14	0
For letters 1s. 4d. paper 3s. letters 3s.	0	7	4
To Sir James Cockburn of Ryslaw	0	10	0
To contrabution for Irish meeting house	0	14	0
To a nurse for Rachy at Edinburgh, July	0	5	0
To Pittcurs [1] nurse	0	5	0
For expence of letters cariing	0	10	0
For powder and sope 1s. more 1 sh. Baillie, surgen's man 2s. 6d.	0	4	6
To fidlers 2 sh. 6d.	0	2	6
To Litildanes [2] nurse and midwife	0	10	0
To Ms. Robertuns nurs 5s.	0	5	0
To Medina [3] picture drawer for Jerriswoods my oun and the two bairens's pictures drawing	20	0	0
For cariing letters to Mintto,[4] etc. 5s. drinkmony for lodging	0	9	6
Aug 12 For Grisies proclamation in the church to	1	1	6
To the door of the house on the 16	0	10	0
To her poket on the 17th	1	1	6
To her she gave John Baillie Murrays servant	2	3	0
To Prestonhalls [5] servant for useing their rooms	0	5	0
To poket given Grisie	2	0	0
To poket 10 sh.	0	10	0
For a moneths chamber rent in Ms. Burns	8	11	0
To the fidlers	1	1	6

[1] Haliburton of Pitcur.
[2] Kerr of Littledean Tower on Tweed.
[3] See p. xxvi.
[4] Belonging to Sir Gilbert Eliott.
[5] Roderick Mackenzie of Prestonhall, raised to the Bench as Lord Prestonhall. His wife was a sister of George Baillie's mother.

	[Sundries]	[Sterling]		
		£	s.	d.
Novr. 8	To expence at Ginelkirk [1] comeing in £1 going out 6 sh	1	6	0
	To drinkmony at Brughton [2] .	1	13	6
	For snuff and tobaca to cary to London	0	11	0
	For a nights lodging at Linton [3]	0	11	6
	For 6 weeks chamber rent in Ms. Rumes [4] at 5s. per night .	10	10	0
	For chaire hyre 6 sh. more 2s.	0	8	0
	To Androw Lambs expences at fairs and head courts 1710, 6s., more 1s., 2s., 2s. 6d. . .	0	11	6
	To the pyp and drum for 2 fairs .	0	9	4
	To Mr. Steall for Grisie .	0	12	0
	For letters by post, etc., per Francy Newtons account .	2	3	6
	To Thorindick 18s. for a horse to Greenlaw 6s.	1	4	0
	To Ms. Richison for her rooms .	0	8	0
	For cariage of a box from London .	0	8	0
July	To a servant of the Banck for bringing dook [?*lege,* doun] the books	0	2	6
	For fraught of the Spaw watter, etc.	0	16	9
	For paper 1s. and caring letters befor the election 12	0	13	0
	For the Acts of Parliament .	2	9	6
	For 2 years news papers pay'd Francy Newton	0	5	8
	For a goun and coat to May Minzies at Grisies marriage . .	8	0	0
	To George Newton for the cart road in the Greenlands . . .	0	5	0

[1] Channelkirk, a place about half-way between Edinburgh and Mellerstain.

[2] Belonging to Sir David Murray of Stanhope, Bart., whose eldest son married Lady Grisell's daughter Grisell.

[3] A village lying between Jerviswood and Mellerstain.

[4] See p. xxxviii.

[Sundries]	[Sterling] £	s.	d.
To Geordy Newton more for that road a fou oates . .	0	3	4
For 3 concave chimnys and 120 foot hewin lintells and rebets for highting the House hewin by James Brady 10s. chi[mney]; 4d. foot	8	10	0
For wright, measone, and glazier work, etc. about the House	26	0	0
For bring stons from Greenlaw to J. Ormston at 5d. per day .	0	5	0
To the nurses house rent 16s. $1\frac{4}{12}$d. John Browns 11s. $1\frac{4}{12}$d. .	1	7	$2\frac{8}{12}$
To the scoolmasters salary this year	0	16	8
	S. 158	09	$05\frac{8}{12}$

Mellerstaine, Janry. Account of Sundry Expences. 1714

		£	s.	d.
	For mending the fine virginall at London . .	12	10	0
	For Fraught of them cariing out of Edn . .	2	0	0
	For the church Bathel at Edn	0	2	6
	To Collonell Hamilton 5s. to others 4s.6d. more	0	9	6
	For a Book 1s.4d. another 1s.	0	2	4
	For cleaning pistols 1s. .	0	1	0
	To Mrs. Howie . . .	0	10	0
Edn	To Robert Mandersons doughter Grisells nurs . .	0	5	0
March 7	For booking my seal in the Goldsmith's Chope .	0	1	0
10	For Poket Tolbooth church .	1	4	0
	To Drinkmoney at Lienhouse .	1	0	0

	[Sundries]	[Sterling]		
	To Drinkmoney at Calder[1] and to coachman and stables	0	10	0
	To powder and ball 4s. .	0	4	0
	For letters 6d. more 6d. .	0	1	0
	To Poket 1s. 6d. drinkmony at Ridbreas	0	2	0
	To Mary Plumer 1s. Abernathys Nurs 5s.	0	6	0
	For a Prognostication 3d. .	0	0	3
	To Hillons[2] Nurs 5s. Kimergham[3] 6s. Dunglas[4] 10s. .		1	0
	For Horse at Berwick 4s. to Adam Mershall for the Mares	0	5	0
	To Drinkmoney at Ridbreas 5s. Nickle 1s.	0	6	0
	To the Nurs at Dunglas	0	5	0
	To the fidlers two times 3s.6d. .	0	3	6
	To Drinkmoney at Dunglas the 2d time 5 garner 2s. groom 2s.	0	9	0
	For letters 6d. more 6d. more 6d.	0	2	6
	For James Duncans holding court at Langshaw .	0	4	0
May 15	To John Walker for the chair rent a year	0	5	0
	To the pys and drum July fair .	0	4	0
	For fairins and for fruit	0	8	0
	For a coat to Baillie Youll 4s.4d. makeing 8	0	5	0
	To Mr. Anderson the Minister, etc.	0	3	6
	For a book . .	0	1	0
	To Hary Fouls the Rent of Collin-			

[1] Lord Torphichen's. See note, p. 23.

[2] Johnston of Hilton. Lady Grisell's grand-aunt, Sophia Hume, married Joseph Johnston of Hilton.

[3] Belonging to Lady Grisell's brother Andrew Hume, raised to the Bench as Lord Kimmerghame.

[4] Anne Hume, Lady Grisell's sister, married Sir John Hall of Dunglass.

	[Sundries]	[Sterling] £	s.	d.
	tons House the last year we was in it and which clears all due him . . .	33	6	8
	For a lb. Rubarb	1	4	0
	For a lb. sealing wax	0	5	0
	For a gun and 30 swords 4£ packing 4s. 6d.	4	4	6
	For cariing letters and letters .	0	11	0
Aug. 8	For expences of going to Wooler	3	10	0
	For cariage of boxes from London	0	11	0
	For expence of coming by sea to Newcastle	3	7	0
	For 3 horses from Newastle to Mellerstaines . . .	2	5	0
	To Docter Gibson . . .	1	1	6
	For chamber rent at Edn 2s. 6d.	0	2	6
	To Smelholm boge .	0	10	9
	To Drinkmoney at Minto and Newton	0	14	0
	To Rutherfoord boat and cochman	0	2	0
	For 29 Guns and Bagginets .	18	4	1$\frac{4}{12}$
	For a barrill Powder weighe 7½ stone	3	6	8
	To James Pringle surgen account	4	0	0
	To Docter Gibson's surgen account . . .	4	11	9
	To John Craw's bill at the last Election	7	10	0
	For Powder for shooting craws, etc.	0	8	8
	To the fidlers	0	5	0
	For carting a box from London .	0	9	0
	To Mr. M'gie	1	1	6
	To Pyp and drum octr fair 4s. for fairins 1£ 4s.	1	8	0
	To Drinkmoney at Kimergham 7s. Ridbreas 7s. . . .	0	14	0

	[Sundries]	[Sterling] £	s.	d.
	To Drinkmoney at Stewartfield,[1] etc.	0	8	6
	To Drinkmoneyat Longformakus[2] and Horses	0	10	0
	To David Weems[3] a guiny his horse 2s. 6d.	1	4	0
	To Poket at Earlston	1	14	0
	To the Bathel of Earlston.	0	2	6
	To Nans Walker and Sandy Broun	0	6	0
	To Poket 1s.	0	1	0
	To Piter Broun for measuring the Hill	0	5	0
	To Drinkmoney Redbreas.	0	17	6
	To Drinkmoney Dunglas.	0	18	6
	For shiping goods 2s. more 15s.	0	17	0
	For Drinkmoney Ridbreas	0	5	0
	For Account books from Mr. Mcgie	1	0	0
	To Mr. Megic for teaching book keeping	3	2	0
	To James Kilpatrick	[illegible]	[illegible]	0
	Breast Mills doughters[4]			
	For a chair			
	To Poket Earlston, etc.			
	To Jean Lambs Bridle		1	
	To Poket Servante, etc.			
London				
Deer. 18	For Servants Tam youll and Katie Hearts fraught to London victualls furnisht by the Skiper	1	10	0
	To Tam and Kate when they went a shore, etc.	0	10	0
	For 5 places in the stage Coach from Edn to London	22	10	0

[1] Now known as Hartrigge. Seat of Col. John Steuart, killed by Sir Gilbert Eliott of Stobs in an election brawl in 1726.
[2] Seat of Sir Robert Sinclair.
[3] See p. 45.
[4] George Baillie's nieces.

	[Sundries]	[Sterling] £	s.	d.
	For booking money	2	0	6
	For cariing bagage one the coach over and above 20 lb. weight for each of us	2	7	0
	For our expences on the road for ourselves five and litle Robie Pringle [1] 13 days from Dunglas	10	0	0
	For James Grive's expence and the horses on the road .	1	17	6
	For shoes to the coach mares at Dunglas to Mouse Mare same road on, basts and cords to trunks etc.	0	14	0
	For fraught of goods from Berwick in three ships . . .	3	8	0
30	For warfage porters carts to the Lodging etc. .	1	9	1
	For fraught of 4 half barrills herins	0	6	0
	For warfage bale and cariing to the Lodgine .	0	2	6
	For fraught of boxes from London in Aug: last and cariages .	2	0	0
	For 8 quare white paper gote last sommer .	0	4	8
	For squaring and binding 2 count books	0	8	0
	For a spectickle eye 1s. letters 2s.	0	3	0
	For puting the Coach in currant	0	3	6
	For a cover to Grisies bible 8d. to her 1s. . .	0	1	8
	For letters 1s. . . .	0	1	0
	For binding the Atlas's	0	7	0
	To John Walker for the chairs rent till White 1715 .	0	18	4

[1] See p. xl.

[Sundries]	[Sterling] £	s.	d.
To Nurses House rent	0	15	0
To Will Mills Housereut .	0	5	$6\frac{8}{12}$
To John Gifferts house rent .	0	5	0
	£183	8	6

London, January 1715. Sundry Accounts, Deb.

12 day	For 4 weeks House Rent payd Mr. Broun	14	0	0
	To Grisell Robison . .	0	10	9
	For the Mous Mare stabling 19 nights shoes 1s. .	1	11	0
	To Docter Shien . . .	1	1	6
	To Rachy a play . .	0	5	6
	For letters 4s. Ms. Boyds childs toy 2s. 6d. . .	0	6	6
26	For a chair and coaches since we came	1	10	0
	To poket	0	3	6
	For a coach 1s. more 2	0	3	0
	To Margrat Robison .	1	1	6
	To cards lost at Dutches Montroses[1]	0	5	0
	To the French Mistres Taucour for a moneth . . .	0	10	0
	To Mrs. Wests Nurse	0	10	9
	To Captain Kirton[2] for lose on Raches Lottary Ticket		1	6
	For 300 Limes and 90 frute trees went to Scotland the frute trees was 4£ 1s. 6d. the limes	4	1	6
	For caring them to Greenwage to a ship for Berwick	0	7	0

[1] See p. 282.

[2] Captain Kirkton, R.N., son of the Rev. James Kirkton, and thus a first cousin of George Baillie. There are a good many of his papers at Mellerstain.

	[Sundries]	[Sterling] £	s.	d.
	For Goldbaters Lieff 1s.	0	1	0
	For a french book 2s. a psalm book 2s.6d.	0	4	6
febr. 22	For the Elections last Parliment and this new election giveing in the two returns to the Crown Clark	0	9	0
	For a hood and Mantle to Ann Kenady[1]		0	0
	For 8 plays at a croun to my Nices and doughters .	2	0	0
	For a book 1s.6d. .	0	1	6
	For News Powder and oyl pay'd John Baillie he gave out	1	0	0
	For Mastregs Coller .	0	1	6
	To Major clelands Nurs .	0	5	0
	For 3 laches 3s. .	0	3	0
March 8	For coach's and chairs to this day	1	12	0
	For 2 losens to a window .	0	2	6
	To John Scote for phisick and wateing on me . .	1	1	6
9	To Mr. Broun for 2 Moneth Lodging	28	0	0
	For the Lady Mannerhall	0	10	0
	For 300 Lime Trees sent to Mellerstaine and cariing	5	0	0
	For a watch and gold chean to Rachie from Massie	27	0	0
ditto	To Mr. Dumbar Franch Master for a Moneths teaching		l	6
	For Straffords tryell 16sh. staffords tryell 2s. 6d.	0	18	6
	To Mr. Isack for a Moneths Dancing to Rachy	3	4	6

1 Probably the daughter of Lady Kennedy afterwards mentioned.

	[Sundries]	[Sterling] £	s.	d.
	To Monsieur La fever Mr. Isacks violer a moneth . .	0	10	9
	To poket 2s., coch 2s., Ink 2s. .	0	6	0
	For dying Ms. Turnbuls goun 4s., lineing and makeing 19s.	1	3	0
	To Monsieur Isack a Moneth for Rachels Dancing and La fever	2	14	3
	To Mr. Dumbar French Master	1	1	6
Ap. 6	To Mr. Broun for 4 weeks Rent	14	0	0
Ap. 20	To Mr. Massys man .	0	1	0
	For a play to Rachel Dundas and May Menzies, gallarie .	0	4	0
	For Thomas a Kempes .	0	4	0
	For letters 1s. 1s. 6d. more 4s. 1s.	0	7	6
	For 6 weeks news to July 1st 9s. 2d., more 11s., 1s. 6d. .	0	11	7
	For coaches 4s., chairs 7s. 1s., 1s., 1s., 1s., 1s., 1s., 1s., 2s. 6d. .	1	0	6
	For Acts of Parliament .	0	3	0
	To Chair men for removeing our goods to the new house 6s. 6d. more 12s.	0	18	6
	For a play to Rachy	[illegible]	[illegible]	[illegible]
	For play Captain Murrays Lady		1	
	To George Drumond			
	To Andrew Kenady[1]			
	To Lady Kenady[2] .			
	To Mr. Baldwine Coachmaker in paint 25	25	0	0
	To pamphlets 1s., church Bethell 4s.	0	5	0

[1] Probably the son of Lady Kennedy.

[2] Perhaps Jean Douglas, daughter of Captain Andrew Douglas of Mains, R.N., and wife of Sir John Kennedy of Culzean, Bart., two of whose sons afterwards became Earls of Cassillis. She had twenty children, fourteen of whom died young. Amongst the six who survived was a daughter Anne, who married John Blair, younger of Dunskey. It is quite likely that she had a son Andrew amongst those who died young.

	[Sundries]	[Sterling]		
		£	s.	d.
	To Mr. Dumbar French Master for a Moneth	1	1	6
	To Johny Stewart for a play	0	5	0
	To John Simmerall .	3	4	6
	For a moneth Lodging payd Mr. Broun . . .	14	0	0
	To tax for the death of the Cows [1]	0	[illegible]	[illegible]
	For a French book .	0		
	To poket . .	0		
	To plays for Grisie and Rach	0	1	
	To Ms. Hurnes litle Girle	0		
May 28	To Captain Clivelands coachman	0		
	For a pair orrs to Richmond and back again to London	0	7	0
	For Morklet rols and wt Mrs. Cockburn . . .	0	2	0
	To Mr. Hays for 2 coach horses a quarter the 9 May 25	25	0	0
	To Mr. Hays for 2 horses to Twittenhame .	0	10	0
	To a Rafle given John Scote	0	10	0
	For 2 reports to send to Scotland	0	7	0
	To Rachy of poket money	1	1	6
June 21	For marled paper 2d. a sheat .	0	0	6
	For scouring all the wanscote of new house at 20d. a day without meat	0	17	0
	For white washing the House 1s. a roof	0	15	0
	For news prints 1s. 6d. .	0	1	6
	For the last two moneths of our lodging payd Mr. Broun .	28	0	0

[1] The tax here mentioned was no doubt imposed to meet the expense incurred in connection with a cattle plague which broke out in London and the neighbourhood in the preceding autumn, when many thousands of cows were destroyed by orders of the magistrates, the owners receiving compensation at the rate of 40s. per cow.—*Calendar of Treasury Papers.*

	[Sundries]	[Sterling] £	s.	d.
	To Mr. Broun for spoyling his furnitur	0	10	2
June 24	For Repairing the Rooff of the new house	0	2	6
	For 50 Reports of the secret Committy to send my father .	1	5	0
	For stoping Grisies Teeth with leed and some things to clean 'em	0	10	0
	To James Minzies to begine a stock . .	1	1	6
	To Mr. Isack for 3 moneth and to Mr. La fever .	8	12	0
	For Andersons pills . . .	0	2	6
	For drinkmoney at Twettenham to all the servants . .	1	7	6
	To Richmont ball with Mrs. Boyd and bairens	0	4	6
July 30	For newspapers 1s. 7d. Aug: 3s. 10d. . .	0	5	5
	To Lady Buts[1] Nurs .	0	5	0
	For painting the house by Muns at 3d. a yeard . . .	5	7	6
	For Glazing the windows 1£ 5 cleaning them all 10s.	1	15	
	The Smith account of Reparations to the house . . .	1	5	0
Aug. 7	To Earls Mitting House .	0	10	9
	To lose at Carts .	0	9	0
	For a necklace hook to May Menzies	0	1	0
	To Dickson joyner for reparations 5sh. . . .	0	5	0
	To John Colecot joyner for shelf to the house, etc.	0	12	0
	To Mr. Burnets servant for bringing the picturs . . .	0	5	0

[1] Lady Bute, Lady Anne Campbell, only daughter of first Duke of Argyll, and wife of James, second Earl of Bute.

	[Sundries]	[Sterling] £	s.	d.
10	To Mr. Dumbar French Master	1	1	6
	To Robert Baillie was taken by the Turks	0	5	0
	For a coach fram to a glass pay Mr. Baldwine . . .	0	2	6
	For a Nightgoun to my sister Graingmoor	2	15	0
	To Grisie 1£ 5s. . . .	1	5	0
	To Lady Kilraick [1] .	1	1	6
	For 3½ yd. yellow satine at 28d., for curtine to the coach	0	8	2
	To Rachy 3s. 2d. . . .	0	3	2
Aug. 26	For new prints to Turnbull .	0	1	0
	For writting the Lease from Coll Mckenzie of Mrs. Smithes house	1	5	0
	To Mr. Baldwine in pairt for the coach 20	20	0	0
set here by mistake	To Mr. Turin for a glase in two pices 84 inches high and 28 inches broad with a glas Muller			
	To Mr. Turin for a chimny glass in ane pice 54½ by 22½ . .			
	To Mr. Turin for a walnut tree writing Desk			
	For ane Apron to Raplocks doughter [2]	0	16	0
	To Grisie . .	1	1	6
	For 2 fans for my Nices Grisie and Anny Humes [3] . . .	0	7	0
Sepm. 17	For news prints 18d. more 22d. more 21d. 1s. 7d. . .	0	6	8

[1] Elizabeth Calder, daughter of Sir James Calder of Muirton, fourth wife of Hugh Rose of Kilravock or Kilraick.

[2] Jean, only child of Gavin Hamilton of Raplock by Lady Margaret Keith, daughter of John, Earl of Kintore. She married Francis Aikman of Brambleton and Ross.

[3] Daughters of Lady Grisell's brother Lord Polwarth. Anne afterwards married Sir William Purves of Purveshall; Grisell died unmarried.

	[Sundries]	[Sterling] £	s.	d
	For chairs 1s. 6d. 1s.	0	2	6
	For cariing my brothers box to this house . .	0	2	0
	For letters 6d., 3d., 6d. . .	0	1	3
	To lose at Carts at the Duke of Montroses . .	0	11	0
	For wax and wafers 2s. .	0	2	0
	To let Lady Shusan Hay see the wax works	0	3	0
	For the Court and country Cook	0	5	0
	For Howards Cookry	0	2	0
dit. 18	For a book of choise recepts .	0	2	6
1 Oct.	For 2 weeks news papers .	0	3	9
	For a weeks papers more Saterday 1st Oct.	0	2	4
	For gazets that time .	0	0	4
	For letters 1s., more 1s. 6d. F.N. more 4d., 3d., 10d., 6d., 6d. .	0	4	11
	For coaches 3 sh., more 1s., 2s.6d., 1s., 1s., 4s., 1s. .	0	13	6
	For scouring 3 pr pistols .	0	6	0
	For writting a Factory to receive mony from Bank .	0	1	6
	To Francy Newtons expence in going to Jerriswood 2s. .	1	0	0
	For a weeks papers Saterday 8 Oct 1s.	0	1	6
	For news papers Saterday 22d	0	3	1
	For News papers Saterday 29 .	0	1	4 $\frac{6}{12}$
	For cuping Rachy in the Banyo	0	5	0
	For collection to build Andersons Meating house . . .	0	5	0
	To Grisie .	1	1	6
	For coaches and chaires 2s., 1s 18d. 1s., 3s.	0	8	6
	For cleaning three pair pistols better	0	0	6

	[Sundries]	[Sterling]		
		£	s.	d
	To old Mrs. Colvill .	0	[illegible]	6
	To lose at Carts in Dick Montroses			0
	To the Mob : on Princes birthday			6
	To poket 2s., 5s., more 5s. .		1	0
	To Will Brown for his book .		1	9
	To Brother Andrew lent him .			6
	To lose at Carts in the Duke of Montroses	0	4	6
	To a Necklace to Jeanny Billingham [1]	0	1	0
	For a Ridinghood to my sister Julian [2]	1	10	6
	To the Dutches of Montroses son Ld George's Nurse	1	1	6
	To Rachy	0	5	0
	To the scaffinger a quarter at Michelmas	0	2	6
	To the watch a quarter at Michelmas	0	2	6
	To Mr. Hays for 2 coach horses for a quarter due the 8 of Septmr. last	25	0	0
Novr. 5	For News papers Saterday 5 Novr	0	1	4
	For letters 1d., 6d.	0	[illegible]	7
	For News papers Saterday 12			$1\frac{6}{12}$
	For News papers Saterday 19th			$4\frac{6}{12}$
	For letters 1s. 2d., 16d.			6
	For a coach 1s.			0
	For news $1\frac{6}{12}$d. new papers Saterday 26 1s. 6d. .	0	1	$7\frac{6}{12}$
	For May Minzies going and coming from Twittenham .	0	2	6
	For Raches going to the Biano to cup	0	6	0

[1] Lady Grisell's niece, daughter of Lady Julian Billingham.

[2] Lady Julian Billingham, Lady Grisell's sister.

	[Sundries]	[Sterling] £	s.	d.
	For wax 2s. 10d. .	0	2	10
	For a Thomas of Kempes for Rachy	0	2	6
	To Rachys poket . . .	1	1	6
	To Mrs. Wilkison . . .	1	1	6
	To John Simmerrell	1	1	6
	For a pair coach whiels 5£ got 1£ for the old ons .	4	0	0
	To Mrs. St clair . . .	1	1	6
	For a ½ lb. sealing wax 3s. .	0	3	0
	For 2 yd Caffa for helping the coach 1£ 4s.		4	0
thursday Decmr. 1	For 2 picturs of King George in Toliduse [1]	0	5	0
	For News prints Saterday 3d .	0	1	6
	For Queen Anns Acts of Parliament the last sessions	2	3	0
	To my Dears poket .	14	10	0
	To lose at Carts Lady Lowdens [2]	0	10	0
	For the Attalantes [3] .	0	12	0
	For a St Andras crosses 1s.			
	For letters 1s. more 1s. 6d.			
	For a coach 1s. . . .			
	To lose at Carts Lady Marr [4] and Duplins [5] and Dutches Montroses [6]	1	0	0
	To Androw Bell on account of books 10 guinys .	10	15	0
	For servantes and horses at the Tour two times . . .	0	4	0

[1] Taille-douce. Engraving on a metal plate with a graver or burin, as distinguished from work with the dry point and from etching.

[2] Lady Loudoun. Lady Margaret Dalrymple, daughter of first Earl of Stair, and wife of Hugh, third Earl of Loudoun.

[3] See p. xxv.

[4] Frances Pierrepont, daughter of the Duke of Kingston, sister of Lady Mary Wortley Montagu and wife of the Earl of Mar.

Abigail, youngest daughter of the Earl of Oxford, wife of George Henry Hay, Viscount Dupplin.

[6] See p. 282.

	[Sundries]	[Sterling] £	s.	d.
	To Mrs. Couper	0	5	0
	For 3 coach glasses . . .	3	15	0
	For 2 frames and covering them for the coach glasses .	0	7	0
	To the Laird of Wedderburn [1] when in prison .	5	0	0
	To Mrs. St clair . . .	1	3	6
	For 4 weeks news papers Saterday 31 Decmr.	0	5	6
	To the wathman a quarter at Christenmas	0	2	6
	To Mrs. St clair. . . .	1	0	0
	To the Church Bathel in Mr. Earls meeting house	0	2	6
	To Major Boyds son James christening where I stood God mother 28 Decmr. 4 Guinys .	4	6	0
Decmr. 29	To the servant at Twittenham of Drinkmoney . .	1	1	6
	To the Twittenham stage coach for 6 coming in . . .	0	12	0
	To the servants christenmas box half a croun each .	1	0	0
	To John Stewart to go to a play	0	5	0
	To lose at Carts at Lord Lowdens [2] Lady Strafford [3] etc. .	0	8	0
	For $5\frac{3}{4}$ Callico to Mrs. Crafoord at 3s. 6d. pr yd . . .	1	0	$1\frac{6}{12}$
	For a coach man and two horses payd Mr. Hays for a quarter due the 8 of Decmr. 1715	25	0	0
	For 6 moneths House Rent at Christenmas Mrs. Smith	22	10	0
	To John Simmerell .	0	5	0

[1] See p. xiv.

[2] See p. 39.

[3] Anne, only daughter and heiress of Sir Henry Johnson and wife of Thomas, third Earl of Strafford, whom the Commons at this time were anxious to impeach.

[Sundries]	[Sterling] £	s.	d.
To Mr. Alexr Guthery writter for Ballencrieffs affair in full of all he can ask	7	18	0
To the Heralds for our coat of Armes . .	0	10	0
To Pate Hunter for a coach Mare stabling	0	18	0
For fraught of young trees to Berwick .	0	15	0
For sclating Langshaw house by Thomson . .	1	16	0
	448	0	$2\frac{6}{12}$

London

January 1st, 1716. Sundry Accounts. Deb. to Cash.

		£	s.	d.
6	For a coach 1s. 3d. .		1	3
7	For letters 6d., 6d., 8d., 1s., 3d., 1d	0	3	0
	For a chair and coaches 5s.		5	0
	To Poket I. 5s. .	0	5	0
	For a pair spectickles mending etc.	0	2	
	For a moneths news .	0	4	
	For a pair spectickles	0	2	
	To Grisie 1£ 1s. 6d.	1	1	
	To Rachy for a Raffle lost	1	1	6
	For Thomas a Kempes to the servants . .	0	2	0
feb.	For letters 5d., 6d., 6d.	0	1	5
	For chairs and coaches 4s. 6d., 2s. 6d.	0	7	0
	For a weeks news papers 1s. $6d\frac{6}{12}$.	0	1	$6\frac{6}{12}$
	To Rachy for a Play	0	4	0
6	To John Simmerall	1	16	6

	[Sundries]	[Sterling] £	s.	d.
	To Cess for the poor three quarters at Ladyday next . .	1	2	6
febr. 10	To a joyner for puting out the closet door . .	1	0	0
	For news Saterday 11th 1s. 2d 2s. 1d$\frac{6}{21}$., 2s. 8d$\frac{6}{12}$.	0	6	0
	For chairs 7s. 6d., 2s., 1s. . .	0	10	6
	For letters 1s. 6d., 9d., 3d., 3d., 3d.	0	3	0
	For water. tax half a. year from Midsomer to Christenmas .	0	10	0
	To John Simmerall	1	1	6
	For mending the watchmans box 1s. to him 1s. . .		2	0
	To St leonards[1] son Patrick Ingles		10	0
	To the Bannew for Grisie .	0	5	0
	To the Bannew for Rachy	0	5	0
	To the Opera for Rachy .		10	9
	For a fram to Captain Kirtons[2] Pictor	2		0
	To Mr Doll the painters man .	0		0
March	For chairs 2s. 7d., more 2s.	0	[illegible]	7
	For news papers 1s. 3d., 1s. 2d., 1s. 6d., 1s. 2d.	0	5	[illegible]
	For letters 6d., 5d., 7d. .	0	1	
24	To the watchman a. quarter at Ladyday . .	0	2	6
Ap	For news 1s. 1d$\frac{6}{12}$. 1s. 2d., freeholders 3s., 1s. 2d., 1s. 2d. .	0	7	7$\frac{6}{12}$
	For letters 1s. 3d., 1d., 1s. 2d. .	0	[illegible]	6
	For mending Rachels watch .			
	To Mr. Frazer Minister			
	To Rachy for a Play and ane opera		1	
	For tuning the spinets .			
	For 8 yeards lutstring to Raplochs doughter[3]	2	8	0

[1] Mr. James Ingles, fourth son of Cornelius Ingles of East Barns, married Elizabeth Holburne, and purchased the lands of St. Leonards.

[2] See p. 31. [3] See p. 36.

	[Sundries]	[Sterling] £	s.	d.
	For a bed to Johnie Stewart 2 weeks	0	5	0
	For a coach, 1s. 1s. .	0	2	0
	For window tax. 3 quarters from Midsomer to Ladyday 1716 .	1	2	6
	For seeing the lyons in the Tower	0	1	6
May 5	For news 1s. 5d., 4d., 1s. 6d.	0	3	3
	For letters 1d., 7d., 1d., 9d.	0	1	6
May 10	To Docter Arburthnet[1] for Rachy	2	3	0
	For a coach 1s. . .	0	1	0
	For Rachel Dundas's going and comeing from Twittnem	0	1	6
June	For 2 weeks news 2s. 4d., more 1s. 6d., 3s. 2d.	0	7	0
	For letters 3s. 6d., 3d., paper 10d., letters 6d. 7d.	0	5	8
	To Jamie Scugald . . .	0	5	0
	To P. at Mr. Andersons .	0	10	0
	To Mr. Andersons Bathel	0	2	6
	For 2 gallary tickets to ane opera	0	3	0
	To Barnackie's[2] benefite 2 tickets to the opera	2		0
	To Mrs. Betsons Nurse .	0		0
	To Poket 2s. 6d.	0		6
	For a coach 2s. 6d., 2s. 1d.	0		7
	For a soliter	0	[illegible]	0
	To Mr. Scote Garner at Chelsy for dressing the Gardine, etc.	2	12	0
	For 3 dusone mother pearl fish 6s. pr du:, 6 duson counters 4s. dus.	2	2	0
	To Mr. Baillies Poket of Ladyday quarter	12	14	0

[1] Dr. John Arbuthnott, Queen Anne's favourite physician, author of several works; frequently mentioned in the *Journal to Stella*.

[2] See p. xlix.

	[Sundries]	[Sterling] £	s.	d.
	To Mr. Scote in Chelsy for puting the Garden in order . .	0	2	0
	To John Colcat for the partition in the seller 28s., etc.	1	14	0
	To the watchman a quarter at Midsomer . . .	0	2	6
	To Mr. Andersons meeting house building . . .	0	10	0
	To my brother Polwarthes man went to Hamburgh	0		0
June 26	For mending the coach by	0	3	0
	To Mr. Baldwine coachmakers excqueters in pairt	10	15	0
	For a Burnisht Gold fram to my brother Polwarths picture .	1	6	0
	For a glass to the coach 1£ Mr. Turnbulls man for geting it 1s.	1	1	0
	For 2 Lottery tickets I gave Cap Murrays bairens	0	10	0
	For 2 Quarters to Mr. Hays for 2 coach Horses from 8 Decmr. 1715 to June 8th 1716	50	0	0
July	For coach 2s., 1s., 2s.	0	5	0
	For letters 2s. 2d., 7d., 9d., 1s., 1s.	0	5	6
	For news 2s. 5d., 1s. 4d. .	0	3	9
	For a horse hire to a servant to woonsour .	0	7	0
	For Rachel my doughters picture drawen by Cummine .		1	6
	For 2 setts of vots to my father and Torphichen . . .	2	3	0
July 18	To my Dearests poket 10 guinys	10	15	0
	To the Lecterers[1] tax a year at Midsomer last . . .	0	3	6

[1] A class of preacher in the Church of England at this period, often Puritans, usually chosen by the parish, whose duty consisted mainly in delivering afternoon or evening lectures. They are said to have been supported by voluntary contributions, but this entry would indicate a regular assessment.

	[Sundries]	[Sterling] £	s.	d.
	To my Dear	0	5	0
	For giveing in and writting Grangemoors Memorialls	1	6	0
	To Walstons [1] Nurse	0	5	0
	For 3 yd. yellow sheveret for a curtine to the coach .	0	9	0
	For cords, etc., to the curtine .	0	1	1
	For a pound sealing wax super fine	0	5	0
	For Rachys Bathing and cuping at the Banio Long Aiker	0	6	0
	To Grisie	1	1	6
	To Mr. Frazer . .	0	2	0
	To lose at carts at sundry times	3	15	0
July 31	For half a years house Rent at Midsomer last payd to Mark Dickson in Broad Street	22	10	0
	For spectickles . . .	0	6	6
	For Pamphlets . . .	0	2	0
	For Pamphlets .	0	2	0
	For drinkmoney at Mr. Wests [2] son christening .	3	4	6
	To a watch man .		6	
Aug.	For news 1s. 2d., 6d.		1	
	For letters 3d., 2s. 6d., 1s.		3	
	For a coaches 5s. . . .		5	
8	To David Weems [3] . . .		3	
	To Martha Johnstons Nurse		5	
	For mending the Kitchin sink		10	
	To my Dearests poket at Bath	22	18	0
	For expence of Publick divertions at Bath	8	10	0

[1] John Baillie of Walston, Lanarkshire.

[2] Probably John West, son of Baron De La Warr, and afterwards first Earl De La Warr.

[3] Perhaps the son of Elizabeth Baillie, George Baillie's sister, who married Mr. Robert Weems of Grangemoor.

	[Sundries]	[Sterling] £	s.	d.
	To Raffles at Bath . . .	4	10	0
	To Docters and Apothicarys at Bath	5	5	0
	For cleaning all our Teeth at Bath	1	14	0
	For chairs to the pump and otherwise	3	0	0
	To Mr. Chanler, etc.	3	0	0
	For pumping and drinkmoney at Bath . . .	5	10	0
	To Rachys poket a moydor	1	7	6
	For coaches to and from Bath by oxfoord . .	20	0	0
	For seeing Blenhome and oxfoord Collages	1	5	0
	For cariing servants to Bath .	3	18	0
	For cariage of trunks to Bath .	6	14	0
	For 8 weeks lodging 4 rooms and garets at Bath . .	18	6	0
	To the Cook and maids	2	3	0
	For Musick books to Grisie	1	0	0
	To my Dears poket at Bath .	2	0	0
Oct. 13.	For the coach from Robert Hays from the 8 of June till the 8 Aug: and for the coaches standing 9 weeks at 18d. a week and horses 3s. to Hamtoncourt	18	17	0
	For news 1s. 9d., 1s. 2d., 3d., 11d.	0	4	1
	For letters 6d., 6d., 1d., 6d 3d., 3d. . .	0	2	1
	To my Dearests poket .	[illegible]	[illegible]	[illegible]
	For a coach glas La saget 1£ 5s. .			
	For 2 Snuff Mills La Sashet		1	
	For a kain string .			
	To Grisie			
	To David Weems [1] to clear his accounts and cary him home	15	0	0

[1] See p. 45.

	[Sundries]	[Sterling] £	s.	d.
	For a years scafangers tax from Michelms 1715 to Mich[s] 1716 .	0	10	0
	To Androw Bell in pairt of ane Account for books . .	10	0	0
	To the Poors tax from Ladyday to Michalmes 1716	1	2	0
	For ane Apron to Mrs. Turnbull	0	6	0
Novr. 8	To water tax three quarters at Michalmes last .	0	15	0
	For a Piew in King Streat chapel a quar. at Michel[s]	0	9	0
	For 2 brass hinges to the coach 6s. puting them on . . .	0	7	6
	To Poket	0	7	6
	To the Countes of Pickburgs[1] footman . . .	0	3	0
Novr. 16	For Pamphlets 5s. 6d., 1s.	0	5	6
	For letters 1s. 10d., 6d., 3d., 1s. 8d., 6d., 2d., 1d. .	0	5	0
	For news pamphlets 2s. n. 3s.6d., pam. 8d., 2s. 3d., 1s. 2d., 1s. 2d.	0	11	9
	To Mr. Weems Apothecary in full of his account .	5	1	6
wrong	For fraught and cartage of 5 duson fish from Hadinton	0	13	0
25	For poket 6s., Mr. Andersons 10s., Jamie Scugald 5s. .	1	1	0
	For mending the water pyps 7s.	0	7	0
	For lose at carts 8s. .	0	8	0
	For a pen glas to a window 10d.	0	0	10
	For a chair 1s.	0	1	0
	For scaffingers tax for a quarter at Christmas 1716 . . .	0	2	6
	For Christmas box 8 servants 1£ watchman bellman 2s.	1	2	0

[1] Countess of Lippe and Buckenburg (in French Piquebourg), one of the Ladies of the Princess of Wales.—*Diary of Lady Cowper.*

[Sundries]	[Sterling] £	s.	d.
For Apoticars man, strewer 5 waterman 1s. shoemakers 2s.	0	8	0
To Drum trainbands 1s., dustman 1s.	0	2	0
To the Princes footman for a crose 10s. 9d. .	0	10	9
For copping a musick book £1 1s. 6d., ruled paper 10	1	11	6
For Meeting House rent Christmas quarter	0	8	0
For half a years house rent at Christmas payd Mrs. Dickson	22	10	0
To poors tax a quarter at Christmas	0	11	0
For tuning the Spinets 2 times	0	5	0
To Dickson for puting out the four windows in the litle drawing rooms in Broad Street .	7	0	0
	373	8	5

London, January 1st, 1717. Account of Sundry Expences

For paveing the streat .	5	4	0
For laying the plain stons before the door	2	0	10
To Mr. Frazer	0	2	6
For newspapers 1s. 2d., 1s. 2d., 2s. 6d. .	0	4	10
For letters 1s. 6d. 6d. 6d. 6d. .	0	3	0
To Mr. Mitchels Christening hs son James . .	3	4	6
For a fan Rachy gave Mrs. Mitchel	0	5	0
For covers of Fans sent to Utright to Lord Binning . .	0	10	0
For ruled paper to Grisie .	0	12	0
For lose at Carts by Grisic at Lady Marrs [1] . . .	2	3	0

[1] See p. 39.

	[Sundries]	[Sterling] £	s.	d.
	For 2 plays to Gris and Rach	0	8	0
	For a Desk to Grisies spinet	0	2	6
	To the watchman to Drink	0	2	0
	For a Purs to my Lord Ghram	0	7	6
	To the watchman drinkmony	0	2	0
	To Poket of Christmas quarter 5 guinys	5	7	6
	To my brother John Baillie	1	1	6
febr.	For news 14d., 2s. 6d., 1s. 6d., 1s. 6d. . .	0	6	8
	For letters 1s. 6d., 6d., 6d	0	2	6
	For stamp paper to write Turnbuls Factory	0	2	0
	For a chair 18d., 1s., 2s., 3s., 1s., 4s., 2s., 3s., 2s., 5s.	1	4	6
	To Alexr Hume of Whitehouse [1]	1	1	6
	To lose at Carts at Duke Roxburgs, etc	0	12	0
	For ane opera ticket to Rachy .	0	10	0
wrong	For 18 botles Ale from Dorathy Halliwall	0	8	0
	For 2 tooth picks 2s. Tho. Hervie 2s. 6d.	0	4	6
	For helping Mr. Johnstons strong box foot	0	1	6
March	For letters 1s. 6d., 3d., 1s., 1s. 6d., 1s.	0	5	3
	For News 1s. 6d., 14d., 1s. 6d., 1s. 6d., 1s. 6d. 1s. 3d., 1s. 2d.	0	9	7
	To the watchman half a year at Christmas last	0	5	0
	For A—— poyam dedicat to Rachy on the Princes .	0	10	9
	To old Frazer 2s. 6d.	0	2	6

[1] Perhaps Alexander Hume, son of George Hume of Whitefield, who along with his father was taken prisoner at Preston and was at this time in prison.

	[Sundries]				[Sterling] £	s.	d.
	To Mrs. Hume Whitefield [1]				1	1	6
	To my Dearests Poket 5 guinys .				5	7	6
	To Grisie .				1	1	6
	To lose at carts at D Roxburgs, Rotheses and Mrs. Verners				1	12	6
	To Mr. Barnackies [2] man for sinorina the Dog . . .				0	5	0
	To Docter Cheine for Rachy				1	1	6
	For opera tickets from Mrs. Robison [3]				2	3	0
	To Mr. Cuningham of Acket [4] 7 guinys				7	10	6
	For tickets to Castruches [5] Musick meeting					1	6
	For 3 seats in a Pew in King Streat Chapell at Lady day ½ year .				0	18	0
	For Pasing Graingmoors warrant for Collecter at Alloa .				1	13	6
	To my Dears Poket of Ladydays quarter				11	13	4
	To the poors Tax a quarter at Ladyday				0	11	0
March 8	To the water tax half a year at Ladyday				0	10	0
	For 2 Coach Horses from the 12 of October 1716 to the 12 of April 1717 . .	50	0	0			
	For sadle Horses in the above sd time at 3sh pr day from Robert Hay in full of all accounts	4	10	0	54	10	0

---

[1] The wife of George Hume, who was taken prisoner at Preston and was at this time in prison.

[2] See p. xlix.

[3] See p. xlix.

[4] Probably another unfortunate of the '15.

[5] See p. xlviii.

	[Sundries]	[Sterling] £	s.	d.
	To James Hume[1] of Aiton my Ld Humes brother	1	1	6
	For writing Musick 1£ 1s. 6d.	1	1	6
Ap. 12	To the lecterer[2] half a years tax at Ladyday	0	2	6
	For window Tax a year at Lady day 1717 . . .	1	10	0
	To Whitelich Coachmaker in full of all Acctts .	9	1	6
	To the Kings Houshold Drums 5s. footmen a guiny .	1	6	6
	To the Gard Drums 6s. Cadogons Drums 5s.	0	11	0
	To the parish wates 5s. Toun Trumpets 10s. 9d.	0	15	9
	To the yemen of the Guard a guiny		1	6
	To the Princes footman 10 9d. for a poyam 10s. 9d.	1	1	6
	To the Kings watermen	0	7	6
May 1st	For chairs 1s., 1s., 3s., 2s., 2s., 1s., 5s., 2s., 4s., 2s.6d., 2s.6d., 1s. .	1	7	0
	For letters 6d., 2s., 1s., 2s. 6d., 4d., 2s. 2d., 3s. 2s.	0	13	6
	For Newspapers 1s. 2d., 2s. 6d., 1s. 6d., 2s. 3d., 6d., 1s. 2d.	0	9	1
	For a book bound to set doun the visiters	0	4	6
	For 14 yd. Masarin blew ruban for the order . . .	0	12	0
	For wax candles 6d.	0	0	6
	For cheana cups, basons, etc. .	2	12	0
	To a Herper came with Mr. Isack		1	6
	To watherburn[3] 1£ 1s. 6d. Aitton a guiny[1]	2	3	0

[1] Taken prisoner at Preston, and then in prison. [2] See p. 44.

[3] See p. xiv.

	[Sundries]	[Sterling] £	s.	d.
	For lose at Dice in Lord Staires .	1	18	0
	To the Clark of the Crown for the return of Election and giveing in the write	1	11	6
	For materialls for my mothers elickses 5s. 5s. . .	0	10	0
	For 4 Tickets to Mr. Barnackies[1] opera	4	6	0
	For 2 tickets to Berenstats[2] opera	2	3	0
	For a purs to the Duke of Montrose	0	5	0
	For snuff mills, etc. in full from Lasaget	0	7	0
	To my sister Graingmoor .	20	0	0
	For a pair Garters in a present	0	10	9
	To Rachy	0	7	6
	To Carts at Rotheses	0	13	0
June	For chairs 1s., 1s., 4s., 1s., 1s., 1s., 1s., 1s., 4s., 2s., 5s.	1	2	0
	For News 1s. 2d., 1s. $1\frac{6}{12}$d., 1s. 2d., 1s., 1s. 2d., 1s. 6d., 1s. 2d 4s.	0	12	$3\frac{6}{12}$
	For letters 6d., 3s. 7d., 1s., 2s., 5d., 2s. 8d., 1s., 4s., 1s. 6d. .	0	16	8
	For paper 1s. pills 18d. snuff Milne 3s.	0	5	6
	For Glasing the windows	0	4	6
	For glas tee cups to sister Julian at 3d. a Tee pot 8s., glas cups etc. 5s.	0	13	3
	To Mary Hamilton . . .	0	10	0
	For cloath to be a peticoat G. I. .	2	5	0
	For tuning the Spinets 2s. 6d. .	0	2	6
	To Mr. Bradberys House	0	2	6

[1] See p. xlix.

[2] See p. xlix.

	[Sundries]	[Sterling] £	s.	d.
	For dressing the Gardine	1	4	6
	For a piece flowrd Indian Callico to sister Julian .	4	0	0
	For linen to the Callico 1£ 3s. .	1	3	0
	To the bairens for operas	0	16	0
	For the Pilgrams dress 1£ 12s. 12s.	2	4	0
	To my Lady Lockart lent and never payd		1	6
	For 2½ yds scarlet cloath for Docter Abernathys son George	2	5	0
July 8	For 3 Monethes dancing to Mr. Isack for Rachy .	8	2	0
	For standing God mother to Mr. Johnstons doughter Lucie	5	7	6
	To Poket of the Midsomer quarter	12	2	0
	To cards at Duke Roxburghs [1] 4s. more 2s. 6d. . . .	0	6	6
	To scaffingers tax a quarter at last Ladyday 1717 . . .	0	2	6
	To the watch half a year at Midsomer 1717	0	5	0
	To James Kilpatrick	0	2	0
	For rubans to give in presents .	1	0	0
	To Grisie 1£ 1s. 6d. To Grisie 2£ 3s.	3	4	6
	For a gold watch to Monsr Bernackie [2] the Italian	25	0	0
	For a gold chean to the watch .	4	10	0
	For a coat to Grisie Turnbull	0	14	0
	For scaffingers tax a quarter Midsomer 1717	0	2	6
	For Mr. Isacks Jamie 1£ 1s. 6d.	1	1	6
	To Vilpontu for drawing Grisies tooth	0	10	9
	For a hat to Patrick Dickson .	1	1	6

[1] See p. 284.

[2] See p. xlix.

	[Sundries]	[Sterling]		
		£	s.	d.
	For Grisie and Rachys lose at Carts	1	0	0
	For my own lose at Carts 10s	0	10	0
	For a string to My Lord Grahmes tortishel staff . . .	0	4	0
July 30	To May Minzies to buy a gown .	10	0	0
	To Frazer 30d. .	0	2	6
	For copping songs by Bernackie[1]	0	12	0
	To Mr. Dickson for half a years rent at Midsomer 1717	22	10	0
Aug. 5	To Androw Bell by a bill on Midleton in pairt paymt	20	0	0
	For a sadle house and hulster caps	6	18	6
	For shiping goods aboord when I went to Scotland payd Hendry Mill in full of all acctts . .	1	5	4
	For stoping Rachys tooth with Leed	0	5	0
	For a curtine of Calamanka to the coach	0		
	To Betty Dundas . . .	0	5	0
	For news while I was in Scotland at Lond.	1	0	$2\frac{6}{12}$
	For letters at London while I was in Scotland	0	11	9
	To Hays for horses to Twittenham Barnet and 18d. a week for the coach standing when we wrought not his horses . .	5	18	0
Eden.	For a coach and six horses to carie us to Scotland in 9 days .	32	15	0
Aug: 14	For expences of 5 in the coach on the road to Scotland till we came to Tiningham on the 14th Aug:	14	13	9
	For expence of a servant and a horse	1	15	0
	To my Rachy	4	3	0

[1] See p. xlix.

	[Sundries]		[Sterling] £	s.	d.
	To Docter St clair[1] and John Baillie		4	10	0
	To My Rachys Proclamation, etc		4	6	0
	To Mr. Robertsons men		0	5	0
	To Mr. Dickson for writing bonds etc . . .		4	10	9
	To Mr. Aickman[2] in pairt for picturs .	21 0 0			
	In full payd for the picturs at 5 guinys sitting and 5£ coppys	31 0 0	52	0	0
	For Drinkmony at Tiningham[3] when My Rachy went home	15 0 0			
	For all Drinkmoney while at Edn. and traveling about the 6 monethes I was in Scotland	29 10 0	44	10	0
	For chears while at Edn. .		4	14	0
	For Dails and trees bought by Cap. Turnbull .		33	12	8
	For 16 cart to bring the above sd timber from Berwick		5	9	4
Edenburgh	For 32 nights chamber rent in Mrs. Rooms . . .		6	12	6
Sept. 3	For $7\frac{1}{2}$ weeks chamber rent in Mrs. Cytons		8	0	0
	To my Dears Poket in Scotland		9	9	0
	For Tickets to Consorts . .		0	15	0
	For lose on guinys when cry'd doun		2	5	0
Decemr.	To Androw Kerr writer on account of my brother James Baillie		3	0	0
	For house rent of chairs in full of all at 6s.8d. a year each chair		1	10	0

[1] Dr. Matthew St. Clair.

[2] See p. xxvii.

[3] The seat of the Earl of Haddington.

[Sundries]	[Sterling] £ s. d.
To Pate Hunter Stabler for horses while we was in Scotland being 6 monethes	4 9 8
For 2 pr gloves to my father at Rachys mariage .	0 6 0
For 2 pr gloves to Mr. Hamilton Minister	0 5 0
For fraught and cariages by land for goods from London to Edenburg etc	4 16 6
For Gloves to Lord Hadingtons servants	0 17 0
For fraught of 2 servants to Edn and up again . . .	6 4 10
To the servants at the Bank at recpt of the Intr^st^ .	0 2 0
For a cover to Grisies dressing box	0 5 0
For writing bonds and persuing wood cutters .	0 10 6
For cariage of a Trunk from London	1 0 0
To John Vint shoemaker my brother Johns Acctt . .	0 18 4
To Mr. Will Hall man Arch: Stewart	1 11 6
To Docter Gibsone [1] for Grisie .	1 1 0
To Domany for a years writing .	0 10 0
To repairing the horse furniture in Scotland . .	0 7 0
Decmr. 29 To P. at Earlston and Bathel	0 15 0
To a Councel post .	0 5 0
To Betty Dundas Grisic Dundas George Sim Mrs. Olifers bairens and Mr. Turnbuls etc. and to servants and others of Hansels	2 18 0

[1] Fellow of the Royal College of Physicians, Edinburgh. Appointed an Examiner in 1725.

	[Sundries]	[Sterling] £	s.	d.
	To a surgen at Berwick for my brow	0	11	6
	For 5 places in the stage coach the 11 Jany that brought us to London the 25 January 1718 wher of Tam Lesly payd 2£ 10	21	16	6
	For expence of a man and horse along with us . . .	1	16	0
	For sadles mending boots and whips at London . .	1	12	0
	For cariage of a box from Scotland	0	12	6
	To the stage coachman of Drink-money	0	5	0
Dec 30	For Acts of Parliment 5£ 3s. 6d. more books 14s. 8d.	5	18	2
	For chairs 3s. . . .	0	3	0
	For mending the glas windows .	0	6	6
	To Christenmas box dustman 1s., watch 2s. 6d., water 2s. 6d., Boes man 2s., news boy 6d., Brewer 1s.	0	9	6
	For the votes . . .	1	1	6
	For coach horses to Hamton Court payd Hays .	4	0	6
	To my Dear for his journey on the Road to Scotland and back to London again and for Poket money besids the 9£ 9s. he gote at Edn. 86. 16 from 5 Aug. to coches and chairs included	86	16	0
	To the watchman half a year at Christenmas . . .	0	5	0
	To the poors tax at Christenmas 1717	2	4	0
	To the scaffinger at Christenmas half a year	0	5	0
	To my Grisies Poket 5 guinys	5	5	0
	To Labushier surgen .	1	1	0
	For lose by a horse bought at			

[Sundries]				[Sterling] £	s.	d.
7£ 18s. and sold at 6 guinys to carie a servant to Scotland and back again				1	12	0
For expences in getting out the Debenturs[1]				1	12	0
To the water tax 3 quarters at Christenmas . . .				0	15	0
For writeing in three years 1714, 15 and 1716 to James Massy				1	10	0
For 7 tarms Cess for Mellerstaine from March 1715 till March 1717 inclusive . . .				37	6	6$\frac{8}{12}$
For repairing Houses at Langshaw in 3 years 1715, 1716 and 1717 . .						
Milne by Park	1	19	0			
Coumslyhill given doun 16s., 4s. .	1	0	0			
Sclats Langshaw house	0	10	0			
more for reparations on Parks acct .	0	10	0			
repairing Langshaw Mill	1	18	2			
on Parks acct divits	0	10	0			
wright work by James Blakie in 3 years	6	6	10			
Meason work in sd years	0	18	10			
To a sclater for Langshaw house	1	15	10			
				14	8	8
For 10 tarms Cess of Langshaw from March 1715 till December 1717 inclus				32	7	3$\frac{2}{12}$

[1] The word 'debenture' was at this time generally used to denote the acknowledgment issued by a Government Department either for goods supplied or money lent. In this case Mr. Baillie had no doubt been lending to the Government. His balance-sheets show that he held debentures of considerable amount.

[Sundries]	[Sterling] £	s.	d.
For Trees and seads bought from Samuel Robson in Kelso	9	3	0
For slating the Towr of Meller. 17s. by Thomson	0	17	0
For a kevelmell 18½ ℔. 9s. 3d., 2 hows 2 gote 1715 Meller.	0	11	3
For young thorns from Newcastle	1	5	0
To a fferrier for the Coach geldine	0	12	0
To James Blakie Messeger for bussines pr acctt and recpt. .	0	11	8
For 3 spades 11s. a shuvel 20d. this year to Mellerstaine .	0	12	8
For mending glas windows at Meller in 3 years by Miller	0	19	2
For 160 bolls lime laid in at Mellerstaine . . .	4	0	0
For yron and nails furnish'd by Liedhouse in 3 years Meller	1	8	8
For charges of my brother John Baillies Funarels . . .	11	16	6
For smith work by Pat Newton shoeing horse and mending work lumes in 3 years . . .	2	13	$5\frac{6}{12}$
To the Nurs 3 years house rent White. 1715, 16 and 1717 .	2	5	0
To Tame Hilandman 3 years house rent Whit. 1715, 16 and 1717 .	1	13	4
To Will Mill 3 years House rent abovesd 3 years .	0	16	8
To Androw orniston a years rent White. 1717 .	0	15	0
for 100 firrs gote from John Humes father . . .	0	8	0
For Measone work in building dicks at Meller in 3 years	3	1	6
For wright work at Mellerstaine in 3 years 1715, 16, 17 .	2	6	10

[Sundries]				[Sterling] £	s.	d.
For the basan in the toun of Mellerstaine 1717 . .				7	10	8
To the 5d. men at planting dicking and quarie in 3 years				37	17	4
The windows tax for half a year at Christen^{ms} 1717 .				0	15	0
The Cess of Jerriswood payd at White. 1717 and preceedings 7 Tarmes in all .				9	16	$7\frac{8}{12}$
To Wilsone writer in Lanark for warning tenants .				0	6	6
To the nurs 3 bolls oats every year of Crops 1714, 15 and 1716				4	10	0
To Captain Turnbull [1]						
3 bolls bear at 10s.	1	10	0			
To him of the rent of Jerriswood Park for 3 years 1715, 16 and 1717 grass	36	11	0			
248 hens at 5d.	5	3	4			
60 capons at 8d.	2	0	0			
To Captain of the Park rent	3	18	0	49	2	4
For sundry small things given out by Cap. Turnbull .				7	18	0
For trees and seeds .				7	16	0
To sundry workmen at Mellerstaine etc				3	0	0
To Mr. Turnbulls expences in going to Langshaw, etc				2	1	0
To expence of holding courts, writings etc in 3 years				1	15	0
To the pyp and drum at the fairs for 3 years				1	5	8

[1] Seems to have been the factor staying at Jerviswood and being paid largely in kind.

[Sundries]	[Sterling] £	s.	d.
For paper to Cap. Turnbull .	0	13	0
	993	13	8

Edenburgh, Januer 1st, 1702. Howsekeeping.
Debt to Cash.

	[Housekeeping]	[Scots] £	s.	d.
	For a muchkin sinamon water	2	8	0
	For ginger	1	4	0
2d.	For 2 pices of clarit gotten from my brother John . .	120	0	0
	For a boll meall bought from Lady Hill . .	5	0	0
	For cariadges by Lesly	2	0	0
	For 2 little swine .	8	0	0
	For 3 lb. 2 ounces suger .	2	17	0
20	For 2 bolls pies to the mairs and swin	7	6	8
	For a salmond	1	10	0
	For 2 hams .	4	0	0
	For 5 fous of oats from Mellersteans crop 1701 .	5	0	0
	For 10 lods colls . . .	7	0	0
	For 8 lb. brown suger	5	0	0
	For gins bread . . .	1	10	0
	For a lb. cannell 7£ 2 ounc mace 26s. per ounce . . .	9	12	0
	For 4 ounce nutmug 9s. per ounc, 4 ounc cloves 9s. per ounce	3	12	0
	For ½ lb. white paper 12s. a pot cofeced ginger 1 li. 2s. .	1	14	0
	For 2 loafs candibrod suger at 18s. per pound	5	7	4

[Housekeeping]		[Scots] £	s.	d.
	For 5 fous oats to the mairs from Mellers.	4	0	0
	For bringing from Glasgow 8 galons wine 5 marks at the port 14s.	4	0	8
	For 5 fous ots for the mairs from Mell.	4	0	0
	For 8 galons 4 or 5 pints seck from Cap: Broun	89	4	0
	For a barrill Lews herin to Mr. Johnston	6	0	0
	For gardin seeds from Ms. Willie	9	12	0
	To James for bringing in the horss and out	1	12	0
	For green oyntment to the mairs hills	1	9	0
	For oats	0	12	0
	For a scon to the bairens .	0	18	0
	From Mellersteans of oats one boll and 4 fous	7	0	0
May 14	From Mellersteans of ots one boll	5	0	0
	From Mellersteans of pies one boll	[illegible]	[illegible]	0
	For beans to the hunting mair .			
	For expenc of bringing in corn .			
	For pits at Mellersteans .	1	1	
	For yron to shoe the horss 1li. 5s.			
	For markums balls from Ingles		1	
	For foulls bought by Androw L. sinc Decm[r].	14	13	0
	For chickens bought by A. L. this munth	2	0	0
	For howse and horss expences in small things from Novr to this day . . .	8	18	6
	For my expences at Ginelkirk and Mellers.	9	0	0
	For yron for horss nails and other			

	[Housekeeping]	[Scots] £	s.	d.
	things got from Liedhowse marchant	16	15	0
May	For 18 loads colls . . .	12	12	0
	For oyl from Lady Greenknow [1].	4	0	0
	For sweeping all the chimnys .	1	17	0
	For whiting the howse roofs and all	5	4	0
12	For malt got from Preston in Lith in full payment . . .	111	10	0
	For colls that cleard of the old colyer	7	14	0
begins this years colls	For 5 scor lods colls to Edmistons [2] man	60	0	0
1702	For 2 bottles oyl .	4	16	0
	For 12 pecks of oats	3	12	0
	For gresing the mairs at 6d. [3] a pice 36 days . . .	21	12	0
August 10	For gresing the mairs 36 days at 6s. a day	21	12	0
26	For 8 bolls malt got from John Wight	64	0	0
	For casting truffs . . .	00	14	0
	For going out and in to Ed. with horss, etc.	5	14	0
	For fouls brought to Ed. .	8	7	6
	For howse at Mellerstean such as salt, etc.	1	0	0
August 27	For foulls bread etc. since the childrin cam ther	4	0	0
	For sevarall things given out by Androw Lamb .	3	0	0
	To pay ane old account of Georg Lasons for 1699 .	9	0	0
	For wax and waffers	00	15	0
	For 5 seor loads of colls	60	0	0

[1] The wife of Pringle of Greenknow.
[2] John Wauchope of Edmonstone.
[3] 6d. Sterling or 6s. Scots.

	[Housekeeping]	[Scots]		
		£	s.	d.
	For my expences at Ginelkirk going, coming	[illegible]	1 [illegible]	0
	For Trumbels bring in oats		1	0
8	For 2 furlits of oats			0
	For materialls to a dyet drink			0
	For a scor colls from Carlips	1		0
	For oats to the mairs			8
	To the barber 6s. more 7s. Sutherlands man 14s. 6d.	1	7	6
	To Lesly for cariadges	6	14	6
Oct. 12	To Lesly for cariadges in full of all	10	0	0
Meller-	For a veall £6	6	0	0
steans	For 4 ship brought from Andrew Lamb	12	0	0
29	For a stack of hay bought in the toun	39	10	0
	For 2 ston cotten 6 in the ℔. at £4 6s. 2 ston rag 6 ℔. one ston 8 in ℔. 2 ston 12 in ℔. 2 ston 20 in the ℔. at 3£ 6s.h	33	16	0
	For a fatt cow bought at the fair	20	0	0
	For 2 ship from John Wight	10	0	0
	For 2 ship from T. Liedhowse	6	0	0
	For 3 ston best chease at 2℔. 4s. the cowrs cheas being at 1£ 16sh. 9 ℔. of it 1£ 6 4	7	5	4
	For 2 swin	20	0	0
	For 17½ staks pittes	35	0	0
	For 27 stack of pitts out of our moss			
	To Davi Youll to goe in with the ass	1	7	0
	For a pot oyntment to the mairs	[illegible]	[illegible]	0
	For a stack of hay from Person	2		
	For shoeing horses at Mell.			
	For a chair		1	
	For starch			
Nov. 20	For cariadges			

	[Housekeeping]	[Scots] £	s.	d.
	To cochman and groom in arles	1	9	0
	To a ferriar for the mairs	0	14	6
	For corn to the mairs	7	14	0
	For powder and starch .	0	8	0
Novr 1	For 2 ruks hay to the ases	30	0	0
	For a lofe suger at 14s. 6d.	2	6	0
	For stabling horses payd in full to Pat. Hunter . . .	43	2	0
	To Sir Robert Chiesly ane old accumpt of ale .	78	0	0
	For mending the coach harnis .	5	0	0
	For 3 days chairs .	2	7	0
	For washing linin brought from the book .	90	12	0
	For meall from Jerriswood 2 bolls at £5			
	For backing payd Capn Mitchell	60	0	0
	For brandy got from Sir Georg Hume in Decmr 1700	61	8	0
Decmr 30	To Bartie Gibson for the coch mairs soeing, etc. from Jany 8 1701 to Nov. 13th 1702	30	0	0
	From James Gray 2 bolls meall at £5	10	0	0
	For meall at Mellersteans of crop 1701, 18 bolls and 4 fous at £5 per boll	94	0	0
	For corn to the horss at Mellersteans of the crop 1701, 14 bolls at £5 per boll . . .	70	0	0
	To foulls and swine crop 1701 at £5 per boll, 3b. 2f.	17	0	0
	To the ass of ots from Mellerstens and to the foulls 8 fouss, of the crop 1702 . .	8	0	0
	For bear for the ases from Mellersteans crop 1702, 3f. . .	3	0	0

	[Housekeeping]	[Scots] £	s.	d.
	For shild pies from Mellersteans 2 peck out of 5 p. 1701 raw .	2	0	0
	For 3 ship to the servants and salt at Mellersteans .	9	14	8
	For 10 hens, 10 ducks wild foull 14s.	1	10	0
	For saim and girthes to the horss	1	19	0
Dec. 24	For 18 pecks bran to the horss £3 12s.	3	12	0
Meller-steans	For fish . £3 6s. Candle £1. Salt 10s. since 1st November last .	4	16	0
	For drink to them since November 1st to this day .	2	0	0
Ditto	For fish 11s., spice 1s., sop 3s. 8d., to the servants candle .	2	5	8
	For warping ale 6s., sow 6s., sop for naprie 7s.	0	19	6
	For salt pitter to 6 lambs £1 10, salt £1	2	10	0
	For a forpit of malt to the mairs	0	3	0
	For blooding the horses .	0	10	0
	For washing more this year	1	8	0
	For bear 5 fous	6	0	0
	From the book of small accumpts for the monthes of Janr, Febr, March	334	8	0
	For the month of Aprill .	41	15	0
	For the month of May £48	48	1	4
	For the mounth of Juny . .	132	12	4
	For the monthes of July and August . .	122	4	6
	For the mounthes of Septmr. .	94	0	2
	For the month of October .	41	14	2
	For the monthes of Novr and Decmr. . . .	145	14	4
Decmr 30	For corn to the horses at Meller-steans this winter of the crop 1702	5	0	0

[Housekeeping]	[Scots] £	s.	d.
For threves oat stra to the horss	80	0	0
For meall at Mellersteans this winter of crop 1702	15	0	0
For meall from Jerriswood was forgot to be fill'd up on the other side .	10	0	0
For 10 bolls malt browm in Edinburgh 1702 pay'd to Thomas Preston at 7li. and 6li. per boll	68	0	0
For a cow bought by Francy Newtons wife .	17	10	0
For brandy from James Marjoribanks . .	228	3	0
For 3 barralls herin whereof 2 sent to London	36	0	0
For bringing herin from Glsagow	5	13	4
S.	3154	06	2

Edenburg, January 1st, 1707. Houshold Expenc.
Deb. to Cash.

For 12 dals of colls from James Ballinton . .	68	8	0
For ale browen by Ms. Howie of my own malt . . .	30	11	10
For frute	6	0	0
For 2 duson of French aples .	1	4	0
For 1 ston cotten, rage one ston, gotten from Johnston, candlemaker	9	0	0
For a bottle sweat oyl from Ms. Wyllie . .	2	8	0
To Alexander Wood for cariing £1 10s.	1	10	0
For rubarbane ounc £1 16s., beries 2s.	1	18	0

	[Housekeeping]	[Scots]		
		£	s.	d.
	For limons £1 2s. more £19 12s. 4s.	20	18	0
	For 5 bottles clarit wine from tenants	3	15	0
	For chestons 14s., suger and spices £4 9s., frute £2 10s., Hungarie water £1 16s.	9	9	0
	For taking out horses, etc. given out by Tam Youll	2	7	0
	For a bottle Queen Hungary water	0	16	0
	To Frazar for ale from Octr 10 to Jan^r 1st 1707 .	33	4	0
	For stra to the mairs £7 6s. 6d. till Decm^r 30, 1706	7	6	6
	For oyl to the coch £1 14s. £1 17s. £1 17s.	4	8	0
April 8th	For coalls from Ulmatt £14 16s. .	14	16	0
	For Mugwart water 5s. .	0	5	0
	For stra to the mairs 19s. 16s. 15s. 15s. 15s. 15s. 6d. £1 4s. £4 18s.	10	17	6
	For a bottle Hungary water 16s.	0	16	0
	For tows to jack 4s., tobaca 14s. 2s.	1	0	0
	For severall smalls given out by James Carrin	7	5	0
	For ale by Ms. Howi of my own malt	20	17	6
	For 3 bolls mallt from Preston in Lieth at £5	15	0	0
	Stochton's drops 14s. . .			
	For a hogshead cherie seck from Hugh Mountgomerie .	200	0	0
	For 2 little swin at Kelso £4 .	4	0	0
Ma. 8	To Patrick Hunter in full of all accounts of stabling .	22	16	0
	For 3 bolls one fou oats from Meller. Crop 1705 at £5 .	16	0	0

[Housekeeping]		[Scots]		
		£	s.	d.
15	For 14 galons small bear from Abay Hill at 1s. per pint	5	12	0
May 20	For a hogshead clarit sent by Gawin Plumer to Mellersteans			
	For 10 pints brandy—by Sandy Inis to Edinburgh	20	0	0
	For 4 galons brandy sent by my brother James to Mellersteans	57	12	0
	For a suger lofe . . .	3	7	6
	For 4 galons ale from Ms. Howie and £10's worth Ms. Monro .	12	8	0
June 6	For a hogshead clarit laid in from Plummer at Edinburgh			
	For corks and botleing it at Lieth and cariing the bottles 1s. duson cariing doun emty and 2s. per pice duson full ther being 19 duson of chapin bottles and 3 duson of muchkins, and drink-mony	4	8	0
	For expence at Ginelkirk 9 men and 5 horss . .	3	12	0
	For 14 turs stra at Edinburgh £14; 4 load grass, 10s. per load	13	16	0
	For oats 12 bols 2 f. at £3 made in meall wherof 66 ston spent at Mellersteans betwixt the 4th of October till the 10 June 1707 by 4 servants and swinglers 7, 3, days and one a month to serve also 2 pecks grots and 6 pecks to Edinburgh and 18 ston meall	37	4	0
Meller-	For 4½ lb. candibrod suger	3	16	6
stean	For courser suger .	2	18	0
June 10	For a lb. capers a lb. cucumbers £1 7s.	1	7	0
	For ounc nutmugs 9s., ½ cloves 5s., 1 lb. spice 18s. . .	1	12	0

[Housekeeping]		[Scots] £	s.	d.
	For 4 ℔. rise £1 4s. . .	1	4	0
	For bread at Edinburgh from October 10 to June 10 .	26	0	0
	For 1½ fows malt to servants in Meller[steans] in winter .	1	15	6
	For a sow to Edinburgh from widow Wight . . .	14	0	0
	For sop 5s., blew 2s. 4d., thread 3s. 2d., sand and oyl 2s. 6d., ale 2s., quicknin 1s. this in winter at Mellerstean by Mary Muir .	0	17	6
	For ale Aprill 1st 10 pints werping 2 pints .	1	4	0
	For 6 sheep from Mellerstains to Edinburgh	20	8	0
	For ale from Ms. Monro .	10	0	0
	For 4 dales colls from Ulmatt in full of all account . . .	16	4	0
Ditto	For corn to the horss at Mellersteans crop 1706 at £3 3s.—31 bol—till the 2d of October	97	10	0
	For light corn to the horss £1 4s. at 28s. per boll . . .	2	2	6
	For corn to the swine crop 1706 at £3 3s. per boll 4 b[olls] 1 f[irlot]	12	11	0
June	For 66 threves oat stra at 4s. per threve at Mellerstains . .	12	18	0
	For pies to the swine crop 1705, 1 f. 2 p.	1	7	0
	For bear to the swine 2 bolls 1 f. £5 per boll . .	11	0	0
	For swine and fouls till Oct. 3d 7 bols oats at £3 3s.	22	1	0
	To the mairs sent to Edinburgh in winter 9 bols oats at £3 3s. .	28	7	0
	For a ℔. tobaca £1 4s. .	1	4	0
	For mum from Ms. Monro	7	1	0

	[Housekeeping]	[Scots] £	s.	d.
	For a punshon small bear from Lieth	6	0	0
	To Alshy Wood for cariages £2 4s, 6d.	2	4	6
June 10	For 12 bolls 4 fous at £3 4s. of oats made at Mellerstains wherin ther was 53 ston meall and 2 pecks and a half of grots 6 pecks scads of on kilfull in the other kilfull 42 ston and 4 ston to the fouls and 4½ pecks grots 6 pecks seads	41	0	0
July 20	For 6 bolls 2 fous oats made in meall at £3 3s. per bol .	20	4	6
Aug. 10	To expene at Ginelkirk with 5 horss	2	14	0
Aug. 26	For meat and drink at Edinburgh a fourtnight with 3 servants .	62	0	0
	To expenc at Ginelkirk with 6 horss	3	11	6
	For 5 load gras to the mairs in May	2	5	0
	To Patrick Hunter, stabler, in full of all accounts .	10	10	0
	To Alshi Wood, cariar, £3 14s. .	3	4	0
	For a load Scarsburg water	22	0	0
	To Hendry Youll for a boll malt makeing £4 more .	5	8	0
	For 6 bolls bear for malt at £5 per bol	30	0	0
Sep. 24	To Alshy Wood in full of all accounts .	3	0	0
	For ale to Grace Brunfild at Greenlaw	3	0	0
	For canlle from Agnes Smith in Kelso from June the 10th till the 1st of October 4 ston 2 lb. wherof a stone ½ cotten at			

	[Housekeeping]	[Scots] £	s.	d.
	£4 per ston comon candle £3 12	15	9	0
Sep. 29	For sope from Thomas Chato in Kelso from June 10th to this day at 6 shilline per pound .	10	16	0
Ditt.	For starch and indigoe to said Chato .	1	0	0
Ditt.	For severall small things to the house from said Chato such as veniger, spice, gatt, same, etc.	6	0	0
	For half a ston of candle more from Agnis Smith .	1	16	0
	For 9 ℔. wight candle 5 last winter and 4 in Aprill when Jerriswood was out	1	16	0
	For a thousand herins . .	6	0	0
	For expenc of horses bringing to Edinburgh	2	16	0
	For 14 loads colls .	2	5	0
	For a ℔. tobaca £1 4s. .	1	4	0
	For soap at Mellerstains last winter 12s.	0	12	0
	To sow piges	1	3	4
	For bringing wine from Lieth mans expences .	0	13	0
	For salt at Mellerstains last winter from Oct. 1st to June .	4	10	0
	For 16 seor ewes milk 2 days for cheases	5	6	6
	For sundry expence with horss at Broxmouth, etc., payed Tam .	2	15	0
Oct. 2d	For 30 threve oat stra to the horse at 4s. per threve . . .	6	0	0
ditt.	For 78 threve bear stra at 2s. 6d. per threve . .	9	15	0
	For pies to horss at Edinburgh 1 bol 2 f., horse at Meller[steans] 4 fo: 4l.	8	16	0

[Housekeeping]	[Scots] £	s.	d.
To the swine of pies 1f. 1l.	0	16	0
For 6 pound snuf tobaca .	3	0	0
For last winters candle from Cochran . .	43	0	0
For 10 pints brandy payd Gawin Plumers man .	21	6	6
To Patrick Hunter for M'gies horse	1	9	0
For 20 stacks piets casten for other 20 bought at £2 per stack	40	0	0
For 11 rucks hay at £9 and £8 per ruck .	93	0	0
For 14 lambs from the Park kild	14	0	0
For 19 sheap at £4 per pice from the Park	76	0	0
For ane ox and a cow from the Park kild	50	0	0
	1620	10	0
Brought from day book this year	827	10	0
	2448	0	0
By 11 ruks hay of Coltcrooks park	93	0	0
By 8 horse grased on Coltcrooks park at £12 per pice . .	96	0	0
	S.2637	0	0

Mellerstaine, January 1st, 1709. Housekeeping.
Deb: to Cash.

	£	s.	d.
For $2\frac{1}{2}$ fous of shield bear for broth from the Milne .	4	3	0
For $4\frac{1}{2}$ ounce of indigoe at 7s. per ounce		1	6

	[Housekeeping]	[Scots] £ s. d.
4th	For 2 boll malt from Hendry Youll . . .	16 0 0
	For 4 ℔. sope £1, more 10s. 10s. 10s. 10s. 15s. £1 15s. 10s. 10s.	6 10 0
18	For candle 9s. pay'd in full for candle from Greenlaw . .	4 13 0
	For muton to the servants £3 5s. more £2 6	5 11 0
	For 13 bolls bear at £7 per boll from the tenants .	48 11 8
	For makeing 2 stip of mallt of the abovesaid bear .	6 0 0
	For ale given the maltman for a steep at Huntly Wood .	0 8 0
	For ale to John Shiels's stiep of malt . .	0 12 0
	For 2 ℔. suger .	1 0 0
March 24	For a ℔. spice from Kelso	1 4 0
Ditto	For George Dods expence to Edinburgh, etc.	1 16 0
	For 23 pints of brandy bought by John Monro	48 6 6
	For half a barrill of Glasgow herins	5 10 0
	For a ½ fow bear meall	0 17 0
	For 2 swine from the milne	24 0 0
	For 1 ounc cinamon at 10s. oune, cloves 9s., ounce nutmugs 10s.	1 9 0
	For 1 ounce mace at £1 6s., 2 kitchen suger 12s. .	1 18 0
	For 4 ℔. 4 ounces loaf suger at 14s. per ℔. .	2 19 6
	For a chapin cucombers £1, a ℔. capers 16s.	1 16 0
	For a muchkin oyl .	1 1 0
	For 2½ ston butter at £3 10s. per stone, salt 1s.	8 16 0
May 1	For wild foull from Bowir to this day	1 10 0

	[Housekeeping]	[Scots] £	s.	d.
	For butter from Kelso £8 .	1	17	0
	For 2½ stone butter from Ms. Bilingham	9	0	0
	For veniger, 2 pints	1	4	0
	For bief from Kelso	2	0	0
	For 4 ℔. hopes at 14s.	2	16	0
	For suger 6s. . . .	0	6	0
	For 8 ℔. starch 8 ℔., powder at 4s. per ℔. .	3	4	0
	For salet oyl 6s. tobaca pips 8s. .	[illegible]	14	0
	For a ℔. tobaca .		[illegible]	
	For sweat butter .			
	For foulls		1	
	For 2 duson oranges		1	
	For drink in John Shiels's			
May 6	For 12 bolls and a fow of oats at £9 per boll wherin there was 12 stone twise shild meall and 43 ston houshold meall and 31 ston for fieding fouls and 8 pecks grots	109	16	0
	For 2 furlits pies shield .	5	0	0
	For a furlite bear meall from Widow Wight . . .	1	14	0
	For 4 ℔. hops . . .	2	16	0
	For 3 botles white wine £2 8, veniger 6s. .	2	14	0
	For 12 ℔. suger 5s. 12 ℔. 8s. cariage 14s.	12	8	0
	For trouts	1	4	0
	For 2 firikins butter wighting each 4 stone 13 ounces including the barrills one at 13 sh. 6d. the other 14 sh. and a sivenpence cariage from Anick to Wooller	17	3	0
	For veniger 12s. a ℔., butter 6d.	0	18	0
	For a quarter of bief at Kelso .	7	12	0

	[Housekeeping]	[Scots] £	s.	d.
	For floor at Kelso .	0	18	0
	For mirr 4s. tobaca and pips £1 12s. waffers 4s. bread £1	3	0	0
	For mending the jack 12 sh. wild foull £1 5s.	1	17	0
June 23	For half a firiken of sope . .	5	11	0
	For pigeons 12s. . . .	0	12	0
	To Ms. Oliphent for suger	3	4	0
	For tobaca 14 sh. . .	0	14	0
	For 2 dusone hard fish from Patton one at 12 sh. one at 14s. and cariage .	14	13	0
	For . ston cotten candle at . and . . . stone rage weeked candle at	30	0	0
	For candle at 4s. 6d. per ℔. clears all from Greenlaw	3	12	0
	For blew 12s. blew £3 4s. at 8 per ounce	3	16	0
	For a fou of bear for meall £2 12s.	2	12	0
Aug. 12	For 2 ℔. sope 10sh. 10s. 15s. 10s. 10s. 10s.	3	5	0
	For 65 stacks peats casten in the moss, £1 10 for 30½ of them .	45	15	0
	For spices, pickles, etc. from Ms. Oliphant . .	4	8	0
	To William Mitchell pairt of his fathers account for backing	110	0	0
	For corks from Edinburgh £7 2s.	7	2	0
	For limons and orangs £7 8s. more £4 16s. . . .	12	4	0
	For sundry things sent by Ms. Monro such as solan gees, herin, bread, etc.	12	8	0
	For brandy at £2 2s. per pint	48	6	6
	For a barrill of herin . .	5	10	0

[Housekeeping]	[Scots] £	s.	d.
For diner at Channelkirk going to toun . .	6	0	0
For linin washing while 14 days in Edinburgh	10	8	0
For 3 bolls malt from Preston of ane old account in full of all he can ask or crave 15	15	2	6
For cariing bagage	0	6	0
For spirit of wine 14 sh., 2 ℔. pouder 10s. . . .	1	4	0
For 4 ℔. suger . . .	2	8	0
For 8 hunder Dumbar herins .	6	4	0
For a cariage and a half pay'd John Waugh to Edinburgh .	2	5	0
For a stack piets from Robert Hope in winter .	7	0	0
For 3 veals	6	10	0
Sep. 26 To William Burnit for couper work since 9 Sept. last	12	0	0
For 8 darg troves casting at 6 pence per day . .	2	8	0
For 51 loads colls from Itell [?Etal] Hill at 6d. per load .	15	6	0
For a stone and a ℔. butter from John Mair in Jerriswood	3	8	0
For 1 ℔. suger 18s. more 18s. 18s. 14s. £1 16s. . . .	5	14	0
For a four gallon barrill being $1\frac{7}{8}$ aghtendeel wite boonties and $1\frac{15}{16}$ aghtendell graw errete[1] was 16 gulders 3 sturs the profite and exchange of mony by Lewis Pringle in all is	19	9	0
For a firikine Dutch sope from Lewis Pringle . . .	9	12	0

[1] Aghtendeel wite boonties=eighth part of white beans (harricot beans), and aghtendell graw errete=eighth part of grey peas. The words are old Dutch phonetically spelled.

[Housekeeping]		[Scots] £	s.	d.
	For a leg beef and the trips of it	4	1	0
	For 2 dusone hard fish from Will Patton	14	13	0
	For veniger	1	10	0
	For a botle of oyl	2	2	0
	For half a dusone aples to Grisie	2	14	0
	For a botle oyl	2	2	0
	For frawght and other expences of bringing the Spaw water from Lieth to Edinburgh	11	6	0
	For a veall from Munga Brounlies	2	0	0
Oct.	For candle £2, more £3 12s. more 12s.	6	4	0
	For 1 ℔. spice	1	4	0
	For cheas at £2 2s. per stone	1	16	0
	For brandy at £2 16 per pint	6	17	0
	For tobaca	2	6	0
	To workmen for clineing the closes	1	10	0
	For 24 bolls 2 fous 2 pecks meall made in Jan[r] last and put in the ark at £5 10s. the boll oats	132	0	0
	For 31 bolls oats to the horses at £6 the boll betwixt the 2d Oct[r] 1708 and the 1st Sep[r] 1709, that the horse was taken in	186	0	0
	For 5 bolls horse corn in the abovesaid time £3	15	0	0
	For foulls that was fed 1 bol, 2 f. at £6	8	8	0
	For feading all the fouls in generall and swine 3 bolls 3 f.	21	12	0
	For peas to the horse in abovesaid time 2 bols 1 f. at £7	15	8	0
	For pies to the fed swine in abovesaid time, etc. 2 bols 4 f.	19	12	0
	For 12 bolls 2 fows oats made			

[Housekeeping]	[Scots] £	s.	d.
in meall in May last wherein there was 84 stone houshold meall and 10 stone twise shield meall and 8 stone given to Munga Park for Langshaw milnetake of £11 4s. for Mun[g]a Parks the oats comes at £6 to	63	4	0
For horses in the abovesaid time 6 bolls 1 f. 2 p. at £6 .	37	16	0
For light oats at half price, 7 bols, 1 f. 2 p. . .	21	18	0
For pies to the horse 1 bol 3 f. at £7	9	4	0
For pies to swine, pigions, etc. 3 bols 1 f. .	22	8	0
For bear stra to the horse at 8 per th. 19 th. . .	7	12	0
For 200 threve oat stra at 12 per th.	120	0	0
For 19 th: bear stra at 8s. per threve . .	7	12	0
For 3 cows gras in the Mains	12	0	0
For milk £2 2s. cheas £2 2 sh.	4	8	0
For a leg bief . . .	3	4	0
For a stone butter .	3	6	0
For spices suger etc. from Charles Ormiston . . .	12	0	0
For spices £1 18, starch £1, tobaca and snuff £3 10s.	6	8	0
For expences in botleing the clarit and puting 14 dusone a bottles in shiepboord for London .	9	18	0
For 1 stone 3 quarters candle from Greenlaw since Oct.	6	0	6
For three bolls of wheat bought from Rutherfoord .	36	0	0
To Alexander Wood for cariing all this year and pairt of the last .	18	4	0

[Housekeeping]	[Scots] £	s.	d.
For bringing pigeons 6s.	0	6	0
For two milk cows from the Park	7[illegible]	6	0
For 2 veals from the Park			
For five cows from the Park kild	13		
For 34 sheap kild in the house	13		
For 9 sheap salted in the ladner			
For 11 lambs kild to the house			
For bringing pigions 6s. .			
Decm[r] 1 For drinkmony for pigions from Rutherfoord	0	12	0
From daybook for this year .	173	12	0
For suger pickles, etc. from Ms. Olifent	50	0	0
For 14 rucks hay at £9 per pice	126	0	0
For graseing 13 horses .	156	0	0
	S.2603	0	8

Mellerstaines, January 1710. Housekeeping.
Deb. to Cash.

	Sterling		
For 14 bolls bear for two steeps of malt at £8 10s. Scots which is in English moony 14 sh. 2d. .	9	18	4
For makeing the two kills full of mallt at Kelso	0	18	10½
For 2 stone barlie 6s. 4d	0	4	6
For 8 ℔. paper 16s., 1 lb. nutmugs 10s., a botle oyl 3s. 6d. .	1	9	6
For 4 ounces blew 3s. 4 ℔., starch 1s. 6d.	0	5	6 [sic]
For a muchkine orang floor water 2s. 6d. . . .	0	2	6
For 6 dusone limons and 2 duson oranges .	1	0	0

	[Housekeeping]	[Sterling]		
		£	s.	d.
	For 7 pints of mum . .	0	11	8
	For suger at 1s. 2d. per lb. from Sir Robert Blackwood . .	1	13	6
	For bisket to my L[ord] Marches childreen and Lord Grahme	0	3	0
	For 4 botles of white wine at 4s. per pint . . .	0	9	0
	For a barrill of Liews herin £1 1s. 8d. cariing from Lieth 10d. .	1	2	6
	For brandy at 4s. 10d. per pint	6	5	8
	For 4 botles brandy at 4s. 8d. per pint and cariing 2d. .	0	9	6
	For 3 dusone and 4 hard fish .	1	10	8
	For washing linins in Edinburgh near 10 weeks . . .	1	1	2
	For starcht linins dresing and washing said time .	1	2	0
	For expences going in to Edinburgh and comeing out	1	10	0
	For cariages in that time by Wood .	0	16	0
March 1	To household expence in Edinburgh near 10 weeks brought from daybook this year .	8	7	8
	For 2 stone candle from Greenlaw at 6sh.	0	12	0
	For 13 ells seckin at 10d. per ell .	0	1[illegible]	[illegible] 1
	For a peck floor . .			
	For a back say and a rump of bief			
	For a for leg of veall			
	For half a leg of bieff . .			
	For ½ tobaca 1s. 1⅓, pips 2d½, chark 3d½	0	1	7⅓
	For 12 flasks Burgundy at 7s. per flask	4	4	0
	For a ℔. cinamon 10s., ½ ℔. cloves 5s. ½ mace 12sh. . .	1	7	0

[Housekeeping]	[Sterling] £	s.	d.
For 2 stone rice at 8 sh. per stone	0	16	0
For half a pound Bohea tee	1	1	0
For ¼ lb. green tee . .	0	5	0
For a barrill salt cod from Bailiff Fall in Dumbar .	1	3	4
For cariage of the cod from Dumbar.	0	2	6
For a boll oats to the mares	0	13	4
For cariages payd Alexander Wood	0	3	6
For pigions .	0	2	0
Ap. 3d For a pint of oile [?] to the werping . .	0	0	2
For a fatt oxe from Thomas Turner to kill 2 0 0 For corn to the above-said oxe at £7 10s. per boll . . 0 17 6	2	17	6
For 12 bolls of oates made of meall at 12 sh. 6d. per boll, there was of houshold meall 48 ston, of meall for sour cakes 5 stone, for meall to the foulls 30 stone, there was three pecks of grots	7	10	0
For twelve bolls oates made in meall 103 stone 103 stone [*sic*] and 6 pecks of grots, thire oats was at 12sh. 6d. per boll .	7	10	0
The meall of thire 24 bolls oats was begune to on the 23d of November last 1709			
For 15 bolls oates to the coach mares preceeding the 1st of Aprill at the Christinmas fiers £7 10s. Scots . .	9	7	6
For 3 bolls to straingers horse preceeding the 1st of April	1	17	6

[Housekeeping]	[Sterling] £	s.	d.
For 3 fous oates to the cart horses	0	6	6
For 2 bolls 2 fous to the swine and fouls preceeding 1 Aprill	1	8	4
For 9 bolls light oates to the folls and other 3 horses preceeding the 1st of Aprill at 5sh. per boll	2	5	0
For 3 fous peas to the mares at 15 sh. per boll . .	0	9	0
For 1 boll bear made in meall at 15sh. per boll . . .	0	15	0
For a sow from Adam Hutchison . . 1 0 0			
For a boll oats to feed the abovesaid sow 0 12 6	1	16	3
For a fow of peas to the sow and 1 peck 0 3 9			
For 10 forpers[1] of peas reckon'd 1 furlit and a peck at 15 sh. per boll given to the pigions	0	3	9
For 2 forpets peas to the house	0	0	9
For 1½ fows peas to the mares at 15s.	0	4	6
For ½ fow bear meall from Widow Wight . . .	0	1	8
For limons and oranges at 2s. 6d. per duson	0	8	0
For 2 duson limons .	[illegible]	[illegible]	[illegible]
For brandy at 5sh. per pint			
For a stone butter . .			
For 100 herins . .			
For salt pitter 8d. 4d.			
For 6 bolls 4 fous and 3 fourtperts came to the horse oats . .	4	1	8
For half a stone of pouder 4d½	0	3	0

[1] Forpet, forper, or fourtpert is stated by Jamieson to be the fourth part of a peck, or in other words a lippy. Lady Grisell, however, makes it the fortieth part of a boll, or equal to 1⅗ of a lippy. This entry is arithmetically wrong.

	[Housekeeping]	[Sterling] £	s.	d.
	For 6 gross of corks . .	0	7	6
	For a botle of spirits	0	2	0
	For severall small things for Rachels backing . . .	0	6	5
	For killing 3 swine .	0	1	0
	For the coches going in for Colonel Stewarts lady . .	0	1	6
	For the cartes going to Edinburgh for the kavie etc.	0	2	5
	For 4 ℔. small candle 1s. 6d.	0	1	6
May 27	To Alshy Wood for cariing	0	4	0
	For 2 ℔. hopes 2s. 4d.	0	2	6
	For 22 gooslings from Togoe [*sic*]	0	11	0
	For a firikine of sope as it cost at Newcastle	0	18	0
	For 10 ℔. Cheshire cheas	0	3	4
	For whittining to the wals 1s. 3d. Glew 1s. 6d.			
	For bring[ing] the firikin sope from the Hirsile .	0	1	0
June 16	For wild foull from Bowir 3 sh.	0	3	0
	For sundry small things in Edinburgh 3sh. more 2sh. . .	0	5	0
	For Ginelkirk bill going and comeing the first of June	0	9	0
	For boord wages to three servants in Edinburgh . . .	0	8	0
	For the coach mares at Kelso with Lady Rutherfoord . .	0	1	2
	For eight dargs of truffs casting by Mowit	0	4	0
	For 2 swine from Adam Hutchison	1	17	6
	For servants beds, etc. at Edinburgh . . .	0	1	0
	For a cariage of clarit and another of cloathes	0	5	0
	For 4 ℔. candle 1s. 8d.	0	1	8

	[Housekeeping]	[Sterling] £ s. d.
	For 1½ gros korks 2s. 5½ ℔. almonds 1s. . .	0 3 5
	For 500 herin 5s. 10d., 500 herin 5 sh.	0 10 10
	For tobaca a ℔. 1s. 10d .	0 1 10
	For wildefoull plivergs [*sic*] gray at 6d. green 5d. per pair, ducks 6d. per pice small tiel 4d. per pice	0 5 8
Sep.	For bringing wine from Dumbar etc. M. Brounlies .	0 10 4
	For salt from Munga at 4d. ⅔ per peck	0 8 6⅔.
	For cariages of Spaw water, etc., by Alshy Wood . . .	0 16 0
	For suger at 8d. a pound got by Lady Couston . .	1 1 6
	For pears and aples at the second hand a gess[1] of both .	0 8 0
	For a gess of aples from Purvis Hall	0 7 6
	For frute at the fair	0 3 6
	For barberies in drinkmony	0 1 0
30 Oct.	For cariages by Alshy Wood preeceeding this day . .	0 8 0
	For 22 wild foull at 6 pence a pice	0 11 0
	For 2 bolls meall from Jerriswood at £6 per boll	01 0 0
Decm^r	For wine from the Taverin in all £4 wherof £1 set in d[ay] book	3 0 0
	For colls at Edinburgh from midle November till January, £1 16s. 6d. wherof £1 4s. 8d. set in day book	0 11 10
	To Alshy Wood for cariages from 8 Novr till January, £1 6s. 6d.	

[1] Gess or guess applied as a measure for apples and pears two or three times, but no information as to its meaning has been found.

[Housekeeping]	[Sterling] £ s. d.
wherof 8s. 6d. more 2s. in day book	0 16 0
For bread sent to Mellerstaines .	0 3 6
For ale from Baillie Hay when Grisie was maried .	0 16 8
For brandy	0 17 8
For drags to the efflixar	0 4 0
For a pice of wine at Grisies mariage from Doc: Melvin .	28 10 0
For aples bought at Kelso	0 6 8
For a lofe suger at 1s. 1d.½ per lb.	0 7 6
To Ms. Howie for linins to our beds	0 2 6
For spices . . .	0 6 0
To Alshy in full of this years cariages . .	0 2 6
For milk from Adam Hutchisons ewes at 2d. per pint . .	0 3 4
For butter bought from John Main in Jerriswood at 5sh. 4d. per stone, 13½ ston more 3 lb. wight . .	3 12 0
To Provist Brown ane old account taken on 1705	011 0 0
For meall to fead foulls from Widow Wight at 16d. per ston 12 stone	0 16 0
For 2 st. 3 lb. cheas from her at 3 sh. per stone . . .	0 6 6½
For 4 fous malt to the servants in winter	0 14 8
For 19 stacks of piets being a foot larger then the £4 staks I payd Tam Youll 4sh. 2d. ster. for 9½ stacks . 3 10 10 For 10 double stacks piets casten by Mowit and Lindsay at the same price for 5 stacks 1 17 6	5 8 4

	[Housekeeping]	[Sterling] £	s.	d.
	To William Mitchell in full of his fathers account for bakeing . . .	7	13	4
	For wine seck brandy at Grisies mariage from George Christy	7	12	6
	For 4 Turkies bought in September at Ripath . .	0	8	0
	For seck ale etc. furnish by Ms. Monro 16 Aug. . .	1	10	0
	For 47 loads cols quherof 6 small from Itell .	1	2	0
	For Androw Lams expence at the colls . . .	0	1	0
	For sundry things bought by Androw Lamb such as bread, fish, butter, wild foull, etc.	3	9	6
	For chickens bought by Lamb	[illegible]	1[illegible]	[illegible]
Aug.	For stoktens draps 2s. 2s. .			
	For oranges and limons . .		1	
	For brandy		1	
Sep^r^	For tobaco, etc. .	0	10	10
	For severall things bought by Francy Newton as oysters, solan geess, limons, snuff, etc.	1	6	0
	For meat bought in the Market of Edinburgh by Robert Mandersons bill	7	10	0
	For spices at the mariage .	0	7	0
	For one boll oats to fead two swine and 2 fous at 17s. 6d. 1 0 0 For 3 fous bear at 13s. 4d. per boll 0 8 0 For 4 fous peas at 16s. 8d. 0 13 4	2	1	4
	For 2 bolls 1 fow bear given for 2 bolls malt from Sticher 13s. 4d. boll	1	9	4

[Housekeeping]		[Sterling] £ s. d.
To the foulls of bear 1 fow	0 2 8	0 12 8
To the foulls of oates 4 fous	0 10 0	
For peas to the pigions 12 forpets [1] at 16s. 6d. per boll is about		0 5 1
For 3 fous peas to the mares at 16s. 6d. is about		0 9 10½
For oates to the mares, etc., till 3d September 3 bols 1 fow		2 0 0
For oats to straingers horse abovesaid time 4 B: 2 f. at 12s. 6d.		2 15 0
[...]all crop 1709. Made in meall 12 bolls 4 fous at 12s. 6d. per boll is		7 10 0
For a boll bear for feeding the borr		0 13 4
For bear to the milne for servants 9 fous		1 4 0
For oate stra at 6d. per 200 th[reve]		5 0 0
For 40 threave bear stra at 4d. per threve		0 13 4
For 40 th: peas stra at 6d. being very ill		2 0 0
For hay this year from Coltcrooks meadow		9 15 0
For a veall calf from John Hope		0 5 0
For 28 fatt sheap bought from the Park at 9s. 2d.		12 16 8
For 5 fatt nowt from the Park		11 9 8
For 6 sheap and a cow to the servants from Park		2 15 4
For 14 lambs from the Park at 4s. per pice		2 16 0
For 3 more sheap to the servants		0 15 0

[1] See p. 83.

[Housekeeping]	[Sterling]		
	£	s.	d.
For meat to Georg Baillies man	0	1	2
For 2 bolls malt from Androw Broun that was brown in strong ale in October . .	2	0	0
For 2 sheap to the servants .	0	5	6
For expence for the tenant bringing meall Brughton . .	0	6	0
For suger, frutes, pickles, etc. from Ms. Olifent . .	6	5	0
For sundry things from Char: Ormston per account	1	15	10
For a firikine soap . .	1	0	6
For ewes milk from Georg Newton	0	3	4
To Charles Hay, baxter, for backen meat at one diner when Grisie was maried . . .	5	0	0
To Thomas Fenton for confections and milk one diner at Grisies mariage . .	11	15	0
For household expence at Mellerstains from 1st March till 1st July, brought from Day book .	7	5	$6\frac{8}{12}$
For household expence in Edinburgh, June and July . .	17	3	3
For household expene at Mellersteans, Aug. and September .	1	8	$6\frac{6}{12}$
For household expence Novr and Decmr at Edinburgh .	10	4	2
For 13 rucks hay from the Park at 15sh. per pice	9	15	0
For graseing 12 horses at £1 the pice	12	0	0
	£345	18	$9\frac{2}{12}$

Mellerstaine, Janr. 1st 1714. Houshold Expences.

	[Housekeeping]	[Sterling] £	s.	d.
	To Mrs. Liver for six turkies .	0	10	9
	For $44\frac{3}{4}$ pints Brandy from Will Robison in Aymouth in part payment	4	15	0
	To expence of the horse that caried the Brandy . .	0	0	10
March 26	To John Baillie Surgen in full of all Accounts	1	17	7
	For half a stone starch	0	2	8
	For expences at Faladam [1] going 6 and 8d. Ginelkirk coming home 7 and 8d. .	0	14	4
	For washing at Edn: till 10 March	0	18	0
	For small thing such as powder and oyl, etc. .	0	2	0
	For three chopins of Hunny .	0	6	0
	For Brandy at 4d. the pint	7	12	0
	For snuff 5s.	0	5	0
	For suger and other small things given out by myself . .	0	8	6
	For a Milk Cow at Faladam .	2	16	8
	For corks to the cherie and botleing of it at Lieth .	0	2	7
	For 30 dusone oranges, 20 dusone limons at 15d. p duson, out of which I had 8 gallons orrange wine and large twelve gallons of pansh and 2 dusone oranges beside to preserve . .	3	2	6
	For a cariage of cherie and customs	0	2	7
	For cariing trunk 6d., drinkmony 6d., horse brecking	0	1	0

[1] A small village lying between Edinburgh and Mellerstain.

	[Housekeeping]	[Sterling]		
		£	s.	d.
	For 2 bolls 2 fows Malt from stonerige Tividale measure .	2	6	0
	For 10 bolls oates at 4£ 15d. Scots pr boll out of which there 1s. 6d. stone twise sheeld Meall two pecks of Meall which is recond duble Meall and sixty three stone of servants Meall 8 pecks of scads	3	19	2
	For three bolls one fow Malt from Berwick at 15s. the Lowthien boll 3£ customs 4d.	3	0	4
	For $7\frac{1}{2}$ stone butter last year from Jerriswood at 5s. pr ston	1	17	6
	For bolls Meall from Jerriswood to Edn. .			
Ap. 14	For sope, candle, etc. from Liedhouse Merchant haveing cleard all with him this day	0		0
	For cariing by Wood	0	6	0
	To carrin for snuff 1s. ornistons stable 1s. . .	0	2	0
	For cards 1s. 4d., $3\frac{1}{2}$ lb. resins 1s. 5d.$\frac{6}{12}$, wax 4d.$\frac{6}{12}$ . . .	0	3	2
	For Brewing 7 bolls Malt by Mrs. Ainsly	0	10	0
	For a ston hopes to the said Malt out of which I had a puntion very strong Ale 10 gallons good second Ale and four puntions of Beer	0	14	0
	For Diets from Hume Mose this winter	2	8	6
Ap. 21	For salt a boll	0	8	0
	To the English Butcher for making a sow in hambs	0	2	6
Ap. 28	For a firriken sope from Newcastle 1£ 1s. 6d. cariing 1s. 6d.	1	3	0

	[Housekeeping]	[Sterling] £	s.	d.
	For cariing hopes etc. 6d. . .	0	0	6
May	For 5 lb. butter from John Person 2s. 6d. more 18 lb. more 9d. . For 14 lb. at 5d. 5s. 10d. . .	0	17	4
	For 3 old Geess at 8d. 6 young ones at 6d. almost at full gruth	0	5	0
	For baling at Preston 1s. 6d. At Ginelkirk 4s. . .	0	5	6
	To Mrs. Crafoords Maid 1s. Francy Newtons 2s. 6d. John Barr 1s.	0	4	6
	To mens boord wages at Edn. .	0	4	0
	For pometum to the bairens	0	2	6
	For 47 pints of Cherie from Gilbert Stewart . . .	6	5	0
	For 2 duson and nine botles muchkins of fruntimack from Will: Carss . . .	2	5	0
	For a veal calf from the hird .	0	5	9
	For drink at Dunce 1s. 6d., drink at Langshaw 1s. . .	0	2	6
	For floor from Berwick 3s., suger 2s.	0	5	0
	For 8 pecks Meall for fouls at Kelso	0	9	0
	For Bieff 5s.	0	5	0
	For 1 ston wight figs and resins .	0	6	$2\frac{8}{12}$
May	For bread and drink at Edn. in Francy Newtons Lodging .	0	3	0
	To servants of boord wages .	0	2	0
	For Tee from Lewis Pringle in full of all accounts . . .	2	18	0
	To William Robison in Aymouth in pairt payment of $44\frac{3}{4}$ pints brandy at 42d. pr pint .	4	15	0
	For goosberies to botle at 3d. a pint 2s. 6d., cheries to preserve at 3d. 600	0	4	0

	[Housekeeping]	[Sterling] £	s.	d.
July 15	For wild foull . .	0	5	0
	To men with 7 horse with 13¾ bolls Meall from Jerriswood .	0	1	10
	For 13¾ bolls Lithgow measure Meall from Jerriswood at 8 sh. the boll	5	10	0
	For 5 duson of limons to be joyce . .	0	5	0
	For 8 fous wheat from Ridbreas at . .	1	16	0
	For 11 gallons and a pint brandy at 27d. pr. pint . . .	10	0	0
	For bringing the brandy from Dunglas . . .	0	2	0
	For a barrill of Herins from Hempsead . .	0	16	8
	For 5 bolls 4 fous Bear got from George Newton at 7£ Scots pr boll	3	10	0
	To Robert Hume for makeing the steep Malt . . .	0	5	0
	For 8 lb. sope 4s., 2 ounce blew 16d.	0	5	4
	For 3 kislips 2s. . .	0	2	0
	For 3 dusone Arrack 12s. gallon and packing	5	19	0
	For 3 lb. Tee and boxes . .	2	16	0
	For 6 fous Malt from Stenrige .	1	3	0
	For 4 ston chease from Widow Wight at 4s.	0	16	
	For 14 lb. courser chease at 3s.	0	2	
	For a ston Meall for foulls	0	1	0
	For drink money for frute	0	15	0
	For Searsburg water 5 dusone botles	2	0	0
Aug. 18	For 8 pecks salt 18 Aug. 10 pecks Salt	0	9	0

[Housekeeping]		[Sterling]		
		£	s.	d.
	For swine chease Milk and all Gorg Newton can ask or crave	3	0	0
	For corn eaten by swine and fouls allowed George Newton .	2	0	0
	For Bieff from Kelso	0	10	0
	For some small things given out by myself	0	7	6
	To Wood for carıng	0	2	0
	For 12 broom bussoms .	0	0	6
Septmr.	For a years work payd Will. Burnit the Couper	0	10	0
	For coupıng L. Rutherfoords barrills .	0	2	6
	For tinkler work . .	0	3	0
	For 6 bolls Bear from Mr. Gowdy at 12s. 6d. pr boll for malt .	3	15	0
	For 7 bolls oats for Meall at 9s. 10d.	3	4	2
	For casting 12 darg trufes with meat	0	6	0
	For 2 half Barrills of Herin from	1	10	9
	For suger at 9d. and at 13d. comes to . . .	4	1	0
	For Alloes and bay Berries	0	2	8
	For 2 guess Aples .		1	
	For pears			
	For sand 2s. 6d. .			
Oct. 30	For cariages		1	
	For ry bread 4 loves .		4	
	For candle 4£ 1s. 8d.		5	
	For bran 1s. 3d., corks 1s. 2d. .		2	
	For 8 galons Ale the Princes[1] birthday at the Bonfier .	0	10	8
	For Mr. Wilsons Horse .	0	1	2
	For a Bea Skep cariing by John Hope	0	1	0

[1] The birthday of the Prince of Wales, afterwards George II. Old style 10 Nov. N.S.

	[Housekeeping]	[Sterling] £	s.	d.
	For sundry things such as sope candle from James Liedhous	0	12	0
	From Day Book the 26 of Nivember that I left Mellerstaine .	22	16	0
	For small things given out by myself	0	10	0
	For cariing 1s. 6d. more 1s. more 9s.	0	11	6
	For expence at Faladam and Dalkieth	0	16	0
	For dry fish 8s. Hempsteed	0	8	0
	For a lb. Tee from Blair .	0	17	0
	For a botle snuff 5s.	0	5	0
	For Butter at Hardis Mill	0	18	6
	For Aples 4s. 6d., chickens 2s., tinker at Kelso 2s. .	0	8	6
	For couper work payd Androw .	0	15	0
	To Jesper when he went to Edn. with the Horses . .	0	2	0
Decmr 1	To Charles Ormston in full of all accounts	4	15	0
	For ½ lb. Jocolet . . .	0	2	0
Edn	For washing cloathes 5s. .	0	5	0
	For a lb. of Tee from Mr. Blair	0	18	0
	For ½ lb. Tee Gilbert Pringle	0	11	0
	For suger spices and sundry other things from Mrs. Olifer	8	0	0
	For 300 loods of Colls from the English side and some expences in bringing them the great at 6d. the small 3d. at the hill and what I hired in was eliven pence small and fourteen great .	9	19	0
	To Charles Ormston in full of all accounts	0	2	0
	To Alexr Lamb Candlemaker in full of all accounts F.N.	7	1	7
	To Bailiff Fall in Dumbar in full accounts R.T. of wines .	18	2	0

	[Housekeeping]	[Sterling] £	s.	d.
London	To Will Robison in full of all accounts of wines etc. R.T. .	14	5	0
Decmr 18	For drinkmony for the Kings venison etc. .	1	9	0
	For a porter to carie it	0	3	6
	For boord wages to Kate and Tam for ten days	1	0	0
30	To account of John Baillies boord wages was resting him when I came news powder oyl etc. .	1	0	0
	For a chaldron of colls from Tod	1	12	0
	For 250 billets . .	0	3	0
	For seller rent of Cariage of 6 barrill Herins from ffife .	0	7	0
	For cotten to be candle .	0	3	6
	For 3 duson botles Malligo from Gil. Stewart . . .	3	3	4
	For 51 b. 2 fous oates to the horses at 5£	21	8	4
	For fouls and swine 11 bolls .	4	11	8
	For 13 bolls oates to straingers horses	5	8	4
	For 7 bolls light corn at 50d.	1	6	8
	For peas to pigeons 9 fows at 15s. boll . . .	l	7	0
	For 200 threve stra beside beding at 6d.	5	0	0
	For 12 bolls oats for Meall and 4 fows	5	6	8
	For 24 bolls more for straingers horse Meall etc. . .	10	0	0
	For light bear at 5d. pr boll to the Ases	0	10	0
	For Ry at 15s .	1	1	0
	For Bear 2 bolls at 12s. 6d. .	1	5	0
		S. 279	19	6

London, January 1715. Houshold Expences.

	[Housekeeping]	[Sterling] £	s.	d.
	For 10 lb. Westfalia Hamb at 11d. pr lb. . .	0	9	2
	For cloves and Nutmug half a pound of each at 5s. 6d.	0	11	0
	For half a pound cinimon .	[illegible]	[illegible]	6
	For a lb. white peper			
	For 8 lb. Barlie at 3d. pr lb.			
	For a litle botle hungary water			
	For a lb. Bohea Tee 16s. Fergison		1	
	For a lb. Beco Tee 24s. Fergison			
	For ¼ lb. fine green Tee cal'd Heyson Tee at fergison .		8	0
	For a lb. firriken of sope		0	6
	For two Milk .	0	0	6
	For a lb. tobaco—Fergison		2	0
	For 2 duson Arrack at 14s. the galon Fergison .	4	4	
1st	For 2½ chaldron colls from Tod .	4	0	0
	For a Tun of Scots Coll .	1	16	0
	For 250 billets 3s. 25 brushes 1s. 9d.	0	4	9
	For 2 barrills of sope	1	5	6
	For Mutton chops Ms. Boyd and we in the city	0	3	0
	For sope blew 4s. 3d.$\frac{6}{12}$, blew 3s., more 1s.	0	8	3$\frac{6}{12}$
	For 2 lb. wax candles 5	0	5	0
	For bread 9d., toungs 1s., herin 1d.$\frac{6}{12}$ . .	0	1	10$\frac{6}{12}$
	For Aples 100 18d., a duson 2d.	0	1	8
March 1st	For a firriken of sope brock up this day	1	8	0
	For bread from Day Book from 18 Decmr to the 1st March .	2	17	3
	For Bear from Day Book from			

	[Housekeeping]	[Sterling]		
	18 Decmr 1714 till the 1st March	£	s.	d.
	1715	5	8	0
	For Houshold Expences from Day book from the 18th Decmr 1714 till the 1st March 1715 . . .	37	11	10 $\frac{4}{12}$
	For 3 botles Cinamon water	0	13	0
	For 3 cakes Ginger bread 4 lb. each	0	6	0
	For blew 8d.	0	0	8
	For tobaca 2s. Ale 2s. powder 1s.	0	5	0
dit	For 2 chalder of colls from Ghrame all charges	3	0	0
ditt	For 500 billets	[illegible]	[illegible]	[illegible]
dit	For half a Tunn of Scots coll		1	
	For blew and starch 3s. 4d.			
	For wine from a frenchman			
	For 4 botles of oyl and a half		1	
	For cinamon water . . .			
	For stacktens drops 2s. Drogs 4s.			
	For Lisbon suger at 7d. a pound			
	For the fraught and other expences of a barill with barly starch blew and two barrills of			
Ap. 20	butter .	1	10	0
May 13	For 4 lb. powther 1sh. 8d., two wash bals 6d., a comb 6d.	0	2	8
	For 4 lb. power at 5 a lb., irise root powder at 17d. . .	0	3	1
	For 1½ chalder of Colls from Tod	[illegible]	[illegible]	[illegible]
	For lb. rosted coffie .		1	
	For Balsamick cyrop			
	For confected pears			
	For Almonds 6d. .			
	For blew 8d., powd. 5s., 2 month wash ball 6d., bleck 6d.	0	6	8
	For spice and barly from Mrs. Abercromby . .	0	5	6

	[Housekeeping]	[Sterling]		
		£	s.	d.
	For 5 weeks washing of great linins only	2	3	6
	For 2 weeks sope 5s. 10 for washing 2 gouns and coats 6d.	0	6	8
	For fine suger and 13d. course lofe at 10d. 2 loves . .	0	9	11
	For fraught of 5 dusone clarit and a box with prints .	0	6	0
	For expences of bringing them out of the ship . . .	0	9	0
13	For a weeks sope another weeks sope 9 lb. ½ at 6d. .	0	4	9
	For sope 11d. for 3 weeks sope till 22d. June 9s. .	0	9	11
	For sope from 2d June till 15 August .	1	5	6
	For paper a lb. 3s. 6d., barly 2s. 3		5	9
	For tobaca 2s., pyps 6d. .	0	2	6
	For a pain of glas to a window .		1	3
	For Bear from 1st March till 1st May . . .	4	15	0
	To drink to wrights and chimny sweap . .		1	
	To Tam youll at Twittenham		1	
	For sope 1s. 3d.	0	1	
	For tobaca . .		2	6
	To Polwarths man for Spa water 1s. more 1s. .	0	2	0
	For drink bread and cheas to the scourers, etc.	0	2	6
	For sope and sand to scour the house . . .	0	3	0
	For speaping all the chimnys of our new house	0	2	6
	For fraught of 2 hampers wine 5s. other expences 5 .	0	10	0
	For nailing up the vine tree .	0	1	8
July 4	For 10 chaldron colls with half a			

[Housekeeping]	[Sterling]		
	£	s.	d.
chalder into them being 12 cart fulls 12 seeks each $1\frac{1}{2}$ chaldron more . . .	16	3	6
For $8\frac{1}{4}$ lb. fine suger at $12\frac{6}{12}$d.	0	8	8
For $6\frac{1}{2}$ lb. suger at 9d.	0	4	$10\frac{6}{12}$
To litle Charles bell 1s. .	0	1	0
For a lb. wax candle for tobaca lighting	0	2	6
To wonsar park keeper for 2 bucks of the Kings venison .	2	3	0
For cariing the 2 bucks from winsour park . .	0	6	0
For a duson lb. mold 6 in the lb. candle . . .	0	7	6
For half a Chalder cols owing Gryms since winter .	0	14	6
To Tam at Twettenham and Hamton Court . .	0	3	0
For greens to the parlour chimny	0	1	6
For frute 2s. 1s. more 3s. .	0	6	0
For triming $10\frac{1}{2}$ chalder Cols in the seller	0	1	6
For 12 botles Spa water .	0	15	0
To Charles Hays Nephew ane old account of backing	0	10	9
For fraught and cariage payd Mill for 5 dusone Clarit and 4 botles snuff . .	1	3	0
For cariing my brother Kimerghams box . .	0	3	0
For frute by May Minzies to the bairens	0	8	0
For starching linins and sope 4s. 2d. . .	0	4	2
For pometam . . .	0	1	6
For Houshold expences from day book from the 1st March till the first May	32	12	$2\frac{6}{12}$

	[Housekeeping]	[Sterling] £	s.	d.
	For Houshold expences from day book from the 1st of May till the first of July .	32	4	$10\frac{3}{12}$
Aug. 26	For half a pound Bohe Tee from Mrs. Johnston .	0	9	0
	To a Butcher for Bieff and mutton the Bieff at 3d. the mutton at $3\frac{6}{12}$d. pr lb. from the 12 July till the 1st September Jo: Betson	7	12	0
	To John Wright Backer for bread and floor, etc. from the first of March till the Last of August for the use of Thomas Broun Backer .	8	2	0
	To Ambrose Jackson for Bear from the first of May till the last of August at 10s. 2 moneth and 9s. 2 moneth .	7	12	0
	For — lb. finest suger at 12d. a lb.	0	11	6
	For — lb. of courser suger at 9d. $\frac{6}{12}$	0	4	6
	For — lb. of coursest lofe suger at 8d. . .	0	5	0
	For Lisbon powder suger at 6d. .	0	5	6
	For 4 botles Spa water at 14d. a flask 4 8 . . .	0	4	8
	For 6 lb. sago . .	0	18	0
	For a lb. Tee 16s., ½ lb. Tee 12s. 6d	1	8	6
Sep. 10	For 3 Chaldron of Colls to fill the cole house up .	4	5	0
17	For 4 weeks sope till this day	0	12	8
	For a lb. tobaca . .	0	2	0
	For 6 botles Spa water .	0	7	0
18	For Houshold expence from the 1st July till the last of August from day book .	22	1	4
Sep. 18	For a duson pound 10s. in lb. candles molded frenchman .	0	6	6

	[Housekeeping]	[Sterling] £	s.	d.
	For 12 botles Spa water	0	14	0
	For a lb. bohea Tee 17s., a lb. coffie 4s., a lb. Spice 3s.	1	4	0
	For $17\frac{4}{11}$ lb. westfalia hamb at 11d. . . .	0	15	7
	For 4 lb. Bohea Tee Fergison	4	4	0
	For 12 lb. candle .	0	6	6
	For 2 lb. Indigo bought in Scotland	1	0	0
	For 56 lb. of Starch bought at Edn. . .	0	18	8
	For 7 stone Pearl barly bought at Edn.	1	8	0
	For 2 ston shield peas bought at Edn. . .	0	5	4
	For a barrill and pock to put the abovsd things in	0	2	0
	For a botle of snuff	0	4	6
	For a bill loadening and putting them in the ship .	0	4	0
	For a barrill for the butter 1s. payd Marion Hempsteed fishing	0	15	0
	For cariing and boxes 1s. 10d. more 10d. .	0	2	8
	For a hamb at 14d. a lb. a botle oyl 3sh. 6d.	0	19	10
Octr. 1	For 100 billets a string of roots 50 brushes	1	1	6
	For a dusone Spa watter .	0	14	0
	For setting 2 hogsheads wine by Mr. Douglas's cuper	0	10	0
	To Captain Douglases Maid for Tee, etc. .	0	2	6
	For 2 Dusone Mold Candles 10 in the lb. . .	0	13	6
	For past to wash hands, etc. and to Mrs. Colvile . . .	0	4	0

	[Housekeeping]		[Sterling] £	s.	d.
	For a botle spirits 1s. 8d.		0	1	8
Oct. 28	For 7 lb. 14 ounce suger at 13	0 8 $6\frac{1}{2}$			
	For 6 lb. 6 do. suger at $9\frac{6}{12}$d.	0 5 $0\frac{3}{12}$	0	15	$3\frac{6}{12}$
	For 4 lb. suger at 5d.	0 1 8			
Nov. 8	For 2 dusone Mold Candles 6 and 10 in the lb. at $6\frac{6}{12}$d. . .		0	13	0
	For a dusone Spa water 14s., half a lb. Tee 8s. .		1	2	0
Ditto 28	For a thousand billets 12s. 5 brushes 3s. 6d. . .		0	15	6
Ditt.	For sope from the 23 of Sepr till the 28 Novr . . .		1	3	8
	For sope more gote in the abovesd 10 weeks		0	2	0
	For powder 2s. 6d. more 10d. .		0	3	4
	For saffron 4s. 2d. lead ure 6d. . .		0	4	8
	For genever and Rubarb 3s. 10d.		0	3	10
	For Tee 9s. 6 wax candles 3 lb. 12s. 6d. . .		1	2	0
	For a Hogshead of Clarit from Archbald Hamilton .		30	0	0
	For a Hogshead of Clarit from Major Boyd		30	0	0
	For $\frac{1}{2}$ lb. Tee		0	8	0
	For 13 lb. suger at $9\frac{1}{2}$d. pr lb.	. 0 10 $3\frac{6}{12}$			
	For 11 lb. 10 ounces suger at $12\frac{6}{12}$d. pr lb.	0 12 $1\frac{6}{12}$	2	13	1
	For 16 lb. powder suger at 6d. 18 lb 6 ou at 9d. . . .	. 1 10 8			
	For a Tun of Scots Coll		1	16	0
	For 6 botles champyne at 7s., 2 botles Harmtage 12s. Dutches		2	14	0

	[Housekeeping]	[Sterling] £ s. d.
	For 10 dusone botles Port wine from Bonnet .	9 0 0
	For 16 lb. resins at 4d., 8 lb. curran: $5\frac{6}{12}$d. .	0 9 0
Decmr. 31	For Bear from Ambrose Jackson from 1st Sptb. till the date here at 9s. per barrill and a croun more for stronger Ale .	7 8 0
	To John Betson Butcher from 1 Septmr. till 31 Decmr. .	18 14 0
	To Arther Grumball Backer from 1 Sepmr till 31 Decmr. 19s.	5 19 3
	For Houshold expene from day Book from 1 Sepmr. till 31 Decmr.	48 17 0
	For sope from 28 Novr. till the last of Decmr. . .	0 15 0
	For wine from Gilbert Black .	22 0 6
	For miscount page 352 .	1 0 0
		S. £441 4 $10\frac{3}{12}$

London, January 1st, 1716 Account of Housekeeping

	For 4 lb. powder 1s. 8d. more 2s. 2d.	0 3 10
	For a weeks sope 2s. 6d. . . .	0 2 6
21	For 3 weeks frut 4s. 6d. Bought myself . . .	0 4 6
ditt	For Candle 6 dusone 6s. and 6 dusone 10s. in the lb. .	3 18 0
	For snuff at 4s. the lb.	0 4 0
	For sope this moneth .	0 9 8
	For a lb. paper 3s. mace 1s. 3d. .	0 4 3
	For ¼ lb. orange pill ¼ lb. cordicitron	0 1 6

	[Housekeeping]	[Sterling]		
		£	s.	d.
	For 1 lb. Tee 1£ 1s. 6d., cimone water 4, paste 18d., pamatum 1s.	1	8	6
Febr. 1	For 12 lb. powder 5s. 4 wash balls 1	0	6	0
	For washing my brothers shiets .	0	5	0
	For 4 ounces Rubarb at 18d. ounce	0	6	0
	For 3 lb. Pistashi nuts at Mr Toom's	0	6	0
	For 2 weeks 6s. 9d. news .	0	6	9
	For fraught of 3, 8 gallon barrils with Meall Berwick . .	0	7	6
	For a bote to Hungerfoord stairs	0	2	0
	For a cart to Broad Streat with the meal . .	0	1	10
febr. 10	For a porter to help with it 3d. warffage 4 . .	0	0	7
	For a lb. Bohe Tee from Mr. Hamly	0	18	0
	For a lb. green Tee . . .	0	16	0
	For a dusone Nutmugs .	0	5	0
	For a lb. Green Tee Mr. Hamlie .	0	16	0
	For a litle barrill Sturgen from Mr. Heart . .	0	8	0
	For ane old account of Spa water	1	12	0
	For a suger lofe at $12d\frac{6}{12}$.	0	8	0
	For sope for this moneth .	0	11	3
March 8	For 2 lb. ½ all sorts dry sweatmeets at 3s. 6d., paste at 2s. 6d. ½ lb.	0	10	0
	For 1 lb. al sorts white confits .	0	3	0
	For a box prunellas 1¼ lb. .	0	2	0
	For 3 glases wate[1] sweatmeets at 6d.	0	1	6
	For ½ lb. waffers . .	0	1	0
	For a suger lofe at $12d\frac{6}{12}$. a lb. weight 6½ lb. .	0	6	9

[1] Wet, moist.

	[Housekeeping]	[Sterling] £	s.	d.
	For 4 ounces Coffie powder	0	1	6
	For ½ ounce Nutmugs	0	[illegible]	5
	For sope this moneth		1	0
	For powder and hungary water .			6
	For Billets and brushes .		1	0
	For 25 brushes . . .			0
	For a Hamb from Gumly at 10s. 6d. a lb.	0	10	0
	For 2 lb. Bohea Tee	1	16	0
	For half a lb. Tee . . .	0	9	0
31	For Bieff and Mutton for 3 Monethes payd John Betson Butcher Bieff 3d. Muton 3d $\frac{6}{12}$. shins 8d.	15	1	0
March 31	For bread in three moneths from Arther Grumble . . .	5	14	0
	For 1½ chalder Colls from Ghrames	2	2	0
	For a suger lofe . . .	0	7	9
Ap. 16	For 6 duson of Mold candle 6 in the lb. at 7d.	2	2	0
	For ½ lb. Tee Mrs. Abercrumby in full of all acctts .	0	9	0
	For Candle 10s. in the lb. 3 duson	0	1 [illegible]	[illegible]
	For a lb. Tee from Mr. Hambly		1	
30	For sope in this moneth .			
	For Coffie 18d. oranges 3s.			
	For Coach 1s.			
	For News 2s. 6d. plays operas			
	For letters 6d., 2d. .			
	For suger			
	For wash balls 6 .			
May	For 5 Dusone Botles Clarit got from Major Boyd	8	6	0
	For suger at 12d. a lb. .	0	7	6
	For sope in this moneth .	0	13	6
	For 25 lb. Jacolet made by Mr. Scots orders	5	3	0

	[Housekeeping]		[Sterling] £	s.	d.
June 1st	For 12¼ Chalder Colls from Ghrames		17	1	2
	For 2 botles Champain 9s., 2 botles Burgundy 8s., Chovet .		0	17	0
	For 3 gallons Rack Mr. Hambly		2	8	0
	For 1d. botles . . .		0	2	6
	For a lb. Tee, Hambly .		0	16	0
	For a du. Stockton drops 13 or 14 to the dusone . .		0	9	0
	For 6 flasks Clarit . .		1	4	0
	For a kit of three salmonds the salmond .	0 15 0			
	For the kitt boyling and veniger, etc. .	0 4 0			
	For frought to London	0 2 0	1	1	0
	For 2 botles Champaine		0	9	0
	For 2 botles Champaine		0	9	0
	For suger and 12 botles Spa water		1	3	6
	For suger . .		0	18	10
	For sope in this Moneth . .		0	16	9
	For 6 flasks Clarit Muns : Chovet		1	4	0
	For 4 botles Champaine .		0	18	0
	For 3 gallons Rack from Hamly		2	8	0
July 16	To the Keeper of Wonsour Park for a Buck . . .		1	1	0
	To the Carier for bringing it home		0	3	0
	For powder		0	6	0
	For a lb. of Tee . . .		0	16	0
	To lose at Carts . . .		0	14	0
Pd in	For a hogshead Clarit from Gilbert Stewart	18£ 0 0			
Scotland	For french duty 7£ 3 $\frac{6}{12}$d. custome house dues 9s: 6d. .	7 12 7$\frac{6}{12}$			
	For a duble cask and packing .	0 7 10$\frac{6}{12}$	26	0	6
	For fraught 10s. London duty				

	[Housekeeping]				[Sterling]		
					£	s.	d.
	1£ 2s. 6d. other expences given out by Hendry Mille 12s. 9d.				2	5	9
July 31	To the Park keeper for a Buck a guiny the carier 3s.				1	4	6
	For spermacity 18d., Lozanges 2s., saffron 3s. 6d., Baino Rachel 6 and spice 1s. 6d. .				0	14	6
	To the servants at Newgate Prison 2s. 6d.[1] . . .				0	2	6
	For sope this moneth					2	
	For suger 1£ 2s., oyl 6s. 6d.					8	
	For Meat bought in the Market					18	
August	For sope the first week .					4	
	To poket . .					2	
	For suger					8	
	For Mrs. Smithes glass					1	
	For sope					2	
	For cheries to Brandy .					8	
	For sope to scour blankets, etc. when I was at bath				0	14	0
	For cleansing the house of office				0	15	9
	For meat to 4 servants when I was 9 weeks at bath from 8 Aug. till 8 Octr. from Betson .	0	15	2			
	For bread in that time	1	2	2			
	For candle chease roots etc. in that time	0	6	6			
	For Bear	0	18	0	3	1	10
	For sope and sand to the house while at bath .				0	3	8
	For Meat, bread, bear, and all provisions at the Bath from the 9 August till the 12 of October .				38	0	0
	For Meat and Lodging going and coming from Bath being 9 days on the roads .				11	18	0

[1] See p. lii.

	[Housekeeping]	[Sterling] £	s.	d.
	For 24 lb. white sope brought from Bath . . .	0	11	0
	For washing linins at Bath and starching	8	10	0
	For a lb. Tee	0	16	0
	For fraught of 8 lb. green Tee from Holland . . .	1	16	0
	For 8 lb. Tee bought from Mr. Jerrard at Raterdam .	6	1	0
	For scouring the Hamer cloath .	0	2	0
	For fraught of ginger bread from Lord Bining	0	4	6
	For Modera gote from James Douglas	8	0	0
	For a hamb at 12d. another at 14d. a pound . . .	1	10	6
	For a Hogshead Pontack wine bought at Bourdaux by my Lord Stairs all expences came to	34	16	$7\frac{9}{12}$
	To Hendry Mille for bringing it home . . .	0	10	0
	To the Banio for Rachy .	0	8	0
	For 5 dusone botles Clarite gote from Major Boyd to send to Bath 7£ 10s. 16s. botles and corks	8	6	0
Oct. 17	For suger at 8d. 5s. and 6d. fine at 12d. 6s. 6d. . .	0	12	0
	For 4 dusone of lb. Candle 10s. in the lb. at $6\frac{6}{12}$d. .	1	6	0
	For 7 duson lb. Mold Candles 6 in lb. at 7d.	2	8	0
	For 2 lb. Bohe Tee . . .	2	0	0
	For a dusone 12s. in	0	6	0
	For 7 lb. suger . . .	0	7	0
Oct. 30	For 5 Duson 6 botles Clarit from Major Boyd	8	6	0

	[Housekeeping]	[Sterling] £	s.	d.
	For billits 15s. 6d.	0	15	6
	For expences of meat going to Windsor	1	5	0
	For drinkmoney at Mrs. Johnstons in Twitnem	0	10	0
	For 2 botles Hermitage 8s. 2 botles champaine 10	0	18	0
	For confections to diner	0	12	0
	For 2 botles cinamon water		8	
Oct. 20	For a muchkine botle snuff		3	
	For suger at 8d.		4	
ditt.	For 2 bushal charcoll		9	
31	For Bread flour, etc., payd Arther Grumbald from the first of Aprill till the last of October .	8	12	0
	For Meat payd John Betson Butcher from Ap. 1st till the last of october .	24	12	0
	To Mr. Tod for Bear gote from Ambros Jacson from January 1st till 1st August	17	12	0
Novr. 6	For a fine suger lofe at 12d. a lb	0	5	11
	For cooling seads 1s. Ales Milk 16s.	0	17	0
	For glasing the House brock by servants	0	7	6
	For pomatum 1s. .	0	1	0
	For strong Ale from .		12	
	For sope 4s. 6d.		4	
Nov. 16	For sope 3s., 3s., 7s., 4s.		17	
	For powder 6s., 1s., 3d.		7	
wrong	For 6 monethes window tax at Michelmas 1716 .	0	15	0
	For a hamercloath $2\frac{1}{2}$ yd. at 6s. 9d., lace 3d. and 2d. lining 3s. making 5s. .	1	9	$4\frac{6}{12}$

	[Housekeeping]	[Sterling] £	s.	d.
friday Decmr. 21	For 6 duson candle 10s. a lb. and a 1d. to R. and M. .	2	5	6
	For expence of foul, fish and other provisions from day book .	149	7	0
	To John Betson Butcher for Bieff and Muton in Novr. and Decmr.	10	18	6
	To Arther Grumble for Bread in Novr. and Decmr.	3	0	8
	For salmond from Berwick	1	5	6
	For fraught Meall, etc.	1	10	0
		S. 506	6	$2\frac{3}{12}$

London. January 1st, 1717. Account of Household expences.

		£	s.	d.
	For 14 lb. fine suger	0	14	0
	For 2 lb. at 11d. 2 lb. at 8d. powderd suger .	0	3	2
	For 2 lb. resins at 4d., 2 lb. currins at $5d\frac{6}{12}$. 2 lb. pruns $3d\frac{6}{12}$. .	0	2	2
	For ane ounce Coffie powder	0	0	5
	For 3 dusone Candles 6s. in the pound at 7d. . . .		1	0
11	For a woman to wash 1s. and 2 weeks sope 7s. .	0	8	0
	For a thousand Billets and half a hunder Brushes .	0	16	0
	For powder .	0	3	0
	For 2 lb. rise 10d., 2 lb. barly 5d., a lb. suger 5d., Mace 8d. .	0	2	4
	For a woman to wash 1s. 4 lb. sope	0	3	0
	For a lb. Tee from Fergison	1	2	0
	For a barrill of sope from Mr. West a lb. salt and peas	1	7	6
Feb. 4	For 4 lb. ½ sope 2s. 3d., 6s., 3s	0	11	3

	[Housekeeping]				[Sterling]		
					£	s.	d.
	For half a Hogshead strong Clarit L.P.	10	0	0			
	For half a Hogshead smaller at	7	0	0			
	For the French duty payd by Lewis Pringle .	7	12	0			
	For botles corks and botleing	2	10	0			
	For 3 casks and packing 22d. and 2 botles in all .	0	7	6	27	9	6
	For frought						
	For suger suger [*sic*] and fruts				1	0	0
	For 2 botles cinamon water				0	8	0
	For 4 lb. wax candle 10s.				0	10	0
	For fraught of 2 punchens Meall and the corper . .				0	10	0
	For bring them from the ship all expences				0	6	0
	For pometam 2s., more 1s., emeticks 1s.				0	4	0
15	For 2 dusone candle 10s. in the pound for R. and M. .				0	13	0
	For fraught and other expences by Hendry mills acctt for the Kinary and herin from Duke Montrose				1	2	0
	For 2 hambs from Matucks at 13d. pr lb.				1	0	0
	For 2 botles cinamon water				0	8	0
March	For sope 3s., 3s., 3s., 3s. .				0	12	0
18	For a thousand billets and ½ hundred brushes .				0	16	0
	For suger 7s. 6d. 10s. 3s. 6d.				1	1	0
	For a Hogshead syder 2£ 5 cate etc. bring in 2s. 6d. .				2	7	6
31 March	To John Betson Butcher for Bieff						

	[Housekeeping]	[Sterling] £	s.	d.
	and Mutton in 3 monethes	14	8	0
ditto	To Arther Grumble for bread flowr etc. in three monethes from 1 Janr. till 1st Aprill	4	8	0
Aprill	For sope 4s. 3d. 3s. 9d.	0	10	9
	For powder 3s. Almond powder at a 4d. p lb. 1 . . .	0	4	0
	To a Duson of candle	0	6	6
	For 3½ Chalder of Colls gote in the 2d March	6	10	0
May	For sope 1s. 1d. 4s. 2d. . .	0	5	3
	For champain	1	8	0
	For 7 Chardron of colls bought by Mr. West	10	0	0
May 1	For sope 3s. 10d. 14s. 10d.	0	18	8
	For wax candles 2s. 6d.			6
	For chesier cheas at 3d.$\frac{6}{12}$ a lb.			0$\frac{8}{12}$
	For a hamb at 6d. a lb. .			4
	For suger at 11d. . . .		1	7
	For a lb. Bohea Tee			0
	For Spa water pd Captain Kirkton . .	3	12	6
28	For 2 dusone of small candles	0	13	0
June 4	For sope 5s. 2d. 3s. 10d. 4s. 11d. 4s. 4d. starch 6d. 5s. 2d.	1	3	11
	For Candle from Wansour at 6 and $\frac{6}{12}$ pr. lb. . . .	3	5	6
	For pils 1s., pills 18d.	0	2	6
	For starch 6d. . . .	0	0	6
	For 4 botles Arrack from Mr. Hambly	1	1	6
	For 12 lb. powder 6s.	0	6	0
July 11	For sope 4s. 6d., starch 6d. 4s. 4d., 4s. 6d. 3s. 8 strch 1s. .	0	18	6
	For 2 dusone Candles .	0	13	0
	For lose by James Grieve he aither lost or miscounted	1	0	0

	[Housekeeping]	[Sterling] £	s.	d.
	For the cariage of a Buck and drinkmoney . . .	1	4	0
	For Bieff and Muton from Betson Butcher in Apr. May and June in full of all accounts	12	0	0
	For Bread from Arther Grumble from the 1st of Aprill till the 14th of July . . .	5	6	0
	For white bear 5 barrils at 10s. .	2	10	0
	For the custom and charge of 57 lb. hambs sent from Holland by my Lord Binning	1	3	0
	For a thousand billets ½ hunder brushes .	0	16	6
	For 2 wash balls 4d. Drinkmoney 2s. 6d.	0	2	8
	For 3 botles Arack more 2 botles	1	10	0
	For some small things by James	0	4	0
Aug. 5	For sweeping chinny .	0	1	6
	To Arther Grumble for bread since 14 June	1	5	0
	For Bear from Sam: Willis from 29 Aug. 1716 till the 5 of August 1717	21	2	9
	For ½ hogshead Clarit from Alexr Baird	18	0	0
	For some things bought by May Minzies	0	16	0
	For six kipper Mrs. Dalrimple .	0	10	0
	For a box and shiping the fish	0	1	6
	For 6 Ling. Fall . .	0	5	7
	For 4 stone-chease from Tweddal	0	13	4
	For ninteen ston Pork at 2s. 11d. pr ston barrills for salting etc. 12 toungs 8d. salting 9d.	3	17	3
	For Cheas from Newton and Wight tenants at 4s ston	1	0	0
	For powder and wash balls	0	13	10

	[Housekeeping]	[Sterling] £	s.	d.
	For tobaca 2s., snuff 4s.	0	6	0
	For Candle while I was in Scotland spent in Lond: besids 1£ 15s. worth left in the House	3	0	0
	For sope at London while I was in Scotland	2	10	9
	For seting razors 2s. 6d. .	0	2	6
	To the Coachman and servants expences at Barnet	0	4	0
	For expence of the servents at London from the 13 Aug: till the 17 of Semtm[r] . . .	5	0	0
	For bring the Barbatos waters and sweatmeats . .	1	1	0
	For 7 Chaldron of Colls in octo[br]	10	15	0
	For 2 lb. tobaco	0	4	0
Edenburg Aug. 17	For wine from Gilbert and Lewis Pringle .	16	0	0
	For Meat from the Cooks etc.: from 18 Aug: till the last of Decm[r] .	34	18	0
	For washing	6	9	0
	For Confections Plumcaks and Bisket from Mrs. Fenton at my Rachys mariage . . .	15	3	0
	For 100 lb. weight starch at Edn	1	16	8
	For 100 lb. powder . . .	1	16	0
	For 21 pint Brandy Mcnill at 2s. 8d. pr pint .	2	16	0
	For dry cask to it and puting aboord all	0	6	10
	For Casks to powder and starch	0	2	0
	For expences of servants and horses traveling about in 6 monethes	8	13	6
	For 4 botles snuff . .	1	0	0
	For 150 lb. Pork at 4d. lb. salt, etc. to be hung	2	14	0

	[Housekeeping]	[Sterling]		
		£	s.	d.
	For Meat, drink, coll, and candle the two times we was at Mellerstaine	14	4	6
	For a pice of Clarite from Major Boyd .	30	0	0
	For confections in full of all acc^tt	3	3	0
	For a Doe at Christenmas	0	10	6
wrong	For lose one Guinys at London	0	15	0
wrong	To the Kings footmen and Beefeaters		1	0
	To Shiriff at Ginelkirk was owing by servants	0	5	0
	For locks and bands by flint to doors and gates at Meller.^tne .	0	10	0
	For snuff sent to London by James Carren	2	0	$3\frac{6}{12}$
	For Meall to the Barnman Meller	2	7	8
	For Meall to the poor at Mellerstaine	1	7	2
	For servants expences in Pate Hunters	0	5	0
	For 16 bolls oats at 10s. made in Meall and sent to London in 1715, 16 and 1717	8	0	0
	For our carte horse at Mellerstaine in 3 year 10 bols .	5	0	0
	For 6 bolls ots in meall while I was in Scotland	3	0	0
	For Boord wages to the barman at 7s. 4d. a moneth	4	8	0
		364	5	$8\frac{2}{12}$
	From the Day book for 11 Monethes	175	2	$6\frac{9}{12}$
		S. £539	8	$2\frac{11}{12}$

	To Servants fies	[Scots] £	s.	d.
1693	To Margrat Flimin her fie .	18	0	0
Apr[ll]	To Sandy Frazer in full of his fies	12	0	0
May 2d.	To Ann Faa in full of her fies	18	0	0
Ditto 7.	For cloathes to servants	18	0	0
	To fieing and arls to servants	18	18	0
	To Isabell Johnston	2	18	0
Sept[r] 6	To Sandy Corbett in full of his fies	6	3	0
	To David Makcom quhich pays all his fies . . .	9	0	0
	To Babi Tamson in full of all her fies	8	0	0
Jun.	To Mary Sincklar her fie .	8	6	0
1694 Jun.	To Nany Christy of her fie	4	0	0
	To Nany her shoes for Whit. 94	1	8	0
	For shirts to John Broun	2	2	0
	For Grises nurses goun	6	8	0
Sep[tr]	To Shusan Brown for her shoes Mertimas 94	1	4	0
	To Shusan of fie . . .	2	0	0
	For shoes to Davi Nickelson and to John Broun	4	8	0
	For making cloathes to the men	8	4	0
Nov[r] 26	To Nany Christy of fie .	12	0	0
	To David Nickelson in full of his fie .	38	0	0
Decm[r] 14	To Sara Semple in full of her fies	60	0	0
	To Shusan her shoes for Whit. 95	1	6	0
	To Grisies nurs in full of her fie	50	0	0
1695	To Nany Chr[d] her shoes for Mert. 94	1	6	0
Febr. 23d.	To her of fie 10s. to her 6lb. 8	6	18	0
	For stokins to Davi 1lb. 3s. a hat to John 18	2	1	0
May	To Nany for shoes for Whit. 95	1	6	0
	To Nany 1lb. 6 . . .	1	6	0

	[Servants]	[Scots] £	s.	d.
	For helping the mens cloathes	2	10	0
	To Adam Owin a rest of fies owing by my mother .	39	6	0
	For stokins to Johny 12s., shoes to him 1lb. 4s.	1	16	0
Jun. 26	To Nany Chr. 12s.	0	12	0
July	To my Robis nurs . . .			
August 9	To An Forrist	4	0	0
Sept.	To Ann Forrist	[illegible]	6	0
	To Shusan shoes for Mert 95			
	For shoes to John .		1	
Novt. 1st.	For helping mens cloathes		1	
	To Mary Marchall of fie .			
	To Nany her shoes Mert 95			
Decmr.	To Nany of fie			
	To Frances Newton per recept to John Wight	45	0	0
	To Frances Newton for shoes	6	0	0
		S. 358	6	0

To Servants fies 1696

To An Forrist

		£	s.	d.
January	It. caried from the — page	12	0	0
Aprill	To her of her fie	12	0	0
July	To her	2	10	0
	To her	8	0	0
Decmr.	To her	6	6	0

To Shusan Broun

		£	s.	d.
January	It. caried from — page .	5	16	0
16	To her of fie	2	4	0
	To her 1lb. 10s. Febr. 10 to her 14	2	4	0
Aprill	To her her shoes for Whit. 96	1	6	0

	[Servants]	[Scots] £	s.	d.
	To her of her fies	4	19	0
21	To her 1lb. 4s.	1	4	0
Septm.	To her for shoes for Mertimas 96	1	7	0
Octor. 1	To her	1	11	6
	To Mr. Robison for 16 ells stuffe to her	12	16	0
	To Nany Christy			
January	It. caried from — page .	33	6	0
15	To her of her fie .	4	0	0
Febr.	To her . .	2	4	0
July	To her her shoes for Whitsunday 96	1	9	0
	To her 2lb. 2s. . . .	2	2	0
Octor. 7	To her	3	0	0
	To Rachys nurs for her fie	40	0	0
	To Francy Newton caried from	45	0	0
Febr. 10	For shoes to Johny and brehes helping	1	13	0
Aprill	To Francy for shoes 2℔. 8	2	8	0
	For a coat to Tam 6℔. 18s. stokins and shoes to him and a wastcoat	9	8	0
	For blew stokins to Tam 1℔. 1s. briches to him 2℔. .	3	1	0
	For a hat to Francy and dresing to him	4	16	0
	For shoes to Tam 1℔. 9s. a shirt to him, shoes 1℔. 11s.	3	14	0
Decmr. 1	To Francy Newton	60	0	0
	For briches to Piter Broun 2℔. 8	2	8	0
	in this year	S. 192	0	0

[Servants]		[Scots]
	To servants fies 1697	
	Mertimas 1694, Ann Forrist her fie £24 00 00	
		£ s. d.
	Item, brought from pagees	040 16 00
Janury	To her	006 10 00
Aprill 21st	To her	003 07 00
Agust 1st	Item, to her	014 16 00
	Item, to John Rainalds for her	002 08 00
Mertimas '97	Item, to her quhich pays her fie and shoes . . .	016 12 00
	Candlmas 1694, Shusan Broun fie in the year £16 00 00	
	Item, brought from page	
	Item, to her shoes for Whitsunday '97	001 08 00
May 24th	Item, to her	005 16 00
July 8	Item, to her	000 14 00
	Item, payd my sister for hangins she got from them	007 18 00
	Mertimas 1693. Nany Christy in the year £16 00 00	
	Item, brought from page	045 17 00
	Item, to her shoes for Whitsunday '97	001 06 00
Novr. 1697	Item, to Jean Brown her full fie and shoes for 3 quarters	013 04 00
Ditto	Item, to John Innis his full fie for half a year	009 00 00
Ditto	Item, to James Carrin his fie for a quarter	004 10 00
	To menservants cloathes	

[Servants]	[Scots] £	s.	d.
Item, stokins and shoes to Tam Herrit	004	00	00
Item, 2 runing wastcoats 8 ells at 14s. per ell, linen to them and draurs	008	00	00
Item, making the wastcoats with butons of the same	001	00	00
Item, for making a p[air] drawers 2s. mending 4s. . . .	000	06	00
Item, a plush cap 1li. 8s. shoes to Rob 2li. 4s. .	003	12	00
Item, stokins to John Inis 1li. 12 shoes to him 2li. 4 bootmending 13s.	004	09	00
For mendings 10sp. to arls to Jamie and fieing 14s. 6d., 10s.	001	14	06
For 4 ells ¼ blew cloath at 7s. 6d.	019	16	00
For cloth to a groms coat 2 ell ½ at 8s. 6d. sterling . . .	012	18	00
For blew cloath for a groms big coat 3 ells at 9s. 6d .	017	02	00
To 4½ ells blew serg for linin, and 5 ells yellow at 16s. . .	007	12	00
To yellow for facing and 3d. ü hair, buttons, and 14 ells serg 16d.	013	16	00
To silk and threed and buttons per Francy Newtons acount	009	00	00
For blew facing 1li. 10s. molde to buttons	002	00	00
To John Hume for making, to acount 5li. 5s. . . .	005	05	00
For cloathes making to Georg Taylor	002	00	00
For John Inises coat and Robs making	002	04	00
For a hat and string to Rob: 1li. 7 shoes to him 1li. 10s. .	002	17	00

[Servants]	[Scots] £	s.	d.
For 7 ells blew cloath for chair coats at 3li. 3s. per ell .	022	01	00
For blew serg to Johns coat linin	002	00	00
To my childs nurs to acount .	008	14	00
For the servants mornings dressing	010	00	00
To John Hume for making cloathes quhich pays all precidings .	008	06	00
For furnitur to cloathes per Mr. J. Hums acount . . .	10	18	0
To Francis Newton per recept .	100	00	0
S.	367	0	0

Edenburgh, 1700, charg of servants. Deb: to cash.

	Gawin Cluther			
January	To him in cash and cloathes .	9	15	0
	Francis Brumigham			
	For cloathes to him	12	0	0
	Judith Malbank			
Fbry.	To her in cash . .	6	0	0
	To her in full of her fie .	54	0	0
	James Cannell			
	His wage is in mony in the year £36. All cloathes except linins.			
	To him for 3 month month he came befor the tarme	15	0	0
	To him for a sadle he lost	5	16	0
	To him 16s., more 14s., more 12s. he keep't	2	2	0
	James Carrin			
	His wages in the year is of mony £24.			
3d.	To him in cash 2li. 18 6	2	18	6
	To hime more 1li. . . .	1	0	0

[Servants]		[Scots]		
	Nany Christy			
		£	s.	d.
May	To her for shoes . .	1	8	0
	To her her fie in full . .	40	0	0
	Dina Ridpath			
	Her wages is 20 pounds in the year and shoes 22 16			
	To her 1ti. 8s. more 1 tl. 8s. more 2ti. 2s. . . .	4	18	0
	To her in full of her fies .	17	18	0
	Hellin Garner			
	Her fie is in the year 16ti. and her shoes 18 16.			
	To her for her gown . .	6	8	0
	To her canar 2ti. more to her 3ti. 6	5	6	0
	Janit Robison			
	To her in full of all her wages .	12	0	0
	Margrat Ingles			
	To her in full of all her wages	18	0	0
	Cloathes to the men.			
	To James Carrins shoes 2ti. 18s. Cannei stokins and shoes 2ti. 18s.	5	16	0
	To Carrins shoes 2ti. 18s. and cloathes makins 12s. .	3	10	0
	For serges to them and yellow cloath per accumpts	61	12	0
	For hats to them .	6	0	0
	For serg 7ti. 2d. Cannells frok 2ti. 6. Carrins shoes 2ti. 2 .	11	10	0
	Cannels shoes 1ti. 16s. Franks shoes 1ti. 16s. . . .	3	12	0

[Servants]	[Scots]		
	£	s.	d.
For cloath to servants at the Pa[r]liment[1] . . .	16	0	0
Georg Trumble			
His fie is in the year 22li. 2 pairs shoes and stokins £26 and a fow of bear . . .	1	8	0
To him in mony . . .	5	0	0
To him for shoes and stokins	1	19	0
To him a furlit of oats	1	0	0
	331	16	6
To John Wight for this year £40	40	0	0
S.	371	16	6

Edenburg, 1701. Servants cloathes. Deb: to Cash.

	To Francis Brummigham when he went away	20	0	0
	To Cannell and Carrns shoes	3	18	0
	To a taylor 6s. skins to ther briches 1li. 6s. taylor 1li. 4s. .	2	16	0
	To account for stokins etc. payd Ms. Abercrumby .	8	0	0
	For a sword and belt to Georg Edger	3	18	0
	For boots to Georg Edgar	5	17	0
Octobr.	For a hatt to Canell 1li. 6s. for bonnits to the men 17s. 6d. .	2	3	6
	For pladin to Black 6s. 8d.	0	6	8
	For shoes to Isabell Lamb 1li. 11s.	1	11	0
	For a coat and shirts to Tam Plendarlith	4	5	4

[1] At the Riding of the Parliament the members for the shires rode each accompanied by two footmen. See note p. 224.

	[Servants]	[Scots] £	s.	d.
	For linin to runing drawers 15s. makeing cloathes 1ti. 18	2	13	0
	For stokins to Canell and runing 2ti.	2	0	0
	For shoes to Georg Edgar .	1	16	0
	For briches to Cannell 1ti. 16s. for serg at 16s.	4	16	0
	For 17½ ells blew livery cloath at	85	0	0
	For stuf to be a frok to George Edgar	2	0	0
	For threed	0	6	10
	For 19 days work of a taylour at 4s. Georges coat 2ti. 8	6	8	0
	For silk and moolls	1	10	0
		S. 159	5	4

Edenburgh, servents wages. Deb: to Cash 1701.

	Katharin Robison came to my service at Whitsunday 1700, her fie in the year is £48			
July 8	To her	12	0	0
August	To her in England and when we went ther for goun rubans and 2 shi. sterling more, goun 54ti. ruban 2ti. 18s.	58	18	0
	This stuf taken to myself so could not be rekoned to her.			
	Grisell Robisone came to me Mertimas 1700 her fie in the year is £24 0 0			
	For perfiting her in sowing .	12	0	0
	James Carrin came to my service at Whitsunday 1699 his fie in the year is £24 0 0			

[Servants]		[Scots] £	s.	d.
	I give him all his cloathes except linins			
May	To him 1li. 10s. To him 8li. .	9	10	0
	To him when he came first home again	8	0	0
July 8	To him 14s. 6d.	0	14	6
	To him of fie from Mertimas 1701 in the year £30 0 0			
Decmr.	To him	3	5	0
	James Cannel cochman came to my service at Whitsunday 1700 his fie in the year £36 0 0			
	I give his all cloathes except linins			
May	To him	36	18	0
	To him 9s.	0	9	0
	Jean Boge came to my service, Martimas 1700, her fie and buntith is £22 16 0			
	To her	1	8	0
	For her shoes 1li. 6s. To her 1li. 5s.	2	11	0
Octor.	To her	10	0	0
	Georg Edgare came to my service Lammas 1701, his fie is in fie the year £36 0 0			
August	To him in England .	19	15	0
	Agnis Christy came back to my service at Lambis 1701, her fie and bountith in the year £22, 16s.			
Feb.	To her 1li. 8s. To her 1li. 18s. 6d. To her 14li.	17	6	6

[Servants]	[Scots] £	s.	d.
Georg Trumble barnman came to me Mertimas 1700, his fie stokins shoes in the year is £26.			
A furlit of bear .	1	8	0
To him 12ti. a furlit of bear	12	19	0
To him 2ti. 10s. more 6ti. more 14s. 6d. more 6s. 6d., Novr. 22d. 10ti. . .	19	6	6
Hellin Garner came to me Martimas 1699, her fie and shoes is in the year £18 16. .			
To her 1ti. 10s. To her 1ti. 6s. To her 5li. 10s. quhich complits	8	6	0
S.	234	14	6

Edenburg, January 1704. Servants Wages. Katharin Robison Deb: to cash.

May 20	To her 2 dollars .	5	16	0
	To her	[illegible]	[illegible]	0
	To her in March . . .			
	To her		1	
	To Francis Newton on her accumpt	76		0
	To Lapairl on her accumpt	15	12	0
	Grisell Robison came at Mertimas 1703; her fie in the year, £24 0 0			
	To her fie in full of all she can crave	24	0	0
	Margrate Carr, came to my service at Whitsunday 1703, her fie in the year is £20 0 0			
Janr. 20	To her £1 lining her goun 8s. .	1	8	0

[Servants]	[Scots] £	s.	d.
To Francy Newton on her acumpt	7	9	0
To her by Katharin £3, 16s. 6d., more £4, 6s.	8	2	6
To stuf for a goun £15, 4s., more £2, 18s., more £2, 2s. 6d., £1, 13s. . .	6	13	0

Mary M'Intosh

To her by Kat: £1, 14s. 6d.	1	14	6
To her in full of her fie . .	54	0	0

Jean Cuningham came to my service at Christinmas 1703 for chambermaid, her fie £18 0 0; her shoes in the year is £2 18 0.

To Jean for 5 monthes service .	9	0	0

Maorin Rule came to be chambermaid, Whitsunday 1704, her fie in the year £16, her shoes £18 18.

To her £1, 10s.	1	10	0

James Carrin

To him by Kat: for a pan, 4s.	0	4	0
To Isabell Ramsay on his acumpt	2	8	0
To him 5s. more £1, 9s. more £1, 9s. more £1, 9s. . .	4	12	0
Decemr. 7 To him	26	0	0

Ms. Tulip came to waite on the childrin Martimas 1704, her wages is in the year £36 0 0, besids the expene of bringing her.

	[Servants]	[Scots]		
	For cariing her cloathes £2, 6s. for some of the expenc by the road she layd out herself, £2, more for her cloathes .	8	10	0
	To cary her back £9, to her wages for 3 monthes . . .	18	15	0
	For bringing her doun . .	4	8	0
	John Harla			
Janr. 15	To him 14s. 6d. . . .	0	14	6
August	To him	5	16	0
Novr. 20	To Francy Newton on his account	2	0	0
	To his wife	19	5	0
Novr. 24	To him by Kate: £1, 9s. more £1, 4s. more by her £2, £1, 10s.	6	3	0
	To Androw Lamb for this year	13	6	8
	For a hat and 2 cravats to him	2	14	0
	Dick Rule			
Feb.	To him 2 dollers .	5	16	0
	To him by Androw Lamb	3	10	0
	To him at Wooller .	1	17	0
	To Francy Newton on his accumpt	5	2	0
Oct.	To himself in sumer .	3	0	0
	Margrat Lamb			
	To her fies for a year and a half	24	0	0
	To her shoes	4	10	0
	Margrat Ross, came to keep howse at Mellerstean, Whitsunday 1704, her fie in the year £20, shoes £22, 18.			
Oct.	To her by Androw Lamb	2	10	2
	To her for a years fie .	20	8	0
	Georg Trumble			
	For shoes to him £1, 16s. 6d. hose to him 9s. hose again 9s. .	2	14	6

		£	s.	d.
	[Servants] Margrat Robison, came to wate on the childrin, Whitsunday 1704, her fie in the year £66 13 4	[Scots]		
Novr. 1st	To her	20	0	0
Dito 20	To her	13	6	8
	Katharin Munro, came to serve as chamber[maid], Whitsunday 1704, her fie in the year £20, her shoes £2, 16, £22, 16.			
	To her, May 20	0	14	6
	To her, £1, 11s., more 14s. 6d. 10s.	2	15	6
	Nany Christy came to my service as cook at Martimas 1704, her fie in the year is £20 0 0 and her shoes.			
	To her	11	0	0
	For 16 ell stuf at 10sh. per ell .	8	0	0
	To her £1, 9s., payd James Miller taylor £1, 16s.	3	5	0
	To her £1, 9, more £1, 6	2	15	0
	S.	185	03	6

Edenburgh, January 1704. Servants cloathes. Deb: to Cash.

To arle Margrat Robison	0	10	0
To arle Margrat Ross, chambermaid	0	7	0
To J. Miller taylor for mending servants cloathes	2	10	0
For Dicks briches making 8s. linin and pokets 13s. .		1	0
For mending James Carrins cloathes	0	8	0

	[Servants]	[Scots] £	s.	d.
July 2d	For makeing 2 suts cloathes to Dick and John .	4	12	0
Aug. 4th	To one Devison upon a decriet gott against him .	3	0	0
	For hose to Dick, 12s. 6d. Dicks shoes £2 . . .	2	12	6
	For threed, silk, pokets	4	0	0
	To a taylor 15s. 10s. £3, 11s. 6d. .	4	16	6
Novr. 22	For stokins to Geordy Dods 18s. shoes to him, 2 pair one of them running ons at £1, 15 the other	0	1	
	at £2, 3s.	3	1	
	For shoes to James Carrin	2		
	For stokins to Geordy Dods 16s.	0	1	0
	For mending servants cloathes	3	8 [illegible]	
	For making furniter to Dicks blew coat	5	5	0
	For 4 ells cloath at 6s. 6d. per ell	1 [illegible]	1 [illegible]	0
	For 6 ells stuf 7s. 0 per ell		1	
	For 8½ ell black serg at 13s. per ell			
	For 4 ells serge 13s. per ell			
	For hardne, stentin, etc.			
	For harden			
		S. 65	02	0

[Servants' Wages, 1707]

Mary Menzies [1]

June 18	To her 2 years wages	200	0	0

Margrat Ritchy

June 10	To her a year and a halfs fie being all her time	63	0	0

[1] See p. xlvi.

	[Servants]	[Scots] £ s. d.
	Grisell [*sic*] came to be chambermaid June 17th, her fie in all is £20 a year.	
	To her arls 3s.	
	She entred not home but went to Ms. Monro.	
	Mary Muir	
	To her for shoes £1, 5s.	1 5 0
Oct. 2	To her £2, 8s. for 2 pair shoes	2 8 0
	To her	4 0 0
	To her shoes 3 pair by Androw Lamb	3 18 0
	Meg Mill	
	For stuf to her goun	9 18 0
	For pack threed bodies £1, 9s. ane ell muslin 19s. .	2 8 0
	For stentin and goun making 18s.	0 18 0
June 5	To Meg Miln £1, 9s. for a suts haed cloathes 19s.	2 8 0
	For ane apron 18s. . . .	0 18 0
June 10	For a plad to her . . .	11 0 0
July 2	To her, Tams wedin, 14s. 6d.	0 14 6
	Janit Kirk came to be cook, Martimas 1706, her fie in the year is £30.	
Feb. 26	To her	1 9 0
May 15	To her for half a year .	13 11 0
	To James Carrin	
March 12	To him when he went back from Durhome 2 guinys and 15 sh. ster.	34 16 0
	To James by Margrat £1, 9s. .	1 9 0
	To him a guiny at 22s. 10d. ster.	13 14 0

	[Servants]	[Scots] £	s.	d.
	To Isabell Ramsay on his account for musline	4	7	0
	To him a duson of servits for many he destroy'd	6	15	0
	To James for a key 6s. for glases he got the mony of	1	16	0
July 2	To him, Tams wedin, 16s. 6d., for 8 ell towils £2, 5 .	3	1	6
	To him, July 1708, £12, 18s. to him by Francy Newton £6	18	18	0
	Margrat Broun, came to be kook at Whitsunday 1707, her fie is £20 in the year and her shoes £1, 6s. in all £22, 12.			
	To her for half a year	11	9	0
	To Isabell Brounlies for washing 4s. pd. wringing 2 . .	1	9	0
	John Frazer, came to serve at Martimas 1706, his fie in the year is £36 0 0.			
Ap.	To him £3, To him £33, for a year	36	0	0
	John Harla			
	To him his fie for Whitsunday 1707	24	0	0
Sepmr.	For a stone wooll payd John Wights widow for him .	5	12	0
	To him for shoes got from Androw Lamb . .	1	16	0
	To Alshy Blith on his account .	0	18	0
Oct. 4	To him, £3 to the marchand on his account £1 18 . . .	4	18	0
	Alison Brounlies entred to service again at Whitsunday 1707.			

[Servants]		[Scots] £	s.	d.
	To her for ten day dightin £1 10 brewing 13s. . . .	2	3	0
Oct. 4	To her in full of all . . .	8	0	0
	Geogre Dods			
Aug.	To Will. Dickson for his childs boord	18	0	0
	To Tam Youll by Androw Lamb	1	3	2
	To James Ormston for threshing	12	0	0
	To James Carrine, January 1709	12	0	0
		S. 543	6	2

[1707. Servants clothes]

	For the rid clok dying . .	2	0	
Febr. 12	For shoes to G. Lamb	1	10	
	For stokins to G. Lamb .	1	2	
	To an ell musline to Marie Muir	0	19	0
June 10	For serg to line Jameses cloathes at 10s. per ell . . .	3	15	0
	For shoes to Tam Youll	1	16	0
	For shoes to Geordi Dods	1	19	0
	For shoes to Geordie Lamb	1	10	0
	For makenig Geordie Lambs black cloathes	2	12	0
	For skins for pokets 7s. at 5s. 6d. per pice	1	18	6
	For threed 11s. butons 11s. 4s.	1	6	0
	For shoes to Geordy Dods	1	14	0
	For shoes to Georg Lamb	1	13	0
	For shoes to Georg Dods 2 hose £1, 3s. 2	3	3	2
	For shoes to Nicoll Marchell	0	10	0
	For stokins to Lam £1, 6s.	1	0	0
	For blew hair and threed	5	6	0

[Servants]	[Scots] £	s.	d.
For wastcoat and drawers and runing briches to Dods .	6	10	0
For butons threed and for Jameses coat	2	6	0
For mending the servants cloathes	7	7	0
For mending boots 7s.	0	7	0
S.	50	3	8

Mellerstaine, January 1709. Servants wages. Deb: to Cash.

	May Minzies			
	To her . . .	100	0	0
S.	To her over and above her fie for her care of the bairens when they had the fever	333	6	8
	Betty Navell. At candlesmas last I ingag'd her for £36.			
June 29	To her	18	0	0
	To her at Edinburgh	12	0	0
	Margrat Mill			
May 7	To her £1, 4s.	1	4	0
June 29	To her	9	0	0
	Bessi Clark			
	To her £1, 4s.	1	4	0
	To her	2	14	0
	To her	6	0	0
	To her £3	3	0	0
	To her in full of her wages	11	0	0

Nans Lindsay came at Martimas 1708, her fie in the year £14 and her shoes £16 8 0.

[Servants]	[Scots] £	s.	d.
To her	1	4	0
To her	1	4	0
To her . . .	2	0	0
To her in full of her fie pay'd by Adam Hutchison . . .	12	0	0
Grisell Wate came to be under cook Whitsunday 1709, her fie in the year £14 and shoes £16 8 0.			
George Mathy came to serve at Lambes 1709, his fie in the year is £36			
To him by Francis Newton .	1	10	0
John Frazer			
To him at Edinburgh	12	0	0
To him from his master at London by his account	28	6	0
To him for briches he bought at London . .	4	4	0
He is fully pay'd			
Tam Youll, he was made coachman at Whitsunday 1709.			
To him at John Shiels's .	0	12	0
To him for George Dods loss of work when drunk and lam'd his leg	7	4	0
George Lamb			
For shirts to him .	3	12	0
George Dods			
March 25 For a velvit cap he spoilt	2	8	0

[Servants]	[Scots] £	s.	d.
For 1 yeard and a half musline	3	3	0
For 6 cravats from James Liedhouse	3	14	0
To him at severall times that he never gave account of .	2	5	0
John Clark came to thresh in the barn at Martimas 1708, his fie in the year £20.			
To him pay'd by Will Halliwall .	20	0	0
To him over and above his wage	4	2	0
To Tam Youll for 10 days threshing at 4s. per day .	2	0	0
Androw Lamb, toun officer			
To him for a year . . .	3	0	0
To him by his officers land	36	0	0
John Hope came to be garner Martimas last 1708, his wage in the year with a house to his wife is £48, and if he have not the house it is £60.			
To him a bed at £8	8	0	0
To him	12	16	0
To him £3, more £5, 1s. 4d.	8	1	4
Oct. 22 To him	15	0	0
To him	8	2	8
In whole for this years fie being more then bargone.	52	00	0

Mellerstains, January 1709. Servants cloathes. Deb: to Cash.

For 6 ells course white plain for briches at 6s. .	1	16	0

	[Servants]		[Scots] £	s.	d.
	For dying the said cloath at 3 sh.		0	18	0
	For hand bands to slives			10	0
	For mending Tam Youlls boots				
March 11	For shoes to Tam Youll .				
	For shoes to Geordy Dods £1 10, his sons 6s .		1	16	0
	For 5 ell linin to Geordy Dods drawers £3, strings 2s. .		3	2	0
	For 3 pairs stokins at £1 10 per pair		4	10	0
	For boots to George Mathy		6	0	0
	For helping cloathes and altering Lambs cloathes pay'd A. B.		2	0	0
	For shoes to Dods £1 10 .		1	10	0
	For 20 ells linine for cloathes at 7s. 6d.		7	10	0
	For shirts to George Lamb payd his mother		3	0	0
	For 1 stone 4 lb. wight sorted wooll for a gray wab at £7 per stone of waild wooll is	£8 15 0			
	For oyl to said web .	0 18 0			
	For working the said wab 20 ells by John Muckle . .	3 0 0	15	13	0
	For dressing the gray wab . .	3 0 0			
	For half a stone waild wooll for pladine to be hose at £7 £3 10		3	10	0
	For working 12 ells of the pladine 3d. per ell		1	16	0
	For shoes to Geordy Lamb		1	14	0
	For 4 cravats to George Lamb at 14s.		2	16	0

[Servants]	[Scots] £	s.	d.
For threed to sow the servants murnins	0	16	0
For pokets to them	1	8	0
For buckerram threed button molds and to their murnins .	1	19	0
For a hat to Tam Youll .	1	8	0
For a hat and stokins to Wight .	3	12	0
For other necessarys for their cloathes	1	10	0
To a taylor 16s. pladine for hose £1 10s.	2	2	0
To Will Dickson taylor for makeing their murnings	1	10	0
For threed	0	14	0
For pladin for hose . .	1	10	0
For dying yellow cloath .	0	6	2
	S. 77	6	2

Mellerstaines, January 1710. Servants wages. Deb: to cash.

		Sterlin		
	May Minzies			
March 6th	To her 10s. more £1	1	10	0
	To her	3	10	0
	To her	3	6	8
	Betty Navell			
	To her 10sh.	0	10	0
	The chair glas brecking of the drinkmony			
	To her	0	10	0
	Margrate Brown, came to be kook at Whitsunday 1709, her wage in the year is 2 10 0.			
	To her	1	05	
	To her 2sh. more £2, 10sh.	2	12	0

	[Servants]	[Sterling]		
	Margrate Milne	£	s.	d.
	To her for shoes .	0	4	0
March 9	To her for shoes .	0	2	0
	To her 2sh.	0	2	0
	To her fathers house rent White [sunday] 1710 . . .	0	5	6⅔
Ap. 12	To her 2sh. more by Androw Lamb £1	1	2	0
	To her which compleats her wages for 5 years time . . .	1	5	0
	Grisell Wate			
March 9	To her for shoes . .	0	2	0
	To her 2sh. more by Androw Lamb £1	1	2	0
	To her for shoes 2sh.	0	2	0
	Jean Ridpath, came to take care of the fouls and swine, her wage in the year with her shoes at 2sh. sterling is (she came at Martimas 1709 year) 1 4 0			
	To her far shoes .	0	2	0
	To her 3d. more £5 Scots which is her wage for 5 month	0	8	[illegible]
	Alisone Brownlies, entred to serve in the kitchen, March 8, 1710, her wage in the year is 1 3 4 her shoes 0 4 0			
	To her 10s. by An'd^{r}. more 17s. 4d	1	7	4
	Jean Glen, came to wash and spin at Whitsunday 1710, her wage is with shoes in the year 1 10 8.			

[Servants]		[Sterling] £	s.	d.
	To her by Androw, 4s. .	0	4	0
	To her which compleats a years fie	l	6	8
	George Mathy			
	To him by his master at London £1, 0s. 6d., more £1	2	0	6
	To Alshy Blyth for him 1s. 2d. more 14s. 6d. more 17s. in full of all	1	12	8
	Thomas Cockburn came to be Mester Houshold, at White-sunday 1710, his wages is in the year 4 0 0.			
	To him his wages for half a year .	2	0	0
Novr. 12	To his wages for half a year longer at £5 a year	2	10	0
	John Hope			
	To his house rent, this besids his £4 of fie	0	11	1½
Ap. 3	To him 5sh. . .	0	5	0
	To him for Pringles shoes	0	2	10
	To him by corn from Widow Wight	2	16	8
	To him a stone wooll at 6s. 8, more 8sh.	0	14	8
	To him which clears his wages from Martimas 1709 till Martimas 1710, etc. .	0	0	10
	Tam Youll			
	To him by his brothers oats	2	13	4
	To hime by Androw Lamb	0	11	8
	To him by Meg Hendersons bear	0	16	8

	[Servants]	[Sterling] £	s.	d.
	Rob: Wight came to be bred buttler at Martimas 1709.			
	For learning him to shave at Edinburgh		1	6
	George Dods			
	To him in Edinburgh	0	6	0
	To him payd Will: Hutchison	3	7	0
	John Clark			
	To him of oats at £8 Scots 3 fous 3 pecks .	0	10	0
	To him a boll bear from Widow Wight .	0	16	8
	To him by the tenants in the Mains corn and mony	0	19	0
	To Tam Youll of lott as it came to 15sh. bear, 13sh. 4d. oats, 15sh. peas	1	14	0
	To a porter at Grisies mariage	0	5	0
	To a cook and two men .	1	11	6
	To Robert Manderston £1, 10s., Roberton Master Houshold £1, 1s. 6d.	2	11	6
	Androw Lamb			
	To his expences in Jan^r and Febr.	0	2	6
July 6	To his expences 1s. 4d. more 8d. and 8d.	0	2	8
	To him his wages this year	3	0	0
	To a cook at Edinburgh caled Margrat Wabster . . .	0	3	6
		S. 54	4	$7\frac{2}{12}$

Mellerstaines, January 1710. Servants cloathes. Deb: to Cash.

	[Servants]	[Sterling] £	s.	d.
	For cloathes, etc. for Rob: Wight. ridin coat	1	9	0
	For makeing Robert Wights riding coat	0	2	0
	For a frock to Wight	[illegible]	[illegible]	[illegible]
Ap. 8	For 4 pair shoes to George Dods			
	For Rob: Wights riding coat			
	For threed 1sh. 8d.			
	For shoes to Rob: Wight .			
	For shoes to Tam Youll			
	To James Watson for makeing mens cloathes . . .	0	3	0
	For 12 ounces threed .	0	1	11
	For 21 ell plain for blew cloath at 7½ . .	0	13	1½
	For a chopin of oyl for livera wooll . .	0	0	10
	For 2½ ston wooll for levera cloath and linine; this wooll was all sorted and clean wail'd	1	5	0
	For butter 5s. [buttons ?] .	0	5	0
	For 42 ells six quarters cloath working at 3d. per ell, J: M: .	0	10	6
	For 21 ell lining ell broad at 1d.½ working	0	2	7½
	For shoes to Robie Wight	0	2	0
	For shoes to Tam Youll .	0	2	6
	For shoes to Tam Youll, Geordy Dods, and Rob: Wight .	0	9	0
	For 2 hats to Tam Youll and Geordy Dods . . .	0	8	0
	For dresing a hat to George Mathy . .	0	1	0
	For galoun to the hats 8sh. 9d. .	0	8	9

[Servants]		[Sterling]	
	£	s.	d.
For stokins to Rob. Wight, Tam Youll, Geo: Dods . . .	0	7	6
For stokins to Rob: Wight	0	1	6
For a hat to Rob. 2s. 6d. Dods 1s. 1d.	0	3	7
For shoes to Rob. 2s. 8d. shoes to Geordy Dods shoes 3sh.	0	5	8
Decmr. For boots to Tam Youll cochman	0	10	0
For shoes to James Kilpatrick .	0	2	4
For a hatt and galune to Wight .	0	9	0
For galuns and tracing to the rest of the servants to finish them	0	2	0
Aug. 16 For Robie Wight cloathes and furnishone . . .	2	0	0
For makeing and furnishing Wights cloathes .	0	6	6
For stokins shoes and buckles to Wight . . .	0	6	0
For linins to Wight, Youll and Dods	1	4	6
For stokins to Dods and Youll .	0	5	6
For 4 ells bustin for Dods's runing wastcoat 3s. 4d. strings and threed 9	0	4	
For furniture for cloathes from Cha: Ormston .	0	10	6
S.	16	01	1

Account of Servants wages 1713.

May Minzies

To her . . . £1 0 0

Margrat Finla

Edn. To her 6s. 8d. more
from my doughter 5s. 0 11 8

	[Servants]				[Sterling]		
					£	s.	d.
Edn.	To her 5s., 2s. 6d., 9s. 10d. . .	0	16	10			
	To her in full of her wages	2	9	10	3	18	4
	Ann Bell came to waah and spine at Marts 1712 her wage in the year with 2s. each half year for shoes is 1 14 0						
	To her 2s. more 2s. .	0	4	0			
	To her a chist .	0	8	7			
	To her in full of her wages . . .	1	19	9	2	12	4
	Alison Brunfield came to be chamber Maid Whit. 1713 her wage with shoes in the year is 1 14 0						
	To her wages for half a year	0	17	0	0	17	0
	Peggy Johnston came at Whitesunday 1713 her wage in the year is 1 16 0						
	To her wages for half a year	1	16	0	1	16	0
	Dorathy Gilroy came to be Kitchen Maid at White 1713 her wage in the year is 50s. fie and drinkmony						
	To Dolly wages for half a year .	0	13	0	0	13	0

Date	[Servants]		[Sterling] £ s. d.
	To Dolly Cook Maid a quarters wages and cariage	0 18 0	0 18 0
	Thomas Youll Coachman [1]		
	To his wife when they were sick .	0 5 0	
	To his Lambes Rent 1712 . . .	0 15 $2\frac{6}{12}$	
febr. 2d	To him at Edn Decmr. last .	0 4 0	
	To his Candls Rent 1713 . . .	0 15 $2\frac{6}{12}$	
July 28	To him 3s. more 5s. to Docter Gibson 1£ 1s. 6d. .	1 9 6	4 11 7
	To his Lambis Rent 15s. $2\frac{6}{12}$d. 1713 shoes 3s., 2s. 6d., 2s. 6d. .	1 3 $2\frac{6}{12}$	
	Will Brounlees came to be footman at Marts 1712 his years wages for stokins shoes and alltogether is 2 10 0		
	To him for shoes 3s. stokins 2s. 3d. .	0 5 3	
	To him in full and for other work for ½ year . . .	1 13 4	1 18 7
	John Hume		
March 11	To him 6 bolls oats Lithgow measure at		

[1] The items here entered against Thomas Youll are included in the fuller statement on p. 148.

	[Servants]				[Sterling]		
					£	s.	d.
	4£ 2 bolls Bear altogether comes to 32£ 4d. . . .	2	13	8			
	To him of his wages	0	16	8			
	To him a ston 4 lb. wooll . . .	0	9	7	7	16	10
July 20	To him 13s. 9d., 8s. to him 2£	3	11	9			
	To his House rent .	0	15	0			
	John Clark entred at Marts						
	1712 His wages in the year is 2 0 0						
	To him payd over and above his account of days work .	1	0	0			
July 15	To him for 4 bolls oats and two ston Meall	1	15	0			
	To him 2s.	0	2	0	2	17	0
	Androw Lamb						
	To the officers land .	2	0	0			
	To Matha Blacks land	1	0	0	3	0	0
	Tame Youll came to be barnman Whit 1713 his wage is in the year 50s., and hose and shose each half year.						
	To him 10s. more.						
	Thomas Youll came to be footman White 1713 his wage is 2£ and for stokins and shos 10s. in the year in all 2 10 0						
	To him stokins 2s.						

[Servants]				[Sterling] £ s. d.
shoes 3s. more 3s. more 3s.	0 11 0			
To him 1s. 2d.	0 1 2			0 12 2
To Barbry Hardy for hay working 16 days . . .	0 5 0			0 5 0
To a washer 6d. more 18d. .	0 2 0			0 2 0
Tam Youll Barnman has gote of late Crop .	1 12 8			
1712 4 bolls oats at 4£ 12s. Scots 4 fows more a boll 4 fous bear at 7£ Scots	1 1 0			2 13 8
				S. 23 16 10

Thomas Youlls Account[1]

	For wages from White 1706 to White 1709	4 10 0	
1707	To him by Androw Lamb .		0 2 0
1708	To him by Androw Lamb .		1 13 4
	To him by corn and stra .		0 9 6
1709	To him by John Shiels		0 1 0
	To him by lose of Dods services and his own drinking		0 10 0
	To him		0 2 0
	For wages at 2£ from Whit 1709 till Whit 1712 . . .	6 0 0	

[1] This statement of accounting with Thomas Youll is written on a separate piece of paper pinned into the Account Book.

	[Servants]				[Sterling]		
					£	s.	d.
1710	To him by Androw Lamb . .				0	11	8
	To him by Androw Lamb Henderson .				0	16	8
	To him by his brothers corns at severall time and allow pat: in his rent . . .				6	10	0
1711	To him .				1	0	0
	To the Lambes Rent 1711 .				0	15	$2\frac{6}{12}$
	To him for drinking at Makerston, etc. .				0	10	0
	To George Dods for him . . .				0	13	8
	To the Docter 1£ 1s. 6 his wife 5 drogs 10 .				1	16	6
	For wages at 2£ 10s. from Whit. 1712 till Marts. 1714 .	6	5	0			
1713	To him 3s., 5s., 3s., 2s. 6d., 2s. 6d. .				0	16	0
	To him at Edn 4s. 3s. 4d. R D 2s. 6d.				0	9	10
	To him 3s. 6d. more 3s.				0	6	6
	To the Ferrier of horse hire . . .				2	0	0
	By his rent for 3 year at Lambs 1714				4	11	3
		16	15	0	23	15	$1\frac{6}{12}$
	ballance over pay'd .	7	15	$1\frac{6}{12}$			

Account of Expence of Servants Cloathes 1713.

To Alison Brunfield of Arls .	0	0	6
To Dolly kilray of Arls and bringing her home	0	2	0

[Servants]	[Sterling]		
For going Whissen bank May Minzies and Androw Lambs	£	s.	d.
expence with one horse	0	2	9
bringing home bella 2s. 2d. James young arls 6d. .	0	2	8
For bustine to make oat a wast-coat at 11d. .	0	2	$2\frac{8}{X}$
For brew hair 6d. pr ounce and threed 6: 0	0	2	0
For 15 ell Gray working six quarter broad at 3d. . .	0	3	9
For 8 ells Bustine for runing cloathes	0	9	0
For arls to wemen 1s.	0	1	0
For working 15 yeards gray at 3d. pr yd . . .	0	3	9
To spotswood taylor for mending cloathes . . .	0	2	0
	£1	11	$7\frac{8}{12}$

Mellerstaine, Janry 1714. Account of Servants wages.

May Minzies

Ap. 24	To her . .	1	0	0			
June	To her . . .	1	0	0			
	For dying her goun .	0	7	0			
	To her .	1	0	0	3	7	0

Fanny Bell Entred at White 1714 to be House keeper her wage in the year is

£ s. d.
5 0 0

To her . .	2	0	0	2	0	0

[Servants]				[Sterling] £ s. d.
Jeany Forsieth Entred at Marts 1713 to be chamber Maid her wage in the year is £ s. d. 2 0 0				
To her half a years wages . .	1	0	0	0 0
Katharin Kenady Entred at White 1714 to be chamber Maid her wages in the year is 2 0 0				
To her for half a year	1	0	0	1 0 0
Katharine Heart Entred to be Landry Maid and washer at White: 1714 her wage in the year is 34s. and 4d. and her two pairs shoes at 2s. a pair . .	1	18	4	
Isabella Rickelton entred to wash and Milk cow at Martimas 1713 her wage in the year is with her shoes at 2s. 1 10 8				
To her 2s. $1\frac{6}{12}$.				
To her in full for a year	1	10	8	1 10 8
Bella Robison entred to be under Cook at Marts 1713 her wage in the year is 2 . 0 0				

	[Servants]		[Sterling] £ s. d.
Janr.	To her 5s. more 2s. 6d. more 5s. one s to her . .	0 13 6	
	For stuff to her goun	1 0 0	
	To her linin to it 2s. 6d. makeing 1s. 8d.	0 4 2	
	For two Aprons James Liedhouse .	0 3 0	
	For changeing a plate	0 1 6	2 2 2
	Peggie Sharp entred to be under cook at July 8 her wage in the year is 1 10 0		
	To her for half a year	0 15 0	0 15 0
	To the Nurs 3s. 4d. more 3s. 4d. .	0 6 8	
	To her 6 bolls oats at 5£ 16s. 8d. .	3 6 0	3 12 8
	Alexander Hume Entred at White 1713 to be Butler his wages in the year is 2 0 0		
Janr.	To him . . .	1 0 0	
	To him for boots .	0 10 0	
	To him for cheno and other things he brock .	0 10 0	2 0 0
	James Grieve Entred at Marts 1713 to be Butler his wage in year is 2£ but if he pleases me it is to be 3£ 3 0 0		
Octr.	To him . .	1 0 0	1 0 0

	[Servants]				[Sterling] £	s.	d.
	Thomas Youll Coachman						
	To the fferriers account 1£ 10 a horse hire to the coch when the Mare was spoilt 0 10 0	2	0	0			
	To him for shoes 3s. 4d. from R D 2s. 6d. . . .	0	5	10			
	Candles rent 1714 Lamb rent 1714 1£ 10s. 5d.	1	10	5	3	16	3
May 15	he is over payd at White 1714 5£ 19 1d.						
June 3	To him 3s. 6d. more 3s.						
	John Hume Garner						
	To him 5s., 2s., more 10s. ston wooll 8s.	1	5	0			
	To him in full of his wages at Marts 1714	2	6	8			
	For his bbolls oats and 2 bolls bear Lithgow measure .	2	13	4			
	For his House Rent	0	15	0	7	0	0
	For his Cows meatt and grase.						
	John Clark						
	To him shoes 3s. 2d. Meal 2s. 5d. more 2s. 1d., 15s. 4d. .	1	3	0			
	Androw Lamb his expences at fairs 2s. more 3s. .	0	5	0			

	[Servants]			[Sterling]
	To Androw Lamb for his land		3 0 0	£ s. d.
	To Dick . . .		0 6 8	4 14 8
	Thom Youll footman			
	To Tom 3s. 6d.		0 3 6	
July 14	To him 5s. more 2s. more 6d more 3s. 6d. .		0 11 6	
	To him 3s.		0 3 6	
	To him which pays him for a year and a half		2 6 0	3 4 6
	To Tamas Youll the Barnman a years wages payd him at Whitsunday 1714			2 17 4
	Thomas Bell Entred at White 1714 to be Barnman his wage in the year is three pound and two pair shoes and 2 pr stokins 10 .	3 10 0		
	To him 5s. to him his whole fees for 6 monethes			1 15 0
	To 5d. men for going errands thresing etc. for a year		1 4 2	
	To Meg Henderson two Aprons 3s. shoe 2s. 2d. .		0 14 2	1 18 4
	To her 2s. and to Barbry Hardy for her 1s. more in full			

28 6]

[Servants]

Account of Servants Cloathes and other expences 1714.

		[Sterling] £	s.	d.
	For a pair boots to Sandy Hume	0	10	0
	To Fanny Bells Arls 1s. .	0	1	0
Ap. 14	To Liedhouse for threed last year	0	2	0
Ap. 26	To Alexander Blyth for makeing and mending cloathes to this day haveing cleard accounts with him	0	8	6
	For cariing Jean Forsyth and her trunk from Newcastle .	0	12	6
	For bring Fanny Bell out of toun 1s. bringing Katharin heart 2s.	0	3	0
	For bringing Katharin Kenady from Berwick 1s. .	0	1	0
	For bringing Pegie Sharp from Berwick	0	1	0
		1	19	0

London, January 1715. Servants wages.

May Minzies

	To her		1	6
Aprill	To her which compleats all her wages till Lambes last 1714 .	19	11	6
Aug. 26	To her 1£ 10sh. Decmr. 2 to her 2£ 3s.	3	13	0

	Katharin Hearts wages I highted when I came to London from Candles 1715 to 3 0 0			
March 8	To her	1	12	0
Aug. 26	To her	1	1	6

Jean Housnem came to be Cook

	[Servants]	[Sterling] £ s. d.
	the 16 day of Dcemr 1714 her wage in the year is £8.	
	To her for 2 Monethes caried away by constables . . .	1 7 4
	To Marie Swan cook for a week	0 2 6
	To Hana Stivens cook	0 8 0
	Sara Lies came to be Chamber Maid the 21 Decmr. 1714 her wage in the year is £4 0 0	
1715 Janr. 11.	To her for 3 weeks wages	0 5 0
	Hellen Williams came to be Housemaid the 12 her wage in the year is . . £4 0 0	
	For a mug 2 more for 6 weeks 6s. 2d.	
Aug. 26	For constables and cariing befor a justice of peace 8s. 2d. .	0 16 4
	Ann Frazer came to be chamber maid the 22d febr. her wage in the year was . 3 0 0	
Aug. 26	To her for a fourtnights wages 3 weeks more	0 7 6
	Sara Thrift came to be Housemaid the 10 of March her wage in the year is . ·£4 0 0	
	To her for a week .	0 2 0
Ap. 8	To Doraty house made for a week	0 1 7
	Lattes Hall entered to be Cook the 26 of March her wage in the year is . 8£ 0 0	
	To her for a moneth wages 13s. 4d. . . .	0 13 8

	[Servants]	[Sterling] £ s. d.
	To Winifrid Rollands for a monethes wages. .	0 16 8
Aug. 26	Katharin Loid came home for one night only	
Sep. 18	Amee cook a day . . .	0 2 6
	John Baillie came to be Jerriswoods servant at White 1714 his wages in the year is £5 0 0	
1715		
Janur. 11	To him half a years wages . .	2 10 0
May 1	To him in full of his wages	2 10 0
	Thomas Hewie came in John Baillies place his wage 4£ 0 0	
	To him for half a year tho he was only from 6 May till 28 Sepr . . .	2 0 0
	James Grives wages I highted after I came to London at Candles 1715 to (in the year) £4 0 0	
Aug. 26	For a Mug 1s. a fork 1⁰sh. . .	
	I highted James wages at Lambes 1715 to £5 0 0	
	Tam youls is to continue at in the year £3.	

	[Servants]				[Sterling]		
					£	s.	d.
	To his wifes Candles rent 1715	0	15	$2\frac{6}{12}$			
	To her Lambes rent 1715 .	0	15	$2\frac{6}{12}$			
Aug. 26	For plewing his land this year . .	0	18	10			
					2	9	]
	Betty cook for a moneth	0	10	6			
Aug. 17	To her for days wages	0	8	0	0	18	6
	Jean Forsith entred to be house Maid at Whitsunday 1715 her wage in the year is £3 0 0						
Aug. 26	To her a pair shoes .	0	4	6			
	To her . . .	1	1	6			
	To her fraught come-ing up beside her wages	0	10	0			
	To her in full of 11 moneths wages at 4£ a year . .	2	0	0	3	16	0
	Nelly Ormand came to be Cook on the 17 August her wage in ye year £5 0 0						
	To her for 6 moneths	2	10	0	2	10	0
	Robert Anderson came to be Jerriswoods footman Sepr. 28 his wage in the year with Liverras is £5 he furnishes shoes and stokins—stayd a week.						

[Servants]	[Sterling] £ s. d.
George Midcalf came to be footman october 1715 his wages in the year without stokens and shoes is 5 0 0	
	S. £48 16 2

		£	s.	d.
	To Hellen Williams arls	0	0	6
	For a Big coat to Tam Youll lined and brass buttons	2	5	0
	For a Big lin'd Coachmans Coat .	2	10	0
	For a hatt and laceing two with old lace I had by me .	0	6	0
Ap. 20	For a blew coat to Tames Youll	2	5	0
May 28	For 4 pair Stokins to the Liverras	0	14	0
	For shoes to Tam youll	0	4	0
	For dresing and cuting two hats	0	2	6
	For a sute Liveras to James Grive at 4£ 1[0]sh.	4	10	0
	For a big Blew coat to James Grive . .	2	10	0
	For a sute Liverras to Thomas Hardy and a big coat .	7	0	0
	For a coate to the coachmas Nicolles . .	1	10	0
	For a wastcoat and briches to make Tam youll a full sute	2	5	0
	To Robert Anderson arls to be Jerriswoods footman .	0	1	0
Aug. 26	For gold lace to two hats	0	17	2
Sep. 18	For shoes to Tam youll .	0	4	6
	For a hat to George Midcalf 8s. lace to it 3s. . . .	0	11	0

[Servants]	[Sterling]
For a pair plushes and with shambo briches to George .	£ s. d. 0 16 0
For a pair of shoes to Tam youll .	0 4 6
	S. £28 16 2

London, January 1st, 1717. Account of Servants wages.

May Minzies

	To Mr. Hambly for a piece of chints	6 0 0
	To her at Lambes 1717 in full of all wages	4 15 6
	Katharine Heart	
	I highted her wages at Whit 1717 to . 5 0 0	
	To her full and compleat payment at White 1717 .	5 16 2
	Katharin Lasell came to be chamber Maid to my doughters the day of her wages in the year is 5 0 0	0 12 6
	She stayd 6 weeks .	0 12 6
	Mary Pen came to be chambermaid her wage in the year is 6 0 0	
June 2d	To her 1£ 1s. 6d. returned 6s. 6d. pay her for six weeks . .	0 15 0
	Katharin Kenady came to be House Maid the 23 day of Janr. her wage in the year is 4 0 0	

[Servants]	[Sterling]		
	£	s.	d.
I highted her wages at Lambes 1717 to 4 10 0			
To her when she was in Scotland	2	1	2
To her compleat wages at Marts 1717	1	3	0
Jean Dickson came to be cook the 1st febr. her wage in the year is 8 0 0			
To her a moneths wages for a fourtnight	0	13	4
Pegie came to be cook the 18 day of febr. her wage in the year is 6 0 0			
She stayd only a night.			
Betty was cook from 20 feb. to			
To her 10 sh., more 10s. more for 10 weeks 8 10d. .	1	8	10
Ann Phillips entred to be cook Wedensday the 24 Aprill her wages in the year . 7 0 0			
To her in full for 2 monethes and 2 weeks at 8£ a year	1	13	6
Ann Griffeth came to be cook the 9 July her wages in the year is 7£ and 8 if she dos well 8 0 0			
To her 7 Moneth and 3 weeks at 3s. 4d. a week .	5	3	4
James Grieve			
To him full payment of all wages at Martimas 1717	14	19	7

[Servants] [Sterling]

		£	s.	d.
	John Hume Garner at Mellerstaine			
	To him three years wages at Martimas 1717 .	12	0	0
	To him 18 bolls oats and 6 bols bear Lithgow measure at 8sh. pr boll for sd 3 years	9	12	0
	To his house rent 3 years at 15	2	5	0
	To his cows grase and fother in winter.			
	James Park came to be footmas 13 febr. his wages without shoes and stokens is 5 0 0			
	Thomas Youll			
	To him the Candles and Lambs 1716 and 1717 rent .	3	10	10
	For Plewing his Land the sd 2 years	1	17	8
	George Divison entered footman his wages in the year is . 4 10 0			
June	To him 5s. in full of his wages for 8 moneth more	3	0	0
	To Androw Lamb 3 years rent Lambs 1715 16 and 1717 his being 2£ Matha blacks 1£ 2s. $8\frac{6}{12}$—9£ 8 $1\frac{6}{12}$	9	8	$1\frac{6}{12}$
	Dorathy Hunter came at the end of Aug: 1717 to be my Grisies Maid her wages in the year is 5 0 0			
octr.	To her by Francy Newtons account	6	14	$4\frac{4}{12}$

	[Servants]	[Sterling] £	s.	d.
	To her by Mrs. Wisharts account	0	6	0
	To Babie Robison for sowing at half a crown a week .	1	12	3
febr. 11	For a woman to wash 1s. to scour 2 days 2s.	0	3	0
	For washing 1s. 1s. 1s. 1s. 1s. 1s. 2s. 6d. 1s. 1s. 1s. 1s. 1s.	0	13	6
	For scouring 1s. 1s. 6d. .	0	2	6
		S. £96	6	$9\frac{10}{12}$

London, January 1st, 1717. Account of Servants cloathes.

	For stokins to Tam 3s. .	0	3	0
	For mending Tam youls Cloathes	0	5	3
	For 6 duson brass buttons at 18	0	9	0
	For 9 dusone small at 9d.	0	6	9
	For a pair gloves for Park	0	1	6
Marchs	For 3 hats to the servants 15s. lace to them 10s. 4d. .	1	5	4
	For cloath to servants at 8sh. 2 big coats and sute cloathes . The serge linin at 20d. big butons as above for one coat . .	6	5	4
	To Pringle the Taylor for makeing the sute at rates agreed on .	3	12	0
	For a pair hose to Tam	0	3	1
	For a pair shoes to Tam .	0	4	0
	For a hat and galoun to George 5s. 4s.	0	9	0
	For 4 pr scarlite stokens to the servants 5s. on at 6s. 6d.	1	1	6
	For Tams shoes 18d. .	0	1	6
	For $\frac{3}{4}$ cloath for Georges Briches 5s. 5d.	0	5	5

	[Servants]	[Sterling]		
		£	s.	d.
	For shoes to James Park 4s. shoes to George 4s. . . .	0	8	0
	For dresing a hat .	0	1	0
	For a pair boots to James Park 11s.	0	11	0
	For 7 duson guilt bras buttons for 2 coats at 2s. pr du.	0	14	0
	For nin duson waistcoat buttons at 1 sh.	0	9	0
	For a goun to Tams doughter	1	4	0
	For stokens to Tam youll .	0	4	6
	For ane Apron to Nans Haliwall	0	5	5
	For a Blew Ridincoat to Will Mc	1	14	10
Aug.	For cariing Dol Hunters cloaths, etc.	0	11	0
	For boots to George which he lost	0	4	6
		S. £23	9	11

Deburst for Houshold furnitur 1693.

1693		[Scots]		
Aprl 22d	To William Scott for a table, stands and glas .	60	0	0
May 20.	For a sut Aras hangins of 14 ells in 3 pices	96	0	0
	For puther from Mrs. Hervie	39	4	0
Ditto	For sevarall othar things to the howss that stands in ane other book	88	18	0
	For furniture betwixt Octr 12. 1693 and May 12, 1694 .	304	0	0
	For bed bolster and cods .	22	2	0
	For drinking glases .	11	6	0
1694	To Penman, goldsmith, for work as per account and recept .	40	0	0

	[Furnishings]	[Scots] £		d.
	For furnitur to my green bed, etc.	169	19	0
	For dornick	24	12	0
Jun. 20	For a washing ruber .	0	9	0
Ditto	For bottles	57	12	0
Aug.	For dornick at Inerkithin 12lb. 3d. str.	124	12	0
	For liting my coper culrd stuf, etc.	28	1	0
Ditto 26	For 2 ston lint	10	0	0
	For linin for shits .	9	8	0
Oct.	For the litle long folding table	4	4	0
	For the rond table .	3	10	0
	For 6 Holland codwars	6	0	0
	For a bast to a bed .	17	0	0
	For 4 spinell yerin .	4	4	0
Novr.	For a lint whille 3lb. 10 earthin pots 6s.	3	16	0
	For 5 duble preses for books at 13lb. p. pice, collering 7lb. .	72	0	0
	For bakets seals and 3lb. helping the screwtor 18s. .	13	18	0
	For a wanscot chist of drawers .	16	0	0
	For lint spining for shits 6 slips in the pound 14s. p. lb.			
	For cariing the Lady Laws chist	1	10	0
1695 March 12	For stript crap for window courtins at 8s. 6d. per ell	4	8	0
	To 24 ells linin for shits	15	12	0
May 30	For a bason 4, for 6 puther spoones 1lb. 4s.	1	8	0
	For 5 glases 2lb. 6s. a lid to a stand 14s.	3	10	0
	For a washing tub 12s. a ruber 8s. a glas 14d. jacolit stick 10d.	2	14	0
July	For polishing my drawers 18s.	0	18	0
	For 6 lame plats for milk .	1	16	0
	For a key to the closit 8, a poranger 4s.	0	12	0

[Furnishings]	[Scots] £	s.	d.
For a gross bottels from Georg Lason at 2lb. pr duson .	24	0	0
For 36 pint bottles .	19	16	0
For a pott 14s. a ston lint for shits 10lb.	10	14	0
For working crap for curtins .	6	1	0
	S. 1310	14	0

Deburst for houshold furnitur 1696.

		[Scots]		
January	For 2 ston of lint to the toun of Mellerstens	11	18	0
	To a pairt of payment for linin working	4	7	0
20	For a ladle 3s. a flamer 4s. caps 3s. washen brush 6s. .	16	0	0
	For a shovell 14, skull 6s. .	1	0	0
	For 6 drinking glases 3lb. 2 chamer pots 1lb. 7s.	3	7	0
	For tikin to bed and bolster	2	16	
	For buttons for codwars .	1	9	
	For a water stoup wt yron girths		8	
Aprill	For a posit dish		4	
	For drinking glases		4	
	For setting a fixt bed in the nursary	2	18	0
	For 2 pair shits 4lb. linin 14s. .	4	14	0
	For linin working 5 quarters brod at 3s. 4d. per ell.			
	For ane yron draping pan	3	14	0
May 1st	For a pair linin and woolan blanckets	8	16	0
	For scuring 3 piece Arass hangins	2	2	0
	For 6 Dutch wand chiers .	19	16	0
	For 54 ells hair plush at 3lb. 8 per ell for hangins .	183	6	0

	[Furnishings]	[Scots]		
	To Pringle for litting the scarlit crap, etc.	£ 15	s. 0	d. 0
Jun. 18	For rubers hard and washing	1	8	0
	For the Japan table stands and glas	120	0	0
	For 6 chairs at 16sh. the pice	49	12	0
	For a fring to the plush hangins 2lb. 7s. cover to Japan table	5	7	0
	For bliching 43 ells linin at 2s. 6d. the ell	5	8	0
July 19	For tikin to a bed 9 ells	6	15	0
	For a Dutch basket for my cloathes	3	0	0
	For a hather brush 3s. 6d.	0	3	6
	For making 6 cuchines at 11s. pice, linnin to one of them	3	16	0
Decmr.	For 6 water glases	3	0	0
	To Carr, goldsmith for 6 spons 6 forks, etc. per recept	100	0	0
	To put the blads in the silver knives	2	2	0
	For a bast to the door	0	12	0
	For 68 ells cours dornick working bliching, etc.	8	14	0
		S. 600	16	6

Deburst for howshold furniture 1697.

		[Scots]		
Agust 1st	To Carr goldsmith the remains of ane acount	012	00	00
	For a lame bason	000	14	00
	For bustin the big chair	000	14	00
	For a clogbag lock	000	04	00
	For a fish pan	000	07	00
	For puting a blad in a knif	000	12	00

	[Furnishings]	[Scots]		
		£	s.	d.
	For sives and riddels at Mellersteans	002	02	00
Ditto	For a fathirbed bolster and 2 cods	042	00	00
	For a bason 4s. 6d. 4 glases 1ti. 16	002	00	06
	For the shoe yron 10s. a lock mending and key to a trunk	001	00	00
	For a cover to the green chair 4 ell at 2ti. per ell	004	00	00
	For scuring 5 pice of Arrass hangings	003	04	00
	For 2 milk basons at 10s. and 14s. 3 caps at 18sh. . . .	002	02	00
	For a rimin dish 2s. milsy 2s. bason 7sh.	000	11	00
	For 6 knives with horn hefts	001	16	00
	For a lame chamber pot 13: 2 rid ons and a dry stool	001	04	00
	For a harth buson 12 a busom for hangins 11	001	03	00
	For a gros of chapin and a gros muchkin bottels . . .	036	00	00
	For a bed bolster and 2 cods	016	00	00
	For werping and sowing my holland	001	00	00
	For working my holland 43 ells 12s. per ell and drinkmony .	026	10	00
Septm.	For 5 hesps mor yerin to the holland at 1ti. 10 the spinill	001	17	00
	For a clogbag lock .	000	05	00
	To Thomas Carr goldsmith 6 ounces silver	019	04	00
	For 6 ells scarlit crap to my bed at 24 s.per ell	007	04	00
	To Robert Hadden for munting it 6ti. 16, a big cushin 2ti. .	008	16	00
	To the timer of the bed 15ti., rops 2ti.	017	00	00
	To the rods of the bed 4ti. 4ti. .	008	00	00

[Furnishings]	[Scots]		
	£	s.	d.
To stentin silk and threed and takits	007	00	00
To 3 cut Vinıs glases	012	13	00
To 4½ ells Damask table cloath, 30½ ells Damask servits.			
To table cloathes at per ell, the servits at			
For 25 ℔. tow	010	08	00
For 4 pair of linin shits	041	12	00
For 4 pair shits at 5ℓi. 10	022	00	00
For a pair old shits .	004	04	00
For seals and 2 pound wight	004	06	00
For 3 carpit cushins 4ℓi. 10s., a chamber box. . . .	005	12	00
The timber of a bed with rods .	006	00	00
To John Hancha for tables and timer work per acount and recept	027	04	00
To Ms. Henry for pother as per recept	018	06	00
	377	14	0
For plode [? plade] to Mr. Johnston	167	12	0

Edenburgh, January 1703. Houshold Furnitur.
Deb: to Cash.

	[Scots]		
For 12 ells callico to help to line the bed	24	0	0
For 19 bottles	1	18	0
For a large sawse pan	5	8	0
For a skellit pan . . .	2	8	0
To Ms. Willy for 18 glases ale 12s. wine 6s. and 8s. .	7	0	0
For 4 jelly glases .	1	4	0
For 8 jugs at 3sh. per pair	7	4	0
For 2 crewits	1	4	0

	[Furnishings]	[Scots] £	s.	d.
	For a wine glas . . .	0	6	0
Febr. 2	For 17⅞ ells silk and cotten for window curtins .	32	3	6
	For drawing the pand of the white bed	0	18	0
	For 5 bottles	[illegible]	1[illegible]	0
	For 2 little cups to drink out off			
Mar. 13	For a little yetlin kettle .			
	For a little bras pan		1	
	For tining the pan .			
	For calico to line my bed	2		
	For ane earthin pot to pickle salmond .	0	4	0
	To Thomas Carr goldsmith ane ballance of ane old accumpt for silver work in full of all I am due him as per his recept	36	0	0
	For a little wort shill	[illegible]	[illegible]	[illegible]
	For a whisk			
	For a dry stool 10s.		1	
	For 33 bottles			
	For a ridle to the tind		1	
	For tows to the wall last year		1	
Aprill	For wall tows			
	For a jack £4 16s. for smithwork in making the whils	10	0	0
	For cuper work . . .	0	9	0
	For a chamerpot . . .	0	12	0
	For 4 bottles 8s. . . .	0	8	0
	For 11½ ell tickin .	10	2	0
	For nails 9s. seting the kitchin chimny £1 2 . . .	1	11	0
	For 8 bottles 16s. nails 4s.	1	0	0
	For 3 slips yeron 18s.	0	18	0
June 15	For 2 pair sheats for the childrins beds, 12 pillabers .	14	0	0
	For 2 pair sheets to the servants	7	0	0

	[Furnishings]	[Scots] £	s.	d.
	To James Imry smith for work	1	0	0
	To Ernist for my bed making	0	10	0
	For 3 bottles 6s., for a map 7s., a whisk 2s. 6d.	0	15	6
	For a slip yeron 6s., for a rill 6s. 6d.	[illegible]	1[illegible]	[illegible]
	For 3 cups 14s.			
	For a bottle 2s., 5 bottles 10s.			
	For 2 decanters			
	For 12 cheana custard dishes			
	For 2 hand sconces			
August	For a coffie pot			
	For ordinar Dornick	54		
	For 57 ells linin for shits	38		
	For chamber pot	[illegible]	1	
	For 2 ℔. Dutch threed for fringes		1	
	For wirsit to make fringes			
	For a basin 14s.			
	For 18 bottles			
	For 21 ells plading working			
	For 50 ells linin bliching .			
	For a timber morter		1	
	For a skep for meall			
	For a pound and ane ounc Dutch threed	3	4	0
	For knitins 4s., small cords 7s. 8	0	11	8
	For takets £1, a ladle and sowin sive 5 . . .	1	5	0
	For a pair wooll cards £1 2s	[illegible]	[illegible]	10
	For yron for cruks and bearers			
	For a tree stoup 11s. a handy cog			
	For 10 ells harden			
	For ane ston wooll .		1	
	For linin for shits .	1		
	For 3 ston lard wooll at £6 10	1	1	
	For oyl to wooll		1	
	For threed £1, 12 cravat to Steedman 12s.	2	4	0

	[Furnishings]	[Scots] £	s.	d.
	For forcing shirs 2 pair 3s., threed 2s.	0	5	0
	For knitins 4s., while bands 2s., knitins 4s.	0	10	0
	For 50 ell stuf for the little room at 7s. 6d.	17	15	0
	To Steedmans son a mounth at Mellersteans in pairt	08	0	0
Meller	To the couper a years accumpt .	6	11	0
[steans]	For 20 ells strakins at 6s. 6d.	6	10	0
Oct. 20	For 156 days spinin whereof 6 to washen	11	14	10
	For 18 days all at 1s. 6d. per day	1	7	0
	For 30 ells linin at 3s. the ell working	4	10	0
	For 20 ells linin to Frater	3	0	0
	For 30 ells pladin by heart at 2s. per ell	3	0	0
	For 21 ells pladin wrought by Rob: Milne at 1s. 6d.	1	11	6
	For 43 days work by Alshy Blith and his son	8	11	6
	For 29 ells harden for bed and horse shites	7	10	0
	For 2 seeks £4 for a pott 2s.	4	2	0
	For dying yellow fringes .	1	10	0
	For a map 8s., ridle 5s. 8d., tyle for chimny, £1 2s. .	1	15	8
	For takets 8s. 6d. .	0	8	6
December	For scarlit wirsit litting to a fring of a bed	26	10	0
	For green worset to the said bed.	2	17	6
	For bangall for servants towills .	3	17	0
	For cloath to the black riding furnitur at 10s. str.	15	0	0
	For a black coutch with canvis botom	9	0	0
	For a black arme rush chair	3	12	0

[Furnishings]	[Scots] £	s.	d.
For two low rush chairs	4	16	0
For a rush bottomd eassi chair	4	4	0
For a big bufft eassi chair with cushon	18	0	0
For a walnut tree footstooll and buffing	4	16	0
For two rush foot stools .	3	0	0
To P. N. for making a cran and cripit . .	0	8	0
For 2 crook trees bed rods etc. by Pat. N.	1	8	0
For 100 ells cord for curtins .	4	8	0
For furnitur to make beds	2		
For rods to a bed at 3s. per foot	2		
For a larg fire shuffill .	3		
For a fine cutt timber of a bed .	48		
For a ston of douns .	9		
For dying silk fring and cushons	4		
For making 7 cushons	7		
For 2 cutt cornises 3s., drinkmony 6s. . .	2	2	0
For buckarm threed, takets, and to a bed	6	7	0
For lame bouls and basons, etc.	3	18	0
For a pice muslin for window curtins	37	0	0
For 11 bottles £1 2s.	1	2	0
To Stidmans son pays out a month at Mellersteans	12	0	0
To Imrie, smith	2	0	0
For linin to help to line the barens bed . .	5	14	0
For brush to the horse 10 nails, etc.	1	5	0
For setting chimnys .	0	18	0
For table cloathes	9	12	0
To Clark wright in pairt of his account	60	0	0

[Furnishings]	[Scots]		
	£	s.	d.
For tining two pots, another pot, 3 covers	2	0	0
For busoms and brushes and chamber pots . . .	8	0	0
For a frying pan . . .	2	2	0
For 9 ells hardin from Hellin Garner	2	14	0
	S. 807	0	8

Edenburg, January 1707. Houshold Furnitur.
Deb. to Cash.

		[Scots]		
	For glazing the house at Edinburgh	20	0	0
	For the workemanship of a cooler 54 ounces and 13d., a duson spoons 31 ounce 8d., 12 knife helfts 10 ounce 10d., six salts 15 ounce 3d. as per Robert Bruce goldsmithes account	91	8	0
	For 37 ounces 2d. silver of the abovesaid work (the rest being my own) at £3 4s. per ounce	118	16	0
	For severall things mended by Mr. Bruce	8	16	0
	For a bras hand candlestick to the bairens room .	0	12	0
	For 2 smothing yrons £1 8s., mending the rest 7s .	1	15	0
April 1st.	To Sibit Smith in full of all accounts	19	0	0
	For a big bras pan . . .	4	16	0
	For a virginall hammer 16s., a musick book £6 .	6	16	0
	For another big brass pan	4	6	6

[Furnishings]	[Scots] £	s.	d.
For a pair little bras candle sticks £2 8s., 3 pair snuffers £1 10, extinguisher 5 . .	4	3	0
For screw nails from Mr. Inis .	4	16	0
For half a gross bottles £9, cariing them	9	2	0
For mending a pot 1s. 6d., cocks and pales 2s., oven mending 5s. 6d.	0	9	0
For nails 2s. 6d., smith work 14s. 6d., 2s. 6d., 1s., 1s., 6s., 1s., 2s. .	1	11	0
For mending the bucat and girthes 9s., tubs 7s. 6d., 3s. 6d.	1	0	0
For kitchen towils £1 2s., more cours cloath £3 6s. .	4	8	0
For threed 1s. 2s. 1s. 6d., a bair busom 16	1	0	6
For a washing ruber 11s., a ruber 8s., a ruber 12s. .	1	11	0
For keys to back gate 11s., 2 little tubs 11s. .		1	0
For a whipe 12s., a Spanish busom 4s., hard brush 8s. 6d. .	1	4	6
For 4 sillibub glases £2 8s., a glas 10s.	2	18	0
For 11 ells Holland for window curtins	21	0	0
For comb and brush to the mares £1 16s.	1	16	0
For glazing windows £1 16s., a map and whisk 12s. 6d.	2	8	6
For 7 earthen juggs £1 2s. 4d., a tin tanker 5s. 6d.	1	7	10
For a sand glas 6s., a milk sive and pott 6s. .	0	12	0
For a ston douns to the easie chair £8 10s., a rugh head £1 2s.	9	12	0

	[Furnishings]	[Scots] £	s.	d.
	For 4 ells harden £1 2s., a coll ridle 4s. . .	1	6	0
	For a lock to Grisies door 16s., a key to the drawers 6 .	l	2	0
	For helping trunk locks 8s., a cours chamer pot	0	9	6
	For bast 6 ells of 8 bread £2 2s., 3 ells fine 8s. 6d. per ell . .	3	7	6
	For a washin ruber for Mellersteans	0	11	0
	For strings to window courtins 17s.	0	17	0
	For 3 hand candlesticks to Mellersteans	2	2	0
	For 10 duson of bottls	12	0	0
Meller [steans] June 10	For 3 lame basons and chamerpots 4 to Mellerstean basons 7s. p. pots 8sh. p.	2	13	0
Mellerstean	For a saus pan .	2	8	0
June 10	For spoons bought by Mary Muir 6s.	0	6	0
	For 9 ells strakins at 6s. per ell .	2	14	0
13	For a ladle 2s., kitchin knif 3s. 6d.	0	5	6
	For 3 ells bast £1 1s., for harden at 4s. per ell	2	0	0
	For 12 yron scewers 9s., a Spanish busom 4s. 6d.	0	13	6
July 8	To the couper in Earlston in full of all accounts .	4	0	0
	For 5 ells strokins for kitchin aprons, etc.	1	5	0
	For stamping plush 2s. per ell 8s.	0	8	0
	For scouring 16 pair blankets	1	8	0
	For puting up chmneys and doing other things in the house	2	0	0
	For a map 3s. 6d., a filler for Meller[stean] 3s. 6d. . .	0	7	0
	For a glass chirn . .	1	0	0

[Furnishings]		[Scots]		
		£	s.	d.
Aug. 15	For houshold furniture from Moubra in full of all accoumpts acording to his account and discharge	107	10	0
	To Docter Dundas for 2 Ormiston queches	3	0	0
	For helping loks and keys at Edinburgh 8s.	0	8	0
	For 6 duson table napkins and 15 table cloathes bought at Innerkitbin by Ms. Linsday	136	0	0
	For sowing table napkens 6 napkens 3 dusone	1	13	0
	For a damask table cloath from Ms. Orr	6	0	0
	For makeing a brander, etc., in the kitchen	1	4	4
Sep. 29	For another glas chirn the first being broke	1	0	0
	For a lock to the utter door of later meet room	0	16	0
	For a clogbag lock 6s., 2 timber plates 14s.	1	0	0
	For alm to lite coverins 8s., working lint £1 more £2 7s.	3	15	0
	For 2 big timber milk basons, a big plate	2	9	0
	To John Muele for working 5 coverings 8s. per p.	2	0	0
	To the couper in Earlston in full	2	15	0
	To Lethem, smith, ane old account for chimnys, etc.	36		00
		S. 694	19	2

London, January 1715. Household Furniture.

[Furnishings]	[Sterling] £	s.	d.
For 4 litle chena frute dishes	0	8	0
For a dusone wine glases 6£, 2 Ale Glases 1s.	0	7	0
For 2 crewits 1s., 2 water botles 3s.	0	4	0
For 21 water glases 8s.	0	8	0
For 6 litle green Tee cups and sassers	0	8	0
For 4 big dishes from Fergison at 3s. 6d.	0	14	0
For 2 duson of chena truncher plate fergison .	2	0	0
For 4 big Dishes for Frut Fergison	0	8	0
For a big punsh bowl Fergison .		1	
For 2 litle punsh bowls Fergison			
For close stoall 10s., a pan 3s. 4d.		1	
For 2 triming cloath			
For a Tee ketle 0 7 0, a hatshet for suger 1s.	0	8	0
For a spung 6d. . . .	0	0	6
For a new washing tub 5s. 6d., a second hand tub 3s. 6d.	0	9	0
For a wig block . . .	0	4	6
For a linin skreen .	0	7	0
For a coll ridle yron one 2s., timer one 6d.	0	2	6
For a head to Coffie Milne .	0	1	6
For 2 Ale jugs 4s., 3 earthen pans 9d.	0	4	9
For a hard Ruber . . .	0	4	6
For a grater and timber spoon 3d., 2 serches 8d., map 11 .	0	1	10
For a pair sisers for the Dog	0	0	6
For a dusone of knife hafts makeing 4s. pr pice and puting on the creast 1sh., the blads 14d.	3	14	0

	[Furnishings]	[Sterling] £	s.	d.
	For 26 ounces 10 peny wight of new sterline at 5s. 6d. .	7	5	9
	For a dusone of forks workmanship 3s., graveing creast 1s. .	2	8	0
	For 26 ounces 4d. weight of new-sterline at 5s. 6d.	7	4	1
	For a coper knif basket .	0	10	0
	For 2 bowls 1s. 6d., a close stool pan 3s.	0	4	6
	For a coper tanker .	0	2	6
	For a writing table .	3	0	0
	For a close box 10s., a puther pan 3s.	0	13	0
Ap. 20	For mending the Hamer .	0	1	4
May	For a brush to the servants	0	0	10
	For fraught of 5 beds, 12 pr blankets bolster piller twills	0	12	0
	For other expences in bring them out of the ship .	0	9	4
	For a hard ruber 1s. 6d., 2 chamber pots 10	0	2	4
	For a paill 2s.	0	2	0
	For 2 broun china litle plates .	0	5	0
	For ane ovel Dutch table 6 cups and sassers	1	10	0
	For a Honn to sharp razors	0	8	0
	To Mrs. Couper for a blew camblet bed	6	0	0
	For ane yron foot to the Marble table	0	5	0
	For a sea Green Camblet Bed	8	18	0
	For a Japan Lief to hand about Tee	0	5	0
	For 2 dressing Glasses for my self and Grisic with drawers .	2	14	0
	For 3 knives and forks .	0	1	6
	For a duson of wine Glases 8s., 2 glas mugs 2s., 2 Ale glas 2s. .	0	12	0

[Furnishings]	[Sterling] £	s.	d.
For 4 white basons . . .	0	3	4
For brass nails for chimny brushes at 6d.	0	3	0
For 2 hooks of brass for curtins 1s.	0	1	0
For a coper Callender	0	8	0
For a big coper pot for Bear	0	7	0
For a nother les copper pot for bear	0	6	0
For a pair Kitchen Bellis	0	4	0
For a pair bellies to the Landry .	0	3	0
For a brass choffer with bras foot	1	0	0
For a top to the Lanthorn of tinn	0	2	0
For a fether bed bolster and pillows from Mrs. Murray	3	0	0
For a dressing glass to May and Rachel	0	15	0
For mending the stair sconce	0	3	0
For scales and weights and broads and weights . . .	1	4	0
For a hook to hold my keys	0	8	0
For 4 duson truncher plates and a bason of puther .	3	19	6
For 38 foot Mullers dyed pear tree for prints at 6d. and 4d. pr foot 0 15 10 For 19½ foot dyed peer tree mullers the smal picturs at 3d. the midle size at 4d. the largest size at 5d. by Mr. Lasaget . . 2 18 0	3	13	10
For a bed from Mrs. Simson and bolsters	3	0	0
For 2 earthen pots for salting meat	0	2	4
For 2 timber plates for takeing up meat out of a pot .	0	3	6

	[Furnishings]	[Sterling] £	s.	d.
	For a brass tinder box	0	1	6
	For ane English blanket to my own bed	0	14	0
	For a clock pin with 10 pins	0	0	10
	For 6 litle hard brushes 8d.	0	0	8
Aug. 26	For 52 els linin for shiets from May Minzies . . .	3	10	0
	For ane yron scewer with a wight a long one for spiting small foul 4 others lesser . . .	0	1	10
	For a chinny glass in one pice 54½ by 22½ Mr. Turin	14	0	0
	For a large Glass in a Glase fram	25	0	0
	For a writting Dask on wheels walnut tree Mr. Turin .	7	0	0
	For a pair bellies 5sh., a hearth brush 18d. of walnut tree	0		6
	For a pair litle hand sconces	0	6	0
	For 3 pices yellow Damask for window curtius .	18	0	0
	For 6 pices Green Damask for hangins, chairs and window curtins from Piter Hambly	36	0	0
	For Mattine 3s. 4d. to the entry	0	3	6
	For a litle Tee pot 3s. 6d., a plate to it 9d., glas suger box 1s.	0	5	3
	For a brass pestel to a morter	0	1	0
Sep. 18	For 3 litle stools .	0	3	0
	To Mr. Scots man for ane Indian Matt bringing . .	0	1	0
	For a pair tongs, shuvel, and Poker to the Kitchen .	0	8	0
	For a trivit to stove halls .	0	0	10
	For a pair brass tongs and poker	0	16	0
	For a glass Lamp 9sh., the yron to fix it at the door 30d.	0	11	0
	For a Backie for Tee dishes	0	4	0

[Furnishings]	[Sterling] £	s.	d.
For a pair Bellies . . .	0	3	6
For a wire sive for the sinders	0	2	0
For a glass to the wemens room	0	2	0
For 2 basons 1s., a chamber pot 6d.	0	1	6
For a Callico Twilt to the blew bed	1	5	0
For ane yroning blanket .	0	8	0
For 2 porangers 3d., a litle pan 2d.	0	0	5
For a spunge to the chambermaid 6d.	0	0	6
For a saffron botle 3s.	0	3	0
For a large chist of drawers	2	5	0
For a table with Drawers for the Cupboord	0	14	0
For a hanging and 2 corner shelfs to the Cupboord .	0	10	0
For 2 hanging shelfs in my Closet	0	10	0
For 60 clock pins at peny a pice .	0	5	0
For a firr table for dressing of linins	0	10	0
For a furm to the Kitchin	0	5	0
For a Basket for cloathes	0	1	6
For 9 wine glases . . .	0	6	0
For a pair glass sconces to the litle drawin room .	0	14	0
For black Japan Frams for picturs at 2d. and 1$\frac{6}{12}$d. . . .	1	0	0
For dyed pear tree frams at 3d., 4d. and 5d. a foot	5	0	0
For 2 frames to the picturs more	0	2	0
For a pair of Raxes and a chean to the Jack	0	10	0
For a brass fender .	0	15	0
For a chimny pice .	2	10	0
For a yellow Moyhair bed and stuff Tourdelie 2 window curtins	46	0	0

[Furnishings]	[Sterling] £	s.	d.
For a glas 6 foot high .	5	14	0
For 2 chimny glasses with black frams and 2 pair of glas sconces . .	7	0	0
For a lage glass with black frame	7	0	0
For a large Glass with glas frame	13	0	0
For a chimny glass with guilt frame	3	0	0
For a chimny Glass with glas frame . .	4	15	0
For a litle chimny glass wt black frame	1	9	0
For a large Glass with black frame	5	10	0
For 2 black japan tables with green plush . . .	3	5	0
For 2 blew Bundet window curtins	3	0	0
For a japan Tee Table .	1	10	0
For a litle glass with black frame	1	15	0
For 12 japan chairs, 2 Arm chairs, 2 stools	5	10	0
For 6 Kain chairs at 12s. a pice .	3	12	0
For 4 black chairs with rush bottoms	0	8	0
For 2 beds Green and blew for servants 2£ each . . .	4	0	0
For 2 fatherbeds, 2 bolsters, 2 pillows, 2 twilts, 4 blankets .	6	0	0
For 2 folding beds for the abovesd beding for servants	1	4	0
For a large Marbel table a litle table and 2 window solls	6	0	0
For 4 window kain sashes	2	10	0
For a wanescot table for 8 sitters 10s., one for 5 sitters 5s.	0	15	0
For a book case with looking glass	7	18	0

[Furnishings]	[Sterling] £	s.	d.
For 2 Portigal Matts for floors	1	0	0
For 2 litle guilt sconces .	0	6	0
For a japan corner cupboord with a table fixt to it . . .	0	10	0
For 2 wanscots tables and a blacke one each 4s.	0	12	0
For 3 chimny graits of one sort with yron fenders tongs etc. .	5	2	0
For a grate	0	15	0
For a Landry grate and grate for heating yrons . .	0	5	0
For a hearth and endyrons and brass tongs and shuvell	1	17	0
For a smothing table 8s., a long brod for washing on starch 8s.	0	16	0
For the stair lantron 6s., 2 stair sconces 7s. . .	0	13	0
For a House Lader 8s., a Horse for drying linins 7s.	0	15	0
For a coper for washing .	3	0	0
For a banch 5s., 4 tubs 10s., a water tub 6s., litle standert 6d.	1	1	6
For a Kitchin grate 18s., with cran 6s., tongs, poker, etc. 5 .	1	9	0
For a litle rax and 2 speets 6s., pot hook 1s., a gridyron 18d. .	0	8	6
For a coper pot 16lb 18s., a pot 10lb 10s., 2 stew pans 10s. .	1	18	0
For 2 sauce pans 8s., a brass Ketle 14s., a bras morter 2s. 6d.	1	4	6
For a driping pan and foot 3s., a truncher stand 8s., frying pan 18d.	0	12	6
For a brass ladle and skumer 2s., a trivet 2s., a plate rack 3s.	0	7	0
For 3 brass candle sticks, snuffers 9s., 2 yron ons 1s.	0	10	0

[Furnishings]	[Sterling] £	s.	d.
For a floor barril 1s., tinn candle box 1s., a folding table 3s. .	0	5	0
For ane yron coll basket 3s., a roling ston 18s. . .		1	0
For a Red and white Marbel table at 5s. a foot . . .	1	10	0
For Rid japan Bellis and brush 6s., bought on ye Tems[1] .	0	6	0
For a brun vernisht tee brood bought on the yce on Tems[1]	0	2	0
For a purple and white Devonshire Marble table 5s. a foot	1	2	6
For sume wrong caried over page 368	0	3	0
For a shad shuvel .		1	6
For a puther chamber pote	0	2	6
For green tape and silk to the chairs	0	2	7
For a fine slap basone .		5	
For a litle Tee broad		3	
For a pittipan to ane ashet		1	
For a grate for Jerriswoods closet		16	
For a pair bras tongs and shuvel		14	
For a brass fender .		2	
For a coper scutle .		1	
For a new fashond coper scuttel		0	
For 18 bras pins at 3d.		4	
For a hearth and dogs		3	
For a back to the Hearth		5	
For a pair Bellows—walnut tree		4	
For ane extinguisher		1	
For ane browning yron		4	
For a stiel to warm water		2	

[1] 'In the winter of 1715-16 the frost was again so intensely severe that the river Thames was frozen over during almost the space of three months. Booths were erected on the congealed river for the sale of all kinds of commodities and all the fun of the fair of 1684 was revived. On 19 January 1716 two large oxen were roasted whole on the ice.'—*Old and New London*, by Edward Walford.

	[Furnishings]	[Sterling] £	s.	d.
	For a coll rack 2s. .	0	2	0
	For a tinn'd Basket for Plates .	0	6	0
	For a litle china Tee pot a saffron pot at 5s.	0	5	0
	For 4 pieces of the Green Damask of my furnitur .	24	0	0
	For a Cavie for chickens .	0	5	0
	For a silver stand for small wax candle weight 6 ounces	1	18	0
	For a case to the bige knives etc.	1	4	0
	For a pair Glas Branches	0	12	0
	For 11 litle picturs glased .	0	5	6
	For a litle wooden cooller .	0	2	6
	For a table bed with canves Bottem to the Landry .	1	5	0
	For 2 large glas sconces from Turin	3	10	0
Novr. 16	For a powdering tub 6s., a meal barrill 1s.	0	7	0
	For 8 yd hollon for one sheat at 4s. the ell	1	8	0
	For a powdering tub	0	6	0
	For 9 yd a quarter holland for the uper shiet 4s. 6d. the ell .	1	12	$11\frac{6}{12}$
	For the easie chair with rid Damask cushon .	4	1	0
	For a Balband screen	1	1	6
	For 12 knives weight 26 ounces and 3 peny weight at 5s. 6d. .	7	3	9
	For 12 forks 12 spoons weight 33 ounc 1 peny 5s. 6d.	9	1	9
	For the fashon of knif 9s., spoons and forks 2s. 6d., engraveing 1s.	10	4	0
	For a case to them 1£ all made by Platel	1	0	0
	For ane fine blanket to my own bed	0	14	0

[Furnishings]		[Sterling] £	s.	d.
	For a Blanket to my Doughters bed			
Scotland	To Ocheltry for working 20 yd. Damask Table cloathes .	5	0	0
Scotland	For boyling 27 spinell yeron .	0	4	6
Scotland	For winding werping and dresing the yeren	0	6	2
Scotland	For Blitching the Table cloathes	0	16	8
	For changing the big salver weighting 58 ounces at 5s. 7d. and 1s. the ounce workmanship	2	4	6
	For puting a handel in the Milk pot . .	0	2	6
	For puting the extinguisher to the Tee Ketle and mending it	0	10	0
	For Damask Table cloath and 12 servits . .	4	11	0
	For a steling to the iner seller 7s., a shelf 2s. 6d. . . .	0	9	6
	For 2 sumter trunks	4	0	0
	For scouring 35 pr blankets at Mellerstaine . . .	0	6	0
made by Moor	For 10 walnut tree chairs wt mated seats 1£ 8s. .	14	0	0
made by Moor	For 2 stoolls of the mated chairs .	2	3	0
made by Moor	For a yellow Callamanca easie chair	5	0	0
made by Moor	For a litle folding walnuttree table	1	0	0
made by Moor	For 10 chairs stuft back and seat beside the Damask at 1£ 15s. and 4 squar stools of the same at 1£ 6s.	22	14	0
made by Moor	For a settie stuff of the same above	4	6	0
made by Moor	For a fram to a fire screen .	1	1	6
made by Moor	For a walnut tree book case	3	0	0
made by Moor	For a fram to a marbel table .	1	10	0
made by Moor	For 4 litle stufft stools these in to the bargon			

[Furnishings]	[Sterling]		
	£	s.	d.
The Dininroom great and harth grate 2£ 5s. hearth 4£	6	5	0
For a fish Ketle weight 18 lb. at 2s.	1	16	0
For makeing 8 Damask window Curtins with 4 seats two pieces of hangins all furniture but the Damask by John Sanderson	26	0	0
	£559	0	$4\frac{6}{12}$

	Deburst for cloathes	Scots		
Aprill 1693 Ditto	To ane acount pay'd to Mr. Robert Blackwood per recept	37	14	0
May 12	To acount to Baillie Pat Johnston quhich is all presiding this day	213	6	0
	For a white Damask wastcoatt .	17	16	0
	For strip muslin for cravat and slives	5	8	0
	For 2 pair shoes . .	5	8	0
Jun. 30	To John Ross for shoes quhich is all he can crave .	4	16	0
	For shoes from Georg Ross	13	4	0
	For linint for shirts and froks	33	6	0
	For a hat	7	16	0
Novr. 22d.	To James Richy acount of cloaths got befor Sept. 1691 and all acounts preciding this day	174	0	0
	To the night goun Jeany[1] got .	36	0	0
1694 Apr. 20	For black crap for a goun and coat at 1lb. 5s. per ell .	24	0	0
Ditto	For lace to shirt hands at 2lb. per ell	25	14	0

[1] Lady Grisell's sister afterwards married James, seventh Lord Torphichen.

	[Clothing]	[Scots] £	s.	d.
	For 3 ells galoun to a coat .	2	4	0
July 18	For buff to be briches	13	4	0
August	For boots 13lb 4s. shoes 2lb. 4s.	15	8	0
	For 2 pair shoes from Andrew Baird	3	8	0
	For making the buff briches and gloves	1	16	0
Novr. 1st	For ternin for a goun to Gris .	2	4	0
Decmr.	For 3 ells ½ Belliden silk fring 1lb 16, making Grises goun 1lb. 16 . .	2	12	0
	For shoes 2lb. 16, for black cloath for goun at 23sh. st. per ell .	78	4	0
	For shoes to Robin 9s., froks to him, pladin to him 3lb. .	3	9	0
1695	For stays to my Robin 1lb. 6s. .	1	6	0
	For 4 ells muslin for morning for the Quin	13	4	0
	For rubans 1lb. 6s., black shoes 2lb. 8s., shambo glovs 2lb. 14s.	6	8	0
May	For a bongrace to my Robin 12, one to Gris 12s., thread 2s. .	1	18	0
	For a love hud 3lb 10s. For a snuf-napken 2lb. 10	6	0	0
	For under stokens .	0	18	0
	For making Grises goun 1lb. 16, shirts and wascoats to her and Robin	9	3	0
	For worsit for strips 1lb. and working 2 pair .	1	18	0
	For a mask 1lb., cuting shoes 8s., dying and washing 3lb. 12s. .	5	0	0
	For a campain wig from Manson 5 dollars	14	10	0
July	For a pair cotten stokins .	4	0	0
20	For 2 pair shoes 4lb. 16s. to the man 3s. 6d.	5	19	6

	[Clothing]	[Scots] £	s.	d.
	For furnitur to a peticoat	0	18	0
	For pladin to my Robin .	0	18	0
	For a pair silk slipers with silk and waltin furnisht	1	4	0
	For lace to the bairnes and	13	10	0
August	For holland from Holland	29	0	0
	For plying to a goun 1lb. 16 for flanen 2lb. 12	4	8	0
	For dressing the rid ridin coat 4lb. 8	4	8	0
	To shoes to Gris 12s. for flanell 2, 12s.	3	4	0
Sept.	To Grahme for a hat	12	0	0
	To linin for Robin 3lb. 4, stuff to him 1lb. 4s., blew base to him 1lb. . .	5	8	0
Novr. 1st	To a frok to Gris 2lb. 3s., for lace to her 1lb. 10	3	13	0
	For 2 pair shoes 5lb. 10, Forone pair 2lb. 14	7	4	0
	For pladin to Robin and stuff to Gris 2lb. 6s. .	2	6	0
	For bustin 2℔. 8, for flanell 2℔. 2s. 3 ells lace 2℔. 14s. .	6	14	0
	For blew shirts litting and Grises goun litting .	3	0	0
	For linin 17s. For making Grises goun 3℔. stokins 11s. .	4	8	0
Decmr.	To Mr. Robert Blackwood per acount	22	3	0
	To Lapairl tags for crap	1	0	0
		S. 914	0	0

	[Clothing]	[Scots]		
	Deburst for cloathes for 1696.	£	s.	d.
January	For 10 ells Flanen at 16s. per ell	8	0	0
	For gloves to Grisie 9s. 6d. en ell flanen	1	13	0
	For linin for litle cloathes .	[illegible]	1[illegible]	0
	For 2 pair understokens .			
	For stokens to Gris .			
	To mor linin for litle cloathes			
Febr. 10	To muslin for 3 napkens .			
	For a pair understokins .			
	For shoes to Grisi: 10s. F.		1	
Ditto 28	For my childs dead linen [1]	1		
	For pladin to Rachy 1l. 3s. linin for her froks and for shirts	10	3	0
	For camrick to slives	[illegible]	14	0
	For linin to be shirts	1	0	
	For a muslin cravat . . .	1	16	
	For shoes 2l. 18s. . . .		18	
	For a long wig from Manson	2	0	
	For a blew cock to a hat, For shoes to Grisie and a bongrace	2	12	0
	For 2 ells muslin for a cravat	6	0	0
	For 2 ells muslin for a cravat	4	16	0
Aprill	For a blew cock to a hat, for a ruban to a staf . . .	1	11	0
	For butons to shirts, for ane apron	[illegible]	1[illegible]	0
	For 6 ounces worsit for stokens			
	For under stokens . . .			
	For a snuf napken . . .			
	For a pair shoes to my self .		1	
May	For whit bustin for a coat at 2l. per ell	10	0	0
	For a whit fring to it	3	6	0

[1] 'My Robin' died 28 February 1696, and was 'buried by his grandfather Robert Baillie in the Grafreers Churchyard 3 quarters from Mortons stone.' From a note by Lady Grisell in a book of MS. songs.

	[Clothing]	[Scots] £	s.	d.
	For whit flard bustin at 2l. 4s. the ell	11	0	0
	For 9 ells black silk stuf for a coat at 4l. 16s. the ell . . .	43	4	0
	For making Grisie a goun .	4	2	0
	For a black fring to my coat at 3s. st. the ounce . . .	27	0	0
	For a black gos hood	1	12	6
Jun.	For bustin to Jeriswoods wast-coats and furnitur to them .	6	0	0
	For 2 napkins—snuf ons .	2	3	0
July 1st	For a wige from Manson Campain	15	0	0
	For dying a coat black .	2	0	0
	For muslin for cravats 5½ ells at 3l. 3s.	26	14	0
	For shoes to my self	3	8	0
	For shirts to Rachy 2l. 12s. 6d., shirts to Gris 2l. 15s. .	5	7	6
Agst.	For stokins to Rachy 18s., Linin for drauers 4l. 10s.	5	8	0
	For 2 caps fo my sisters .	15	12	0
	For 2 ells bustin for a wast coat .	1	12	0
	For dresing a cap to Gris 3l. Shoes to her 1l. 6s.	4	6	0
	For washing 9 pairs gloves 1l. 16s. Understokens 1l. 4s. .	3	0	0
Novr.	For dresing boots 18s. for butons to wastcoats 6 duson .	1	14	0
	For 2 shoes to Gris 1l. 8s. For pladin and making cloath to Ra	3	6	0
	For making Grisis sadculerd goun and a rufflin to it	7	1	0
	For shoes to Gris 17s. tape for cloathes 10s. 6d. .	1	7	6
	For a strip flanell coat at 1l. 12s.	4	0	0
	For a sute of cloathes from John Hoburn of cloath .	81	2	0
	For an alamod skerf	20	10	00

[Clothing]		[Scots] £	s.	d.
	For stript stuf to Grisie	6	0	0
Janr.	For shoes and slipers to J	7	4	0
	For making a velvit cap 12s. to cambrick and muslin to cravats	9	12	0
	To Roses wife an account for shoes	8	2	0
		S. 476	00	00

	To the expence of cloathes 1698.	Scots		
Janr. 10 1698	To a sute of black cloathes taken of in Janr. 1697 .	54	0	0
	For a sute of black cloothes from Mr. Blackwood, Mar. 1696 .	73	15	0
Ditto	For lace to shirt hands .	26	15	0
11th	For 4¼ ells stript flanill at 1li. 16s. for 2 wastcoats . . .	7	13	0
	For muslin I bought at Preston pans	85	05	0
	For gloves to Grisy .	0	15	0
	For muslin to my self	9	14	0
	For a mask	0	18	0
	For 10 ells blew camlit to a riding coat	17	00	00
	For sowing of things when I went to England	6	00	0
	For bustin to a wastcoat	2	15	0
	For lining to Rachys shirts and drawers to Grisy 14 ells	7	04	0
	For lining bought from Ms. Abercrummy	9	5	0
	For lace to the bairens	5	07	0
	For gloves to Grisy	0	4	0
	For rabitt skins to lin briches with	0	8	0
	For making Grisies goun .	3	12	0

[Clothing]	[Scots] £	s.	d.
For shoes to Grisy	0	16	0
For gloves to Gris	1	10	0
For a bongrace to her	0	12	0
For wirsit to be stokens to her	0	15	0
For eggin	0	13	6
	S. 313	16	6

Edenburgh, January 1702. Cloathes. Debet to Cash.

		Scots		
	For 2 pair gloves to the bairens .	0	12	0
	For 3 ells lace at 18s. the ell .	2	12	0
23d	For 4 yeards white rubans to the bairens	3	16	0
	For lace to shirt hands at £3 the ell	7	10	0
	For shoes to Grisie .	1	2	0
	For boots bought from Brutheresteans	11	12	0
	For drinkmony	0	7	0
	For 2 pair gloves .	1	4	0
Febr. 27	For 3 pairt of shoes from Brutheresteans in pairt of payment at 4s. 6d. the pair .	6	10	0
	To Cowin Taylor to a pairt of his accumpt	6	10	0
	For working stokins to Jer. 18s. for on stokin 10 .	1	9	0
	For spining wirsit for stokins and ½ ℔. bought	1	16	0
	For black gloves .	1	0	0
	For 2 pair of gloves .	1	4	0
	For 20 ells Maskarad for gown and peticoat	30	0	0

	[Clothing]	[Scots] £	s.	d.
	For strip flanen coats to the bairens	4	0	0
	For serg to line a wastcoat	1	10	0
	For taill borders the bairens	0	15	0
	For linin to the bairens	2	5	0
	For a pair black gloves	0	15	0
	To calico the bairenses gowns is made of .	15	19	0
Aprill	For a wige from Shin 3 guinys .	42	12	0
	To Cop for puting up the wige and finding it for me .	1	9	0
	For wires 2s. For making up ane old goun 18 . .	1	0	0
	For 13 ells lace from Jean Cheasly	2	14	0
	For a pair of cloath shoes makıng	1	16	0
	For makeing up my old goun	0	18	0
	For a side of a night goun of strip satin	14	0	0
	For a fan	0	18	0
	For working a pair of stokins to J	1	10	0
	For plading to pice a plying of a goun . . .	0	16	0
May	For 11 ells of lace for the bairens	11	0	0
	For making Grisies and covering Rachys gouns . . .	5	0	0
	For shoes to Grisie £1, more £1 4	2	4	0
	For 24 ells stuf working at 5 per ell, etc.	7	4	0
June	For a cravat from Ramsay	7	4	0
	For 2¼ ell strip bustin for a wastcoat	2	14	0
	For gloves £2 10s., for shoes £2, muslin £4 18s. . . .	9	8	0
	For muslin to cravats	16	4	0
	For 2 pair under stokins .	3	0	0
	For 50 ells linin for shifts	50	0	0
	For holland for shirts	42	0	0

[Clothing]		[Scots] £	s.	d.
August	To Francy Newton for muslin paid accounts for cravats and childrin and my own morning	41	0	0
	For silk handcurchefs to the childrin	7	4	0
August	For 2 pair black stokins	8	14	0
29	For hatband and black gloves	5	16	0
	For calico to the childrin .	15	0	0
	For snuf handcurchefs 6 .	20	0	0
	For a black fan £1 12s. 3 masks £4	5	12	0
	For necklace and eyrrings £1 8s. white silk gloves £3 12 .	5	0	0
	For a black silk belt 18s. .	0	18	0
	For tape threed shoestrings etc. per F. N.	11	10	0
	For shoes to myself £1 16, shoes to Gris, £2	3	16	0
	For cleaning and dying the camlit goun, bairens gouns, etc.	4	4	0
	For a black sword £7 4s. for 3 quarter shed muslin 3sh. sterling	9	0	0
	For working stokings £1 10s.	1	10	0
	For a hatt £5 16s., strings 6s., butons for shirts £1, Le'pairls 14s. 6d.	7	16	6
	For threed £1 16s., for sowing by my Ant Couls[1] maid 18s.	2	14	0
	To a taylor at Mellersteans £1 18s., a pair gloves 16s. .	2	14	0
	For shoes to myself £1 16s., shoes Grisie and R[achel] £1 16s.	3	12	0
	For stokins to John Hume	0	18	0
	For 6 ells eggine .	1	10	0
	For lining to a satin night wastecoat	1	1	0

[1] A sister of George Baillie's mother married Sir Alexander Mackenzie of Coul.

[Clothing]		[Scots] £	s.	d.
Novr.	For muslin to the bairens	7	4	0
20	For 20 ells linin for ther shifts .	12	0	0
	For ther second mourning gouns last year	25	6	0
	For 11 ells black crap to line a goun .	10	0	0
	For a black crap hood .	5	8	0
d. 23	To John Haburn for hats and gloves old account	27	8	0
	For twill and burds eye for drawers	5	0	0
	For black silk cord for a necklace	0	10	0
Novr. 30	For 4 pair stokins to the bairens from Ms. Abercrumie	4	0	0
	For 9 ells blew grounded callico at	16	4	0
	For strong shoes to Mersser	3	14	0
	To Rachi's calico nightgoun from Ms. Hogg	15	1	6
	For spining wirsit at 18s. per lb	0	18	0
Decmr.	From strong shoes from Merser [*sic*]	3	14	0
	For 2 spinell wirsit for stuff	2	10	0
	For a belt to Grisie	0	18	0
	For pins 6s., to a taylor 8s., gloves 5s.	0	19	0
	For a muff to Rachy .	0	18	0
30	For a sute black cloth $2\frac{3}{4}$ ells at £13 10s.	37	2	6
	For 11 ells black linin for 2 sutes £1 2s. .	11	16	6
	For $5\frac{1}{2}$ ells black shagrin at £3 6s.	18	9	0
	For 6 ells lace . .	6	0	0
	For shoes at Kelso to the bairens	5	2	0
	For a white satin paticoat from Lisie Rainalds . . .	24	0	0
		S. 729	2	0

Edinburgh, January 1st 1707. Cloathes. Deb.
to Cash. [Scots]

	For a pair boots from Mersser .	12	0	0
	To Merssers man .	0	7	0
	To Merstone 2 pair Campagn shoes	7	8	0
	To him for a pair marican, ap: calf lather	5	8	0
	For my Poplin goun and coat	97	0	0
	For helping my Tipper £1 16s., safer for the juell £1 10	3	6	0
	For stript muslin for heads £5, more £4 5s., more £2 12s., £2 5s.	14	2	0
	For shoes to Rachy lac'd £2 8s., serg tair border 16s. .	3	4	0
	For strips to J.	1	4	0
	For serge for lining . .	4	4	0
	For a duson kids to my self at Pearth 12sh., 6 pair to Rach: 6s. 6d.	11	2	0
	To drink mony to a taylor 14s. 6d.	3	12	6
April	For last somers drogat dying and stokins	7	0	0
	For 9 ells drogat dy'd over again	1	16	0
	For a pair stokins dying	1	5	0
	For shoes to Rachy £1 1s., 2 black neckleses 8s.	1	10	0
	For eggin £2 13s., washing 3 pair gloves 10s., 6s. 6d., 6s. 6d	3	16	0
	For black ruban to slives £1 6s., 3s.	1	9	0
	For stokins £1 8s., silk 7s., threed 8s. 6d., 1s. 6d.	1	17	0
	For a taylor in the house £1 8s. .	1	8	0
	For patches 6s., blew serg for Grisies coat helping £1 1s. .	1	7	0
	For mending the bairens dust-gouns	1	12	0

[Clothing]	[Scots] £	s.	d.
For gloves £2 4s., £2 8s. 6d.	4	12	6
For 3 ells black silk for aprons at 8s. per ell . .	15	12	0
For rubans to the borders and strings of the aprons .	1	5	10
For cotton threed 3s. 10d., shoes 3s. 6d.	0	7	4
For ane ell plain muslin £3 6s., threed 5 8d. . .	3	11	8
For linin to Rachys calls [?collars] 11s., for 11 ell linin for 6 shifts to her	6	11	0
For muslin to Grisie £2 16 gas handcurchefs £5 14 for 2	8	10	0
For a pair black silk gloves £3 6s.	3	6	0
To Grisell Robison for sowing	3	12	6
For a big staind satin nightgoun	48	0	0
For 18¼ ell egin at 11s. 6d. per ell £10 10s. more £2 4s. 8d. .	12	14	8
For 10 ells satin to line Grisies taby goun . .	26	0	0
For Scots muslin for night cloathes	5	6	0
For a hatt £4 4s., shoes £2 18s stokins £1	8	2	0
For gloves to the bairens and myself last year .	18	12	0
For stript muslin £13 14s. 6d., eggin £13 10s.	27	4	0
For threed 10s., 3s. 6d., 3s., 4s., 14s., tape 6s. stentin 4s. 4d., threed 8s. 4s.	2	17	2
For 8½ ell camlit for sourtoot 4d., butons to it £3 6 per el, £3 4	21	1	0
For sarge to line the coat	9	0	0
For stokins £1 4s., a handcurcher black and white £1 9	2	13	0

[Clothing]	[Scots] £	s.	d.
For fine musline a sute £7 17s. 6, 2½ strip camrik £4 10 .	12	7	6
For 1½ muslin for Bachy	4	7	0
For shoes to Grisie and Rachy made by John Blyth .	8	18	0
For 1 ell[?] musline to Rachy £3 6s.	3	6	0
For threed £2 10s., laces 15s., tape 2s. 4d., knitins 10s. .	2	17	4
For 3 ell linin for calls £3, 3 ell Scots cambrick plain .	2	8	0
For 14 ells stript Scots cambrick, different prices . . .	20	10	0
For shoes 5s. 6d., nidles 4s. 6d., a comb 11s., shoes 6s.	1	7	0
For a belt to Grisi 18s., knitons 5s., nidles 3s. ¼ 100 . .	1	6	0
For threed and silk 15s., p. tape 7s., ruban 6s., pins 7s. 2s. .	1	17	0
For a scor linin for drawers	10	16	0
For a pair slipers £1 6s., half ell moskarad 11s., threed 6	1	17	6
For 6 ells silk waltins	0	18	0
For 25 ells cloath for shirts to my self and the bairenses shirts at £1 2s. 6, 26 ells at £1 6d., 21 ell at 10s. per ell for drawers	55	0	0
For 2 ell plain cambrick	3	18	10
For ane ell stript cambrick and ane ell musline .	3	5	0
For a black lace 9s., a pair wirsite under stokens . . .	1	10	0
To Will Cowin taylore	40	0	0
For a pair threed stokens 13s. 6d. riding stokens 14s.	1	7	0
For 18 ells Holland £2 19 per ell for shirts	53	2	0
For 2 ells cambrick . . .	3	8	0

	[Clothing]	[Scots] £	s.	d.
	For 4 ells lace at 3sh. per ell	7	4	0
	For 24 shirts sowing at 3s. per pice, etc.	4	12	0
	For silk 13s., tape pins £1, yellow ruban £2 2s.	3	15	0
	For one ell ¼ kelt for gramashes	2	5	0
	For 12 ells unblitcht linin at 12s. per ell . .	7	4	0
	For 20 ell drogate bought by Milne	3	0	0
Octr.	For 21 ell Holland from Francis Newton, shirts .	62	16	0
	For a lutstring hood of 2¼ ell from ditto	8	2	0
	For calico to the bairenses 2 gouns outsid and in .	18	18	6
	For a lutstring hood 2¼	8	2	0
	For 2 ells Holland 4s. 8	5	12	0
Octor. 3	For 10 ells musline and a half for sutes from Francis Newton since Martimas last at sundry prices	34	6	6
	For a black gaz hood £2 5, black gloves 2 pair £2 6s.	4	11	0
	For 11¼ ell fin cambrick for ruffils at sundry prices from Francis Newton since Martimas last	52	14	6
	For rubans in ditto time F. N.	27	7	0
	For 2 fans £2 8s. 2 p.	2	8	0
	For patons £2 8	2	8	0
	For threed lupin pins, etc.	23	16	0
	For 10 ell stript musline at 6s. 6d. per ell, 10 ell plain muslin 6s. 6d., 10 ell stript at 6s. got from Francie Newton and taken to London with me .	114	0	0
	For 4 ell lace to shirts	7	4	0

[Clothing]		[Scots]		
		£	s.	d.
Oct. 3d	For cloathes in full of all accounts to Will Cowin . . .	50	0	0
	For a sute black cloathes from Sr. Ro: Blackwood .	72	0	0
		S. 1171	8	10

Mellerstaines, January 1710. Cloathes. Deb. to Cash.

		Stg.	
For cloathes to Grisie and Rachell in Edinburgh when they were in morning	12	14	0
For cloathes to my self in Edinburgh	0	15	0
For gloves to Jerriswood .	0	17	0
For patches pins etc.	0	2	0
For a stone gray cloath petticoat	1	10	0
For some small things at Kelso for my mornins . . .	0	5	6
For black cloath to help my goun	1	05	0
For black shoes 2 pair .	0	6	0
For plain musline .	1	1	8
For love hood 10s., black gloves 4s. 6d.	0	14	6
For black silk gloves 6s., vellam 1s., serge 2s.	0	9	0
For stokins 2s. 6d., plain shoes 3s. 4d.	0	5	10
For Grisie and Rachy musline .	2	0	0
For cloath to help Grisies goun .	1	5	0
For shoes to Rachie 6s., stokins 2s. 6d.	0	8	6
For a neckles 10d. .	0	0	10
For a gas napken 5s., lining silk to help a goun	0	7	9

	[Clothing]	[Sterling] £	s.	d.
24 14 1	For silk gloves to Rachell	0	6	0
17 0	For ruban 6d. all the abovesaid for mornings excep for gloves			
23 71 1	17s.	0	0	6
	For 8 ells holland for Grisies goun at 6s. 6d.	2	12	0
March 1	For pins threed, etc.	0	2	6
	For 4 yard plain musline at 5s. 6d. per yard	1	2	0
Ap. 4th	For 5 ell prying to Rachys night goun	0	3	0
	For 5½ ell plying to my callico goun	0	3	10¾
	For lining to help nightcloathes	0	0	8¾
	For bustine for pokets .	0	2	6
	For 6½ ell cambrick for night-cloathes	1	18	9
	For 2 pair gloves to Rachy	0	2	0
May 31	To William Dickson taylor for 15 days	0	5	0
	For a silk lace . .	0	1	0
	For 40 ells linin for shifts and aprons at 2s. the ell from James Ainsly	2	0	0
	For 17 ells linin for drawers at 1sh. 4d. from James Ainsly	1	2	8
August	For 40 ells linin for Grisies shifts from Lithgow . . .	5	0	0
	For pins, etc.	0	2	0
Aug. 16	For holland cambrick musline and severall other things at Grisies mariage as per Francis Newtons account	38	11	0
	For altering two gouns by Finlisone	0	5	0
	For 20 ells linins for the bairens's shifts	1	13	4

[Clothing]	[Sterling] £	s.	d.
For 21 ells linin for my own shifts at 2sh. 4d.	2	9	0
For musline for night cloathes, ruffles, tukers, etc.	3	4	0
For 2 snuf handkerchiefs	[illegible]	[illegible]	[illegible]
For a silk handkerchief .			
For 2 litle blew and white napkins			
For gloves for Jerriswood			
For shoes to Rachell			
For a pair of boots from Messer	1	0	0
For drinkmony to his man and for liquering boots .	0	01	0
For gloves to Rachy 6s., washing gloves 2s. . .	0	8	0
For gloves to Jerriswood 2sh., washing gloves 4sh. 8d.	0	6	8
To Grisie Lamb for sowing shirts at 3d.½ per pice . . .	0	2	8
For black silk for ane apron at 6sh.	0	9	0
For gloves 1s. 6d., working frienge to my aprone 6d $\frac{6}{12}$	0	2	0 $\frac{6}{12}$
To Mr. Weems for my Tabie goun and coat and lining .	11	7	0
For sowing Grisies holland coat 18s. the ell square	2	12	6
For a pice musline got from Provist Broun 1705	5	10	0
For gloves from Liviston at Grisies marriage	4	10	0
For altering two gouns to Rachy by Ms. Duncan .	2	0	0
For 6¾ ells fine lace at 26sh. per ell for a head sute to Rachy from Lewis Pringle . . .	8	15	6
For a taill border to Grisies sowed coat	0	5	6

	[Clothing]	[Sterling] £	s.	d.
	For severall small things such as pines, tape, threed, etc. .	0	8	6
	For a pice knitins . . .	0	0	6
	For Grisies brids favorits .	3	10	6
	For 4 ells ruban 12s. and silver tasels 10s. for her brids garters	1	2	0
	For ruband for the brids garland thats brock over her head	0	3	0
	For a head sute fine laces to Grisie £10 9s. 9d., ruffels £5 8s. .	15	17	9
	For lace to shift tuckers and egins, etc. . . .	15	6	0
	For Grisies best night cloathes and ruffles	3	12	0
	For a linin to the sow'd goun .	3	16	0
	For two pices of holland by Ms. Crafford	9	9	0
	For a headsute of narrow lace to Grisie and ruffles . . .	4	10	0
	For lace for tuckert and egin .	2	10	0
	For fine musline for Grisies apron and heads, etc. .	1	14	0
	For rubans to Grisies night cloathes . .	0	12	0
	For ruffels to Rachys fine head .	[illegible]	[illegible]	[illegible]
Aug:	For egine to a sute to Rachy .			
	For sowing linins at the mariage			
	For a gold and white handkerchieff			
	For Grisies slipers . . .			
	For 2 pair slipers and a pair shoes			
	For gloves at the mariage from Ms. Burn	1	0	0
	To Ms. Lyon manto makers account	1	0	0
	For shoes to Jerriswood	0	5	0
	For a hatt at the mariage	0	9	0
	For a sute cloathes trim'd with silver for Grisie, a sute trim'd			

[Clothing]	[Sterling] £	s.	d.
with silk to Rachy, a skerff to each, and stokins, shoes, rubans, fans and handkerchieffs and 3 big night gouns and stays for Grisies mariage .	112	8	6
For small things from Char: Ormstons	0	7	4
For green satine to Grisies peticoat	2	7	3
For gold galoun to the green peticoat	1	6	3
	S. 315	1	9

London, January 1st, 1717. Account of my Dearests Cloathes.

		Stg.		
	For 5 yd cloath at 17s. 6d..	4	7	6
	For 5 yd black cloath at 17s.	4	[illegible]	0
feb. 28	For a hat	1		
	For scouring 2 pr stokens	0		
	For silk stokens . . .	0	1	
	For a seabert to a sword	0		
	For Black gloves 16d.			
	For a Duson of gloves .	0	1	0
	For Musline for Cravats at 7s.	3	5	6
	For makeing 3 suts cloath by Whisle at 2 guinys the sute I furnishing linin and buttons to coat and wastcoat .	6	9	0
	For some linin he bought for the cloathes .	1	8	
March 2	For a wige from Robert Boe	3	4	6
	For 16 yd shagreen at 3s. 6d.	2	16	
	For 15 yd drogat at 3s. 6d.	2	12	6
May 28	For 16 yd shagreen for the sute			

	[Clothing]	[Sterling] £	s.	d.
	and 6 yd for the Bragad wastcoat	4	4	0
	For a yd more linin to the wastcoat	0	3	6
	For 3 pr under stokens 10s. 6d., 2 pr stryps 6s. .	0	16	6
	For 3½ yd Gold Brogade for a wastecoat	10	10	0
	For a wige	3	4	6
	For a pair silk stokens .	0	17	0
	For cleaning stuff coats, cleaning black cloathes 1s. . . .		2	0
	For 4 pr shoes from Broun	1	4	0
	For mending a sword	0	1	0
	For gloves 8s. 8d. . .	0	8	8
	For 3d. 3 buttons at 2s. 6d. 3d.½ at 12d. 2 wastbands 3d.	0	11	10 6/12
	For a hatt 1£ 1s. 6d., 2 hair skins 3s., another 3s. .	1	7	6
	For a pair silk stokins 15s., scouring cloathes 2s. 6d. .	0	17	6
	For a cotton satine goun 2£	2	0	0
wrong	For a glas weight for Lady Margrat Hamilton	0	7	0
	For holland from Cycell Wray	1	4	10
	For a powdering goun .	0	10	2
Edenburgh	For 2 wigs bought at Edn: 2£ 10 and 1£ 5		15	0
	For a wig from Bowie octr last .	3	3	0
	For 6 pr gloves 7s. 6d., a pair stokens 15s. . . .	1	2	6
	For Holland for shirts	2	8	0
	For rubans, etc. 8s. .	0	8	0
	For shoes 1£ 10 .	1	10	0
	For Black Cloath from Elliot	4	9	3
	S.	76	10	9

London, January 1st, 1717. Account of my own Cloathes.

	Stg.		
	£	s.	d.
For 27 yd White Indian quilting at 4s. 6d. and 5s. 6d. .	4	13	6
For dying my green goun 7s., my callico and lining scowring	0	6	0
For glazing my white lining 1s. and the green above not drawn out	0	8	0
For 8 yd lining to the green at 5s. 6d. . . .	2	4	0
For gloves washing 1s., hood washing 1s. . . .	0	2	0
For 2 ounces threed and tape	0	2	6
For $1\frac{3}{4}$ yd cambrick for a sute at 11s. pr yd	0	18	3
For a girdle 1s., washing 3 hoods 18d., gloves 2s .	0	4	6
For 5 yd white callico at 28d. a yd	0	11	8
For 9 pr gloves 18s. 9d., silk gloves 6s. 3d.	1	5	0
For $2\frac{1}{2}\frac{1}{8}$ yd lann at 4s. 6d., 10s. 6d., sowing 4 shifts 6s. 8d. . .	0	17	2
For Dutch Manto to be body and slives to my black goun 6s. 3d.	0	9	0
For satine laceing 1s., pluf 6d., a cypres hood 2s. . .	0	3	6
For some small things 3s., pins 1s.	0	4	0
For a pair gloves 2s. 2d., 2 pair stokins at 7s. and 5s. .	0	14	2
For $1\frac{1}{2}$ yd cloath for a peticoat .	1	8	6
For 14 yd egin at 5s. 6d. 3 19 9			
For a yd $\frac{3}{4}$ $\frac{1}{8}$ lan at 1 2 6			
For Musline and making a handkerchief . 0 2 6			

	[Clothing]	[Sterling] £ s. d.
	For a wire makeing and starching ye head 0 . 4 6	
		5 9 3
	For a floorisht hood and Apron .	0 13 0
	For a yd Cambrick . . .	0 10 0
	For a Marsyls wastcoat	1 0 0
	For 2 pr Cotten slives 2s., a pair green shoes and lace 6s.	0 8 0
	For Holland for shirts at 4s. 6d.	1 17 0
	For dying a pr stokins 1s. .	0 1 0
	For egine at 5s. 6d. valentians ground and severall other things from Mrs. Pearks this is above inceart.	
	For a fan 2s. 5s., lan at 12s. 1£ 5s. 6d., alamed hood 8s. .	2 0 6
	For a pr green lacd shoes 6s., plain 3s.	0 9 0
	For 6 snuff handkerchieff at 28d. pr piece	0 14 0
	For 25¾ yd Green strypt Lutstring at 10s.	12 17 6
	For 5 combs 9s., sweat waters 2s., lace for shoes 11d.	0 11 11
	For silk gloves 6s. 3d., more for gloves 18s, more 16s. . . .	2 0 3
	For 9 yd green lutstring for linin and ane aprone .	3 3 0
	For making my scarlet peticoat 4s., 2 pr threed stokins 6s. .	0 8 0
June 28	To Mrs. Lindsay Manto maker in full of all accounts	6 4 6
	For a piece satine 14½ yd ¾ broad	4 10 0
	For a piece pertian of 10 yds .	3 2 6
	For 9 yd green lutstring 3£ 3s. 22 yd pench 3£ 4s. 6d. .	6 7 6
	For ½ piece pertian 1 12s. 3d.,	

	[Clothing]	[Sterling] £	s.	d.
	girdles 10s., scowring white linin 2s. 6d. . .	2	4	9
	For 2 allamod hoods 1£, a gass hood 6s., rose ruban 2s. 6d	1	8	6
	For 2 pieces chints 10 a pice scarlet Damask 5£	15	0	0
Aug. 3d	For a yellow satine night goun 2£ 8d., a pr stays 2£, opening body 10s. . . .	4	18	0
	For linin from old silk shop to this day . .	7	0	0
	For Camrick frome Cicel Wray, etc.	4	0	0
Aug. 5	To Mrs. Lindsay manta maker in full of all accounts to this day . .	4	4	0
Edinr,	For some things bought by May Menzies, Lond: . . .	[illegible]	4	0
Sept. 3	For gloves from Livingston kids 2, lambs 14d .	4	12	0
	For severall small things at my Rachys mariage . . .	4	0	0
	S.	116	9	11

London, January 1st, 1717. Account of my Grisies Cloath.

	Stg.		
For a green and gold Attles	16	0	0
For 8 yd green lutstring for lining it at 6s. 3d. . .	2	10	0
For 11 yd fring for a head sute at 8d.	0	9	4
For gloves washing 1s., 1s. 6d.	0	2	6
For a white Apron 6s. 6d.	0	6	6
For 5 years green lutstring for a skerf at 6s. 3d. . . .	1	11	6

[Clothing]	[Sterling]		
	£	s.	d.
For making the skerf by Mrs. Gray	0	7	0
For a scarlet apron 7s. 6d. .	0	7	6
For 27 yd Black velvet for goun and coat at 17s. .	22	19	0
For 8 yd Black Italian Lutstring lining .	2	10	0
For severall small things 8s., a girdle 1s. .	0	9	0
For 18 yd white Persian for the Caposhins dress . . .	1	13	0
For 6 yd ruban 3s. 9d., pins 1s.	0	4	9
For 10 yd fringe at 8d. .	0	6	8
For gloves 18d. 15d.	0	3	9
For 11 yd quilting for coats at 5s. 6d.	3	0	6
For dying the blew Damask goun without a linin .	0	7	0
For Green Ruban at 9d., 2s. 3d., fan 3s., a hook 6d.	0	6	6
For 22 yd green and white stript Armozeen at 13sh.	14	6	0
For 4 snuff handkerchiefs at 28d.	0	9	4
For combs 3s., lining to a peticoat 7s.	0	10	0
For dying peticoat linin 3s., 5 yd Damity 10	0	13	0
For a pair buckles 3s. 9d., a visard 6d.	0	4	3
For small things 4s. 10d., a duson gloves 1£ 5s. . . .	1	9	10
For thick Musline 9s., a Hoop 1£	1	9	0
For boning a hoop 5s., a pair threed stokins 6s. 6d., shoes 16s.	1	7	6
To Mrs. Lindsay Manta maker in full to this day . . .	5	6	0
For blew ruban 4s., shoes 11s., fan 18d., hat 10d. . . .	1	6	6

	[Clothing]	[Sterling] £	s.	d.
	For 12½ yd. Gindgum ell broad for a goun	2	10	0
	For .girdles 9s., green lutstring 9s. 8d., a glas weight 5s.	1	3	8
	For half piece china taffito 2£ 17s. 6d., a girdle 2s., wires 1s..	3	0	6
	For ½ piece pertian to Grisies old chinse 1£ 12s. 3d. . . .	1	12	3
	For black egine 5s. 6d., white egin 6s. 4d., ruban 2s. 6d. . .	0	14	4
	For shoes 6s., lining hatt 1s., white Damask goun scowring 6	0	13	0
	For ane alamad hood 10s., small things 5s., more 2s.	0	17	0
	For scouring wraping goun 4s. 6d threed 1s., laceing 1s.	0	6	6
	For a dusone of gloves 1£ 8s., shoes 14s. 6d., fans 6s. 6d.	1	19	0
	For 4 yd crimson ruban 3s. 4d., a piece chints 5£ . . .	5	3	4
	For 8 yerds gingem to line the gingem goun	1	0	0
	For a piece gellow Damask, ½ a piece Taffita	7	10	0
	For covering breast wt white tabie 5s. p jumps 10	0	15	0
	For dressing box 1£ 12s. 3d., lace from Mrs. Dessliger	4	18	9
Aug. 3	For lutstring for gouns and linins from old silk shop	11	0	2
	For camirick 1£ 4s., gloves 6s	1	10	0
Aug 5	To Mrs. Lindsay Manta maker in full of all acctts .	3	0	0
	For Clasps	0	3	0
Sep. 3d	For sundry things bought by May Minzies	2	13	6
	For sundry things to her at her sisters mariage . . .	7	14	0

[Clothing]	[Sterling]		
For Gloves from Livinston kids	£	s.	d.
2s., La: [lambs] 14d .	4	12	0
For 2 pieces Indian Pertian	5	19	0
For 2 pr shoes at 16sh. . .	1	12	0
S.	£151	2	11

Account of money given Rachel Dundas.

	For shoes	0	4	6
	For 26 yd white Cotten satine at 2s. 9d., 12 yd white sesnet 27sh.	5	0	2
	For 6 pair gloves I give her .	0	12	6
	To Piter Hambly for a pice of Chints	6	0	0
April	To her	1	12	0
	For ¾ lace 2s.	0	2	0
	To her by Captain Turnbull, etc., in Scotland	3	5	0
11	For a pice chints	5	0	0
	To her	2	2	0
	S.	23	8	2

London, January 1st, 1717. Account of My Rachy's cloath. Stg.

For a cherie handkerchieff .	0	3	6
For washing gloves 1s., Fan 9s. .	0	1	9
For Fans 5s. 6d. more 7s. 6d. 2s., more 9s..	0	15	9
For a duson and 3 pr gloves .	1	12	3
For a scarlet Apron 7s. pr yd old silk shop	0	7	0
For 27 yd velvet at 17s. .	22	19	0
For 8 yd black Italian Lining for it at 6s. 3d.	2	10	0
For 10½ yd fring for a sute at 8d.	0	7	0

[Clothing]	[Sterling] £	s.	d.
For 1¼ yd thick Musline at 5s. .	0	6	3
For 3 yd pink ruban 2s. 6d., a girdle 1s. . .	0	3	9
For sundry small things .	0	10	0
For 18 yds white persian at 22d. pr yd for her Caposhin dress at the Maskarad . . .	1	13	0
For 12 yd white semet for the Damask goun . . .	1	7	0
For 6 yd rubans 3s. 9d., pins 1s. .	0	4	0
For gloves washing 18d., gloves 2s.	0	1	
For ane Alamod hood		9	
For 10 yd fring . . .		6	
For dresing a head by Mrs. Tuer		2	
For 24 yd Rid and silver stuff at 22s., 8 yd lining . . .	30	6	0
For 7 yerds Indian quilting at 5s. 6d.	1	18	6
For dying the rid damask goun yellow wt out linin .	0	7	0
For scouring the pillen linin and peticoat	0	5	0
For narow valentians lace at 11s. lane 12 makeing, etc.	5	7	0
For a girdle 6s., ane ell ruban 7s.	0	13	0
For cambrick and makeing a sute head cloathes and Ruf .	0	19	0
For Fans 9s., a stra hat 10s., floors 7s., Mask 2s.. . . .	1	8	0
For green lac'd shoes 7s., for 2 snuff handkerchiefs .	0	4	8
For combs 3s., fan 2s., hooks and pendons 3s. 6d. . . .	0	8	6
For rid galoun 5s., rid silk 3d., green silk stokins 11s. 6d.	0	16	9
For lace to shoes 1s., sundry small things 4s. 10 .	0	4	10

[Clothing]	[Sterling]		
	£	s.	d.
For a gase handkerchief 2s., raffleing and mounting a 3£ fan 25s.	1	7	0
For a duson of Gloves 1£ 5s., a Hoop 1£ . .	2	5	0
For 8 yd Indian chekerd linin cald to a Best [?] goun at 2s. 7d. .	1	0	8
For a Riding goun .	2	15	0
For boning a hoop 5 rubans 4s., fan 18d. 3 girdles 9s.	0	19	6
To Mrs. Lindsay Mantua maker in full of all accounts .	1	15	6
For a dresing box 1£ 12s. 3d., green lutstring 9s. 8d. .	2	1	11
For ½ piece china taffita 2£ 17s. 6d, a glas weight 5d., girdles 2s. .	3	4	6
For 4 girdles 12s. 6d., lace Mrs. Waird 1s. 4d., laceing 9d. .	0	14	7
For ruban 2s. 6d., 8 yds lace Mrs. Ward, etc. 2£ 7s. 6d.	2	10	0
For lining a hat 1s., scowring white Damask goun 6 . .	0	7	0
For gloves 6s., shoes at 16s., and slipers 2£ 3s. . . .	2	9	0
For shoes by Reinolds .	2	12	0
For a cloath hat to her riding habite . .	0	13	0
For a naturall black hair wige from Boe		1	6
For 36 yd Holland from Mr. Lind	12	7	6
For ane Alamad hood 10, a pair stokins 6s. a roll 18d. . .	0	17	6
For 1½ yd Damity for pokets 2s. 6d., small things 5s., more 2s..	0	9	6
For robings to a goun 4s. 6d., threed 1s.	0	5	6
For a white satine quilted coat .	2	15	0

	[Clothing]	[Sterling] £	s.	d.
	For a yellow pertian quilted coat	1	15	0
	For 2 dusone 4 pr gloves at 2s. 8d. pr D	3	7	4
	For a pr tickine shoes .	0	5	0
	For 2 Callico Aprons 10 3 jepsies 13s. 2d.	1	3	2
	For laceing 18d., 4 yds crimson ruban 3s. 4d., wires 6d. . .	0	5	4
	For a piece chints 5£, another piece 5£ got befor . .	10	0	0
	For 16 yd gingem for a goun .	2	0	0
	For a pr white stays 2£, covering a pr on breast 5s. . .	2	5	0
	For a pr jumps yellow canves sticht wt green 10 .	0	10	0
	For satine with silver shoes from Green	0	15	0
	For 12 yd rid and white silk at 7s. for wraping goun .	4	4	0
	For 8 yd white lutstring for lining the goun at 5s. 6d. .	2	4	0
	For 20 yd black lutstring at 6s. 3d. for linings and aprons	3	5	0
	For 4d. white sesnet hoods 12s. 8d. more lutstring old silk shop all	1	9	2
	For lining to the old chints goun 1£ 12s. 3d.	1	12	3
	For a sute laces at 4£ from Mrs. Devliger .	30	9	6
	For lace to Night cloathes, Apron, shift, etc. . .	16	4	0
	For $5\frac{3}{4}$ Cambrick .	3	9	0
	For Cambrick night cloathes and ruffles	4	1	6
	For handkerchiefs 2£ 10 .	2	10	0
Aug. 5	To Mrs. Lindsay mantua maker in full of all .	4	9	0

	[Clothing]	[Sterling] £	s.	d.
	For lace and cambrick, etc., from Mers. Perks	11	0	0
Eden-burgh	For 9 yd Dayaper from Rob. Manderson . .	0	12	0
	For sundry things bought by May Minzies . . .	4	18	5
Sep. 3d	For Linins and sowing and gloves and sundry other things at Edn. at her Mariage . . .	36	10	0
	For Bryds favours[1] . .	3	0	0
	For the Brids Garter[1] .	1	3	0
	For the Garland that is brock over the Brids head[1] . .	1	1	6
	For 25 yeards silver stuff for goun and coat	41	5	0
	For a green Podisoy hood and Mantle Trimd wt Gold .	12	10	0
	For a Cotten Satine Night goun to Lord Binning	2	10	0
	For 8 yd lutstring for the silver stuff goun . . .	2	12	0
	For lutstring to slives and necks of gouns	0	9	0
	For a sute loup'd laces from Mrs. Tempest	28	9	0
	S.	361	12	3

1718	My Rachys childs cloathes.	Stg.		
Aug. 16	To Mrs. Lindsay in full	1	0	0
	For scouring gouns .	0	12	0
	For mending lace 5s., a hook 1s.	0	6	0
	For child Bed Linins and every thing she wanted . .	74	4	3
Novr. 19	For egine Mrs. Tempest .	1	4	0

[1] See p. xlv.

[Clothing]				[Sterling]		
				£	s.	d.
For ½ piece jueling for childs day vests				0	16	0
For cleaning a goun py'd Whitson				0	4	0
For quilting a goun .				1	10	6
For 2 baskets . . .				0	6	
For litle wastcoats 3s. .				0	3	
For egins for 3 sute litle cloathes				5	11	
For 4 p. litle threed Mittons .				0	2	
To Mrs. Childs account coats and froks .				4	11	6
For holland from Lind .				4	19	0
For 6 sute litle linins besids the egines				4	15	0
To Mrs. Perks for egins for 3 suts				5	15	9
For a Bed table and chair from Moor						
For more eggine . .				1	10	0
For 4¼ yd Podisoy for a cloack	2	13	0			
For scarlet sesnet at 3s. 6d. .	1	0	0			
				3	13	0
For makeing the clock the lace my own				0	4	0
For loops to the goun				0	9	0
For more eggine .				0	11	6
a pair white shoes with silver .				0	16	0
				113	3	6

Debursments in bussines 1692. Scots

December 27 To Mr. William Chiesly[1] per receipt for Drumkairn's bussi-

[1] William Chieslie of Cockburn, W.S.

	[Business Charges, etc.]	[Scots]		
	nes and extracting ane act against the tenant in Easton .	58	00	00
ditto 30	To Mr. William Chiesly for expeding the gift of Ballancriefs warde[1]	58	0	0
1693 July	To Broun messenger for citing of Tersonce	11	4	0
Sept. 30	To Nicoll Somervill agent for William Melvill, merchant, for ane attestation of the best assignation granted by Banjamin Wirsely	34	16	0
Octr. 2	To Mr. William Chiesly for infefting me in Wariston's Land	21	6	0
	To a consultation in the bussines of Landrick	24	0	0
Novr. 22	To Mr. Chiesly for raising a sommonds for proveing the tenuer of some writs relating to Ridhall	20	0	0
Decmr. 9	To Mr. Chiesly to consult Mr. Brody in Meldrum's affair	11	0	0
ditto 26	To Mr. Chiesly for informations in Landrick affair .	8	8	0
1694 Januar 3	To Mr. Chiesly for extracting decriets against Lanrick, Meldrum and Kemne, per receipt	56	0	0
Ditto 8	To consult Lenrick bussiness .	28	10	0
24	To the decector of the Chancery for passing of my gift of genarell receaver[2]	46	0	0

[1] A grant of ward entitled the grantee to draw the rents of an estate held 'ward' of the Crown, the owner of which was dead, during the minority of the heir, under burden always of the alimony of the heir, widow's terce, etc. The tenure of ward was abolished in 1747 in consequence of the ''45.' In the present case the grant was made for the minority of Alexander Hamilton, heir of his father James Hamilton.

[2] Salary £300.

[Business Charges, etc.]		[Scots] £	s.	d.
	To the servants of the abovsaid .	6	0	0
	To the keeper and under keeper of the great seall and purs dues	100	0	0
	To expences at the privie seall .	13	4	0
Febr. 28	To Mr. Chieslys man Rob Young	8	12	0
May 9	To him for ane execution of arristment against Meldrums tenets . .	14	0	0
July	To Mr. Chieslys servants .	6	0	0
August 2	To Mr. William Chiesly to acount, per receipt . .	240	0	0
23	To Mr. Chiesly per receipt .	40	0	0
	To Mr. Chiesly for a sommonds of valuation of the tinds of Mellersteans .	5	16	0
	For writting memorialls about the poll	2	8	0
Decm.	To 3 consultations with the Kings advocat [1] 2 in Duck Gordons business and on in the tinds of Mellersteans	100	16	0
1695 Feb^r 22	To Mr. Chiesly for Meldrums bussines, per receipt .	100	0	0
	To his men for informations writing .	4	16	0
March 11	To Sir Archibald Moor [2] he gave out in the Duck of Gordons bussines .	43	10	0
	To the sheriffe clark in Aberdien to take infeftment in Meldrums Land 40lib, expences sending ther 4lib 4s. . . .	44	4	0

[1] Sir James Stewart, whose curious actings at the time of the Revolution earned him the sobriquet of 'Wily Jamie.'

[2] Probably Sir Archibald Muir of Thornton, afterward Provost of the city of Edinburgh.

[Business Charges, etc.]		[Scots] £ s. d.
August	To Mr. Chiesly per receipt	66 13 4
Novr. 1st	To Adam Urwin . .	72 0 0
	To Mr. Chiesly to get out the decreat about the hows .	9 8 0
	To a consultation in Duck Gordon bussines	64 2 0
	For executing a sommond	3 4 0
	To Patrick Christy at the infeftment takeing . . .	2 10 00
	Take out Mr. Cheslys mony.	
	lent first . 240 0 0	
	It. more per recept 40 0 0	
	It. more per recept 66 13 4	
	346 13 4	
	The sume of all the rest is	S. 976 14 0

Debursments in bussiness, 1697.		Scots
January	To Sir Gilbert[1] 5 guinys .	0075 00 00
	To Sir Gilberts man for writing informations in the bussiness of Ridhall	0001 09 00

[1] Sir Gilbert Elliot of Minto practised first as a writer in Edinburgh, acting as agent for William Veitch, the convenanting minister, and for the Earl of Argyll, whose escape he secured. He took a leading part in arranging Argyll's Rising, and was actually in arms with him, but escaped abroad. Having obtained a pardon, he passed for the Bar in November 1688 (having failed to pass the examination in the preceding July), was made a Baronet in 1700, and became a judge under the title of Lord Minto in 1705. He and his wife were evidently intimate friends of the Baillies, as much 'drink-money' is entered as having been left at Minto, and it was to Lady Minto that Baillie gave the commission, which evidently caused some amusement at the time, and which is referred to by Mrs. Calderwood (twenty years after his death), viz. 'to get him a fine house at the Cross of Edinburgh with a large garden behind it, that he might both have the pleasure of seeing the street and walking in his own garden.'—*Coltness Collections*.

	[Business Charges, etc.]	[Scots] £ s. d.
Di. 7th	To the clerks and servants for the dues of a decreet of making aristed goods forthcoming against the tenents of Meldrum	0012 07 00
	To the Signit for horning and punding on the decritt .	0001 16 00
	To Jo: Russell for seeking out the process for proving the tener of writs relating to Ridhall .	0001 09 00
	To writting 18 informations for proving the tenar of said writs	0006 17 00
Ditt. 18	To Patt. Christy for doing bussiness Novr. '96 .	0005 16 00
	To consult my brother Wills assignation . . .	0036 00 00
	For a messingers going for Meldrum . . .	0000 14 00
July 10	To Mr. Chiesly for expeding of bussiness, per recept . .	0042 10 00
	To Mr. Chiesly for a decritt of valuation of the tinds of Mellersteans . . .	0006 00 00
Novr. 10	To Sir Gilbert Elliot for the two Taylies of my estate 3 guinies	0043 04 00
	To Sir Gilberts man for writting them . . .	0008 14 00
	To Androu Car the writers man	0001 00 00
	To Mr. Crafoords man .	0001 09 0
		S. 244 5 0

Edenburg, January 1704. Publick Burdins.

Deb: to Cash. Scots

Cess.

The lands of Langshaw for Martinmas 1703 and Candlemas 1704	79 19 4

[Business Charges, etc.]	[Scots] £	s.	d.
For going in with cess by Androw Lamb .	0	7	0
For 3 termes cess by James Gray for Jerriswood .	32	18	0
For 4 tarmes cess out of Meller-steans preceeding the 1st of September 1704 . . .	236	11	6
	S. 349	15	10

Expene at Law. Deb: to Cash.

Febr.	To Alexander Pringle for writting	14	4	0
May 30	To bussines in Landrick pay'd Rob: Dick in full for head courts and all preciding this day	12	13	6
	For the messangers expenc at Langshaw in takeing infeftment	7	0	0
	For a discharge to Androw Bruce	0	14	6
	To Houstons brother	7	2	0
	To Alexander Cuningham writter for Rickertons bussines and others as per his account given in	145	7	4
		S. 197	01	4

Edenburgh, January 1704. Sundry Account.
Deb: to the Rents of Langshaw. Scots

For two monthes cess at Canilmes 1704 payd by the tenants in Coumsly hill .	39	19	7
For 4 tarmes cess payd by John Mudie in Threepwood the last tarme being Cals 1704	5	14	0
For cess at Whitsunday 1704 payd by John Moodie	1	2	0

	[Business Charges, etc.]		[Scots]		
			£	s.	d.
	For cess payd by Thomas Turñer for the tarme of Whitsunday 1704 . .		29	18	6
	To cess payd by John Moody Febr. 26		1	8	0
	Tq cess for Whitsunday 1705 payd by John Mudie . .		1	8	6
	To cess payd by Cumsly Hill Septr. 1st 1704 . . .		39	18	3
		S.	99	08	10
	To loss upon Langshaw rents crop and year 1703, this was of the Parks set to Thomas Ladlay so much doun of the rentall . . .	S.	119	13	8
	For kirk stent payd by John Mudie, Whit. 1704	S.	1	10	0
	To James Hunter for reparing the kirk		38	12	8
August	For the foot mantle of Twidale [1]	S.	17	7	8
	For answering at the head court	S.	1	9	0
	To Will : Nicolson pay'd by John Moodie in Threepwood of few duty for the tarmes of Whitsunday and Martimas 1703	S.	14	15	2
	To Will: Nicolson of few duty payd by Tho: Turner for Mose howses, Coumsly hill and Blainsly for the tarmes of Whitsunday and Martimas 1703	S.	141	8	4

[1] A similar entry occurs in the accounts of the previous year. It was probably an assessment levied under an Act passed in 1661, whereby the commissioners of shires were relieved of the expense of providing the costly foot-mantles worn by them at the Riding of Parliament, which for the future were to be paid for by the shires, to whom they were to be restored at the rising of Parliament. Langshaw lay in the shire of Roxburgh or sheriffdom of Teviotdale.

	[Business Charges, etc.]		[Scots] £	s.	d.
	To Will: Nicolson by Moodie in Threepwood the few duty for Whitsunday and Martinmas 1704 . . .	S.	14	15	2
	To William Nicolson the few duty, Martimas 1704	S.	141	8	4
	To the scoolmasters sallary for Whitsunday and Martimas 1703 payd by John Moodie in Threepwood	S.	0	10	0
	To . scoolmasters sallary by Moody for Whitsunday and Martimas 1704 . .	S.	0	10	0
	To the scoolmaster sallarie by Ladlay, but recept brunt	S.	10	0	0
	To scoolmasters sallary Whitsunday and Martimas 1704	S.	10	0	0
	For a milston to the milne .	Ş.	21	0	0
	For yron work to her £4 13s., wright work £14 12	Ş.	19	15	0
	For lime and meason work to the milne howse £14, wright £6	Ş.	20	0	0
	For puting up Cumsly Hill bire £1 18s. more £1 18	Ş.	3	16	0
	For repairing Will. Marssers bire howse	Ş.	3	4	0
	For a workmans wages 2 days at Thom: Turners .	S.	0	16	0
Oct.	To Mr. Willson of Steapond payd by T. Ladlay .	S.	261	0	0

These artickles marked Ş is caried to the 137 fol. in this book 1705.

Horsekeeping.[1]

	To expencess in horss keeping.	Scots		
Jun. 1693	To James Moor stabler of ane old acount	87	11	0

[1] *N.B.*—Many entries relating to this heading will be found under 'Sundries.'

	[Horsekeeping]	[Scots] £	s.	d.
	To Moffit, stabler per recept .	15	4	
Sept. 22d	For shoes to horsses . .	2	12	
1694	To James Moor stabler .	40	0	
Oct.	For girth 4s. 6d., mor 6s	0	10	6
1695	For caring out horss at severall	4	0	
Decemr.	To James Moor stabler which pays all precidings	60	0	0
	To Moffit stablar per recept	5	16	0
	For shoes to horss . . .	4	1	0
	For hay to horses . . .	18	0	0
	For a bridle to the guilding	0	12	0
	For sevarell things to the gueldings leg . .	4	14	6
	This was mostly at Edn.			
		244	0	0
	To expence of horses at Mellerstane which is caried to leger particularly by itself	500	0	0

To expences in horskeeping 1696

		£	s.	d.
January	To David Denun, sadlar, per recept	46	0	0
March 8	For a gelding	266	13	4
	To Pat. Hunter for horss .	5	10	0
	For horss carrig to Edinburgh	1	12	0
	For 2 horses to Polwart and shoes to the gray hors .	9	4	0
	For bridle to the hors	0	15	0
	For girding	0	7	0
1697 August 20	For a comb, spung, brush, shiers to the horss	2	2	6
	To take horses out of toun	1	0	0
	To gress to the horss at the Dean	10	4	0

[Horsekeeping]		[Scots] £ s. d.
Decmr.	To Mr. Moor, stabler	64 0 0
Janr. 1 1698	To Mr. Moor stabler in full of acounts preciding this day .	24 0 0
	For things bought for the horss at Mellerstean as yron and bindings, etc., go. . . .	4 1 0
	S.	105 8 10

Mellerstains, Janr. 1708. Horses expence.

	Deb: to Cash.	Scots
	For feading at Ginelkirk .	0 14 6
	For feeding at Ginelkirk £1 6, and £3 5	4 11 0
	For feeding by the road 9s.	0 9 0
	For drogs to them . .	0 12 0
Dec:	For 4 coch mares a night at Greenlaw	1 4 0
	For cleaks to the grate cart traces makeing them . .	0 12 0
	To Patrick Hunter in full for stabling this year	39 0 0
	For nets fiet oyls .	2 10 0
	For munting the old chariot	35 0 0
	For a crem and plate to a sadle and stuffing . . .	0 12 0
	For mending a clogbag sadle .	1 0 0
	For a strip lather and strip yron	0 14 0
	For a chean bitt and bosses .	0 18 0
	For a tie to a side sadle .	1 0 0
	For paneling 2 cart sadles one 14s. one £1 4s.	1 18 0
	For a bridle . .	0 14 0
	For a horse comb and a brush to Tam Youll . . .	1 6 0

[Horsekeeping]	[Scots]		
	£	s.	d.
For 2 tathers to the cart horse	[illegible]	1[illegible]	0
For a cart sadle . . .		1	0
For 2 new collers to the horse			0
For 2 pair cart fiets great tows			0
For lamp bleck for the coach			0
For 8 bridles and bitts at 20s.			0
For a pair strips and yrons			0
For a mane comb .			0
For a bridle and curple			0
For 11 ells girding .			0
For 6 pair buckles .		1	0
For mending a side sadle			0
For a sadle mending			0
For 6 ells girdin 12s. 2 pair buckles 4s. Ch: Or . . .	0	16	0
For yron for shoes at Mellerstains this year	25	0	0
For shoeing horse by Pate Newton from 19 Sep. 1707 till Janr. 1st 1709 . . .	20	2	0
	S. 156	12	6

Meller[staine], Janr. 1709. Expence of Coach and Horses. Deb: to Cash.

		Scots		
	For oyl to the coach	1	4	0
	For oyl to horse legs	0	19	0
	For horse shoes . . .	0	14	0
	For expence of horses to George Baillie	4	10	0
	For 3 ell girthin .	0	6	0
	For a ps of 24 ells girthin from John Muckle .	1	4	0
June 29	To Patrick Hunter in full of all accounts	9	0	0

	[Horsekeeping]	[Scots]		
		£	s.	d.
July 30	To Barty Gibsone for 2 coach mares 13 nights and helping the coach	21	0	0
	For mending harnes .	1	10	0
	For glas to the chariot from Mr. Burtone	3	4	0
	For more glases for the chariot	3	17	0
	For shoeing horse and mending sadles		4	0
	For the white mares expence to Cesnock	3	0	0
	For horses expence at Kelso, etc.	10	0	0
	For horse expence at Kelso in full	2	14	6
July 17th	For 1 stone 14 ounces yron for shoes £1 12s. per stone .	1	13	6
Aug. 26	For 22 ℔. yron at £1 12 per stone	2	4	0
Decmr. 12	For 3 stone 4 ℔. 3 ounces yrone at £1 12s. per stone .	5	4	0
	For shoeing horses by Pat. Newton £18 . . .	18	0	0
		S. 91	8	0

	Expence of coch and horses 1710.	Stg.		
	For the coch mares at Ginelkirk with Tam Youll .	0	2	0
	For gat same to the mares	0	[illegible]	[illegible]
	For horse sezers [scissors]			½
	For lamp bleck to the harnes			
	For a pint of oyl to the harnes			
Ap. 17	For 1 ston 1 ℔. yron for shoes		1	
	For lamp bleck 3d.			
	For mending the chariot wheals	0	6	0
	For grase to the powny at Edinburgh 6d. per night	0	2	6

	[Horsekeeping]	[Sterling]		
		£	s.	d.
July 6	To Tam of yron for shoes 1 ston 7 ℔. is 3s. 10d. .	0	3	10
	For tethers to the horses .	0	3	6
	For lamp bleck 7d.½ .	0	0	7½
	To Bartie Gibson ane account of stabling	1	0	0
	To Pate Hunter ane account of stabling	0	17	3
	For bringing the mare and foll from Cesnock	0	5	0
Novr. 1	For 1 ston 1 ℔. 5 ounces yron to Tam Youll 2s. 9d.	0	2	9
	For a pair safe braces to the coach	2	3	4
	For a pad .	0	4	0
	For a clogbage sadle, and furnitur	0	18	0
	For ane account of horse expence pay'd T. Y.	0	11	0
	For oyl to the coach	0	5	0
	For caring out horses 2s.	0	2	0
	For a pair hulsters to the clogbage sadle	0	3	3
	For expence of horses on the road	0	3	6
	To Pat: Hunter stabler in full of all preceeding 4 Decmr.	0	18	0
	To sundry accounts laid out by George Mathy at Kelso, etc.	0	6	0
	For glas to the chariot by Barton	0	13	0
	For horse at Ginelkerk when we went to toun pay'd Shirrifs account sometime after	0	7	3
	For expence of horses at Kelso .	0	4	6
	For shoeing horse, by Pat. Newton from 1 Janr. 1710 till 6 Novr. 1710 £1 4s. 6d. .	1	4	6
	For noult feet oyl .	0	5	8
	For oyl 2d.½, tar 8d.	0	00	10½
	For yron got by Tam Youll	0	2	8

[Horsekeeping]	[Sterling]		
	£	s.	d.
For 2 broad white bridles with bits 14d. a pair, come and brush 27d.	0	3	5
For 8 fathom 9 threed tows 13d.$\frac{1}{3}$, 6 pair girth buckles 9d.	0	1	10$\frac{1}{4}$
For a broad white bridle 14d.	0	1	2
To William Miller garner in the Abay compleat payment of Bartholamew Gibsons account for stabline from 31 Janr. 1710 till 1 Decmr. 1710 .	11	4	8
To Clark in Melrose for head courts	0	2	4
	S. 23	14	7$\frac{10}{12}$

Expence of Horses and Coach 1711. Stg.

Janr. 19	For 3 bolls oates from the Tenants of the Mains to the Horses at 11s. 8d. pr boll	1	15	0
feb. 28	For Horse upon the road 4s. 1d., more 2s.	0	6	1
	For horse at Ginelkirk .	0	3	0
	For stabline at Pat Hunters to this day . . .	0	10	0
	For lintsead oyl to the Horse	0	0	6

For oates to the Horse at 11s. 8d. from 3 Sepr. 1710 till Ap. 12 1711 — 20 15 0 (bracketed total):

			£	s.	d.
For oates to the Horse at 11s. 8d. from 3 Sepr. 1710 till Ap. 12 1711 .	30B	1f	17	10	0
more	2	3	1	10	4
For cart Horse going to toun	0	2	0	4	8
For 6 bolls light oats at 5s. pr boll .	6	0	1	10	0

Total of the above (bracketed): 20 15 0

	[Horsekeeping]	[Sterling] £ s. d.
	For oats more to the Horse 3 0 which is sett doun above sum of all is . . . 42 1	
	For Bear to the Horse at 15s. pr Boll . . . . 1f .	0 3 0
	For Bear to the Horses 1 .	0 3 0
	For shoeing Horses payd John Flint from Novr. 18 1710 till Aprill 18 1711 . . .	0 5 6
May 29	For 19 lb. 7 ounes yron from the Marchant to Tam youll 3s. 3d.	0 3 3
	For a chapine oyl 9d.	0 0 9
Sepr. 21	For 2 Colts gelding the ordiner price is a shillin I gave .	0 4 0
	For gras to Horse at Edn .	0 2 6
	To a Ferrier for the young coch mare . . .	0 2 6
	For a bridle 1s. payd Trotter sadlers account at Kelso 15 .	0 16 0
	For cutting down the Hay in Jerriswood Park . .	3 0 0
	For cutting doun Coltcrooks Meadow	0 15 0
	For horses at Edn. . . .	0 2 6
	For poling sisers 5d. 9 fathom 9 threed tows 15d. strip lethers 16d.	0 3 0
	For a fine bridle 26d. another 18d.	0 3 8
	For 14 Bolls oates at 10sh. from 12 Ap. till 1st Sepm. .	7 0 0
	For 1 boll 1 fou peas at 15s. from Apl. 12 till Sepm. 1 . . .	0 18 0
	To William Miller Gardner in the Abay full payment of Barthola-mew Gibson stablers account	

[Horsekeeping]	[Sterling] £	s.	d.
from 1 July 1711 till 21st Novr. 1711 8s. 8d. . .	0	8	8
To Pate Hunter stabler till 18 August 1711 .	3	6	8
To Pate Newton for shoeing 6 horse from Mart. 1710 till Martemas 1711 1£ 10s., mending the chariot 2s. 8d., rumping 2 horse 1s. . .	1	13	8
To James Hunter wright for the chariot mending . . .	0	5	0
For yron to the coach and Tarr 8s. 6d. from Liedhouse	0	8	6
For dresing a boar skine 1s. 10d. more	0	1	10
For 20 Rucks Hay at 10s. pr Ruck	10	0	0
For Grass to 14 horses .	14	0	0
To timber to the coach wheels 1£ 14s. 4d. yron 1£ 5s. 4d. making them 1£ 8s. 4d., shoeing them 1£, collering 5s. 4d., Tarr 1s.	5	14	4
	S. £73	10	11

Expence of Coch and Horses 1712. Stg.

	Coch etc.			Horses Corn and Stra		
For oyl to the coch	0	4	0			
For a comb and brush	0	2	3			
For hemp sead				0	1	6
For oats to the Horses from the 1st Septmr 1711 till the 22 May 1712 at 10sh. pr boll						

	[Horsekeeping]	b.	f.	[Coch £	s.	d.	Horses Corn and Stra] £	s.	d.
		38	4						
	For strangers horses .	2	0						
May 23	For horses put in the stable chist this day	1	3				21	4	0
		42	2						
	For light oats to the horse 5s. .	4	0				1	0	0
	For pease at 15s. .	0	2				0	0	6
	For Peas Straw at 10d. .	30st.					1	5	0
This stra was 1711 crop and spent last year but was forgot to be incert till the acct was clos'd	For oat stra at 8d. . .	100					3	6	8
	For bear strat at 6d. .	32					0	16	0
	To a boll Langshaw light oats 4s. 2d. .	4					0	16	8
	For bear at 4sh. 8d.	2 fouls					0	4	8
	For helping the chariot by Hunter 8 days .			0	5	0			
	For mending horse furniture .			0	4	0			
	For 100 nails to the coach .			0	1	0			
	To the Ferrier for the Gray Mare . .						0	2	0
	For oyl to the coach			0	1	6			
	For mending sadles by Trotter . .			0	4	0			

[Sterling]

[Horsekeeping]		[Coch etc.				[Sterling] Horses Corn and Stra]	
					£	s.	d.
	For oyle to Gray Mare				0	1	6
	For bran and Drogs when colded . .				0	5	0
	For 12 ells Girthing at 2d. very broad .	0	2	0			
	For 2 pair strip lathers 2s. 3d., buckles 18d.	0	3	9			
	For shoe to a horse	0	0	4			
	For Tarr to the coach 6d., oyl 2s., bleck 3d. . .	0	2	9			
	For expene on the road to Edn . .				0	2	0
	For mending the coach and 2 pair shekles, the shekles with nails 15d. a pair	0	3	6			
	For expences on the road . .				0	3	0
	To a pyper at Red-breas for the horse				0	1	0
Decm. 10	To Patrick Hunter in full of all Accounts for this year				2	12	0
	For two trees for polls	0	2	0			
	For mending of sadles at Kelso, etc	0	5	3			
	For mending sadles by Mrs. Troter	0	1	0			
	For the Hay of Jerris-wood Park last year being still untoucht				6	0	0
	For the Hay of Colt-crooks . .				10	0	0
	For stra which comes to 7£ 5 of crop 1712				7	5	0

[Horsekeeping]	[Coch			Horses Corn and Stra] [Sterling]		
				£	s.	d.
To Pat Newton for shoeing horse from the last March 1712 till last March 1713	2	0	0			
	£4	2	4	35	12	0

[1709]

Estate Management.[1]

The expence of repairing tenants houses.

	Deb: to Cash.	[Scots]		
March 22	For meason and wright work in Langshaw Milne allowed to Thomas Ladly this day . .	44	7	8
	For naills to sclate the house, etc., of Langshaw .	6	1	0
June 8	For a milne stone to Langshaw Milne bought by James Deas .	20	12	0
	For doors to Moss houses .	2	8	0
	For a nather milston from Greenlaw to Langshaw.			
	For sclateing the house of Langshaw by Pat: Thomsone	30	0	0
	To Jamie Blakie 2 days at Langshaw cutting timber .		4	0
	To Mellerstains workmen at Langshaw Dam	5	15	0
	For helping to put up Langshaw Park dicks	28	0	0
	For repairein the stone dicks at Langshaw . .	16	0	0
	For 6 loads lime for Langshaw House	1	16	0
	For divits to Langshaw House	3	6	8
	For thicking Langshaw stables	4	10	0

[1] *N.B.*—Many entries relating to this heading will be found under 'Sundries.'

[Estate Management]	[Scots] £	s.	d.
To a milne wright for repaireing Langshaw Milne . . .	42	0	0
To said milne wright Munga Dick half a boll meall . . .	9	0	0
To Munga Park measone for repaireing Langshaw Milne	48	0	0
For yrone £5 10sh., casting divits to Langshaw Milne £5 12s. .	11	2	0
For nails to the milne by John Boe and other yron work .	7	2	0
For other expences at Langshaw Miln by Ja: Ainsly	4	10	
For reparations in Over Langshaw and Mose Houses .	41	18	8
For glazing Langshaw Houss .	13	0	0
For lime to Langshaw House .	2	0	0
For casting divots to Langshaw Milne . .	7	0	0
For divits leading and other work at Langshaw House	11	0	0
For pan cratch a boll £1 14, Tam Youlls expence a night with a horss going to the Pans for it, he haveing corn along with him 6sh. 4d. and custome .	2	0	4
For pan cratch to the Tour head	1	16	0
For 4 days bringing the cratch at 5s.	1	0	0
For drawing thack to the thicker	0	10	0
For helpnig the pigion house at Jerriswood	1	10	0
For a furlite to Langshaw Milne	2	0	0
	S. 369	9	4

[Estate Management] [Sterling]

Expence of repairing Tenants Houses, 1710.

			£ s. d.
May 15	For repairing Tam Williamsons house and the smithes T: Hop .	0 5 0	
	For 4 days thicking of these houses by Mowit . . .	0 2 0	0 17 0
	For building the smidy belonging to John Flint by Tam H. .	0 10 0	
	For divits to Jamie Ormstons house when he entred to it .		0 1 6
	For repairing Coltcrooks park dick by Kerncorse .		0 9 8
	For 4000 divits for Ormston and Thomsons houses .		0 4 0
	For stinging the barn 9½ day .		0 4 9
	For 56 threve bear stra for stinging the barn at 4d. per threve 1709 crop		0 18 8
	To Hunter for 2 cuples in the smithes house and two in Tam Williamsons house and timering them and helping the nurses house		0 6 8
	For service at the smidy 11 days more at it and T: W: 19		0 12 6
	For 5000 divits for Tam Williamsons house . .		0 5 0
	For building the kitchen payd Munga Dick 3 15 2 .		3 05 2
	To Mungae for the park gate makeing		0 2 0
	For the nurses house repairing .		0 6 1½
	For John Brouns house, for 1709 repairing		0 11 1½

[Estate Management]	[Sterling] £	s.	d.
For repairing Langshaw Dicks	0	15	6
For repaireing Langshaw Milne houses which compleats them at James Ainslys entry payd to Munga Dick	2	0	0
For repaireing Mose Houses payd the said Munga Dick in pairt 0 4s. 5⅓ . .	0	4	5 4/12
For repairing Alexander Pringles houses in Langshaw .	0	7	3
For divits casting to Langshaw Milne house at 12d. per thousand . . .	1	0	0
For lime to the slouse of the milne	0	1	6
For nails and wooud bands to the Milne	0	2	8
To Munga Dick in full of Mosehouses reparations .	0	12	10⅓
For mending Langshaw Miln whiel and traugh .	1	7	6
For 4000 divits to malt barn, etc.	0	4	0
For repairing Coumsly Hill and Over Langshaw payd Munga Dick the timber all cutt on the ground . .	11	4	0
For 3400 divits to Coumsly Hill, and 2400 to Over Langshaw 5000 to Langshaw office houses	3	5	0
	29	8	10 8/12

Reparations of Langshaw Barrony 1711.

	[Sterling]		
For repairing Langshaw Park Dicks when Thomas Turner entred to them Mart. 1710 .	5	10	0

	[Estate Management]	[Sterling]		
	Repairing Houses 1711.			
		£	s.	d.
	For helping the walls of Mains Houses by Imry . .	0	5	0
May 29	For bilding up the Stable and coachhouse by John Wilson .	0	6	0
	For three shovels .	0	3	6
	For cloding Jerviswood Park 5sh. 6d.			
	For building Jerviswood Park door . .	0	1	0
	For 17½ days work at Cochhouse and Stable by John Wilson at 10d. a day without meet. .	0	14	2
	For pan crach to the tour head 2s. 2d. pr boll, cariage 2s. 6d..	0	4	8
	For Nails	0	10	6
	For building the Kitchen payd Mungo Dick 2 15 2 .	2	15	2
	For 53 days work of 5d. men about the houses this year			3
	For 114 5d. days at the Kitchen 2 7 6	2	7	6
	For work about the House and for dails, etc.	25	0	0
	For cariing home the Dails the 100 dails the rest our own horses	0	13	4
	For building the Kitchen by Imry in full of his . 1 8 0 } For building the Kitchen by John Young . . . 1 4 8 }	2	12	8
	For work about the House by Hunter 33 days 10d. pr day .	0	17	6
	For 468 foot pavement at 2d. pr foot in kitchen and trance	3	18	0

[Estate Management]	[Sterling] £	s.	d.
For 45 days work at the quarie for the pavement .	0	18	1
For helping Caltcrooks park Dicks by Tam Hope 5½ .	0	5	6
For Nails from Liedhouse 1s. 6, yron for sundry uses 16sh.	0	17	6
For inclosing the Thack Meadow to the Tenants in Mellerstaine Mains at 8d. pr Rood .	7	3	4
For inclosing the Bogg in Mellerstaine Mains at 8d. pr Rood	12	0	0
	S. 62	14	8

Expence of Repairing Tenants Houses 1712.

					Sterline Money Barony of Langshaw.		
March 24	For puting a band about Langshaw Miston[1]				0	12	6
	For building Malt Barn at 15sh. pr Rood .						
	For 2 days by Hunter at Tho Willisons House . .				0	1	8
	For 5 days at Hall Houses	0	2	1			
July 3	To James Hunter for John Humes House cuples 5	0	5	0			
	For George Dodses chimny and windows 4 days .	0	3	4			

[1] Millstone.

[Estate Management]				[Sterling]		
				£	s.	d.
For Timber payd John Gibson for Fanns Scooll	0	11	8			
For bands to the spinle and armes Langshaw Milne .				0	3	8
For John Boes work at the Spinle and armes .				0	2	6
To Ammers Wright for work 4 days there .				0	3	10
For timber to the Garners house and George Dodses	1	5	8			
For Meason and wright work at Garners house by Munga Dick at 12ds. a day lad 8ds.	2	13	8			
For work by Munga Dick at making a chimuy to Dodses House .	0	1	0			
For puting up Coumslyhill barn, etc. .				1	5	4
For Hillandmans sering Dick 12 days	0	5	0			
For more timber from Park for Garners House .	1	9	0			
For 4 doors crooks and bands to Coumslyhill . . .				0	13	4
	£6	17	9	3	1	2

[Estate Management] [Sterling]

	£	s.	d.
For mending old Ditch Dick in Coltcrooks .	0	0	10
For the Dick and Ditch at 8s. pr Rood in Coltcrooks	0	10	0
For helping Coltcrooks Ditch Dick 10 days	0	4	2
For 10 thousand Divits for Hall House	0	10	0
For 6 days work at Hall House 5d. men	0	2	6
For 3000 divits to Fanns Scooll	0	3	0
For for Coltcrooks park to Munga Dick	0	3	8
S.	£1	14	2

Expence of Repairing Mellerstaine Tour and offices Houses 1712.

		[Sterling]		
	For hair to plaster the Kitchin at 9d. a stone	0	6	6
	For Nails 7s., more 4s. 6 .	0	11	6
May 13	For 400 windows at 2d.½, 200 doors at 5d., 200 planshers at 8d. p hunder .	0	3	0
	For Nails 4s. 4d., 1000 windows, 200 doors, 200 planshers	0	8	7
	For 45, 5d. days at the quarie for payment to the Kitchin, etc. .	0	18	9
	For flooring the Milk House, etc. by Thomson .	0	10	0
22	For 13 days Meason work about the House by David Imry .	0	17	0

	[Estate Management]	[Sterling] £	s.	d.
	For 65 days work of 5d. men about the House, etc. .	1	2	1
	For 24 days 5d. men at the stone quarie	0	10	0
	For work about the dicks by John Clark 25 days at 5d. .	0	8	9
June 24	For biging the Collhouse 9 days, other work 3½ days by Tam Hope	0	12	6
	For building the house of office by Tho Hope 5 days	0	5	0
	For nin score Dails from Eymouth and Berwick to the house only 110 of them at 11d. .	5	0	10
	For bringing home two carts full Daills from Berwick	0	13	8
Ditt 16	To James Miller Glazier 2£ to account in full of all 2£ 1s. 8 .	4	1	8
	For Nails from Liedhouse 2s. 8d., for yron from him 3s. .	0	5	8
	For lead 2lb. 4d., lime 11s. 8d., lime 5s.	0	17	0
	For Nails 5s. 4d., 3s. 5d., 4s., 1s. 8d., and more 5s. 7d. . .	1	0	0
	For 60 Dails from Aymouth brining home . . .	0	6	3
	To William Moor 11s. 6d. .	0	1	6
	To John Smith for makeing and mending smith work 2£	2	0	0
Sep. 2	For wright work about the house by James Blakie 4£	4	0	0
	For plastering 1£, more wright work by James Blakie 2£ 7s. .	3	7	0
	To James Hunter for sawing Dails 10d. a day 6 days .	0	5	0
	For work about house and offices houses by the 5ds. men, etc. .	4	14	8
		S. £33	7	4

Expence of Repairing Tenants Houses 1713.

		Mellerstanes	Langshaw
	For mending Langshaw Milne Arms .		0 2 [illegible]
	For Nails to the park gate . . .		0 0 3
			0 2 4
	For 2600 divits to Fanns House 23 6d. a days work by Jamie Paterson that has it 0 2 9	0 2 9	
	To Munga Dick for work at Fanns house	0 2 0	
		0 4 9	
	For cuting down colt-crooks Hay	0 17 0	
	For 5d. men at Colt-crooks park	0 18 6	
	For hay rakes 6	0 1 4	
	For suples to the barn	0 1 3	
		1 18 [illegible]	
June	To Andrew Lambs expences at fairs	0 1 0	
July 17	To his expence	0 1 4	
	To his expences 1s. 2.	0 1 2	
		£0 3 6	

Expence of Repairing Mellerstean Tour and office Houses 1713. [Sterling]

Date	Item	£ s. d.
	For 8 sto. whitening from Grive in Dunce at 8ds. p stn.	
June 18	For Nails	0 6 4
	For Lead to door crooks . .	0 1 8

[Estate Management]	[Sterling] £	s.	d.
For a mutchkin lientsead oyl 16ds. 2d., white lead 8ds	0	2	0
For a Muchken Lintsead oyl 15ds.	0	1	3
For a botle to hold it 2ds. $\frac{6}{12}$		0	2 $\frac{6}{12}$
For 8 st. whitening Grive in Dunc at 8ds. pr ston .	0	5	4
For a chopine lintsead oyl 14ds., culours for dyill 10ds. .	0	2	0
For 20½ days stinging the house 8ds. and meat .	0	13	8
For 100 threve bear stra at 3ds. for stinging the house .	l	5	0
To Pat Newton for smith work till Lambes 1713 .	l	0	0
To Mean Meason for work about the house	0	6	0
For 5½ road meason work in the garden dick upon the North side by Robert Mean at 11s. 8ds.	3	4	2
For work by 5d. men about the House and Dicks till the 18 day July 1713	0	17	0
For 5d. men at back close till 18 July	0	9	0
For 12 yron snakes for windows at Dunce	0	6	0
For pan cratch 2s. 6d., cariing it 2s. 6d., paynting tour head 2s.	0	7	0
For a wainfull Dails bringing from Berwick . . .	0	6	10
For a rake lime 4s. 2ds. .	0	4	2
For 8 trees and 60 dails from Edmiston in Berwick .	3	15	6
For smith work about the house by Hardy . .	0	14	0
For more smith work at Gordon 5s., more 1s. 2d., more 8d. .	0	6	10
For thicking the kitchin 2s. 6d. .	0	2	6

[Estate Management]	[Sterling]		
	£	s.	d.
For 50 Dails at 1s., 60 at 9ds. from Will. Robertson in Aymouth .	4	15	0
For 4 lb. white leed a chapine lint-sead oyl 2s. 7ds. . . .	0	2	7
For a tree from Park 5 Nails 3s. .	0	8	0
For wright work by James Blackie	3	9	0
	£23	11	$0\frac{6}{12}$

Repairing Mellerstaine Tour and office Houses 1714.

		[Sterling]		
Ap. 14	For yron from James Liedhouse last year haveing cleard all accounts with him till this day	1	2	0
	For lime 11s. last year .	0	11	0
	For 7 loads lime at 6ds., 3s. 6d., An^r expences 9ds. to new house	0	4	3
	For stones to soll the big oven and building up the mouths of Both with new hewen ston and stons for their mouthes and the workmenship with their meat 3 of them 3 days Sanders Mean and his sons a grot to the lads .	1	0	4
Ap. 27	To James Pringle at founding the House 4d., Blakie at Aymouth 2s.	0	2	4
	To James Pringle for building the back office houses 12d. pr day	3	1	0
May 24	To Jamie hunter for work about the house last year	0	9	0
	For Nails to the new house 9s. Nails 7s. 6d., more 5s. .		1	6
	For 3 thousand Divits to the new House	0	3	0
	For 4 days barrowmen 1s. 8d. A. Hardy	0	1	8

	[Estate Management]	[Sterling] £	s.	d.
	For thicking the house 2s. 8d., 2 shuffels 3s. 2d. . . .	0	5	10
	For bring home three wanefulls of dails and trees to the house .	1	0	3
	For glazing the new house 100 ches losens 36 foot wire losens at 3d. and 4d. .	2	0	0
	For pavment and laying the litle close by Alexr Mean	2	7	0
	For days work about the house by him	0	5	0
	For expence of the cart horse going to Coldstream	0	2	0
	For mending the glass windows from Aug. 18, 1713 till July 12	1	3	0
	For Nails at severall times 17s. 2d., 1s.	0	18	2
	For 265 ells Casow at the well back closes at 2d. pr ell without meat	2	3	4
	For 5d. men 69 days at the offices houses in back close . .	1	8	9
Sept. 6	For leveling and leeding stons to the back closes 86 days .	1	15	10
	For 8 days Meason work about the house	0	8	0
	For 100 dals brought home in two wains	0	13	6
	For 4 trees from George Dods	0	5	0
	To Pate Newton for smith work about the house and workmens shuvels and house .	0	13	6
Sept. 11	To 5ds. men 65 days at back wind and sowing dails 6 of them which clears of all the 3 workmen to this day also 18 days work by John Shirra 83 in all .	1	14	7
Nov. 19	To 5ds. men for work at Dicks houses, etc.	2	1	8

	[Estate Management]	[Sterling] £	s.	d.
	For Lime 1s. 2d., 3s., glazing in full to Miller by R. T. 1s. 8d. .	0	5	10
	For bands, locks, and snecks to the offices houses by Hardy Smith in Gordon 1s. 4d., more 2£ 5s.	2	6	4
	To John Mowit for stinging the house and dick		17	6
	For 20 dails from James Blakie 1£, cariing 3s. 4d. . .	1	3	4
Nov. 24	To Jamie Blakie cleard all accounts and payd . .	8	8	0
	For thicking the house by Young 8 days . . .	0	8	0
	For 1 st. 11 lb. yron for quarie work, looms mending . .	0	4	6
	For more yron 4s. 8d., 2 shuvels 3s. 2d.	0	7	10
	For 34 lb. lead 5s. 9d.	0	5	9
		£41	8	7

Mellerstaine, Janry 1714. Repairing Tenants Houses.

	Mellerstaine.			Langshaw. [Sterling]		
To Amers Milne wright for Langshaw Mile Wheel . .				5	19	4
To Munga Dick for over Langshaw barn 10 days 8ds.				0	6	8
To Munga Dick 2 days building up the cross and tronn	0	2	0			
To a Meason to finish out the Malt Kill and barn	1	0	0			
To Ainsly for overlangshaw Houses .				0	6	0

	[Estate Management]	£	s.	d.	[Sterling] £	s.	d.
	To John Gray for doors at Mosehouses				0	5	0
	For a door to Coumsly hill and 2 days work				0	4	8
	For casting Divits to the Malt barn 12ds. p 1000 .	0	5	0			
	For 2 suples 3d. more 2 suples $2\frac{6}{12}$d. .						
	For flals and hudins to Tam Bell .	0					
	For tar to the sheep last year in the toun	0	2	4			
	To Hope Meason 2 days at Jerriswood Park dick .	0	2	0			
	To 5d. men at Jerriswood park dicks and other dicks	2	1	8			
	To 5d. men at Coltcrooks park dick 9 days .	0	3	9			
Septm. 6	For 5d. men at the Hay 27 days being 9 day each	0	11	3			
	For 5d. men at the park dicks	0	7	1			
	For working at the Hay by 5d. men etc.	0	10	0			
	For cuting the Hay in nursary ground .	0	8	0			
	For 2 days at Nurses house . . .	0	1	0			
		£5	15	2	7	1	3

Expense of Garden.[1]

Mellerstaines, Janr. 1709. Expence of the Gardine. Deb: to Cash. [Scots]

	For 2 spads £6, a how £1 16s.	7	16	0
	For men to work with the garner at 5sh. per day .	3	10	0
	For 3 rackes, a howe, a pairin yron, a stalk for a line threed, and a pair of fork grains	2	2	0
	For plants at 4s. per 100 . .	2	8	0
	To Samuill Robsone in Brigend for gardine seeds .	19	11	0
	For spinage sead 4 ounces at Edinburgh . . .	0	11	0
	For 51 day by Tam Youll in the gardine at 5d. [stg.]	12	15	0
Decmr. 12	For workmen at the gardine preceeding this date	29	0	0
	For workmen at the gardine	2	10	0
	For 34 foot glass for hote beds .	7	12	0
		S. 87	15	0

Expence of the gardine 1710. [Sterling]

	For a ℔. peas . . .	0	1	3
Ap. 22d	For workmen at 5d. a day, delving	0	15	0
	To Tam Youll at the boulling green 15½ days .	0	6	5½
	To White in Fans and Black in Mellersteans at the boulingreen	0	9	2
	For plants 3s. 6d., peas 1s. 3d. .	0	4	9
	For gardine seads from Brigend Garner	1	7	0

[1] Many entries relating to this heading will be found under 'Sundries.'

[Expense of Garden]	[Sterling] £	s.	d.
For 8 shuffels .	0	8	6
For 200 days work at the Boullingreen at 5d. per day	4	3	4
	7	10	5 6/12

Expense of the Gardine 1711.			
For Spades 2 at 4sh. 6d., shaffels 4 at 1s. 2d. . . .	[Sterling] 0	13	8
For Gardine seads .	1	5	6
For pursly sead . . .	0	1	4
For a watering cann c. o. .	0	4	4
For 106 5d. days at the Bowlingreen	2	4	2
	S. £4	9	0

Expence of the Gardine 1712.			
For a lb. of white pease	0	0	6
For men to work the ground at 5d. p day	0	15	0
For a lb. firr sead . . .	0	12	0
For inclosing the Nursary 80 5d. days . . .	1	13	4
For 78 5d. days trinching and setting trees and in gerdine .	1	12	6
For 19 days at Jerriswood Nursary more	0	8	0
For 38 days ditchen out the Nursary Dicks	0	15	10
For 25 days more at setting out the trees	0	10	5

[Expense of Garden]	[Sterling] £	s.	d.
For young Trees bought by John Hope which was a perfit cheat	2	10	0
For Elm sead from Hundalie .	0	[illegible]	[illegible]
For 2 shuffels 2s. . . .			
For a line threed 7d.			
For gardine seads by John Hope from Samuell Robsone	1	16	8
For a syth .	0	2	0
For a spade 3s. 8 a shovell 18d. another shovell 14d.	0	6	4
For a spade 4s. 2ds. .	0	4	6
For 5ds. men at the Green 80 days . .	1	13	8
For 5d. men at the Gardine 20 days	0	8	4
	S. £13	14	2

1713 Expence of the Gardine	Sterling		
For a spade Berwick 3s. 6d.	0	3	6
For floors 2s., 2 shovles c. o. 3s.	0	5	0
For a long syth 2s. 2d., sharpening stons 4ds. a pice . .	0	3	6
For a spade c. o. 4s., 3 lb. clover sead 2s. 3d.	0	2	3
For a lb. lime sead 5s. 6d	0	5	6
For 5ds. men and others at the Boulling green and banks .	5	12	6
For 5d. men at the North wall till 18 July .	0	14	0
For 5ds. men at Gardine 4s. 6d. at for close 1£, gravell 4 .	1	5	6
For 5ds. men at the Gardine	0	0	10
For 34 ewe trees from William Miller	5	0	0

[Expense of Garden]	[Sterling]		
	£	s.	d.
For a roling ston from Kimmergham	1	2	6
For Gardin seads and tree seads Samuell Robson . . .	4	0	0
For John Humes expences 2s. 8d., more 1s.	0	3	8
For trees from Earlston	1	19	0
	£21	0	9

Expence of the Gardine and Planting 1714.

		Sterling		
	For trees from Jedbrugh .	1	16	0
	To Sr Pat. Scots Garner for geting the Allers . .	0	2	6
March	For 2 spades at Edn.	0	8	0
	For John Humes expences going about seeds, trees, etc. .	0	4	8
	For a spade from my father 4s.	0	4	0
	For a syth 2s. another syth and 2 sharping stons 3s.	0	5	0
	For Gardine seeds this year	1	13	4
	For 2800 thorns 10s. pr 1000 .	1	8	0
	For Anemonys 4d. Ranunculus 3d. Junquils 1d. Tulips 2d. .	l	5	0
	For 40 plains 1d. pr pice, 1000 Elms 15s.½, 100 geans 2d. .	1	8	4
	For 200 firs 12s. pr 100 .	1	4	0
Sep. 6	For 5d. mens work in the Gardine and at planting 192 days for a years time . .	4	0	0
Sep. 9	For smith work by Pat Newton till this day . .	0	7	0

[Expense of Garden]	[Sterling]		
	£	s.	d.
For Akorns 2s., Mrs. Mean 1s.	0	3	0
For lines 1s. .	0	1	0
	14	9	10

Expence of the Gardine and Planting 1718.

	[Sterling]		
For chestons and Walnuts	1	5	0
For 300 horse chestons	0	6	0
For a sneding knyf 1s. 6d.	1	11	0
	3	2	0
For corn to Cart Horses	2	5	0

Doctors and Surgeons.[1]

To docters and chirurgions.

		[Scots]		
1694 Janr. 4th	To a consultation of chirurgions for my leg . .	34	16	0
March 18	To John Baillie cherurgion for drawing my wife blood	5	16	0
Jun. 6	To John Baillie and Docter Kirton[2] for wateing on me in my flux .	92	16	0
July 2	To Mr. Knox for letting blood	3	12	0
1695	For blooding	3	10	0
	For Sarsa root[3]. . . .	16	6	0

[1] Many entries relating to this heading will be found under 'Sundries.'

[2] Doctor George Kirkton, a first cousin of George Baillie. See p. 31.

[3] Sarsa or sarsaparilla, a still much employed medicine.

	[Doctors, etc.]	[Sterling] £	s.	d.
Augt.	To Docter Sincklair.[1]	11	12	0
Novr.	To Docter Burnits man at two times.	5	16	0
	To John Baillie cherurgion	34	16	0
	For Sarsa root	6	0	0
January	To Docter Sincklar	11	12	0
	S.	226	12	0
	To more expence of Docters, etc.	399	14	0
	S.	626	6	0

1696	To Docters and cherurgions.	[Scots]		
January	To George Kirton for his pains	29	0	0
Aprill	For 3 ℔. sarsaparella	13	10	0
	To Docter Sincklair	46	16	0
9	To Mr. Rainolds per recept	120	0	0
	To Mr. Rainalds	60	0	0
	For Andersons pills .	2	0	0
	To Georg Kirkton 8 rex dollers to account .	23	4	
	To Georg Kirton for blooding	5	16	
May	To Georg Kirton to acount	13	16	
January	To Docter Burnits man	2	18	
1697	To Docter Senclair .	52	0	0
	To his man	2	0	

[1] Elsewhere called Dr. St. Clair. Probably Dr. Matthew St. Clair of Herdmanston, East Lothian, the ancestor of the present Lord Sinclair. He was a deputy-lieutenant of East Lothian, and was in command of the party who went to interview Mr. Hepburn of Humbie, who in 1715 was considered as likely to join the rising. In the skirmish which followed Keith's younger son was killed, 'the first that was killed in the late rebellion.'—Rae's *Rebellion*. In revenge the Highlanders plundered Herdmanston House 'of everything valuable which they could carry with them.'—Rae's *Rebellion*.

	[Doctors, etc.]	[Scots]		
		£	s.	d.
Febr. 12	To Georg Kirton a guiny at 23s. 6d.	14	2	0
Jany.	To Docter Sincklair	69	12	0
1698	To Docter Sinckair . . .	59	14	0
		S. 197	8	0

Small Payments.

	Sundry small things.	[Scots]		
1694 Jun.	For nidles	1	0	0
	For paper, puder, and jasamin	1	4	0
	To Greenocks man[1]	2	0	0
	To materialls to japan[2] .	3	0	0
	For drinkmonv and horss hire at Temple	4	13	0
October	For caring books 14s., for paper and for a coch . .	1	9	0
	For sevarell small things 6℔. for safer of a mufe 2℔ 18.	8	18	0
	For paper, wax, pens, 14s, pins, knitins, 12s. .	1	6	0
1695	For sevarell small things 1℔. 16, sevarell things 3℔. 13	5	9	0
Febr. 23	To Christinins	8	14	0
	For a coch 14s., Greenocks man 14s., flitting the seller 10sh. .	1	18	0
	To Lisi Rainald for my Robins vallantin gloves . .	1	10	0
	To the poor 6℔., to Jedbrughs[3] cochman 14s., corks 9sh.	7	3	0

[1] Sir John Shaw of Greenock.

[2] Japanning must have been a comparatively new art in Scotland at this time, for in 1705 a petition was presented to Parliament by Sarah Dalrymple for leave to carry on 'a japaning manufactory,' which was opposed by two glass makers, 'M. la Blanc and Mr. Scott.'

[3] William Kerr, Lord Jedburgh.

	[Small Payments]	[Scots] £	s.	d.
	For tape thrid 12s., to a barber 14s., to a nurs 3℔. 10 . .	4	16	0
	To a poor woman 1℔. 8, drink mony to nurses 7 . . .	8	18	0
	For a coch 7s. To Reths[1] nurs 3℔. 10, thrid and knitins 2℔. 2s. .	5	19	0
Jun.	To John Formons mariadg for my self and gris	6	10	0
	For letters 13s. Lady Boyis womans mariadg . . .	3	10	0
	For taking Nany to Polwarth Hows and to buy sop .	2	12	0
	To Docter Sincklars childs christining	5	16	0
July	For powder and jassamin .	1	12	0
	To the woman in the tobuith 1lb. 9s. To Tam Noble 1lb. 9s.	2	18	0
August	For letters 1lb. For letters from London betwixt August 94 and this day	9	0	0
	For helpin windows 10s. To Manson, barber, 14s. .	1	4	0
	To Drink mony in the contry	2	0	0
	For letters		13	
	To Adam cochman .		18	
Novr.	To Provist Chis's nurs		6	
	To letters at the post 2lb. 4		4	
	To Greenocks man 14, Torwoodlys nurs 3lb.	3	14	0
Decmr.	To Drumsho boys, etc. .	2	1	0
		S. 122	0	0

[1] Alexander, Lord Raith, at one time Lord Treasurer Depute for Scotland.

	[Small Payments]	[Scots]		
	Sundry small debursments, 1696.	£	s.	d.
Janr.	To Andrew Lamb . . .	0	10	0
	To hansels	10	0	0
20th	For knitins and tap 15s. .	0	15	0
Aprill	For letters 9s. to Ladikins to a poor woman 1l. 11s.	2	0	0
	For threed 1l. 14s., for coch heirs 1l. 9s.	3	3	0
	For letters 1l. 5s. For paper 7s., powder 12l., to An Faa 1l. 9s.	3	13	
	To Justice Clarks[1] nurs	2	18	
	For a bell and cord to the door	1	9	
	For cariing books . . .	1	13	0
	For washing a goun .	1	9	
	To a christining of a child of Breastmills . .	5	16	
	To the woman in Tolbooth	0	14	6
July	For letters 15s., mor 4l. 8s.	5	3	
	To Will Padyen . . .	1	16	0
	For a hather brush 3s., pins 10s..	0	13	
Agust.	For threed 18s., pins 10s., knitins 10s.			
	To the falconer 14s.	0	14	0
Sept.	To the Justice Clarks man	[illegible]	[illegible]	0
Octobr.	To a barber for half a year		1	
1st	For 4 ounces of threed .		1	
Novr.	For letters .			
	To Car when he brought in Rachy			
	To Will: Padyen . . .			
	To gloves to Marin Lidas .			
	To the woman in Tolboth			
	To Meg Vas			
	To Gavin Plumers[2] nurs .			
	To my sister Elisabeth I gave her			
		S. 65	00	00

[1] Adam Cockburn of Ormiston, appointed 28th November 1692.

[2] Frequently mentioned in the *Account Book of Sir John Foulis*.

. .

[Small Payments] [Scots]

Sundry small Debursments, 1697.

		£	s.	d.
January 1st	To hansels and new years gifts	012	00	00
	To Wisharts man . . .	001	00	00
	For letters	000	10	00
	To drinkmony to Conservater and Cap[tain] Drumonds nurses .	005	16	00
Febr. 12	To the barber a quarter .	001	09	00
	For a letter from John	000	13	00
	To Justice Clarks man 1li. 9s., to a poor man 14s. . . .	002	13	00
March	To Provist Chieslys 2 nurses	005	16	00
	To pouther 8sh. 2 quer paper 14s.	001	02	00
	To Jame Carein in arls and to Jacson 14s. 6d. . .	001	01	06
	To my fathers cochman in drinkmony	002	10	00
Agust.	To the old woman .	000	14	06
	To flint and ball . . .	000	04	00
	To my sister Breastmills nurs	004	00	00
Sep:	To An Faa	000	14	00
	For letters to b. . . .	000	05	00
Octor 12	To the barber.	001	09	00
	To fieing and arls . . .	001	00	00
	For wafers	000	02	00
	To Grisies master for cols	000	14	06
	For sweat powther 12s.	000	12	00
	For letters	000	10	00
	To Jamie Carr	002	00	00
	For letters	000	15	00
	To a cochman . .	000	14	06
	For bringing Dorathie Farellton from Berwick . . .	003	12	00
	To chairmen	001	02	00
	For cariing a chair and box twis .	000	16	00
	For sevarell little things . .	007	00	00

[Small Payments]	[Scots] £ s. d.
For pins and other litle things per Francy Newtons account	002 04 00
	S. 62 18 0

Brothers and Sisters' Accounts.

1696	Pay'd to my brothers and sisters.			
January	To Archibald Baillie.	[Scots]		
the 18	To Baillie Faa on his acount	62	10	0
Febr. 24	To him	5	16	0
Aprill	To him .	5	16	0
	To Will Johnston on his acount	17	10	0
May 13th	To John Murduck on his acount per recept . .	12	0	0
	To my mother in law on his acount	66	13	8
	To Archbald per recept .	24	0	0
July 19	To Archbald Bewhauen on his acount per recept .	21	0	0
	To the Lady Gradins[1] servant Marg^rt Ingles on his acount .	2	8	0
	To Breastmill[2] on his acount	19	0	0
	To Hew Mintgumary on his acount	36	0	0
	To John Wight on his acount	36	0	0
	To him brought from the 4 page	986	14	0
	To John Bayllie.			
July 96	To pay a bill for him . .	130	0	0
	To him he pay'd his skiper and conservaters lady .	30	0	0
	To Manson for a wige to him	17	8	0

[1] Helen Johnston, daughter of Lord Wariston, and aunt of George Baillie, married George Hume of Graden.

[2] Dundas of Breastmiln, Linlithgowshire, married George Baillie's sister Rachel.

	[Brothers, etc.]	[Scots] £	s.	d.
	To him he lent a Ham bargeman	17	8	0
	To him when he went away 10 crons, more 1℔. 9	31	9	0
	To pay his chamer rent .	1	0	0
	For Harton to be his night goun	12	17	0
Octor.	For making his goun	0	14	0
	To him by bill to Holland .	120	0	0
		360	16	0

Payd to my brothers and sisters 1697.

		[Scots]		
January	To my sister Hellin .	009	14	00
	To linin to her	007	10	00
	To muslin to her .	001	19	00
	To muslin to her ruffils	001	10	00
	To her ant Johnston on her acount	026	02	00
	To her for flowrd muslin	007	15	

To Elisabeth.

January	To her	002	00	
	To her in mony .	009	14	00
	To her 2 ells strip flanell	005	00	00
	To her 5 ells alamod	012	00	00
	To linen for her . . .	007	10	00
	To strip muslin to her at 3℔. 18 per ell	008	08	00
	To muslin for ruffils at 3℔.	001	10	00
	To her ant Johnston on her acountt	026	02	00
Jun. 22d	To her	006	06	00
Septm.	To her	004	00	00
Novr.	To her 3℔. 12s. .	003	12	00
	To her for flourd muslin .	007	15.	

	[Brothers, etc.]	[Scots] £ s. d.
March	To John Baillies acount to Cowin Taylor	012 00 00
	To Chisim shoemaker on his acountt	002 08 00
Septm.	To Mr. Robison on his acount .	120 00 00
Decmr.	To him a doller . .	002 18 00
	To Cowin taylor in full of ane old acount	010 00

Johns account is £147 6 0.

Febr. 28	To Robert he got for his master .	002 14 00
	To him 10s., to making a wastcoat 12, hat and gloves 11ti. 2s.	012 04 00
March	To 8 pair shoes by Chisim 6ti. 8s., to him 1ti. 4s., puder 10s.	008 02 00
Ditto	To him 1ti. 9, more 1ti. 9, stokins to him 1ti. 6s. .	004 04 00
Aprill	To him 1ti. 10, more 16s. 6d. .	002 06 06
May	To him to go over the water 1ti. 9sh., more 1ti. 9s.	002 18 00
Jun.	To him 1ti. 9s., for writting his book 5ti.	006 09 00
July	To him 1ti. 9s., stokins 1ti. 14s., bukels 16s.	003 19 00
Agust.	To a wige 11ti. 16, ane other wige 2ti. 18s., shoes 2ti. 14 .	017 08 00
	To him 1ti. 9s. To him 14s., muslin to him 1ti. 4s., mending 10s.	003 17 00
Septr.	To him 2ti. 18s., more 1ti., puder 14s. shoes 2ti. 13s. .	007 05 00
	To him 1ti. 9s. butons, threed, shoes, mending and 1ti. 2s. 11d. .	002 11 00
	To muslin to him at 3ti. 8s. .	011 18 00
Febr.	To James to give his master, 8ti. 14s., writting master, 2ti. 14	011 08 00

	[Brothers, etc.]	[Scots] £ s. d.
	To him for books, 10s., shoes 1li. 16s., to himself 10.	002 16 00
	To stokins to him 19s., puder 10s., to ge over the water 1li. 9s.	002 18 00
March	To pay 3 quarters at the scooll	017 08 00
	To stokins 1li. 6s., to his writing master 14s., to him 9s.	002 09 00
Jun.	To shoes 1li. 10s., dressing a hat 6s., gloves 6s. 6d., pokits 6s. 6d.	002 09 00
October	To books to him 2li. 9s., to Lily for him 14s. 6d.	003 03 06
	To stokins 18s., candle to his scool 14s. 6d., to himself 10s.	002 02 06

Edenburg, '99. Mony pay'd my brothers this year.
To Archbald Baillie as follows.

		[Scots]
1699 January	To Georg Drumond in Edinburgh tolbuth	63 12 0
	To Andrew Carr per instructione	57 16 0
Febr. 24	To Robert Spence	6 10 0
	To chamber rent	6 10 6
	To John Rainalds	20 8 0
	To Mr. Dumbar	70 14 0
	To loos a panded coat, the man in Canigate Tolbuth	6 0 0
	To man in tolbuth 9	009 0 0
	To him at severall times 30 19 0	30 19 0
	For Mr. Bonnar	20 0 0
October	For boord to Will Paton per recept	129 0 0
	To William Thomson per accumpt and recept	

John Baillie.

January	To him	81 14 0
	To him which was the last he got befor he counted	38 3 4

	[Brothers, etc.]	[Scots]		
		£	s.	d.
June	To him the ballance of his count that he had his brothers not for	1169	8	4
July	To hime which was the first he got after he counted with his brother	9	8	4
	To his poll	4	0	0
	To his docters . . .	49	6	0
November	To him his principall sume of 333ti. 6s. 8d., intrest 185ti. 8s. 0d.	[Scots] 518	14	8

James Baillie.

Febr.	To him at severall times befor his accumpt was made	32	06	0
	To Baillie Bowdens accumpt the first after his counting .	205	4	4
Decmr.	To him at severall times this year as per Cash book .	155	10	0
S.	The ballance of his last account, Candlemas '99 .	134	6	8

Robert Baillie.

Febr.	To him quhich was the last befor cumpting with his brother .	49	14	6
	To him at severall times after cumpting and per Grahm's account	72	6	0
	To Baillie Bowdens accumpt	317	13	6
	To a bill from Holland	520	0	0
S.	To ballance of his last account, Candlemas '99 £157 5 6			

Edenburgh, 1700. My brothers. Deb: to Cash.

Archibald Baillie.	[Scots]		
To Francy Newton per accumpt .	29	5	0
To Mr. Abercrummie per accumpt	16	10	0

	[Brothers, etc.]	[Scots] £	s.	d.
June	To Mr. Dumbar by instructions	38	0	0
	To Will: Papon [*sic*] for boord and poket mony	194	0	0
	For loosing a bible was panded	5	6	0
August 24	To Will: Cowins accumpt	25		
	To Provist Johnstons accumpt	96		
	To a baxter in town	8		
	To pay Hay, wige maker	9		
	To one Duncan in town	8		
	To him at severall times in cash	14	1	
	To Dinigile Robison	5	1	
Deem. 11th	To William Paton for 6 monthes boord and poket	113	1	0
	To him by Plumer when he was in the Tolbooth	54	8	0

John Baillie.

		£	s.	d.
	To his poll	4	0	0
	To hime per recept	480	0	0

Robert Baillie.

		£	s.	d.
	For his poll	10	0	0
	To Francy Newton per accumpt	7	0	0

James Baillie.

		£	s.	d.
Decmr. 4th	To him at sevarall times as per his recept	121	5	6
Ditto 30	To him being the first after he sign'd his account in Decm' 4th	22	11	0

* *

Edenburgh, January 1702. My brothers. Deb. to Cash.

	Archibald.	[Scots] £	s.	d.
20	To Georg Edgar on his precept	53	3	0
March	To Breastmill for him	3	0	0

	[Brothers, etc.]	[Scots] £	s.	d.
2d.	To my sister Breastmill per his precept	12	0	0
	To Androw Car per hir [*sic*] recept	3	6	0
May 15	To himself	1	0	0
	To my sister Breastmills woman per his precept . . .	14	4	0
26	To my sister Breastmill to accumpt of the above said precept the whole precept being for £60 Scots	15	0	0
	For a skin to his briches and one sent to my sister Breast[mill] .	0	14	0
June 9	To him sent by his man to Breastmill	4	0	0
	To my sister Breastmill on his precept	4	0	0
	For shoes	2	0	0
	For lowsing his brothers watch he panded .	7	10	0
July 18	To Ms. Stothert in Lanrick on his precept	17	16	0
August	To Francis Newton per his precept	61	18	0
	To my sister Breastmill in pairt of a precept of £52 12s. Scots .	36	0	0
	To my sister Breastmill in full of the precept of £52 12s. .	16	12	0
Oct. 6	To Georg Edgar one his accumpt	3	14	0
Novr. 26th	To my sister Breastmill per his precept	57	16	0
	To my sister Breastmills woman in full of the precept abovesaid of £60 Scots	30	16	0

[1698] The expence of my mothers funerals.

	[Scots]		
To her dead linin .	060	00	0
To her coffin . .	076	00	0

[Mother's funeral]	[Scots] £	s.	d.
To charge of her lying in the church	029	00	
For writting the letters and paper	14	10	
For plumkake 18℔. bisket 36	054	00	
For glases	13	00	0
For brecking the ground	14	10	
To the batthels . . .	07	05	
To the kirk tressorar	52	10	0
For the morcloath .	11	12	0
For the grave and turf	08	14	0
To the bell man . . .	02	08	
To the poor	06	00	
For coch and harse	37	04	
For cariing the letters .	08	00	00
For keeping the stairs	01	10	
To the man that drove the harse	02	00	
For cariing letters to the country	03	00	
To drink mony to the surgons man	07	08	
To the wrights man	02	00	
For wins and seck, my oun	129	12	0
To the herralds for her scuchens and horsemunting per ther accompt	210	06	8
	750	9	8

	£	s.	d.	£	s.	d.
Of this mony only payd out presently, the wine being in the howse .	478	12	00			
Heralds and wine together is .. .	339	18	8			
S.	818	10	8			
Given out for sundry small things				68	1	0
				818	10	8

My Father-in-law[1]

Robert Baillie of Jerriswood, Esqr. was eldest son to George Baillie of Jerriswood. His Mother was sister to Sir Archibald Johnston Lord Warriston. After having been educated in the Universitys of Scotland he went abroad to study the law, and, being at Paris when Sir William Lockart of Lee was first time Ambasoder at that Court, he was recommended by Sir William Lockart to the Popes Nuncio then at Paris to travel with him to Rome, which gave him an opertunity of being acquainted with many great men.

Returning to Scotland some years therafter, he was well seen in the Civel Law, divinity, History and whatever else could acomplish a Gentleman and good Christian. Abount the year 1661 he married[2] Mrs. Rachell Johnston, Daughter to the Lord Warriston. When the Lord Warriston was committed to the Tower in the year 1663 Jerriswood came from Scotland to wait of him, and stayed at London untill The Lord Warriston was sent to Scotland. Then Jerriswood went to Scotland and attended him till his Death. It is observable That from the time of my Lord Warristons Death Jerriswood had an impression on his Spirit that he would suffer death for the Cause of his Religion in the same place that my Lord Warriston did, which he told to some of his nearest friends long before his death.

Also about two years before he died, having been long in the fields alone, he came in and told his Lady that he would Certainly Suffer Death at the Cross of Edinburgh for his principles ere long.

Tho' he was a very Bright man he would never accept of any publick Employment, nor be member of parliament,

[1] The words 'My Father-in-law' are in Lady Grisell's handwriting, and are endorsed on the paper. The document itself is not in her hand, and is unpunctuated.

[2] '20 January 1661. Proclaimed in marriage Mr. Robert Baillie of Jerviswood and Rachel Johnston, daughter of Sir Archibald Johnston, Lord Warriston.' —Lanark Parish Registers.

because he would not take the Declaration Test and other Oaths imposed at that time. Yet he lived always peaceably under the government, acknowledged the King's authority, and Declared in his last words that he never intended any thing against the government but to have things redressed in a parlimentary way.

About the year 1677 Mr. James Kirton, late Minester of Edinburgh, who was seized in his own Chamber by Captain Carstairs unwarrantably without any order, Jerriswood, being lodged near by, was Called, and desired the Captain to show his order for apprehending Mr. Kirton; and he having none to produce, Jerriswood Rescued him out of the Captan's hands. Jerriswood was summened to Appear nixt day before the privy Council, and having appeared was fined in five hundred pound Str. and committed prisoner to the tolbooth of Edinburgh. Afterward was sent prisoner to the Castle of Stirlen where he Continued a long time.

In the year 1678 Jerriswood went to London with Duke William Hamilton and the Noblemen and Gentlemen to represent the grivences of the Highland Host invading the West of Scotland.

About the year 1682, when the Duke of York was appointed Commissioner for the parliament of Scotland, Duke William Hamilton, Lord Tarras and many other members of parliament had concerted to Oppose The Duke's being Commissioner because he was a papist, and had the Oppinion of Sir George Lockart and Sir John Cunningham two Eminent Lawyers who thought it was against law. Jerriswood being consulted all along by Duke Hamilton etc. in that affair, tho he was no member of parliament but as a man very Capable of advising them, The Duke of York, being come to Scotland, by his intrest kept the two lawyers from pleading against him; but Jerriswood was looked upon by the Duke with a Jealous eye and as an enimy to the government because of his opposing popery and arbitrary power

About the year 1683 Sir Hugh and Sir George Campbles of Sesnock, Jerriswood, Commissar Monro and several other Gentlemen were seised in London. Jerriswood, being brought before King Charles the Second and the Councill, was charged with tresonable practices and of being Engaged in a plot against the Government, which he absolutly denyed. The King Threatned him with the Boots in Scotland, to which he answeared, His Majesty might give him Spurs too but he Could Say nothing but the truth. He was returned to the gate house and laid in Irions, where he continued Six Months, and afterwards sent down in a Yaught to Scotland with Sir Hugh Campble etc. and there confined Closs prisoner in Edinburgh Tollbooth, where being Called and examined before the Councill and charged with Conversing with and advising the members of Parliament to oppose the Duke of Yorks being Commissioner and several other things Relating thereto of which there was no proof, yet he was fined in Six thousand pound Str. It was then thought their malice would have gone no further against him but he was Still detained Closs prisoner, during which time he was afflected with a fever of Sex weeks Continuance, and before he was well recovered there came an order from Court to pursue him before the Justiciary for his life. It was very remarkable the thursday night before he Received his indictment he had some glorious Manefestation from God, and on the friday morning he wrot out a note which he convey'd by his keeper to his Sister Mrs. Kirton in which he said 'Sister, Praise, praise God with me for I 'have got such a glorious Manifestation of God this night as I would not exchange for Many Many Worlds. They are thirsting after my blood, which they will get, but Some 'of the greatest of them will live Short while after." K Chas: th 2d died febr. 7th 1685.

It was very extraordinary The Justiciary Court proceeded against him on the same grounds and Reasons for which he was fined by the Councill without ever the Councills Sentence being recalled.

On Munday the 22 of December 1684 he received his indictment to Appear befor the Justice Court at ten a Clock the day following, wher Sir George Lockart was made assessor to Sir George McKenzie, then King's Advocat, to plead against him. He was Carried out in his nightgown not being fully recovered of his fever, and was kept in the Court untill one on the Wedindsay morning, returned again to prison, appeared before them again about eleven the same day, and Received Sentence of death to be execute the very Same day betwext two and three in the afternoon. When he returned to prison after Receiving his Sentence, he prayed publickly before all in the room. Some of his words were 'Lord, we take this Severe Sentence from the land of man as a love token from the heart of my God This night Shall I be a piller in the House of God to go furth no more and I shall be with the Generall Assembly of the first born and with the Spirits of Just men made perfect and the Mediator of the new Covenant which is best of all.'

A little before his excecution there came two of the town Curats Mr. Trotter and Mr. Londie to desire access to him, but his Lady and her sisters told them none of them Should come there to trouble him. He pleasantly said he would be content to Speak with the brethren, but he Saw the Sisterhood were not for it and he had little time to Spare. Some of his fellow prisoners came to take their leave of him, asked him what Lord Tarras and others had witnessed against him. He answeared, 'Who Could Remember fire Side discourse Several years ago.' For he could not Remember whether one word of it was true or not. But, tho none of the witnesses agreed in any one point in the proof against him, yet they Thirsted So much after his blood that it was resolved this great and good man Should be made a Sacrifice to Popery and arbitary power. He said also to some of his fellow prisoners they are to cutt me in pices and Send me thorrow the Country but do what they will this body Shall be a glorifyed body in the day of the Resurrection.

Memoradums and derections to Servants and ruels layd down by my Mother both fer their diet and work. Copyd and colected together 1752, made by her Decr. 1743, and the derections given to the severl Servants.

To the Butler

1. You must rise airly in the morning which will make your whole business and houshold accounts easie.

2. Two bells are to be rung fer every meal; for breakfast half an hour after 8 and at 9; for diner half an hour after 1 and at 2; for super half an hour after 8 and at 9. At the first bell for super lay the bible and cushions for prayers. At the stated hours.

3. Have bread toasted, butterd tost or whatever is orderd for breakfast all set ready by the second bell.

4. Consider your business and have a little forethought that you may never be in a hurry or have anything to seek, to which nothing will contribut more than having a fixt and regular places for seting every thing in your custody in order, and never fail seting every thing in its own place, which will prevent much trouble and confution, and soon make every thing easie, when you know where to go derectly for what you want.

5. See that the back doors of the Porch be shut as soon as the last bell rings for diner and super. *N.B.*

6. That all the servants that are to wate at table be ready *in the room before we come.*

7. That you may never have occation to run out of the room for what is wanted have always at the sideboard what follows or any thing ells you can foresee there can be occation for

Bread	Water	peper	vinigar
Ail	wines	mustard	shalot
smal Beer	sugar	oyle	sallad

N.B. 8. Stand at the sideboard and fill what is cald for to the other servants that come for it, and never fill, nor let any other do it in a dirty glass, but as soon as a glass is drunk out of, range it derectly in the brass pail which you must have there with water for that purpos, then wype it.

9. Never let the dirty knives forks and spoons go out of the dinning room, but put them all in the box that stands for that use under the table.

10. When a signe is made to you, go and see if the second course is ready, then come and take away all the first course before you set down any of the second.

11. In like maner when a sign is made take away the second course.

12. Take the napkine of the midle of the table and sweep all the bread and crums clean of all round the table into a plate.

13. Have any desert that there is ready to set doun, always have butter and cheese, and set plates and knives round.

14. When all that is taken away, set doun water to wash.

15. Then take away the cloath and set doun what wine is cald for, with the silver marks upon them, in bottle boards, and a decanter of water, and glasses to every one round.

16. When diner and super is over, cary what leaves of smal beer and bread into the Pantry your self, and the cheese, that nothing may go to waste.

17. As soon as the company leaves the dining room after diner and super come imediatly and lock up what Liquors are left, clean your glasses, and set every thing in its place and in order.

18. Always take care to keep your doors and your cuberts lockt where you have any charge.

N.B 19. The Plate must always be clean and bright, which a little wiping every day will do, when once it is made perfectly clean, which must not be by whitening but a little soap suds to wash it, or spirit of wine if it has got any spots, and wiping and rubing with a brush and then a piece Shambo leather.

20. The Pantry, seler and *Larder* and every thing that is under your care must be kept perfectly clean and sweet, which will require constant attention, but if things are alowed to run into dirt and confution, double the time and pains will not set it right, and every thing that stands in dirty places will soon grow musty and stinking and unfit to be used.

21. Let not the dirty cheney go into the kitchin till the cook be ready to clean it and empty the meat of them into pewter dishes befor it goes to the second table, and see that none of them is brock when you put them by.

22. Who ever breaks cheny, glasses or bottles let me know that day, otherways thay will be layd to your charge.

23. Be exact in giving your pantry cloaths to wash, and in geting them back and keeping them together.

24. Clean everything without delay and put all your things in order after every meal and after tea.

25. Have tea, water and what may be usualy cald for in the afternoon ready, that it may not be to wait for.

26. Every morning clean all the bottle that have been emptyd the day befor, and set them up in the bottle rack, this will save much trouble and make cleaner bottles, then when the dirt is allowed to dry in them, if any has a bad smel or sedement sticking to them, to make them as sweet and clean as new, boyle some wood ashes in watter and make a strong Lee, put the bottles into it befor it is cold, let them soak in it all night, next day wash them well in it, then in clean water, a few hours standing in the Lee may do for those not very dirty, and hang them in the bottle rack with their heads down, the most necessary thing for having good wine and ale is clean bottles and good corking, every bottle must be ranced with a little of the Liquor that is bottling, and one bottle of it will do the whole.

27. Be constantly atentive in looking about to see what any one wants at table and when you take away a

dirty plate take also the dirty knife and fork and give all clean.

28. You must keep your self very clean.

29. At one a clock in the sumer when the servants are at out work all the stable people, carters and maids go to diner, in the winter they dyn at the hour with the rest of the family altogether after we have dynd, but in the sumer you and those that wait at table must dyn after us, both second table and later meat are alowed a clean table cloth every other day, and you must see that all get their vituals warm and in order without confution or waste.

N.B. 30. You must see that all the servants about the stables and out works be out of the kitchin before ten a clock, except when any of them is obliged to wait at super

N.B. 31. The under butler puts on the gentlemens fiers, cleans their boots and shoes, helps you to clean every thing, and to get breakfast and to cover the table, etc.

32. If any of the family is indesposed and eat in their room, require back from the person you gave it to any thing that is under your charge, such as knives, forks, spoons, glasses, linnen, etc., and never allow any thing of that sort to go about the house or to be out of its proper place.

33. Deliver carefully back to the house keeper what ever table linnen you get from her and upon no account make any other use of them, nor dity them by wyping any thing as you have cloaths for every use you can want.

34. *N.B.* Bring up your Account books every monday morning and lay them at my room door.

35. Every servant gets a mutchkin of beer every meal, except when they get milk, which is always when there is any to give them, and then they have only beer for their diner.

36. The servants gets half an Oat loaf at every meal, or if it is broun bread or Ry, the loaf is set down to eat what they want, but no pocketing or waste alowed, and that you must see to, and observe these ruels for bread and beer, for your account of it must hold out with this.

37. *N.B.* If a glass of wine is cald for to company bring

as many glasses on a salver as there is people, and *fill it befor you come* into the room, and leave the bottle at the door in case more is wanted, and have a clean napkin hung over your arm.

The Servants Diet

There is to be brewed out of every Louthian Boll of Malt 20 gallons of small beer, our coper and looms brews 2½ bolls at a time which is 50 gallons, that is 400 Scots pints. From 6 furlets of Malt that is a Louthian boll and half there is 240 scots pints of beer.

	pints
17 servants 3 mutchkins a day each is about 13 pints a day which in 14 days is .	182
For the table 2 pints a day in 14 days is .	28
For second table 2 pints a day is and 2 more .	30
	240

This calculation is when all the servants get beer.

8 stone of meal or broun flower should fully serve 17 servants eight days.

There is 30 loves out of the stone of Oat meal, the same reckoning to be made of broun flower or Ry, backt in half peck,[1] loaves. Beef salted for the servants is cut in pieces of as many pounds as there are common servants, if 15, every pice is 15 pounds, no alowence in that for the second table, they geting what comes from the first table.

Sunday they have boild beef and broth made in the great pot, and always the broth made to serve two days.

Monday broth made on Sunday and a Herring.

Teusday broth and Beef.

Wednesday broth and 2 egs each.

Thursday Broth and beef.

Fryday Broth and Herring.

---

[1] This should surely be half pound ; a peck is a measure of capacity containing about two stones.

Saterday broth without meat, and cheese, or a puden or blood pudens, or a bagish, or what is most convenient.

In the big pot for the 2 days broth is alowed 2 pound of barly or grots, or half and half.

Breakfast and super half an oat loaf or a proportion of broun bread, but better set down the loaf, and see non is taken or wasted, and a muchkin of beer or milk when ever there is any. at diner a mutchkin of beer for each.[1]

Derections for the House Keeper

The servants diet belongs to her charge but I chose to put it altogether.

To get up airly is most necessary to see that all the maids and other servants be about their proper business. a constant care and attention is required to every thing that there be no waste nor any thing neglected that should be don.

The dayry carefully lookt after, you to keep the kie of the inner milk house where the butter and milk is, see the butter weighted when churn'd, and salt what is not wanted fresh, to help to make the cheese and every now and then as often as you have time to be at the milking of the cows.

Keep the maids closs at their spining till 9 at night when they are not washing or at other necessary work, weight out to them exactly the soap, and often go to the wash house to see it is not wasted but made the proper use of, and that there be no linnen washt there but those of the family that are alowed to do it. often see that they waste not fire either in the wash house or Landry and that the Landry be keept clean.

Take care that the Cooks waste not butter, spices, nor

[1] From the data here given the cost of feeding a servant would seem to have amounted to about 3d. per diem, made up thus: bread $\frac{24}{60}$d., beer $\frac{54}{60}$d., meat $\frac{60}{60}$d., eggs or herrings $\frac{24}{60}$d., barley $\frac{12}{60}$d., sundries $\frac{6}{60}$d.—total $\frac{180}{60}$d. = 3d. In this calculation oats are taken at 10s. per boll, barley at 3d. per lb., malt at 15s. per boll, eggs at 2d. per dozen, and meat at 2d. per lb.

any thing amongst their hands, nor embasel it, and that the kitchin fire be carefully lookt after and no waste, let it be getherd after diner and the cinders throwen up that non be throwen out, neither from that nor by the Chamber maid.

Make the kitchin maid keep all the places you have lookt up very clean, also the kitchin, Hal and passages, and see the Cook feed the fouls that are put up right and keep them clean or they can never be fat nor good.

To take care the house be kept clean and in order, help to sheet and make the straingers beds, that the beds and sheets be dry and well aird. get account from the chamber maid of what candles she gets from you for the rooms and see there be no waste of candle nor fire any where.

Keep the kie of the cole house but when it is wanted to get out coals, but be sur it be always lockt at night, that the Turf stack be not tred down but burnt even forward. let them fill all their places with coals at once, that the kie be not left in the door.

To make scimed milk cheese for the use of the family when ever there is milk enough for it. when there are more cows then the dairy maid can milk so soon as they shoud be, let Grisell Wait or any other in the toun I shall name help her and get for doing it a pint of scim'd milk a day.

As every thing is weighted to you give out nothing but by weight.

6 ounces pruens for Cockaleekie or stove.

6 oun. Makerony for a smal dish, 8 oun. larger.

6 oun. vermiceli for a soup.

a pound peas for a puden or soup.

for best short bread 8 lb. flower 3 lb. butter, second short bread 8 lb. flower 2 lb. butter.

For a bun of 5 lb flower 1 lb butter, 2 lb raisins, 1 lb curants, 4 ounces caraway seed, 4 ounces sugar and barm.

The servants sheets is changed once a munth.

One week the body linnin is washt, the second week table and bed linnin and always bouckt when the weather will alow of it, the third week the landry maids must be keept closs at spining and at all times when they have not other necessary business, such as Hay and Harvest and the Barn which the dairy maid goes to when she has a moments time for it, and always to the miln with any melder. the dairy maid, house maid and kitchin maid always to spine when they are not otherways necessarly imployd which they will often pretend to be if they are not diligently lookt after and keep to it.

Thomas Yool, George Carter and postilion do not wash in the house nor

John Hume the Carter.

The other men servants wash in the house or out of the house as I can agree for them, but not at a certainty. when washt out I give 1^{0}sh. a year for each of them.

All the scim'd milk that can be spaird after serving the family or when cheese is not made of it, to be measurd and sent to Grisell Wait who sells it and accounts for it, or gives it away to such poor people in the toun as I give her a note of. but non of them to come about the doors for it.

Take care there be no hangers on, nor santering odd people come about the house, but those that have business and that not at male time, which they will always do if not hinderd.

See that all the maids keep their dusters and washing clouts dry and in order, and not let them ly about in hols wet, which soon rots and makes an end of them.

See that every one keeps what is in their charge in there proper stated places, then nothing will be out of order, or to seek when wanted, nor any hurry.

In general to keep all the servants in order, with some authority and make them obay you and do their duty without feed or favour to any, and to look after every thing with the same care and faithfulness as if it was your own, then few things can go wrong. if diffident or ignorant of any thing, ask derections from me or Mrs. Menzies or any that can inform you.

EXTRACTS FROM BOOK MARKED 'BILLS OF FAIR'[1]

Lord Orknays,[2] Oct. 12, 1715

	Peas soup	relief hame and spinich
boyld chickens with bate butter and slices of bread and limon	pidgion py	stacks with minst meat about them
	sewd bief very tender with sallarly	

2

	Rosted Turkic	
pickled sols		friassy of cocks-combs and sweat breads
	4 rosted partrages	

---

	milk in a boill	
aples Chestons pears	confections	pears peald walnuts aples
	milk	

---

[1] There are one hundred and seventy of these.

[2] Lord George Hamilton, Earl of Orkney, fifth son of the Duke of Hamilton, one of the Lords of the Bedchamber to George I. He married Mrs. Villiers, William III.'s mistress, after the death of Queen Mary. She is commemorated by Swift for her wisdom and ugliness, and according to Lady Mary Wortley Montagu she drew the greatest number of eyes at the coronation of George II. 'She exposed behind a mixture of fat and wrinkles, and before a very considerable protuberance which preceded her. Add to this the inimitable roll of her eyes and her gray hairs, which by good fortune stood directly upright, and 'tis impossible to imagine a more delightful spectacle.'

Duck of montroses [1] super

Scots collips w^{t} marow and black pudins about them

friasy rabits		rost cheas
ratafia cream	frut	earned cream
	rost small wild foull	

Sunday, Christenmas 1715, w^{t} 9 of our frinds 14 at table in all.

Plumb patage with sagoe and a few frute

relief minsht pys

fricascy chickens	Bran [2]	plumb puden
	rost bief	

2

	a rost goos	
cold toung	Bran	oyster loves
	wild foull	

Desert

	Ratafia cream	
butter and chease	sillibubs	Jacolet walnuts and almonds
aples		stewd pears
chestons	Jellys	butter and chease

[1] James Graham, fourth Marquis and first Duke of Montrose, at this time Keeper of the Great Seal of Scotland, married Lady Christian Carnegy, second daughter of David, Earl of Northesk. The Duke and Duchess seem to have been very intimate friends of the Baillies, as their names occur frequently in the Accounts. Lockhart was not unnaturally very sore at the Duke becoming a Whig, and sums up his character as follows: 'He was a man of good understanding yet was led by the nose by a set of men whom he far surpassed, and never in all his by-past life did one material action that was prudent and discreet. His courage upon certain accounts was much questioned, but his unsincerity and falseness allowed by all.'

[2] Brawn.

Lord Orfoords,[1] 28 Deer.

	sup	a relief 2 young geas
rost bief on by table	rost mutton	
cut by servants	———	
	2 *ser*	
2 partrages		Ragow cokscoms
and partrages hasht		
ragow hogs feet		rosted larks and
	———	other small birds
	Deseart.	
Chestnuts	Jellys	aples
butter and cheese		butter and cheese
	Confections	
Bisquet		oranges
	Jellys	

Bishop Sarums [2] Christenmas Dinr.

	Plumb patage	relief Scots colops cokscombs
	little bals and sawsages	
fricasey forst	Bran	orange pudine
meat	Rost Bieff	
and other	———	
things	2	
	Minsht pys	
	Bran stood still	Larks rosted
	a side of lame	
	———	
	Deseart	
Bisquets		stwd pears
	sillibubs	
	Jellys	
	Pears oranges	
stwd aples		Bisquits

[1] Edward Russel, Earl of Orford, at this time First Lord of the Admiralty.

[2] Dr. Gilbert Burnet, Lord Bishop of Salisbury, chaplain to William III. His mother was a sister of George Baillie's grandmother, so they were first cousins once removed. As Bishop Sarum died on 17th March 1715 the dinner recorded must have been his last Christmas dinner.

1715

Jan[r]. at home, 8 at table w[t] the duck of Montros.[1]

Broth — relief of salmond

pudens — hages

sheap head

2

checken py

Lobsters — peas

2 rosted turkies

Duke of Roxburgh,[2] January 3, 1715.

soup with a foull — relief of fish

fricascy chickens — little py of cocks combs

lams stons

leg rost mutton

2[d]

Rosted wild foull 4 or 5

sparagrasse — athine aple py — dry'd whitiens

a rosted turkie

Deseart

Limon Cream

dry'd aples — chestons

confections

shelld walnots — Jellys — pears

---

[1] See p. 282.

[2] John, fifth Earl and first Duke of Roxburgh, at this time Secretary of State for Scotland. He married Lady Mary Finch, only child of Daniel, Earl of Winchelsea and Nottingham, and widow of William Savile, Marquis of Halifax. His Grace had been very closely associated with Baillie at the time of the passing of the Act of Union, being one of the inner circle who directed the voting of the 'Squadrone Volante.' Lockhart describes him as follows: 'He was a man of good sense improven by so much reading and learning that perhaps he was the best accomplished young man of quality in Europe, and had so charming a way of expressing his thoughts that he pleased even those 'gainst whom he spoke.' The Duchess of Roxburgh was said to be the original of the Roxana of Lady Mary Wortley Montagu's Town eclogue.

Gen[l] Erles,[1] 10 May 1715

Green Soup

Makrell colopes

hens w[t] colloflour

2[d]

Rost hear

soles tartes

green peas

Mr. Mitchels, Feb. 29, 1716.

Soup relief salmon

fricascy of rabits a py

rost a saddle of mutton

2nd

3 rost ducklins

rague sweat breads sparagras
truffle and morels

4 rost chickens

April 1717. Duck and Duck Montrose Lord[2] and Lady Rothes

Soup relief cods head with alle sauce

fricascy rabits natle cale 3 boyld chickens

boyld hame

---

[1] General Erles. Probably Colonel Giles Earle, distinguished both in war and politics. He attached himself first to the Duke of Argyle, and was known as 'the Duke of Argyll's Erle.' He was appointed in 1718 groom of the Prince of Wales's bedchamber, and afterwards filled several other posts. He was a coarse humorist who played for his own hand, and eventually became more or less the tool of Walpole.

[2] John Leslie, eighth Earl of Rothes, eldest son of the fifth Earl of Haddington by the elder daughter of the Duke of Rothes, who left no sons. On succeed-

2nd

a rosted fillet of bief Larded with a rague of sweat breads under it

Ptansy | Crawfish | limon puden

rague sweatbreads | | sparagrass

8 rost ducks

Deseart

ratafia cream and gellies

chestnuts | | cheas butter

oranges | confections | aples

cheas | | pistoches

sillibubs

1718, 26 May, At Mr. Jhonstons.[1]

soup with a foule

relief boyld hame and pidgeons

beans and bacon | fricasey of chikens

rost veall with rague saus

relief of rost mutton

---

ing to the earldom of Rothes he assumed the surname of Leslie, and resigned the earldom of Haddington to his younger brother. He married Lady Jean Hay, daughter of John, second Marquis of Tweeddale. He was another of the Whigs for whom Lockhart had not a good word to say, 'being false to a degree, a contemner of honour and engagements, extremely ambitious, ridiculous, vain, and conceited (tho' of very ordinary parts and accomplishments), extravagantly proud and scandalously mercenary.'

[1] Son of Sir Archibald Johnston, Lord Wariston (executed 1663), and uncle of George Baillie. He was for many years Secretary of State for Scotland under William and Mary, but was dismissed over the Darien Scheme in 1696. He was generally known as 'Secretary Johnston,' and at one time was probably the most unpopular man in Scotland. Lockhart cannot find words in which to express his hate and contempt for that 'vile and execrable wretch,' who nevertheless was 'much esteemed' by Queen Caroline for his humour and pleasantry. He married Catherine Poulett, daughter of the second Baron Poulett, and lived latterly at Orleans House, Twickenham, where he cultivated fruit and entertained royalty. Lady Grisell's accounts show that many barrels of herrings were sent to him from Scotland by his dutiful nephew George Baillie.

	2 *Cour*[s]	
frayd eles	a goos	peas
archocks	tarts	cold salmond
	3 chickens	

Dessert

Milk		Milk
	Chirries	
strawberes	silibubs with strawberres	
	sweet meats	
milk	oranges	milk

Augst 1718. Lord Sundrelands,[1] 4 folks at table

Soup without anything init

Hog potch of bief mutton veall

2

boyld sols

fricasy chickens

3

Rost fillet bief

puden

4

	4 patriedges	
bottams of Raeteehocks		broyld eells
	2 young hairs	

Desert

frut	sillibubs	frut
frut	frut	frut
	Limon cream	

[1] Charles Spencer, third Earl of Sunderland, married, first, Lady Arabella Cavendish, fifth daughter of the Duke of Newcastle, and, second, Lady Anne Churchill, second daughter of the Duke of Marlborough. He was at this time First Lord of the Treasury. He was a great book collector, and a most unattractive character. His son succeeded as Duke of Marlborough.

Dinner at Sir William Bairds, 30 Dess. 1718

brown soup
chached calfs head

2nd

stewd carp
asalray seld [1]
rost Lame.

3rd

fasond with Larks about it mintched

pys jellies bran
salmond scoloped oysters
gundie partrages
with pickels and wood cocks.

Lord Anadall,[2] 29 January 1719, 10 at table

Brown Soup
Relief fish

backed pudins stewed Breast of veall
Beef or Mutton py
stewed fillet of Beef boyled chickens

whit soup
relief boyld Turkie with
forsed balls and sagages

---

[1] A celery salad.

[2] William Johnstone, third Earl and first Marquis, married, first, Sophia, daughter and heiress of John Fairholm of Craigiehall, Linlithgowshire, and, second, Charlotte Vanhose, only child of John Vanden Bempole. 'He was a man framed and cut out for business, extremely capable and assiduous; of a proud, aspiring temper, and when his affairs and politics went right, haughty to a great degree; and vice versa the civillest, complaisantest man alive, and a great affecter of popularity.'—*Lockhart's Papers.* He played for his own hand, and was trusted by neither party.

[Bills of Fare]

2d *C.*

Phesan and partrage

sparagras — scoloped oysters

aple tart w^{t} cream

ragu of sweet bread and cockscombs — broyled salmond.

3 Ducklins

Desert

a salver with sweet meats

stweed pears — pistosenuts

butter — chees

sillibubs and jellies — a lagere salver wt sweet meats — sillibubs and jellies

cheese — butter

pistashe nuts — stweed aples

a salver with sweet meats

---

super

confections

Lobster — rost lame

silibubs and jellies — a ring w^{t} wild foull collops and pickles etc. — silibubs and jellies

bran — cold tart

confections

---

febr 23, 1719. Super att home D and Ducthess of Montross Lord and Ladye forster.

4 rost chickens

salmond — collops

Candles

eating poset — fatafia cream

pattie — a salver w^{t} jellies and sillie bubess — a hair ragud

[Bills of Fare]

sago		lemon hatted kit[1]
	Candles
frecasy veals feet	3 Ducklines	drest Lobsters

At home Lady Mary Worthly.[2]

A soup with Marrabon

2
boyld lam
a plum pudine

3
rost turkie with mushrom sauce
and pickles w^{t} a litle bread

Desert
Curds
pears Jelly aples
cream

[1] Hatted Kit, a preparation of milk, etc., with a creamy top. 'Make 2 quarts of new milk scalding hot, and pour upon it quickly 4 quarts of fresh butter milk; let it stand without stirring till it becomes cold and firm, then take off the hat or upper part, drain it in a hair sieve, put it into a shape for half-an-hour, turn it into a dish, and serve with cream and sugar.'—Stevens's *Farm Book*, 1855, vol. ii. p. 299.

[2] The famous Lady Mary Pierrepont, eldest daughter of Evelyn, first Duke of Kingston, and the Lady Mary Fielding, daughter of William, Earl of Denbigh. She married Edward Wortley Montagu, eldest son of the Honourable Sydney Montagu. She was at this time a great friend of Lady Murray, *née* Grisell Baillie, a friendship which came to an end a few years afterwards. In 1721 'the peace of Mrs. Murray's family had been painfully broken in consequence of the brutality of a servant of her brother-in-law, Lord Binning, who, in a fit of drunkenness, burst into her bedchamber in the middle of the night and threatened to put her instantly to death if she ventured to resist his violence. With great courage and presence of mind she succeeded in alarming and calling up the family; but for this crime, which was held to be a capital burglary, the man was condemned to death, though afterwards his punishment

[Bills of Fare]

21 [Novr 1719]. Lady Hindfoord,[1] Ld Sutherland.[2]
10 at table.

1. Broth sheaps head boyld goos and a hagis
2. rost veal 2 easterlings limon pudine collerd pig the relief was fish

Confections and Jellys.

---

14 Decm^{r} (1719). Super at Mr. Cockburn 11 at table
22 persons in al.

head, eating poset in cheana high dish, foot, hauch venison, one side backd pudine, 2 partrages and larks, midle litl dish with sallory sellet made and unmade, othe[r] s^{d} veal collops white sauce, 2 boyd pullets w^{t} persley sauce in the midle pickles of other sort than the comon ones

In the midle of the table a pirimide sillibubs and orang cream in the past, above it sweet meets dry and wet.

---

was commuted for transportation. On the subject of this escape, Lady Mary thought fit to exercise her wicked wit in an infamous ballad, which of course she loudly disclaimed all knowledge of, but of which her own letters to her sister Lady Mary plainly enough betray her to have been the writer. . The subject is repeatedly alluded to in the printed collection of her letters, and still more pointedly in some of those that have not been published.'—Appendix to Lady Murray's *Memoirs*.

[1] Lady Hyndford, daughter of John, fifth Earl of Lauderdale, and wife of James Carmichael, second Earl of Hyndford.

[2] John Gordon, sixteenth Earl of Sutherland. President of the Board of Trade. Took a leading part in suppressing the '15. 'He is a very honest man, a great asserter of the liberties of the people, hath a good rough sense, is open and free, a great lover of the bottle and of his friend, brave in his person which he hath shown in several duels, too familiar for his quality, and often keeps company below it.'—Mackay. He married three times.

[Bills of Fare]

5 June (1720) Mr. Wallop [1] and 8 at table

1. Barly broth with lambs head
2. a chean rost mutton
3. a dish turbet
4. Chickens, hair, peas and cold toung

Deseart

Milk, strawberies, Sillibubs

June 21st. Earle of Staires [2] and eleven at Table [3]

Scots Broth

Remove of Turbet and broild salmond

muton collups   Pigen py   chickins boyld

Boyld Lamb and French beans

2 Turkie poults.

Mushrooms   Peas

Cheries Tart

Lobsters   cream loafs.

a goose.

Desert and

Cream Jellies strawberies

Cheries swetmeats allmond-cream

Lemon Cream

---

[1] John Wallop, afterwards first Earl of Portsmouth, at this time M.P. for Hampshire, and a Lord of the Treasury. He was created Baron Wallop and Viscount Lymington on 11 June 1720, a few days after the date of this dinner.

[2] John Dalrymple, second Earl of Stair, famous both as a general and as a diplomatist. At this time he must have just returned from his brilliant embassy to Paris. He married Eleanor, Viscountess Primrose, daughter of the second Earl of Loudon, and widow of James, first Viscount Primrose. The curious phantasmagoria of the death of her first husband in Rotterdam seen by her in Edinburgh was the origin of Sir Walter Scott's 'My Aunt Margaret's Mirror,' and the circumstances of her marriage with Lord Stair were almost as peculiar.

[3] This Menu is not in Lady Grisell's hand.

[Bills of Fare]

15 July 1720. At the Princess [1]

the Lady of the bed chambers Table at Richmond,

9 at table

a white soup with hearbs

salt rosted mutton

sids fish a large Mackerall

fricassy chickens

bacon and beans

a chicken py

midle a piece bief stewd whole

no relief

2

2 pullets at top

6 pigions at foot

sids peas

broyled herins with butter souce

lopsters

beans

tart in the midle

Deseart

a big dish in the Midle with

connections and frute only

---

22 June Prince Wales Duchess Shrosberries [2] Table.

13 at one and 6 at a litle.

midle soup with peas

top boyld Lamb

foot rost mutton

one s^{d} fish boyld chicken rague

side pigion py, veal colep, fricassy

[1] Carolina Wilhelmina, Princess of Wales, daughter of the Markgraf of Anspach.

[2] Duchess of Shrewsbury. One of the Ladies-in-Waiting on the Princess of Wales. According to Lady Cowper she was rather forced on the princess by the king, but she 'had some extraordinary talents, and it was impossible to hate her so much as her Lord. . . . She had a wonderful art at entertaining and diverting people, though she would sometimes exceed the bounds of decency. She had a great memory, had read a good deal, and spoke three languages to perfection.'—*Diary of Lady Cowper*.

[Bills of Fare]

2 Course

midle	tart with cream
top	pullets
foot	pigions and partrage
side	sturgen, venson pasty peas
side	fryd sols, frensh beans, lopsters

Deseart

2 big dishes frute and confections.

---

20 Novr 1722 at Ld Carlils,[1] 7 at Table.

1. A Dish stewd Meat muton bief veall and crimp cod, the fish set up and rost beaff set down with gravie sauce boyld with shalot on one side and bitrowes wt oyl and veniger on the other side in litle chena hollow plates

2. A pigion py and Mutton collips stewd Ld. Rothes way

3. 5 Ashiets; 3 teel, squab pigions, scollopd oysters, fryd smelts and butterd scorsonera or something of that kind hertickhos cut in thin slices will do better it was cream bet up with butter was on it

4. rid herin and tarts butter on one side and cheas on the other

5. Deseart: oranges, apels, pears, and chestons all the dishes litle and very neat no case with knives on the by table.

---

17 Decmr. 10 at a big table Ld Carlile,[1] etc. 1722.

1st. 7 dishes 2 soups, a terean, stewd pigions wt sweat breads mushrooms etc. with a sauce half rague half

[1] Charles Howard, third Earl of Carlisle, at this time Constable of the Tower of London. He held several important posts under Whig Administrations. He married Lady Anne Capel, daughter of Arthur, first Earl of Essex.

[Bills of Fare]

fricassy, a litle py of toungs etc. veall a la dob with spinag sauce a boyld pullet sallary sauc

2 Releaffes a whole turbot and fryd smelts and rosted veal

Rost Bieff on the By table for any that cald for it

2nd. 7 Dish a Turkic, a Phesant, snyps, partrages, a wild duck and larks round

3^{d}. 7 Dish in chena a large dish crawfish, a tart, fryd solls, Blang mange, sallary and chease, sparagrass, lambs livers whole w^{t} sauce

---

Deseart

Aples in cyrop and raw ones round — pears stewd in a round glass in with a foot and raw pears round them

Jelluy 6 glasses 3 of biskets
hipd as high betwixt each
2 glasses, a high scaloped glass
in midle wet orang chips

Milk in china bowl but I think glas as good — candle — candle — bowl milk

in midle wet orang chips
salver confections in the middle

carrans in cyrop and raw pears round — the like below — aples with cyrop and raw ones round

---

1725, January 22 Duke Hamilton [1] Ld Twedle [2] Rothes [3] Selkirk [4] 10 at Ta.

2 end Dishes soup and Lamb Midle dish bieff py in blood one ashiet in each salt tung w^{t} red cabage and sasages and boyld Turkie with salary sauce.

2 Reliefs salmond and sadle of Mutton

---

[1] James, fifth Duke of Hamilton, married, first, Anne, daughter of the fourth Earl of Dundonald; second, Elizabeth, daughter of Thomas Strangeways; and third, Anne, daughter of Edward Spencer.

[2] Lord Tweeddale. John Hay, fourth Marquess, one of the Representative Peers in six Parliaments. He married in 1748 Frances, daughter of John, Earl Granville.

[3] See note 2, p. 285.

[4] Lord Selkirk. Charles Douglas, formerly Hamilton, Earl of Selkirk, one of the Lords of the Bedchamber to the king; died unmarried.

[Bills of Fare]

2nd *Service*

partrage and wood cock young Ducklins for end dishes the midle dish aple py with cream

2 ashiets on each side, rague with sweat bread, Asparagrass rost oysters on Squers and marrow pudine

Deseart Jelly ratafia cream sweat meats frute etc.

Mr. Dundas of that Ilk [1] Jan. 25 Mr. Dundas Advocate [2]
Sr. G. Eliot [3] and Lady

At the 2 ends soup and rost Mutton pickles in the midle, ane ashet on each side, salt toung and fricassy of rabets, relieff of salmond.

2nd *Course*

ends 2 Ducklins, a Rague of sweatbread pallets etc., Midle dish aple py with cream

2 ashets on each side, Tanzie, fricassy ousters, caparata, Lamb.

Deseart, confections, frute, etc.

April 12, 1725. At the Duke Chandes [4] howse at Cannons. A Duson at Table

1st. a broun soup and a white soup, fricassy, pudine, broun rague, and collopes, ane Eparn in the Midle.

---

[1] Mr. George Dundas of that Ilk, advocate, at this time M.P. for Linlithgowshire, married Alison, daughter of Brigadier-General Bruce of Kennet.

[2] Mr. Robert Dundas, advocate, eldest son of Robert Dundas of Arniston. He was at this time M.P. for the county of Edinburgh. He became Lord President of the Court of Session in 1748.

[3] Sir Gilbert Elliot of Minto, second Baronet, son of Sir Gilbert Elliot. (See p. 221.) He was at this time M.P. for Roxburgh, afterwards a Lord of Session as Lord Minto. He was interested in music, arboriculture, etc. He married Helen Stewart of Allanbank. His daughter Jean was the authoress of the 'Flowers of the Forest.'

[4] Duke of Chandos. James Brydges, first Duke of Chandos, built a magnificent house at Canons near Edgware, where this dinner took place. According to Defoe there were one hundred and twenty persons in family, and the choir entertained them every day at dinner. Pope is said to have drawn his Timon's Villa from this house.

[Bills of Fare]

Reliefs 2 salmond, Lamb, and Chickens.

2d. 3 rings with 5 plates 4 low and one higher in the midle in each, 1st ring a green goose a chicken, a Rabet.

the midle ring, blang Mangie and broun Mangie, brunt cream, custart white and custart green or Tanzie.

3rd. ring, a dukline, turkic pout, 2 pigions, broyld chicken, rabet.

2 ashets on each side, a Rague sweat breads, fryd sols, hartichocs spnch.

---

15 March [1727]. At Ld. Mountjoys [1] 10 at table,
7 and 7 and 2 removes.

1st. a Tareen with Bcafe, veall, etc., ducklins, chickens, pigions, pallets, sweatbreeds, cocks combs, all sorts of roots, Asparagras, sallary, licks, etc.: in midle a rogued Turkic with oysters gisert's livers, Morels and sundry things put on scewars and stuck in it and light broun sauce.

sids: 3 litle pudins, a plumb, a green, a white, and backed one cut and put betwext them, Beef collops stewd tender, Pigions one suortout, and a very smal sadle mutton; at other end white soup and a pullet in it, 7 dishes in all.

Relieffs, a jack with pudin in it, and whitens wt smelts and a good sauce, a ragued breast of veall prety white.

3 young ducks, 4 Turkies, aple tart, and small sweat-meat tarts round it, craw fish, 3 sols fryd and craw fish tails and shrimps, and bodys craw fish brused and put in the sauce and pourd on the midle of them.

3 whole sweatbreads and a piece veall stuft with forst meat, the skiny piece of the veall or lamb the bigness of a large sweat bread and put in the midle; they were all prity white and bate butter and limon, Asparagrass with cream and butter sauce, and tost and fryd sippets [?] round.

---

[1] Thomas Windsor distinguished himself in the wars in Flanders, and was made Viscount Windsor of Black Castle in the Irish peerage. He was afterwards made Baron Mountjoy in the peerage of the United Kingdom. He married Charlotte, daughter of the seventh Earl of Pembroke.

[Bills of Fare]

Deseart: 9 all on guilt cornered salvers, low feet; midle, with one row glass salvers with half inch broad brims with franch plumb, Apricoks, fruts dry, Almond bisket and Ratafia. 8 in all, and wafers put in betwixt them, a salver above that w^{t} 4 frute jellys and wet sweat-meats, with covers, and betwixt them high glasses, white confits on the top, a scolloped glass cornered brim.

2 ends bottom row, Jelly harts horn and limon and ratafia cream, a salver on top with the same cornered brimd glasses as in the midle.

2 sids 1st. row, Aples in sawcers and frensh figs and plumbs, the last pistashe nuts on one and aples in cyrop in the other, the same cornerd brimd glasses as the rest, the 4 corners, 2 slist oranges and 2 almonds and resins, in glass broad cream bowls.

At Lord Hallifax [1] in the Country at Bushy Park,
28 May 1726.

green soup
veal in it

Bacon and Beans   veal stewed   pidgeon pye

carp
Relief Roast mutton

Pidgeans, Chickens,
and young turkies

Ragout of sweatbreads   Pease

Tart

Sparagras   green geese   char

---

[1] Lord Halifax. George Montagu, first Earl of Halifax, married, first, Ricarda Posthume, daughter of Richard Saltonshall, and, second, Mary, daughter of the Earl of Scarborough.

[Bills of Fare]

1727, June 6. Sir Robert Walpoul,[1] Mr. Dodington.[2]

8 at Table.

5 dish, a sop, Pudin, Hamb, 4 boyld chickens, a stwd fillet bieff; 2 releiffs, fish and rost Mutton.

7 dish: 2 young gees, Turrem green pigions, curran tart, peas stewd, burnt cream, hautichok sukers, Angeloty.

Deseart: Confections, frute, Jellys, and Milk.

We was eight days at Twitenham. We had always an Eparn in the midle, 2 dish at first, 4 at 2[d], 6 at the last, the variety was soups, peas, Mager, gravie, rise, barly, vermaselly, variety of meat was rost Bieff, Bran, stwd cops [?], pigions, minsd pys, boyld lamb, rost lamb, boyd foull, rost foull and sasages, jack, hard fish, stewed rump bieff, boyld beaff, rost veall, ragu'd breast veall, Turkic, chean pork, rosted breast of pork, Lamb, boyld and backed pudin, orang pudin, Asparagrass, Brocaly w[t] sasages, vension Pasty, rost venison, rost mutton, wild Ducks, rabets, boyld wild ducks w[t] ounions, larks, rost goos, boyld goos, sturgen, rague sweat breads, hogs pudins and white ones, lamb frys, fricassy rabets, rost rabets.

---

1 Sir Robert Walpole, afterwards Earl of Orford, at this time Prime Minister. This dinner took place shortly before the death of George I., the news of which reached Walpole at Chelsea on the 14th. He is said to have killed two horses in carrying the tidings to the new king at Richmond.

2 George Dubb Doddington, afterwards Lord Melcomb Regis, at this time a Lord of the Treasury. He left a diary which has been published, and which shows the writer in anything but a pleasant light. Lady Mary Wortley Montagu, who never missed an opportunity of saying something spiteful of her quondam friend, Lady Murray, writes in 1725: 'Mrs. Murray has got a new lover in the most accomplished Mr. Doddington.'

[Bills of Fare]

26 Janur 1728. Mr. Onsly,[1] the Speaker, Hadinton,[2] and Marchmont,[3] Coll. Hope, Mr. Johnston, and Mr. Mitchell. 11 at Table.

1st. 7 dish: a soup, a sweatbread and cox comb py, a Lamb, 4 on the sids, a pudin, boyld chickens, ragu'd fillet bieff, Tush. 2 relieffs, Turbet and rost mutton.

2nd. 7 dish: wild foull, cheston py and a goos, on the sids craw fish or white beans and sasages, Asparagras, minsd collips and sasages, burnt cream.

Deseart: Sweatmeats and Jellys and sillibubs, etc.

London, 30 March 1728. Ld Carlyl,[4] Lady Lechmoor,[5] Lady Mary,[6] Lds. Stairs,[7] Hadinton,[2] Marchmont.[3] 12

1st. 4 dish: Soup, Lamb, sids, 4 boyld chickens and a pudin; 2 relefes, crimp hard [?] and forsadle of mutton.

2nd. 5 dish: 2 Duclins, date py, Kidny beans and sheaps toungs rosted; sids, a crab and Asparagras.

---

[1] Arthur Onslow was elected Speaker on 23rd January 1728, so this was no doubt a dinner in his honour. He held this most distinguished position until 18th March 1761, when he retired after thirty-three years 'constant and unwearied attendance in the chair.'

[2] Thomas Hamilton, sixth Earl of Haddington, whose son, Lord Binning, was married to Lady Grisell Baillie's daughter Rachel.

[3] Alexander Hume, second Earl of Marchmont, K.T., Lady Grisell Baillie's brother. He was the third son of the first Earl, his elder brothers predeceasing their father. He married Margaret, daughter and heiress of Sir George Campbell of Cessnock, when he assumed the surname of Campbell.

[4] See note 1, p. 294.

[5] Lady Elizabeth Letchmere, daughter of the third Earl of Carlisle, married, first, Nicholas Letchmere, Attorney-General in 1718 and raised to the peerage in 1721 as Lord Letchmere. 'The discreet and sober Lady L——re has lost such furious sums at the Bath that it may be questioned whether all the sweetness the waters can put into my lord's blood can make him endure it, particularly £700 at one sitting which is aggravated with many astonishing circumstances.' —Lady Mary Wortley Montagu. She married, second, Thomas Robinson of Rokeby Park.

[6] Lady Mary Howard, daughter of the Earl of Carlisle.

[7] See note 2, p. 292.

[Bills of Fare]

Deseart: Jellys and Sillibubs, curds and cream, pears and aples, pistaches and scorcht almonds, Bisket round the milk.

The following three Menus are from a jotting left by Lady Grisell of dinners at Naples shortly before Lord Binning's death:—

18 Decr 1732. Mr. Horner Archer, etc. 12 at Table.

Soup

Boyld veal and colifloor — Lamb — plumb pudin and litle paties round it

Soup

---

2 reliefs fish and muton py

---

4 wood cocks, 4 snyp

a french lof drest with milk — peas

salmagundy[1]

fryd soles

Corainorely [?] Pig — burnt cream

Aples

Biskit — Chesnuts

Drest buter etc. — graps — drest buter upon crots

pistaches — plumb etc. — bisket

Mr. H. Hunters. 16 Folk.

Mr. Horner. 10 at Table, 6 by table.

Mrs. Archer.

Boyld leg Pork

Soup

[?] mustart pickle, etc. — potatos

pudin — rague veal and sweet breads cok comb, etc.

turnips — fish souce

fish

[1] 'Salmagunde,' a dish of minced meat with eggs, anchovies, vinegar, pepper, etc.

[Bills of Fare]

relife, pigion py

wood cocks and partrages

salet	Minshed py	Morells
cold toung		fryd solls
peas		fish sause
	loyn veal	

	Soup[1]	
Peas pudin		Pork and torts
	Boyld Turkic	

relief of fish

	rost udder	
Salmagundy		frogs
	Aple Dumplin	
Turnips		salet
	ragued veal	

The following Menus are from some loose sheets of paper, and relate to a visit paid by Lady Harvey[2] at Mellerstain:—

Super, Thursday, July 15, 1756.

	cold Chickens	
Waffles		colerd pig
	Jelly	
Hartichoks		Salmon
	Collops	

[1] There is no heading to this Menu, but it is on the same sheet as the two immediately preceding.

[2] 'Sweet Molly Lapell,' familiarly known as 'Tom' in the Prince of Wales's circle, daughter of Brigadier-General Nicholas Lepell, at one time Maid of Honour to the Princess of Wales, afterwards Mistress of the Robes to her when Queen. She married John Hervey, the handsome son of the Earl of Bristol, who rather neglected her. She was a great friend of Lady Murray, and stood loyally by her in her quarrel with Lady Mary Wortley Montagu. Indeed, she

[Bills of Fare]

Diner, 16th.

Soup
relif cod

pickls		salad
	rost beef	

---

	chickens	
Tarts		peas
	puffs	
cowhead		pickled salmon
	veal colops	

Diner, Sunday, 18th

Giblet broth
relief salmon
salad
rost beef

	Hagis	
Colerd Eel		peas
pudens	moor foul	cox colms
	Cold Pig	

---

no super
but strawbery

Diner, 21

Rumble of Veal and broth
Salmon

---

was beloved by the whole Baillie family. It was she who attended Lady Grisell on her deathbed, both Lady Murray and Lady Binning being ill at the time. She was noted for her beauty, and seems to have been a charming personality. Her portrait still adorns the walls of Mellerstain. Her husband was a great friend of Lady Mary Wortley Montagu, with whom his wife was not on speaking terms on account of the quarrel between Lady Mary and Lady Murray.

[Bills of Fare]

Loin of Mutton and stakes

Stewed cucumbers Makerony

Moor foul

Super

veal colops

Cream strawberys

fryd eggs

Mellerstain 1748 account of what is spent yearly in the house of meat and drink, etc., in quantity, but not the value.[1]

6 oxen cut in 199 pieces, besides beef from Kelso		6
Wedders		19
Lambs		11
Ewe		1
Calfs		3
Swine		4
Pigs		10
Eggs besides those of our own hens 2284		
Candle Stones		30
Butter for sheep	12 pound	
for greesing wool	8 pd	
in family	300 pd	
	320	
Soap pounds		231
Cheeses		24
Fouls eat or given away.		
Turkies	56	
Geess	22	
Hens	62	
ducks	33	
capons	12	
Chickens	191	
	376	

[1] It must be remembered that Mellerstain was at this time a lady's establishment.

		Bottles
Liquors	Claret	31
	Port	62
	Hermitage	18
	Cotrotee	5
	Canary	33
	Modera	28
	Chirrie	56
	Serainse	9
	Tocky	1
	White wine	11
	Frontiniac	12
	Cyder	54
	Strong Ale	269
	Second Ale	458
	Bottled small Beer	218
	Bottles	1265

Small Beer in Barels 850 gallons Scots
Flower 111 Stone 14 pounds
Oat Meal 264 stone

Mellerstain 1749 Account of what is spent yearly in the house of meat and drink, etc., in quantity, but not in value.

5 Oxen cut in 166 pieces		5
Wedders		18
Ewes		6
Lambs		12
Calfs		4
Swine		5
Pigs		27
Eggs besides those of our own house		3720
Candles, Stones 29, pounds 4		
Soap pounds		228½
Butter, our own pounds	216	344
Butter bought pounds	128	
Cheeses		51

U

Herrings, half Barrels		4
Tusk fish		5
Fouls eat or given away		
Turkies	45	
geess	5	
ducks	22	
Hens	81	
Chickens	181	
Pigions, our own	113	
	447	

Liquors	Bottles
Claret	26
Port	65
Hermitage	10
Canary	25
Shirrie	43
Modera	24
Frontiniac	4
Seraionse	4½
Strong ale	152
Second Ale	572
Bottled small Beer	217
Orange wine	33
White wine	15
Cotrottee	5
Punch besides shrub	34
	1232½

Small Beer in Barrels, 850 Scots gallons
Flower, Stones 134, pounds 8
Oatmeal and Ry, Stones 272

Extracts from small paper covered book marked 'Cash Book begune 22 March 1729. For no use at all.' It deals with a visit to Bath and Bristol. In this book Lady Grisell uses the word 'By' when she means 'Paid to.'

March 22	By May Menzies to account . .	£1	1	0
	By Account payd Ja Johnston .	[illegible]	[illegible]	[illegible]
	,, Fraught, etc. payd Mrs. Towyn		1	
	,, Cariing Allers . . .			
	,, Doc: Gibson's man .			
	,, Plasters . . .			
	,, Limmons sent to Mellerstane		1	
	,, 3 pr under stokins .			
	,, Megilsidler 5s. Pate Allan 2			
	,, Betty and Nelly .			
	,, Kimergham Drinkmoney		1	
	,, Whitehall Drinkmoney		1	
	,, Mr. Halls Carter .			
	,, Sr James Halls Coachman			
	,, John Coachman 7½ Mo wages at 10£ a year,	6	6	0
		14	9	2

By the expence of 6 coach horses and 8 Riding horse from Dunce to Bath .	30	1	9½
,, cariing Bagage	2	2	0
,, guids	0	9	0
,, Turnpicks	0	2	2
,, mending sadles and blooding	0	5	4
,, pistol ball 2s sope 1s.	0	3	0
,, Bassindain and Hume's horss . .	0	4	0
,, Washing on the Road	0	16	2
,, Eating for 5 and Georg in the Coach and 2 maids from Berwick 16 days to Bath .	23	18	6
,, Servants at Dunc .	0	4	0

		£	s.	d.	
	By 7 mens board 16 days at 1s. pr day	5	12	0	
	,, Duncan and John each 5s. of wages	0	10	0	
	,, John Coachman and Tams board 5 days at Bath and Joeys	0	15	0	
Apl 17	,, Horses 5 nights at Bath	6	18	0	
	,, Shoeing horses at Bath etc. .	1	14	8	
	,, Tam to cary home 9 horses	14	14	0	
					£88 9 7½

L: B is to pay the half of this £88, 9s. 7d½.

[Note as to details of £30,1s. 9½d. above stated, contained on a separate piece of paper and not in Lady Grisell's handwriting.]

Berwick a night	1	7	1½
Belfoord a night	1	1	0
Anwick a night	1	1	8
Morpeth a night	1		8
New Castle a night	2		4
Darlington baitting	0		11
fferryhill a night .	1	1	8
Northalerton a night	1	1	0
Borrowbridg a night	1		3
Wetherby baitting	0		1
ffarybridge a night	1		4
Doncaster baiting	0		3
Blyth a night .	1		8
Nottingham a night	1		8
Leister a night .	1		3
Smokington a night	1		8
Coventry baitting	0		10

Warwick a night . .	1	8	1			
Hartfoordbridge baiting	0	4	0			
Mortinmash a night	1	11	7			
Cirensister a night	1	14	5			
Alerton baitting	0	7	11			
	28	9	3½			
Duns . . .	1					
Franc . .	0	12	6			
				30	1	9½

[Note as to Lodgings at Bath.]

	my 3 rooms and one Garet . .	£1	15	0
pr week	L. Bin 2 rooms and half and Garet	1	10	0
	Mr. Mitchell 2 rooms and a half	1	5	0
		4	10	0

p. Month, 18£.

Journel, May 20, 1731, that we went abroad To the October, new still, 1733, that we left Paris. and to the Oct., old style, that we came to London, 1733.[1]

Roterdam 29 May 1731 Old Stil and the 9d of June N. St.

	gdr.	st.	doit.	£	s.	d.
For Boat fraught from the yaught	6	0	0	0	11	0
Diner at .	6	0	0	0	11	0
bagage . . .	2	6	0	0	4	2
a coach .	2	10	0	0	4	6
a scout [2] from Roterdam to Delph . .	5	2	0	0	9	4

[1] Contained in a paper-covered notebook $7\frac{7}{8}'' \times 6\frac{1}{4}''$. The outer column giving the values in Sterling money has been added by the editor. For money tables see p. 421.

[2] Schuit or trekschuit, a public boat drawn through the canals by horse.

[Foreign Tour]

		gdr.	st.	doit.	£	s.	d.
	Paline, etc., at Delph	4	12	0	0	8	4
	Coach hire at Roterdam .	3	2	0	0	5	8
	Coach at Delph .	1	10	0	0	2	8
	Seeing the church ther .	0	12	0	0	1	0
N.S.	for a large hamper and lock and a little hamper for Grisie	3	18	0	0	7	0
June 10. Saterday	Passage of letters to the 11 day . . .	6	9	0	0	11	9
	Exchange for 150 £ Stel. Bag and portage of 521g. 8st.	1	5	0	0	2	3
	the roof in scout from Delf to Leyden each 10s 1 doit Servants in scout, 7s. 1d.	4	8	4	0	8	1
	a hamper for the Drogs .	1	13	0	0	2	11
	2 Tea Kells . . .	6	0	0	0	11	0
	Bagage from Roterdam to Lyden, . .	4	2	0	0	7	6
11.	For Breckfast and diner the last 1g. pr head and for wine	14	2	0	1	5	10
	To Edwards for 2 nights lodging at Roterdam he reckoned it a week payd by J. Gordon	75	0	0	6	17	6
	our intertainment there being 2 diners 2 breckfasts and 2 suppers payd by Gorden	96	15	0	8	17	8
Lyden. June 12.	For diner and super and wine the maids 8	8	16	0	0	16	0
13.	the maids 8, we dining in Mr. Burnets .	0	8	0	0	0	8
	Smalls by John for breckfast and suppers	1	14	0	0	3	0

[Foreign Tour]

		gdr.	st.	doit.	£	s.	d.
	For sugar for Tea at 8½ st. 3¼ lb.	1	6	0	0	2	4
	For washing Roterdam	1	4	0	0	2	2
	For entertainment in 3 days	33	0	0	3	0	6
Leyden June 15.	For milk at a Bours house	0	13	0	0	1	1
	For bagage 1g. 7st. more 2g.	3	7	0	0		1
	For a coach 2g. 16st.	2	16	0	0	6	0
16.	For lodging a week at Lyden	14	0	0	1	5	8
	To Frederick, etc.	3	0	0	0	5	6
	To a man for errands	0	11	0	0	0	11
	For 6 lb. chocalet	13	16	0	1	5	2
	For a lb. Tea	12	0	0	1	2	0
	For lodging 2 nights at Edwards errour in Roterdam this is set down befor.						
	For a Scout from Liden to harlem for the roof and 6 and 4 servants in Scout	6	6	2	0	11	
Amster-dam June	For scout harlem to Amsterdam	3	15	0	0	6	9
18	For bagage	2	6	0	0	4	2
	For tape at Harlem errour						
	For a guid	0	6	0	0	0	6
	For a coach	3	6	0	0	6	0
	For a coach	3	5	0	0	5	11
	For bagage	1	12	0	0	2	10
	For lodging and intertainment 3 nights	64	16	0	5	18	8
	For a scout to utright the whole of it which was devided 20 gul. and drink	15	9	0	1	8	3

[Foreign Tour]

				gdr.	st.	doit.	£	s.	d.
	For diner at Newer Sluce of fish .			24	0	0	2	4	0
Utright									
June 20.	For 4 lb. coffie powder 32 st. and box 18st. .			7	6	0	0	13	4
	a lb. Tea Bohea from Lord Bins landlord .			6	10	0	0	11	10
	2 pair gloves Grisie and I errour								
	For lodging and entertainment at the Castel of Antwerp.3 nights			47	5	0	4	6	7
	For a coach to Syst			5	0	0	0	9	2
	For a coach to Sousdick–			9	0		0	16	6
Gildermause									
	For diner to 6 of us and 2 maids	3	11						
	Servant : .	0	12						
		———		4	3	0	0	7	7
	For 2 Post wagon to the Buss to the wagennears			40	0	0	3	13	4
	To servants at Utright .			2	10	0		4	6
	To the wageneer .			0	12		0	1	0
	For smalls by James .			3	4	4	0	5	11
Buss 25.	For lodging and intertainment 3 nights at the golden Lyon			32	15	0	3	0	0
	To servants .			1	2	0	0	2	0
	To a sergent 11 st. soger 6st.			0	17	0	0	1	5
	For a Berline to Mostrick:.	40	0						
	2 Post wagons	50	0						
	bagage	5	5						
	Commissers Knight		11						
	Wageneers . .	1	8						
		———		97	4	0	8	18	2

[Foreign Tour]

			gdr.	st.	doit.	£	s.	d.
For diner at Lumpt	4	18						
Overbeck a night.	6	5						
maid .	0	6						
bree for breckfast	1	6						
Diner At Ass .	4	10						
			17	5	0	1	11	7
			741	12	2	67	14	5

Mostrick a guiny is 27 Skillins,[1] and each skillin 10 Marks, and each Mark 6 doits.

		Sk.	M.	d.	Stg. £	s.	d.
June 27	For lodging and super and breckfast	36	0	0	1	1	0
	Servants . . .	1	0	0	0	0	7
	For a berline to Aix	32	0	0	0	18	8
	For 2 Diligances to Aix .	45	0	0	1	6	3
	For baggage .	4	0	0	0	2	4
	To the Wagennears	3	0	0	0	1	9
	To a soger to forbear serching . . .	1	0	0	0	0	7
·9 Marks is	For Diner at Gulph	21	0	0	0	12	3
a skillin	To a wageneer .	1	0	0	0	0	7
at Aix	To the 3 servants boord 21 days to 27 June	111	0	0	3	4	9
30	To accounts from John of Smalls for breckfasts and supers	27	0	0	0	15	9
	To smalls by John and James .	7	3	0	0	4	3
	To clear house accounts pd. John . . .	15	8	4	0	9	2
June 9	To clear house accounts more at Aix .	22	8	6	0	13	3

[1] This should be thirty-seven skillings, and is so given elsewhere.

[Foreign Tour] [Stg.]

	Sk.	M.	d.	£	s.	d.
To sundry smalls for house I bought .	31	8	4	0	18	6
For diners 11 days and 2 skillins a head .	195	0	0	5	13	9
cooks maid .	1	0	0	0	0	7
to see the relicks in great church .	17	0	0	0	9	11
a coach .	6	0	0	0	3	6
For 12 nights lodging in Mr. Tewis house	168	0	0	4	18	0
the maid in the house	8	0	0	0	4	8
coffie	1	4	4	0	0	10
For a Berline and 2 waggons to Spa .	88	0	0	2	11	4
3 wagonneers .	3	0	0	0	1	9
	[1] 850	4	0	24	14	0

Spa.

here the guiny is 37 skill and 4 souse, a skillin 10 sous, and a sous 4 liers

		sk.	st.	doits.	Stg. £	s.	d.
July 9	To John . . .	78	8	0	2	5	11
13	To John . . .	74	8	0	2	3	7
		[illegible]		0	[illegible]	[illegible]	[illegible]
	For wood, etc.	1	0				
	To house .		0				1
	To a Copashin		0				
	For a water bottle		0				
20	To John . . .	37	4				1
23	To John . . .	81	16				
		S. 293	6	0	8	11	2

Spa.

This is Lievers, sous, etc.

		French £	s.	d.	Stg. £	s.	d.
July 25	To John . . .	12	0	0	0	13	4

[1] This column is wrongly summed. It should be 847 Sk. 4 M.

[Foreign Tour]

		[French]			[Stg.]		
		£	s.	d.	£	s.	d.
	To make up a former balance .	0	13	0	0	0	9
	For powder 1lb to day 20 a wash ball 7d.	1	7	0	0	1	6
26	To Lady Fannys carnush [?] .	7	0	0	0	7	10
	To John .	18	14	0	1	1	0
30	To John .	18	14	0	1	1	0
	To Neckles Grisie and Mrs. Burnet .						
	To poor pilgrims 1 sk.	0	10	0	0	0	7
Augt 1	For John . . .	18	14	0	1	1	0
	To John . . .	18	14	0	1	1	0
2	To John . . .	18	14	0	1	1	0
	To John .	37	8	0	2	2	0
Monday 6	For a moneths Lodging 9 rooms and a kitchen and 2 beds for men servants, 14 sk. p. week, 10½ guinys and 6 sk. and 3 liers .	196	0	0	11	0	6
7	To John . . .	18	14	0	1	1	0
	To John was forgot to set down . . .	37	8	0	2	2	0
9	To John . . .	37	8	0	2	2	0
	For letters . . .	3	5	0	0	3	8
13	To John . . .	37	8	0	2	2	0
20	For 2 wagons at 3 sk. apiece for 37 days to this and 2 days riding	110	10	0	6	4	4
Augt 20	To John . . .	37	8	0	2	2	0
22	To John 4 guinys	74	16	0	4	4	0
	For the Buckie to the ball	11	0	0	0	12	0
Aug. 25 O.S.	For 12 doz. botls water to Mr. Cockburn						
	To Roclor for the Ball and Super to 70 persons .	196	7	0	11	0	11

[Foreign Tour]		[French] £	s.	d.	[Stg.] £	s.	d.
	To John . . .	37	8	0	2	2	
	To John . . .	18	14	0	1	1	0
	To John .	30	12	0	1	14	5
	To the fidels at the ball	28	1	0	1	11	6
Wednes-	For bread etc. by John						
day 28	To a cook at 1 sk pr day 49 days .	24	15	0	1	7	10
	For 3 weeks lodging to Monday 27 .	147	0	0	8	5	4
	To John at 3 times 3 guinys .	56	2	0	3	3	0
	For a weeks lodging the Sunday 31 Sept.[1]	49	0	0	2	15	1
	For a chaise to the 1st						0
	of Sep. and horses	35	10	0		0	
Septm 3	To John to the 10	74	16	0		4	0
and 10	For Arrack and Limons	10	0	0	0	11	3
	Washing to Saterday 8 2 weeks .	8	13	0	0	9	9
	2 french caps Mrs. Twiles at Aix .	6	18		0	7	9
11	To John .	37	8	0	2	2	0
12	To John .	37	8		2	2	0
	For 12 nights lodging to Saturday 15 at 12 skill	72	0	0	4	1	0
	To the Caposhins	37	8	0	2	2	0
	To the wemen at Geronster Pohon .	18	14	0	1	1	0
	To the wemen at Pohon in Toun .	8	0	0	0		0
Friday 14	To the cook for 10 days	8	10	0	0	9	7
	To the housemaid Ann Mary Nort Livoux, daughter of our landlord . . .	9	7	0	0	10	6

[1] Probably a mistake for 1st September.

					[French]			[Stg.]		
[Foreign Tour]					£	s.	d.	£	s.	d.
	For a wanscote chest and lock .				6	0	0	0	6	9
Saturday 15, we went to Leige	For a chaise 12 days .				35	10	0	2	10	0
16	For the last weeks wash 8 frank .				8	0	0	0	9	0
	For Kains the half				3 [illegible]	[illegible]	0	[illegible]	[illegible]	[illegible]
	For a pr shoes my D.									
	mending shoes									½
	2 pr clogs .				8	10	0	0	9	7
	letters .				8	15	0	0	9	10
	Apoticary's bill .				13	0	0	0	14	7
					[1] 1038	6	0	60	19	4½
	taken out of this washing	8	13	0						
	washing .	8	0	0						
	shoes my D	5	0	0						
	mending shoes	1	0	0						
	2 pr Cloggs G and I	8	10	0	31	3	0			
				S.	1007	3	0			
Leige. 17 Sepm	For 1 lb. Tee				7	10	0	0	8	5
	To 54¼ broad holland for 3 pr shiets at 35 Sturs the ell .				94	10	0	5	6	4
	For 34½ demie holland at 45 Sturs for 7 Shifts to Grisie .				77	12	2	4	7	4
	5 els Muslin for 4 cravats 45 St. . . .				11	5	0	0	12	3
	2 night napkins .				5	6	1	0	5	11
					196	3	3	11	0	3

[1] This column is wrongly summed by Lady Grisell.

[Foreign Tour]					[French]			[Stg.]		
					£	s.	d.	£	s.	d.
	take out the demi holland muslin and night caps . . .				94	3	3	5	5	11
	S. 102				102	00	00	5	14	4
	For 2 chases from Spa to Leige that caried 8 persons .	28	0	0				1	11	6
	A wagon for 2 servants and bagog	12	0	0				0	13	6
	a horse to a servant .	4	0	0						
					44	0	0	0	4	6
	To drink money to Chaises . . .				1	0	0	0	1	1½
	To the poor				1	10	0	0	1	9
19 Sep.	For diner at Barixpay 7 masters 5 servants				14	10	0	0	16	4
	For a kain to Charles Forbes 3 guinys				56	2	0	3	3	0
	pay^{d} his horse from Spa				5	0	0	0	5	7½
	For 5 Nights at the Altas Noble to M^{sr} Pontels				250	0	0	14	1	3
	makeing 4 p^{r} shiets .				3	0	0	0	3	4½
	a blunderbush 2 guin. 2 p^{r} pistols 2 gu.				74	16	0	4	4	0
Namour.										
	For 2 Berlins from Leige	80	0	0						
	a horse to a servant	5	0	0						
					85	0	0	4	15	8
	To Lodging and supers for 4 nights for we									

[Foreign Tour]			[French]			[Stg.]		
			£	s.	d.	£	s.	d.
dined mostly in the Bishops . . .			96	3	0	5	8	2
To the Bishops Servants			45	8	0	2	11	0
For 2 Berlins and a Riding horse from Namure to Shalong 39 guinys 15 the riding horse was 5 of it .			748	6	2	42	1	10
Seeing the Castle of Namure .			11	0	0	0	12	5
For bread etc. by John			2	2	0	0	2	4
†lay at Rosey upon Stra	8	00				0	9	0
†Din[d] at Ritchmount	12	0				0	13	6
For Diner at erriton .	4	10				0	5	1
Super at Mash	6	0				0	6	9
Diner at Runion	4	10				0	5	1
Super at Bostogne	9	0				0	10	1
Diner at Marklange .	5	0				0	5	7½
Super at Arlong impos[d] on	16					0	18	0
Diner at Luxenburg	12	0				0	13	6
†the 2 above should be here ———			77	0	0			
S.			1616	17	2	90	18	4
Sup[d] at Carmine, the first village in Lorain and here the Lewidors[1] is 32 livers	6	10				4	4	0

[1] Lady Grisell seems to use 'Lewis dors' as synonymous to 'guiny,' and the calculations are based on this assumption.

[Foreign Tour]			[French] £ s. d.	[Stg.] £ s. d.
28	breckfast at Pont-mush .	3 10		0 2 4
	lay and sup[d] at Nancy .	32 0		1 1 4
	wine upon the road	1 10		0 1 0
29	dind at Roviell	6 0		0 [illegible] 0
30	Sup[d] at Lunavile	20 0		1 4
	lay at Mercour	15 10		1 4
Oct. 1	Din at Alunavile	7 0		8
	lay at Ish	7 15		2
	Coshers for going out of the road 3 leigs to Lunavile	48 0		1 12 0
	Seeing the Duke of Lorains Palice and the Acadamie	21 0		0 14 0
		——	168 15 0	5 12 6

here the Lewidor is 24 livers

				Sterling
Oct. 2	For diner at Jussie in Burgundy	6 10		0 5 8
	biskets etc.	4 7		0 3 10
	lay at Doncour Chato a private house and left the servants	15 12		0 13 8
3	Dind at Dampier	4 7		0 3 10
	lay at Champain in the Dutche of Burgundy	7 10		0 6 7
	was serched here overly and gote a pass gave the men	3 2		0 2 8
4	breckfast at Ark-surtiel .	3 0		2 7

[Foreign Tour]

		[French]					Stg. £	s.	d.
	lay at Dijon	24	0				1	1	0
	Cyrop copilair[1] suger, etc.	4	15				0	4	2
	Maid at Dijon	1	4				0	1	1
5	Dind at Nuys	10	0				0	8	9
	lay at Beaune	11	0				0	9	7
6	Dind and lay at Shalong up Soan	33	0				1	8	10
	servants twise paid	3	0				0	2	7
	was stop^d at Shalong 3 days by the impertinance of the Bourro and paid lodging, etc	24	14					1	7
	A chase post for Ld Bin and my Dear to Lyons	160	0				7	0	0
	.			361	1	0			
	4 servants in the Diligence to lyons .			48	0	0	2	2	0
	4 trunks 12£ caring out and in 8£ . .			20	0	0	0	17	6
	their supers at Macom 3£ boat men 3^0st.			4	10	0	0	3	11
Oct. 9	For 5 places in the Diligence upon the Soan in 2 days from Shalon to Lyon us 4 women and a footman			60	0	0	2	12	6
	lay at Macom for super			6	0	0	0	5	3

[1] Capillaire. a syrup extracted from the maiden-hair fern ; a simple syrup flavoured with orange-flower water.

[Foreign Tour]

				[French]			Stg. £	s.	d.
11	Dind at Roiotin			5	12	0	0	4	11
	a coach at Lyons 3 hours			3	16	0	0	3	5
	letters 12£ new 1£			13	0	0	0	11	5
Lyon guinys strl 24 Livres.	For Lodging. au Park and entertainment 6 nights .	230	0				10	1	3
12	3 ℔. chocolet	10	15				0	8	5
	2 bottles Genever	1	8				0	1	3
	Suger and other smalls graps etc.	6	10				0	5	8
	Serchers	1	10				0	1	4
	a clogbag a lewidor and 24 sous	25	4				1	2	1
	a clogbag lock		10				0	0	5
	2 Maps	3	0				0	2	7
	harden bags	0	6				0	0	3
	wax cloath to trunks .	2	17				0	2	6
	a pillow and cover	5	10				0	4	10
	mending clogbags	1	10				0	1	4
	phisick bag 10s, Bowers Bag 4£ 18 ℔. .	5	08				0	4	9
	a chocalet pot	9	0				0	7	10
		———		303	8	0			
Oct. 23	For caring 6 chairs over the Alps cald Munt Sines to men to drink			12	0	0	0	10	6
	Sundry things layd out by Bower for Gibson when sick	8	11				0	7	9
	For 4 chases and a sadle horse from Lyon to Turin giveing as dinner and super and car-								

[Foreign Tour]

		[French]			Stg. £	s.	d.
	ing us over the Alps, 40 Lewidors	960	0	0	42	0	0
	to the Camariers from Lyons to Turin	8	15	0	0	7	8
	Serchers the Duan at Novalies . . .	2	0	0	0	1	9
		[1] 1779	13	0	77	9	6

the sequin is 9 livers 10 St. here

1731, Turin							
Oct. 27	For coaches at 8 Livers a day .	28	10	0	1	11	8
	Persico and other waters	6	15	0	0	7	8
	Seeing Palices and other places .	33	0	0	1	16	8
	La Boundanc the foot-mat [*sic*] 30 st. p. day and something to drink	7	10	0	0	8	4
	opera tickets .	12	0	0	0	13	6
	Mr. Banker at Turin Commission for 200£ . . .	37	10	0	2	1	8
	Lodging and entertainment 5 nights and 4 day at Turin	229	13	0	12	15	2
	For drink money upon the road lay at Syany 1 0						
30	dind at Versiles 15						
	lay at Navar 1 0						
	Serchers at Bourg-deversail . 2 10						
	(not summed into account)						
	For 4 chases and a sadle horse from						

[1] Wrongly summed by Lady Grisell.

[Foreign Tour]

						Stg. £	s.	d.
Turin to Rom in twenty days with 2 mails a day 180 sequins	1710					95	0	0
the Coshers to drink 4 .	38		1748	0	0	2	2	3
6 geografical maps			18	0	0	1	0	0
			2120	18	0	117	16	9

Millan, 1 November 1731
a sequin here is 14 livers

						£	s.	d.
For seeing Ecco	4	10				0	3	5
Tomb	4	0				0	3	0
Palaces, Liberrary Hospitall in all	20	0				0	15	0
2 days 2 coaches	36	15				1	7	7
Bourgon footman	4	10				0	3	5
Lantron .	1	0				0	0	9
Cinamon water	1	14				0	1	4
the Countes of Borameas servant brought us chocolet	2	5				0	1	9
Servant St. Bernardo .	0	15				0	0	8
3 Nights Lodging and entertainment .	108	5				4	1	2
a footman	8	0				0	6	0
			191	14	0	7	3	10

Plasentia here a sequin is 20 Julios

For seing Churches Palices etc.	18	0	0	0	9	5
Camarier	4	0	0	0	2	1
	22	0	0	0	11	6

[Foreign Tour]

Parma, here and in all Italy where we went till we came to Naples a sequin is 20 and sometimes 20½ Pol or Julios 10 byoks is a Poul.

							Stg. £	s.	d.
	carred over			22	0	0	0	11	6
	For diner at Parma	28					0	14	7
	The 5 servants	7					0	3	10
	Milk .	5					0	2	7
	Tobaco	3					0	1	7
	wine .	5	0				0	2	7
	finding books was lost .	6	0				0	3	
	a woman in Regio	4	0				0	2	2
	serchers	1	0				0		
	frute	1	0				0	0	6
(name erased)	Sending to Mr.	0	5				0	0	2
				61	0	0			
	To Gosolas servant	3	0				0	1	7
	galary	5	0				0	[illegible]	[illegible]
	Theater	4							
	Palaces	12							
	Coachman	5							
	footman	4							
	camarier	2							
Reggie	For seeng Palaces	3	0				0	1	7
	more .	3	0				0	1	7
	camaries .	3	0				0	1	7
Modena				44	0	0			
	For seeing Paleses	10	0				0	5	2
	footman	3	0				0	1	7
	Passage gilt Severals	13	0				0	6	9

[Foreign Tour]

					Stg. £	s.	d.
	Camarrir	2	0		0	1	0
				28			
Bulonia							
10 Nov.	For sasageses	22	10		0	11	9
	a Scots pint of waters	12	0		0	6	3
	wax cloth to trunks .	8	0		0	4	2
	bad brandy	6	0		0	3	2
	Tobaco .	2	0		0	1	0
	Messages to Dulioly .	1	0		0	0	6
	books	6	0		0	3	2
	2 gramers .	6	0		0	[illegible]	2
	Duan sercher						0
	seing palaces	1					11
	seing instituto						7
	Coledge						7
	Coches	58	0		1	10	3
	footman	9	0		0	4	9
	Lodging and entertainment	102	0				
	Camarier	5	0		0	2	7
				266 10 0	2	13	2
Loretta							
16	For lodging only	1	0			6	3
	fish .		5			1	9
	Seing St. Casa		0			3	2
	Seeing Treasurs		0		0	3	2
	a footman .	2	0			1	0
	to a woman Pilgram .	1	0		0	0	6

[Foreign Tour]

							Stg.		
							£	s.	d.
	a guid to Cascad at Terny .	3	0				0	1	7
				33	5	0			
	To Camariers upon the road								
17	Dind at Matcher-ata	1	5				0	0	8
	lay at Toranteens	1	5				0	0	8
18	Dind Ponta de latravo .	2	0				0	1	0
	lay at Seravala	1	5				0	0	8
19	Dind at Foligna	1	0				0	0	6
	lay at Spoletta	1	5				0	0	8
	Dind and lay at Terne	2	0				0	1	0
	Suger plumbs and frute	4	8				0	2	4
	Dind at Narni	1	0				0	0	6
	lay at Uticoly	1	0				0	0	6
	a Prist at Narnì to see reliks	3	0				0	[illegible]	
	Dind at Chevita costelata .	1	5				0	0	8
	lay at Castle Nov	1	0				0	0	6
		1	0				0	0	6
		1	5				0	0	8
		1	0	24	18	0	0	0	6
				479	3	0	12	9	10

We came to Rome the 23 Novm[r] at one a clock of the day 1731, here a sequin is still 20 Julios or Pols in some payments ½ poul more, a sequin is 2 Phillips, there is half phillips and quater phillips which is 2 and a half Poul. A Powl is 10 byocks, there is half and quarter pouls and 5 quotrins for a byock.

[Foreign Tour]

Rome, 23 Novm^{r}, 173.

			Julios	by.	q.	Stg.		
For passage at the bridge .			1	0	0	0	0	6
Duan serching bagage overly .			6	0	0	0	3	2
At the Port for bagage			5	5	0	0	2	9
Mrs. Cotten a sequin .			20	0	0	0	10	5
Mr. Hays man for wine			3	0	0	0	1	7
wax candle .			3	0	0	0	1	7
a hamper and cords for wine . . .			4	9	0	0	2	4
Suger at 16 byocks the ℔.			8	5	0	0	4	4
Coaches at 12 pouls p^{r}. day . . .			144	0	0	3	15	0
Lodging and entertainment 3 times a day except Tee and suger for 8 days 3 sequins a day at 20 Julios, in all 24 sequins . .			480	0	0	12	10	0
to the cook 2 testoun	6	0				0	3	2
to the camarier	3	0				0	1	7
to the maid a testoun .	3	0				0	1	7
			12	0	0			
to vincent the footman			27	0	0	0	14	1
L^{d} M l's servant			6	0	0	0	3	2
Sir Thomas Derhams servant . . .			6	0	0	0	3	2
Mr. Hays servant			6	0	0	0	3	2
Countes Bolanetis Servants .			6	0	0	0	3	2
Corsini the Pops Nephews servants .			6	0	0	0	3	2
Prince St. Abonys servants .			6	0	0	0	3	2

[Foreign Tour]

				Julios	bv.	q.	Stg.		
	Books of Travels Mr. Elphiston			33	0	0	0	17	2
	For seeing Mosaickwork	3	0				0	1	7
	Bustas	1	0				0	0	6
	St. Chorls Church	1	0				0	0	6
	villa Borghese	4	0				0	2	1
	Borghese Palice	3	0				0	1	7
	Farnesi Palic	3	0				0	1	7
	the famous Bull there .	1	0				0	0	6
	Pamphili Palic	3	0				0	1	7
	Barberini Palice	6	0				0	3	2
	Justiniani Palic	3	0				0	1	7
	the vatican .	4	0				0	2	1
	Villa Pamphili Pal .	4	0				0	2	[illegible]
	seting up coach ther	6	0				0	3	2
	the Amphitheater	1	0				0	0	6
	Collona Palic	3	0				0	1	7
	For entering the Kingdom of Naples .	1	0				0	0	6
	Mala Duan .	4	0				0	2	1
	Naples Duan	5	0				0	2	7
				56	0	0			
Decm 5	For 4 Chases bv the Procatcho and a sadle horse from Rom to Naples in 5 days with 2 Mails a day 26 sequins and 2 to drink			560	0	0	14	10	8
			S	1398	19	0	36	8	2

[Foreign Tour]

Naples, Wedensday, 5 Dec[r] N.S., 1731.

	D.	c.	g.	Stg. £	s.	d.
For 2 Doz Naples chena plats	7	2	0	0	2	11
6 basket chamber pots	0	6	4	0	2	7
5 water basons	0	5	0	0	2	0
6 Chamber ston pots	0	6	0	0	2	5
8 earthen pots kitchen	0	7	2	0	2	11
3 Kitchen pots more	0	3		0	1	2
a big water jar	0	1		0	0	9
2 sauce pans	0	0	8	0	0	3
2 big blew and white bouls	0	3	8	0	1	6
6 Tee cups 10 Coffiecups and saucers and 4 little bouls	2	5	0	0	10	0
6 Ivery Knives and forks	3	8	0	0	15	2
2 Tee pots	0	1	9	0	0	9
a boyling and 2 washing basons	3	8	0	0	1	6
12 cristal wine glases	1	4	0	0	5	7
12 slight wine glases		2	4		1	0
2 cruits	0	2	4		1	0
10 water glayses	0	8	0		3	2
12 small carafs	1	4	4	0	5	9
4½ Doz. wine flasks .	0	5	4	0	2	2
2 salet Dishes	0	2	4	0	1	0
a Tee pot .	0	0	7	0	0	3
	15	9	4			

Janua-

[Foreign Tour]

			D.	c.	g.	£	s.	d.
	Mr. Douglasses man's service .		2	8	0	0	11	2
	Cleaning the house		0	9	9	0	3	9
			19	7	3	3	18	9
Naples	Caried over		19	17	3	3	18	9
	For 33½ can Hagabag for 5 doz. Tee napkins fring[d] .	23 2 5				4	13	0
	4 doz. hagabag napkins 7 ca.	20 3 0				4	1	2
	4 can hagabag 2 tablecloths	2 8 0				0	11	2
	32 Napens and 4 Table cloaths of German Dyaper .	35 0 0				7	0	0
	3 Naples Dyaper Tablecloths	8 5 0				1	14	0
	some second hand linen	16 8 0				3	7	2
	4 lan towels finer	2 8 5				0	11	4
			109	2	0			
	To Francisko footmans wage	8 7 0				1	14	9
	Cooks wages at 6D. pr mo.	14 1 0				2	16	5
	Fransiska the maid 15 carlins pr Moneth to her	0 6 0				0	2	5
			23	4	0			
1731 January 28	For house rent a moneth to this day		40	0	0	8	0	0

[Foreign Tour]

					Stg.		
		D.	c.	g.	£	s.	d.
	making a Chimny	5	0	0	1	0	0
	For coach and horses a Moneth to 6 Jan^r^.	40	0	0	8	0	0
	For coaches to see Presapias, etc. .	3	3	0	0	13	2
	For a Millan Chase	52	5	0	10	10	0
	To Saverios child 2 C. taylor 2 Car. .	0	4	0	0	1	7
	For mending smokie chimny .	5		0	1	2	0
	To a cook .	0	5	0	0	3	2
	To Fransisca the maid of wages . . .	0	8	0	0	3	2
	To Saverio of wages at 10D. pr Month	14	0	0	2	16	0
	To the french cook at 7D. pr. Month .	2	0	0	0	8	0
Feb[r] 4	For the coach a Moneth .	40	0	0	8	0	0
	For House Rent a moneth the .	40	0	0	8	0	0
	For letters .	2	2	0	0	8	10
	For cariing Chease to Rome . . .	2	0	0	0	8	0
	For two Millan chases .	91	0	0	18	4	0
	For bringing home the chases . . .	0		0	0	2	5
	For glasses .	0	6	0	0	3	2
	For a Coach to see Presapias, etc. .	1	2	0	0	4	10
	For a Balcony to see the car	4	0	0	0	16	0
	For a Lodge at the opera a night .	3	0	0	0	12	0
	For 2 trunks .	5	0	0	1	0	0
	To St. Francis Church	0	2	0	0	0	10
	To Saverio of wages	8	0	0	1	12	0

[Foreign Tour]

						Stg.		
			D.	c.	g.	£	s.	d.
	To the French cook John of wages . .		7	0	0	1	8	0
	To Francesca maid in full of 3 moneth wages .		3	1	0	0	12	5
27	For a moneth and a half house Rent to the 12 of March .		60	0	0	12	0	0
March 6	For the coach a moneth this day .		40	0	0	8	0	0
	For making 30 ℔. chocalet in house book							
	24 pound coco nuts	9 6 0				1	18	5
	14 pound powder suger	1 8 0				0	7	2
	4 ounces vinellas	6 6 6				1	6	8
	4 oun cinamon	0 5 3				0	2	2
		18 5 9						

Naples

	From Day house Books from 5 Dec^m 1731 to the 1st March 1732 N.S. . . .	603	9	1	120	15	7
Ap. 14	For House Rent a moneth	40	0	0	8	0	0
	For Saverias wages .	10	0	0	2	0	0
	The Cook a moneths wages . . .	7	0	0	1	8	0
	To Francisco a moneths wages . . .	1	5	0	0	6	0
	To Nicola the Boy a moneth .	1	5	0	0	6	0
	To the Cook at Sorıento of his wages .	1	0	0	0	4	0
	For 95 Can gas at 22 and 24 g. for beds .	21	2	0	4	4	10
	To Nicolla in full wages	0	2	0	0	0	10

[Foreign Tour]

		D.	c.	g.	Stg. £	s.	d.
	For 3 chases to Putsola and Bara, etc. .	3	9	0	0	15	7
	For expenses at Neros Baths, etc. .	6	1	0	1	4	5
	To the Chasemen	0	6	0	0	2	5
30	For House Rent to this day	26	0	0	5	4	0
	For a coach and 2 horses 2 Moneths	80	0	0	16	0	0
	For 20 packs of cards	2	2	0	0	8	10
	For 3 chases to Castle Marc	6	0	0	1	4	0
	To the Chase men	0	6	0	0	2	5
	To French Cook a moneths wages	7	0	0	1	8	0
May 2	To Saverio a moneth this day .	10	0	0	2	0	0
10	To Francisco the Maid a moneth	1	5	0	0	6	0
	To Nicol cook boy a moneth and 2 days .	1	7	0	0	6	10
25	To Francisco cook boy 28 days . .	1	4	0	0	5	8
		[1] 1448	0	4	291	13	2

Naples.

The Furniture for our House
At Portiche and removing

		D.	c.	g.	£	s.	d.
May 3 1732	For Naples						
	3 Doz Plates	1	1	6	0	4	8
	2 soup basons	0	[illegible]	[illegible]	0	[illegible]	1[illegible]
	3 Dishes						
	2 Dishes						
	a boul ½ caraf						
	12 Jelly glases						

[1] This summation should be 1458 0 4.

[Foreign Tour]

			D.	c.	g.	£	s.	d.
	12 Earthen Candlesticks	0 6 0				0	2	5
	6 pr. snuffers	0 6 6				0	2	8
	36 white wicker chairs at 15 grains the peace	5 4 0					1	7
	3 can bedin to cookboy .	0 6 0				0	2	5
	a looking glas	1 0 0				0	4	0
	yron grate to stove hal	0 6 4				0	2	7
	Nails .	0 1 0				0	0	5
			13	0	2			
Portice	Serching our goods at Duan	1 3 0				0	5	2
4 May	ffelucas with goods and ourselves	5 3 0					1	2
	Whiting the house .	3 5 0				0	14	0
	Cleaning house	0 8 0				0	3	2
	chases with servants	2 5 0				0	10	0
			13	4	0			
	nails 4g	4	0	0	4	0	0	2
	Porters for caring goods		8	5	0	1	14	0
	Coper pots 17 qr^{ll}		8	6	1	1	14	5
	yron things, spits, etc		2	0	8	0	8	4
1732 Naples Portice June 2	To Saveria a months wages to this day .		10	0	0	2	0	0
	To cook a moneths wages to this day .		7	0	0	1	8	0
	To Francisco cook in full this day .		0	3	0	0	1	2

[Foreign Tour]

			D.	c.	g.	Stg. £	s.	d.
	To washing table linen		0	8	0	0	3	2
	For 32 can cords to beds	1 0 7				0	4	3
	80 yron rings	0 2 2				0	0	11
	2 ounces scarlet silk	0 6 0				0	2	5
	Taylor 10 days	4 0 0				0	16	0
	more rings, etc., to beds .	0 3 1				0	1	3
			6	2	0			
30	To-day book from the 1st March to the 1st of July being 4 moneths		632	11	7	126	12	8
	To hear Carastin[1] sing		5	0	0	1	0	0
Augt. 16	To cary a bed to Naples		0	6	0	0	2	5
	For the coach to Angelo	36 0				7	4	0
	For the coach to 1 Augt. 7w.	54 0				10	16	0
			90	0	0			
	To the vanditor 4 Moneth 1 Septm^{r}. .	53 00	53	3	4	10	13	5
	To Mr. Saveria of wages .	12 50				2	10	0
	To the cook 2 ms. 2 Aug. .	14 00				2	16	0
	Francisco Maid 2 August 3 m.	4 50				0	18	0
	To Frances Kitchen boy .	2 50				0	10	0

[1] Giovanni Carestini, born about 1705. 'His voice, at first a powerful clear soprano, afterwards changed to the fullest, finest, deepest contralto ever perhaps heard.'—Groves's *Dictionary of Music, etc.* Carestini made his debut in London under Handel on 4th December 1733. He was a tall, handsome man, and a very good actor.

[Foreign Tour]

							Stg.		
				d.	c.	g.	£	s.	d.
	To Joseph Kitchen boy 10 Aug.	3	50				0	14	0
	To Lowrenc a Month 22 Aug.	5	00				1	0	0
				42	0	0			
	To Indian rute			0	5	0	0	2	0
Portice Octr 2	To the Cook 2 moneth 2d. Oct.	14	0				2	16	0
22	To Lorensine to this day 2 mo.	10	0				2	0	0
	To Mushet .	5	0				1	0	0
	To Francisco the maid to 18 Octr.	3	0				0	12	0
	To Joseph cook boy to 10 Novr	6	0				1	4	0
	To Frances coachman	1	0				0	4	0
				39	0	0			
	To Nicola Goveglio, coach 1 Mo. hire . . .			36	0	0	7	4	0
	To Guisc Attanassio on acct. of house rent .			100	0	0	20	0	0
	To Notaro di Roma pr the Policy			1	0	0	0	4	0
	For the coach a Moneth by Toriano			36	0	0	7	4	0
	For coach horses to 1st November from Angelo viti a moneth .			36	0	0	7	4	0
	To venditor at the 1st November for 2 monthes . .			26	6	0	5	6	5
	For carts at 4½ carlins with goods								

[Foreign Tour]

							Stg.		
				d.	c.	g.	£	s.	d.
	from Portice to Naples .	5	75				1	2	11
	porters 2 carl.						0		
	each cart	1	80				0	7	2
	to drink .	0	30					1	3
	Birris at Bridge several times	1	0					4	0
	caring more good	2	40				0	9	7
	bring a press	0	25					1	0
	puting up Damask curtins	0	30				0	1	3
	a cloath to cover the carts .	0	30				0	1	3
				12	1	0			
	For a bed at Mr. Temples			1	2	0	0	4	10
Naples Nov. 15 1732	For a tee boord	1	0				0	4	0
	a hagabag tablecloathe	1	70				0	6	10
	12 rush chairs	1	80				0	7	3
	a coper pot 24 gr ounce .	1	56				0	6	3
	2 doz. Tee Napkins	7	20				1	8	10
	4 can hagabag 7 Carlins .	2	80				0	11	2
				16	0	6			
	To ventitor in pairt of 100 Ducats for 6 moneth beginning the 1st. of Novr 1732			20	0	0	4	0	0
	To Caposhins and Saints Pictors			0	8	0	0	3	2
	For our coach from Angelo for the moneth of Nov^r			36	0	0	7	4	0

[Foreign Tour]

			d.	c.	g.	Stg. £	s.	d.
	To cooks wage to 2 Dec^{r} .	14 0				2	16	0
	To Lorrance to 22 Nov^{r} .	5 0				1	0	0
	To Joseph under cook in full	4 0				0	16	0
	Fransisco Maid to 18 Nov^{r}. .	1 50				0	6	0
	For 2 hatts to John and James	2 40				0	9	7
	To Calabria a moneth 15 Dec^{r}	2 0				0	8	0
			28	9	0			
	To Capt Piels ships crew		2	7	0	0	10	10
	To horses to the Consols coach etc		1	4	0	0	5	7
Friday 14	For chair men etc. .		1	2	0	0	4	10
we came	To Caposhins .		0	4	0	0	1	7
to Naples	From Day House Book from 1st July to the 1st Decem^{br} being 5 Moneths .		765	0	7	153	0	3
1733								
			D.	C.	gr.			
	To cooks wages to 2 January .	7 0				1	8	0
	To Lowrencon to 2 ms. 22 Jan^{r}.	12 0				2	8	0
	To Calabria cook boy full .	1 50				0	6	0
	To Francisco Maid to 18 Jan^{r}.	3 0				0	12	0
	To a Cook Xmas daj . .	2 0				0	8	0
			25	5	0			
	To Angelo for							

[Foreign Tour]

				d.	c.	g.	£	s.	d.
	2 Moneths to the 1st Feb^{r}. . . .			72	0	0	14	8	0
	To the vanditor ın pairt of 100 D^{t} for 6 moneth which is not full 17 D^{t} p^{r} moneth and this maks 60 D^{ts}. .			40	0	0	8	0	0
	For bringing cheases from Hammons			0	3	0	0	1	3
	To Prests .	0	50				0	2	0
	old shiets .	2	50				0	10	0
	James bedin in ship	6	32				1	5	4
	custom house for trunks .	3	95				0	15	10
	rubarb	2	55				0	10	2
		———		15	8	2			
	For repairing cheases .			1	2	0	0	4	10
feb^{r} 2	To Mark Cook boy to 6 feb. 1 mo.			1	5	0	0	6	0
	To House Book in Decm^{r} 1732			165	7	8½	33	3	1
	To D^{n} Guiseppe Attenassio on account of house Rent			50	0	0	10	0	0
	For lock and repairs at Portice . .			4	8	6	0	19	5
Naples 1733 March 26	To the venditor in full for Moneths 5			20	0	0	4	0	0
	For our coach 1 March	36	0				7	4	0
	Ditt to the 27 March	30	0				6	0	0
		———		66	0	0			
	To Portice House Rent for a year			170	0	0	34	0	0

[Foreign Tour]

						Sterling		
			d.	c.	g.	£	s.	d.
To the house at Naples in full of 200 D			50	0	0	10	0	0
For letters by Hammons acott in 17 Mon			52	5	9	10	10	4
To Sigr. Spelteras Journey to England			76	6	0	15	6	5
To Ditt of wages 5£ Str.			65	0	0	13	0	0
To John the Cook in full of wages .			21	0	0	4	4	0
To Fransisco of wages .			3	4	0	0	13	7
To Mark under cook .			3	1	0	0	12	5
For jack boots	2	82				0	11	3
buff britches 1 D. 42g.	2	42				0	9	8
			5	2	4			
To Erasmus Rolland	1	0				0	4	0
Mr. Golds Maid	1	0				0	4	0
Sigr Stefano a hat	3	0				0	12	0
Capusins and Preasts	0	20				0	0	10
the Consul and Tories servants	1	50				0	6	0
Marquis R. .	1	0				0	4	0
Faranta Mr. Temples man	1	0				0	4	0
Gratcia .	1	0				0	4	0
			9	7	0			
For 259 Rottolo hambs 36 of ym	25	90				5	3	7
bring them from Soriento and puting them a boord in the Moll	2	30				0	9	3
3 Parmozan cheases 165 lb. .	43	85				8	15	4
all sent home			72	0	5			

[Foreign Tour] Sterling

		d.	c.	gr.	£	s.	d.
For Maccarony at 7½g. 10, 11, 13, 14 gr pr. Rott. all sent home 69 Rottolo of it . .		8	0	3½	1	12	1
		4501	7	0	902	11	10
For repairing Chases .	13 50				2	14	0
Ditt . .	3 71½				0	14	9
Ditt 2D. 94g. 1D. 73g. .	4 67				0	18	8
days wages to workmen	3 60				0	14	5
		25	4	8½			
For mending sadles .	1 20				0	4	10
caring trunks and sighting ym	3 30				0	18	3
postilions to ty on bagag	0 05				0	0	2½
stra to lay bagage right .	0 07				0	0	3½
	——	4	6	2			
The expense of our Journey in the Kingdom of Naples to Rome		51	1	0	10	4	5
From Household book from 1 January 1733 to the 22nd of March 1733 . .		333	2	5	66	18	0
		4916	1	5½	985	9	8

[1] this in English money at 510 Ducats for 100£ Sterline is 960£ 2 shillins.

[1] Lady Grisell here takes the ducat as worth 3s. 11d. sterling. In the editor's calculations the ducat has been taken as worth 4s.; hence the discrepancy.

[Foreign Tour]

	d.	julio	by	Sterling		
Bring back Rome expenc which is .	554	2	9			
2 crouns is a sequin, a sequin 20 Julios, this in English money is 138 guinys £145 8 6 reckoning 20 Julios or pauls half a guiny						
	£	by.				
Bring back Bolome sum of	1160	13	4			
this in English money 10£ 10 byocks to a sequin 57£ 16 shillins .						

Rome, 1733		crouns	p.	byocks	Stg.		
March 29	For our journey from Terracina to Rome .						
Apl. 22	For our journey from Rome to Florence and from Florence to Balonia . . .	164	8	0	43	4	2
	For seeing Churches Palices and villas 9D 6 P. of it for the great Duks Gallarie .	37	8	0	9	18	5
	For Chease repairs	40	4	0	10	12	1
	For cords 5p. caring cheases . . .	0	6	8	0	3	4
	For greess .	0	7	7	0	3	10
	For porters to Duan, etc.	1	4	0	0	7	4
	For 7 days coach Mezareri week, 20 pouls .	14	0	0	3	13	6
	10 days at 12 pauls	12	0	0	3	3	0
	For 2 coaches 2 days .	5	0	0	1	6	3
	To Mr. Strods contribution . . .	4	0	0	1	1	0
	To Mrs. Cottan .	1	0	0	0	5	3

[Foreign Tour]

		cr.	p.	by.	St. £	s.	d.
	To Mr. Hamiltons servant . . .	0	3	0	0	1	7
	To coachman .	0	7	0	0	3	8
	For a syrang 2 D a box for it 1p 3^d^. .	2	1	3	0	11	1
	For 2 brushes 1p. 5 paper 6	0	2	1	0	1	1
	To Angelo the footman	5	1	0	1	6	9
	To Lowrensin to cary him to Naples .	4	0	0	1	1	0
	To mend boots and baginet .	0	3	5	0	1	9
Florence	For repairs of Cheases 1D 9 washing, etc. 5	2	4	0	0	12	7
	For nails and gemlet 8Sc. and caring chease 2p. . .	0	2	8	0	1	3
	For essenes for us all and orang butter . .	14	9	0	3	18	3
	For 2 ounces apaplectick balsom . . .	1	0	0	0	5	3
	To the house and cook here . . .	1	0	0	0	5	3
	For letters for Mr. Temple 3p. for ourselves .	1	0	0	0	5	3
	For a coach 17 days at 9 pauls p^r^ day	15	3	9	4	0	4
	For pometam	0	1	5	0	0	8
	For Lodging and entertainment at Madam Pettits for 5 days 50 9 wax candle, suger, etc. 5 5 4	56	4	4	14	16	2
	To Ditt 14 Days at 48 Pauls a day and to servants 2D. .	86	7	0	22	15	2
Jossipies	For Ditt at a french house						

[Foreign Tour]

		cr.	p.	by.	Sterling £	s.	d.
May 26 french house	18 days 40C. pr day etc. 3 . .	80	4	8	21	2	4
	brought all from house book . . .	554	2	9	145	7	7

here a sequin is 10 Liners 10 byocks, and 1£ is 2 pauls, and 12 demi is a byock

		£	by	D			
Balonia 15 May 1733	For 2 Cheases to Palazzo Albegote with Lady Essex 12£, voitarins men to drink £4 10 .	16	10	0	0	16	6
	For a coach 23 days at 10 pauls pr day	131	0	0	6	11	0
	For our lodging at 1½ sequin for 26 days .	408	10	0	20	8	6
	For 4 linch pins 2£ rops 7£ . . .	9	0	0	0	9	0
	For puting in cheases 1£ mending pistols	4	10	0	0	4	6
	For a saddle	11	10	0	0	11	6
	To Lowra the maid, 2 pistols at 36 pauls	36	0	0	1	16	0
	From House Book .	420	13	4	21	0	8
	Going Post to Francolina 5½ post pr acct. to be added 123£ to this	1037	13	4			
					6	8	0
		1160	13	4	58	0	8

Vinice 11 June	For 2 piots in 3 days from Francolina 9 florence sequins at 21 paul which is here 21 Linrie

[Foreign Tour]

					Sterling.		
		£	s.	d.	£	s.	d.
	and to the rowers 3£ 8 byoks or soldis devide this in 3 pairts is	126	8	0	8	8	2
	painters maid 2£ paper wax etc. 4£ . . .	6	0	0	0	3	0
	For a Gundala 8 days at 8£ pr day	64	0	0	1	12	0
	For lodging and entertainment in a French house at 35£ per day except Tee and suger	372	0	0	9	6	0
	to servants who served us well .	24	0	0	0	12	0
	for frute and wine in the piot .	4	0	0	0	2	0
	For seeing the Doges Palice and other places . .	12	0	0	0	6	0
	3 glases at glass work	5	0	0	0	2	6
	For a Barchella to Padua 48 the 3ᵈ is	32	0	0	0	16	0
	to Rowers . .	4	0	0	0	2	0
Padua	For Super, breckfast, and diner with Sʳ Rob Broun and Neil Broun Consull . . .	70	0	0	1	15	0
	to the servant . . cariing baggage	1	10	0	0	0	8
	To a scrivener 6£ .	6	0	0	0	3	0
	To the cetcerony a pistol I rekon it	36	0	0	0	18	0
	For 2 Coaches	20	0	0	0	10	0
	For suger wax candle etc. at Vinice .	51	9	0	1	5	9
	For washing at Vinice .	24	0	0	0	12	0
Verona	For grees to cheases . 5 0				0	2	6
	a coach at Verona . 8 8				0	4	2

[Foreign Tour]

		£	s.	d.	Sterling £	s.	d.
seeing churches, etc. there	6 0				0	3	0
		19	8	0			
		877	15	0	21	18	9

This in English money at 2143 £17 7 soldis for £50 is about 21£ 15s. 6.

Frankford

here 4 florins and 15 Karmitens is a unger

	Flo.	k.	
For seeing churches .	2	7	0

this is about 5 shillins sterlin

Vinice

For 1 lb. green 1 lb. Bohe Tea	32	12	0	0	16	4
For 25 lb. Chocalet	112	10	0	2	16	3
For wax candle 1, 17, letters 17£ . .	18	17	0	0	9	5
To sum brought over .	858	7	0			
To Mr. Smiths Commission . . .	64	9	0	1	12	3
S	1087	05	p			

bring down 21£ 15 6 and ad at 22£ in a sequin 228 £18 which is .	5	5	0
	27	00	5

	D.	g.	d
For our Journey from Padua to Aix .	627	0	0

[Foreign Tour]

						Sterling. £	s.	d.
14½ guny	From Padua to Trent 28½ sequins at 22£ .							
15 4 6								
73 16 8	From Trent to Aix							
	a Post Horse	48 38				6	1	7
	eating and lodging	110 34				13	16	5
	odd expences	33 14				4	3	1
	expences of 2 cheases .	Florins 398 16	Kar. 590	42	0	49	15	8
	From Aix to Spa for journey and other things 143½ shillin		L. 71	Su. 15				
4 10 0								
£93 2 0								
	For our journey from Leige to Valensien by a particular account a pairt, which particular I must cary to Leger		327	19	0	14	9	9
	For our Journey from Valencien to Paris by a particular account .		450	4	0	20	12	6
	For our journey from Paris to Calice by ditt.		517	6	0	23	13	11
	To the Master of the Sloup from Calice to Dover		96	0	0	4	8	0
			1391	09	0			

this at 1090 Livers for £50 is near about 63£ Sterling 14 sh.

				£ or franc	S.	liers	£	s.	d.
[Foreign Tour]							Sterling		
Spa							£	s.	d.
10 July 1733	From Day House Book from this date to the 22nd Sepm^r^. about £39, 12Stg.			1464	5	2	85	8	0
Sept. 22	For 2 cheases with 2 horses each to Liege	24	0				1	8	0
	2 riding horses	8	0				0	9	4
	cariage of bagage and postilions	7	15				0	2	0
	diner for 14 at Chairfountain	24	5				1	10	3
Leige, 24	2 night super diner and breakfast, 7 of us and 2 servants at Mutton blanc	40	0				2	6	8
Brusles 25	For 3 nights Lodging and eating, 6 of us .	53	2				3	1	11
	to servant of the house	2	10				0	2	[illegible]
				159	12	0			
				1623	17	2			
	This at 1725£ for 100£ Str is £94 4 6 Stg.								
Paris, October Tewsday 27	From Daybook from 2 Oct. to the date hereof for 5 of our selves and Mr. Horatio Man			320	0	0	14	2	0
	this at 1090 Livers for £50 stg is about 14£ 2 sh. stirling.								

[Foreign Tour]

					Sterling		
					£	s.	d.
For lodging 3 weeks 3 days at le otel der Hambourg	315	315	0	0	13	17	6

	Sterling.		
	£	s.	d.
For our laces at Brusles	63	11	0
Cambrick at Valensien .	17	2	1½
Duty at Custom house for Cambrick .	1	3	6½
For our journey from Dover to London, 6 of us and 2 servants pr. a particular account .	16	8	8
To Mr. Man to clear traveling accounts .	4	8	0
For silver plate 111 ounces and fashion .	31	17	6
For gilding the porangers	1	2	6

Leyden.

Account from the new stil that we came to Roterdam which is 27 May 0 : stil of expenses only for my D Grisie and I.

	G.	st.	D.	£	s.	d.
For washing . .	2	8	0	0	4	5
For a piece of 7 Snuff hander chiefs .	11	10	0	1	1	1
For 5¼ Pertian to line wraper at 28st . .	7	7	0	0	13	5
To a writing Apron 3¼ ell armapre say 28 .	4	11	0		8	4
To James a pair of Stokins . . .	2	0	0	0	3	8
For a pair pockets .	1	7	0	0	2	5
To John a pr. stokins .	2	0	0	0	3	8

[Foreign Tour]

					Sterling.		
		g.	st.	d.	£	s.	d.
	To 2 pr. threed stokins mine .	3	14	0	0	6	9
	For making Grisie's goun . . .	1	14	0	0	8	1
	For a washing	3	0	0	0	5	6
	For a pair pockets .	1	6	0	0	2	4
	For 2 threeds of broad holland 19½ ell 54 st.	28	10	0	2	12	3
	For 50½ ell holl gris shifts at 37 st. .	91	11	8	8	7	11
	For 2 thrids of 49 ells holland at 4 gul. .	130	14	0	11	19	7
	For 16½ holland at 58 sturs . . .	52	4	0	4	15	8
	For Mushets holland 2£ Stirling . .	21	19	0	2	0	3
	To Mushet 30 sh. Str. errour set in Leger	00	0	0			
	To Mrs. Clench for 6 shirts	95	18	0	8	15	10
	For tape at Harlem	10	15	4	0	19	8
	For 2 piece green handerchieff	34	0	0	3	2	4
	For 6 pr thread stockins Grisie . .	21	0	0	1	18	6
	To 5 pr. thread stockins for Grisie 2g 18st .	14	0	0	1	5	8
	For 2 pr collerd thread stockins errour .	0	0	0	0	0	0
	For a piece broun handerchiefs errour .						
	For apron Mushet .	1	9	0	0	2	8
Utright	For a purs Grisie . silver . 17 10				1	12	
	For a purs Rachy ditt . 17 10				1	12	
	For a purs litle gris — 17 0				1	11	2

[Foreign Tour]

		g.	st.	d.	£	s.	d.
For 3 velvet purss to them	4 16				0	6	9
		56	16	0			
For 2 pr. gloves Grisie and I		1	8	0	0	2	7
For washing		8	13	0	0	6	8
For 10 Dutch els yaly ( ) silk for a goan		70	0	0	6	8	4
For stokins Grisie 29 2 st.		2	2	0	0	3	10
For 2 pr under stokins Gris 2 g 2 st.		2	2	0	0	3	10
For a pr baver stokins	3 0				0	5	6
a pr baver gloves	1 4				0	2	2
		4	4	0			
litle coffie pot		2	4	0	0	4	0
a litle lock to coffie pot		0	0	2	0	0	0¼
litle copper ketle		1	4	0	0	2	2
For a pr thread stok under stokins Gris		1	10	0	0	2	9
For 4 piece tape 10, 5, 7, 6	1 12				0	2	11
buttons	0 3				0	0	3
		1	15	0			
For a wagone to loonupstant		6	0	0	0	11	0
expenses at loonupstant [1]		1	4	0	0	2	2
put to Grisies slives							
For 4½ ells hollen for my west coats		9	9	0	0	17	4
For the silver conforture		34	0	0	3	2	4
		740	9	6	67	14	11

[1] This line has been interlined, and no doubt refers to the immediately succeeding entry.

[Foreign Tour]

Mostrick. At this place 37 skillins, and each skilling 10 St. is in a guiny.

					[Sterling]		
		Sk.	Mks.	doits	£	s.	d.
	For Mushets goun at 24 Mark 10 ells	24	0	0	0	14	0
Aix	To chairman for 3 days	3	0	0	0	1	9
37 sk. 4	For a doz glovs L Hervie[1]	15	0	0	0	8	9
Marks in	2 doz Grisie	26	0	0	0	15	2
a guiny	2 doz me	26	0	0	0	15	2
	3 doz to give away	52	0	0	1	10	4
	2 pr gloves Mrs. Terris	3	7	0	0	2	2
	2 kains . . .	5	0	0	0	2	11
	2 nidle cases	3	0	0	0	1	9
	Nidles	15	0	0	0	8	9
	2 p^{r} shoves my D.	9	0	0	0	5	3
	a litle silver plate	37	4	0	1	1	10
	2 biger plates 20 crowns	160	0	0	4	13	4
	callico for 2 bed gouns lining .	7	7	4	0	3	11
	galoun and silk my coat	0	2	0	0	0	1½
	6 p^{r} gloves to my D.	9	0	0	0	5	3
	a floorishd handkerchief Grisie	15	0	0	0	8	9
	3 snuff handkerchief my Dear . . .	24	0	0	0	14	0
	a pair gray threed stokins me . . .	8	0	0	0	4	8
	a pie boban	0	6	0	0	0	5
	2 lb. puder .	1	3	0	0	0	9
	For 7½ els camblet for frok 5 sk.37 4 0					1	10
	furniture buttons, etc. 10 5 7				0	6	2
	making 9 sk. 11 ells lining 15 27 3 3				0	16	11
		75	4	2			

[1] See p. 302.

[Foreign Tour] [Sterling]

			Sk.	Mks.	doits	£	s.	d.
July 4 Aix	For washing		16	0	0	0	9	4
	Chair 8 days to Douse		8	0	0	0	4	8
	17 times each near half an hour at Douse		34	0	0	0	19	10
	Making Grisies seck and mine . . .		10	0	0	0	5	10
	a box for the heads		1	1	0	0	0	8
	servant at Douuse		1	0	0	0	0	7
	For 10½ ell Indian Tafita Gris	66 0 0				1	18	6
	10 ells brountafita me .	60 0 0				1	15	0
	clohth for stay bands	1 3 0				0	0	9
	lining for the sleves	4 0 0				0	2	4
			131	3	0			
	For 3½ ell Dyaper Grisie .	10 4 4				0	6	1
	6 ell holland my D drawers	24 0 0				0	14	0
	6 yd. holland my drawers .	15 0 0				0	8	9
	13½ ell holland 3 aprons	54 0 0				1	11	6
			103	4	4			
			825	3	2	24	1	9

Spa, the 9 July 1731.

		Sk.	Mks.	doits	£	s.	d.
	For a Neclace to me	2	5	0	0	1	5
	a pair breast straps	3	0	0	0	1	9
	13½ ell holl for 4 aprons Grisie 4 sk. .	54	0	0	1	11	6
	2¼ holl for pockets	6	7	2	0	3	11

[Foreign Tour]							[Sterling
		Sk.	Mks.	doits	£	s.	d.
	31½ ell holl gris shifts at 4 skil .	127	9	0	3	14	7
	3 pr spectickles 3 sk. staff string 1½ .	4	4	2	0	2	7
	lace at 15 sk Grisie tuckers .	45	0	0	1	6	3
20	To John erour						
	a waterbotle errour						
	a pr. threed stokins	6	0	0	0	3	6
	To Moushets to buy her goun lining .	0	8	0	0	0	6
		250	4	0	7	6	0
	To the half of the stons and wax frute . .	37	4	0	1	1	10
	S.	287	8	0	8	7	10
	[1]143£ 18 143£ 18s.						
		L.	S.				
21	For 2 weeks washing this 21 sk. 7	10	17	0	0	12	2
	To litle Grisie I owd her on the last account	3	0	0	0	3	5
	To the old woman at well	0	10	0	0	0	7
	To the waganier 5s. Dick Litletons carinish[?] 5s.	0	10	0	0	0	7
	To Grisie and Mrs. Burnet necklaces .	2	0	0	0	3	2
	To a Ball 4 sk. the boy 1 sk.	2	10	0	0	2	10
Aug. 1	For a wash ball 7 2 lb. powder 10	0	17	0	0	0	11
	For a weeks washing saterday 28 July	2	17	0	0	3	2

[1] Lady Grisel here changes skillings, sous, and liers into its equivalent at Spa in French money of livers and sous.

[Foreign Tour]					[Sterling]		
		L.	S.		£	s.	d.
	For a pr gray threed stokins . . .	3	0	0	0	3	4
	For a Jeronstat dyell .	0	5	0	0	0	3
	For a box to Phillips the Jesuit at Liege	1	10	0	0	1	9
8	For a lb. powder 5s a lb. this day 5s.	0	10	0	0	0	7
	For neckleses Mrs. Dalrymple and I .	2	0	0	0	2	3
	To French horns .	1	0	0	0	1	1
	To my Dear	2	10	0	0	2	10
	For a box to Mr. Cartret	1	0	0	0	1	1
	For 4 weeks washing a sk. the day great pieces 6 sturs doz. small 5 st. shirt, cravat, and handkerchief and 3 st. shifts and 3 sturs peticoats	4	0	0	0	4	6
	8 handkerchiefs 4 hoods to Grisie equely and me 14 yd.	31	5	0	1	14	10
18	2 lb. ½ poweder a lb. this day . . .	0	19	2		1	1
	a pr threed stockins	3	0	0		3	5
	lost to Mrs. Spence	12	0	0	0	13	6
18	To my dear	37	8	0	2	1	8
	For washing to the saterday 19 .	10	0	0		11	3
	For a soliter to Grisie	3	0	0	0	3	
	For 3 black neckleses .	3	0	0		3	5
		138	11	2	7	16	2
	take out pocket .	37	8	0	2	1	8
	S—	£101	3	2	5	14	6

Spailing.							
		L.	S.				
28	For 3 lb. powder 2 ysday	0	15	0	0	0	10

[Foreign Tour] [Sterling]

		L.	S.		£	s.	d.
	For a weeks washing Saterday 25	4	5	0	0	4	9
Sept. 6	To Mushet	18	14	0	1	1	0
	Washing .	16	13	0	0	18	9
	Shoes my D. 5£ mending 1£ .	6	0	0	0	6	10
	2 pr clogs Grisie and I	8	10	0	0	9	7
Leige	3 articles in generall account . . .	94	3	3	5	5	11
	fine holland my Dear at 4 livers 20 els	80	0	0	4	10	0
19 Sepm. Leige	The articles of 94 livers 3s 3 on the other side set by mistake in the general account is as followeth :						
	34½ Demi holland at 45 sturs for 7 shifts to Grisie 77 12 2						
	5 ells muslin for 4 cravats 11 5 0						
	2 night Napkins 5 6 1						
	Cambrick fine 46 15 0	46	15	0	2	12	7
	3½ ell Baskest which is cambrick	29	15	0	1	13	5
	For a pr boots to James	6	10	0	0	7	5
	For a pr shoes my Dear	6	0	0	0	6	10
	4 lb. powder and wash ball . .	1	5	0	0	1	4
	Waltins and silk for mantle . . .	1	10			1	9
	Pocket my D. . .	6	0			6	1
	2 pr. stokins to Gr.	5	0	0	0	5	8
	2 Ink horns	0	14			0	9
	John a guiny he has not acc^{tt}ed for . .	18	14	0	1	1	0

[Foreign Tour]					[Sterling]		
	the half of the kams in the box	L. 18	S. 14	0	£ 1	s. 1	d. 0
	S.	369	17	3	20	16	3
Oct. 12, 1731.							
	Lyon here the guiny or Lewidor is 24 livers						
	For 10½ ell floord silk to G. at 20 Livers the ell	210	0	0	9	3	9
	10½ ell my goun at 10 Livers	105	0	0	4	11	10
	lining and borders to goun G.	11	10	0	0	10	0
	lining etc. to mine	6	4	2	0	5	5
	my goun making .	5	0	0	0	4	4
	Grisie goun making	5	0	0	0	4	4
	Maid	1	0	0	0	0	10½
	6 head wires	0	6	0	0	0	3
	mending James boots	1	16	0	0	1	6½
	Mushet for smalls	0	12	0	0	0	6
	a hoop	15	5	0	0	13	4
	washing linin	12	0	0	0	10	6
	ell silk for a sute cloaths .	120	0	0	5	5	0
	The Taylors for lining and making .	72	0	0	3	3	0
	For making my old sack, etc.	7	0	0	0	6	2
	For mending James's cloaths .	2	0	0	0	1	9
Turin	For Dressing a hat and lining .	3	0	0	0	2	7
Oct. 27	For stokins to my D. .	7	0	0	0	6	2
	2 pr uper and 4 under myself .	28	10	0	1	4	11
	Grisie stokins	11	17	0	0	10	4
	washing linins	7	0	0	0	6	2
	spectickles .	1	10	0	0	1	3½
Millan	For washing	1	0	0	0	0	10½

[Foreign Tour]					[Sterling]		
1 Nov.		L.	S.		£	s.	d.
Bolonia	For washing	11	0	0	0	9	7
	washing . . .	15	0	0	0	13	2
		S. 660	10	2	28	17	8

Rome 23 Novr 1731. 20 pols a sequin.

		Poul.	By.		£	s.	d.
	To my Dears pocket	21	0		0	10	11
	a Stafe string	1	5		0	0	9
	a Necklace me	5	0		0	2	7
	Gloves my D	1	5		0	0	9
	Gloves me .	1	5		0	0	9
	Washing the doz. 1 pol the shirts 5 byoks	18	0		0	9	4
		48	5		1	5	1
	26 Carlin in a Rom sequin						
	2 Kain Damaty for 2 p^r pockets Gris at 5 earline 26½	1	0	0	0	4	0
Naples							
5 Deem. 1732	A Kain and a Palm ermasin for one apron 26½ . .	2	7	0	0	10	9
	6 Kanscord silk Rob 36 cor for Grisie .	21	6	0	4	6	5
		25	3	0	5	1	2

A Ducat is 10 Carlins and Teric is 2 Carlins. 10 grains is a Carline, 26 or 26½ Carlins is a sequen, a venetian sequin is 27 carlins, a Ducat is about 4 sh. stirlin.

Naples. Wednesday, 5 Decr. N. S. 1731.

	Duc.	Car.	Gr.	£	s.	d.
Caried over	25	0	0	5	1	2
To a capashin for siringing the ears . .	5	2	0	1	0	10

[Foreign Tour]					[Sterling]		
		Duc.	Car.	Gr.	£	s.	d.
	For 15 Palm Cloath 11 Duc. can .	20	6	2	4	2	6
	For tape 3 Carlins 5 g. .	0	3	5	0	1	5
	For threed and silk	1	1	0	0	4	5
	For paper 8 g., tape 5 car	0	5	8	0	2	4
	For powder 2 car paper	0	3	0	0	1	3
	For black ruban .	0	2	0	0	0	10
	For gold buttons 9 grain big and 4½ gr small the peice . . .	14	4	0	2	17	8
	For threed 4 g	0	0	4	0	0	2
	For a wige to Gr .	3	0	0	0	12	0
	For making and lining my Deirs Cloaths by John .	12	6	0	2	10	5
	For making G. wastcoat and mine	0	8	0	0	3	2
	For 9½ can velvet my goun at 5½ Ducat	52	7	2½	10	10	10
	For a pr. black silk stokins . . .	2	8	0	0	11	2
	For a can blew cloath . 7 2 0				1	8	10
	5 and 4 yellow serge . 3 2 2				0	12	9
	5½ ou. gold galoun 7 1 5				1	8	0
	buttons 0 8 0				0	3	2
	makeing 4 0 0				0	16	0
	———	22	3	7			
1732							
Seteday	For 10 ells Demie holl: G and I .	9	0	0	1	16	0
January 9	For 6 spoons 15 D. 6 C. 5 g. gote for 2 old ones 3 D. 9 Carlins	11	7	5	2	6	9
	To the Italian Master a moneth .	3	3	8	0	13	7

[Foreign Tour] [Sterling]

		Duc.	Car.	Gr.	£	s.	d.
	To Gibson of her 20£ 12 Legu . . .	32	4	0	6	9	7
	For 3 can Dyaper for Dr.	3	0	0	0	12	0
	For threed 3 g.	0	0	3	0	0	1½
	To Musick Master a moneth .	4	5	0	0	18	0
	For coppying Musick	2	6	0	0	10	5
	To my Dears pocket	7	8	0	1	11	2
	For washing 5 weeks	6	0	0	1	4	0
12	For 1½ 1/16 Can Muslin 26 car	3	9	5	0	15	9½
	[1]	246	4	9½	49	6	4

1732							
Janr 22	To the litle Italian Mr.	2	0	0	0	8	0
	For fine sope	0	2	0	0	0	10
	For a hat to James	1	4	0	0	5	7
	For a pr shoes to me	1	0	0	0	4	0
	To Doctor	5	4	0	1	1	7
	To the Mantua Maker me	4	0	0	0	16	0
	To the Mantua Maker Gris . . .	4	0	0	0	16	0
	For my velvet mittons .	1	7	0	0	6	10
	For copiing music at 1 C. the 4 lines	8	1	0	1	12	5
	For 5 Lottery Ticket of Millan .	7	2	0	1	8	10
	For Tuning spinet a month . .	1	2	0	0	4	10
	For a pr. short furd gloves me . .	0	5	0	0	2	0
	To S. Carmany Playing master .	4	5	0	0	18	0
	For St. Josephs pictor .	0	2	0	0	0	10

[1] Up to this point the accounts are given in full detail. Henceforward, in order to avoid repetition, only selected entries are given.

[Foreign Tour]

		Duc.	Car.	Gr.	£	s.	d.
					[Sterling]		
	For Chera de Spanie is wax and jostro. Ink and ostio [?] wafers .	0	1	8	0	0	9
	For 2 Naples handkerchiefs . .	1	8	0	0	7	2
	For 4 Mesma handkerchieffs . . .	4	0	0	0	16	0
	For 3 can of the 10 can strypd armazin for my			0			0
	Rob 25 C.	7	5	0	1	10	0
	For a pr. shoes my D.	1	0			4	
	For 25½ can blew armazin for curtins 22 Carlins	56	0	0	11	4	0
	For 17 can snuff colour linins . . .	37	1	0	7	8	5
	For ½ can black armaz. hats . . .	1	1	0	0	4	5
	For 8 venturs in the Lotery at Rome for us and our grandchildren	20	2	5	4	1	0
	For 8 ventors in the Lotery at Millon for Ditto . . .	18	8	5	3	15	4
	For Jamie Mitchell and Mr. Sausure in Rome Lottery . . .	5	4	0	1	1	7
1732, Naples,	For 3 can strypd armozin of the purple for me 23 C. . . .	6	9	0	1	7	7
12 Mch	For 4 p^{r} spectickles and one case . . .	1	3	0	0	5	2
	For Don quickset	0	8	0	0	3	2
	For a pr. black knit mittons G.	1	0	0	0	4	0
	For 14 palm armazin Cantoush at 24 c. Gr.	4	2	0	0	16	10
	For 1½. 1. p. green g: wraper 22½ c	3	7	0	0	14	10

[Foreign Tour]				[Sterling]		
	Duc.	Car.	Gr.	£	s.	d.
For 2 cans p. green peticoat 22½ C.	5	0	4	1	0	2
For 1 C. 5 palm g: wraper 25 C. .	4	0	6	0	16	3
For 3 Can green for Sultain 22½ C. .	6	7	5	1	7	0
For 2 green aprons G: .	2	7	8	0	11	2
For making Cantush G. . 5 0 0; green peticoat 3 0 1; wraper 5 0 0; ruban to peticoat 2 6 0; Sultain . 6 0 0	2	1	6	0	8	8
For 3 snuff handkerchiefs G. .	1	5	0	0	6	0
For 2 fether Tipits G and I .	1	6	0	0	6	5
For 4 snuff handkerchiefs me	2	6	0	0	10	5
For a p^r shoes my D· broun .	0	9	0	0	3	7
For 4 picturs to George	2	0	0	0	8	0
For 4 pair spectickles	2	0	0	0	8	0
29 To the Italian Master .	3	4	0	0	13	7
To the Playing Master to 12 Mar.	4	5	0	0	18	0
For making 3 gouns me 5 4 0; making 1 to G: 1 8 0	7	2	0	1	9	2
For 2 can black silk my D 2 4 8; making the waistcoat 6 2 2; lineing and buttons						

[Foreign Tour]

						[Sterling]		
			Duc.	Car.	Gr.	£	s.	d.
	making velvet britches .	0 2 2						
		———	9	0	0	1	16	0
Naples 1732	copiing Musick	1 4 0						
	Italian Master	3 4 0	4	8	0	0	19	2
	Churches at Soriento .		1	5	0	0	6	0
	2 handkerchief snuff ones me . . .		0	7	0	0	2	10
	a Dressing glass		1	0	0	0	4	0
	2 fans Gris .		5	0	0	1	0	0
	6 aprons changeing colour 22 C. .		9	6	0	1	18	5
	2 pr yellow stokins Gr.		2	0	0	0	8	0
	a tortoyshel comb, Gr. .		0	9	0	0	3	7
	2 goss handker chiefs G.		1	4	0	0	5	7
	yellow shoes Grisie		0		0	0	3	2
	a rid coffer with yellow nails . . .		5	0	0	1	0	0
	Coppiing musick .		3	2	0	0	12	10
	a subscription for Musick		2	7	0	0	10	10
	Blooding .		1	2	4	0	5	0
May 12	Carmany Gordana playing Mst. . . .		9	0	0	1	16	0
	tuning spinet		0	6	0	0	2	5
	Italian Master Mr. Nicol		3	4	0	0	13	7
	Chuches which is asses at a Terie the whole day and a man		1	8	0	0	7	2
	22½ Can green Pertian bed 11 C. .		24	1	0	4	16	5
	Cutting Grisie's hair		0	8	0	0	3	2
14	binding music books 16 gr. .		1	2	8	0	5	2
	For cutting Grisies hair		0	4	0	0	1	7
	For copiing Corellies Musick . . .		0	2	6	0	10	5
	For 3¼ can Armazin me							

[Foreign Tour] [Sterling]

		Duc.	Car.	Gr.	£	s.	d.
	22 C. changing gold and white .	7	1	5	1	8	7
	To Nicol taylor for all Mantas 18, carlins sultains 8 c., cantush 5 c, peticoats 3 and work in the house 4 carlins p day and meat	9	7	0	1	17	9
	1 can padisoy britches	2	4	0	0	9	7
	a pr garters	0	4	0	0	1	7
	2 pr silk stokins .	6	5	0	1	6	0
	2 pr under stokins	3	2	0	0	12	10
	For 20 gold loups	3	0	0	0	12	0
	20 gold buttons .	0	8	0	0	3	2
1732	Account of Marbel bought at Naples.						
May 24	For 2 Marbel Tables Fiore de persico from Don Michel Dicalabria	56	0	0	11	4	0
	2 wooden cases .	2	0	0	0	8	0
	Shiping in the Barcelona and custom house officers . . .	2	3	0	0	9	2
	For the whole Marble Tables	3846	0	4	769	4	2
		3906	3	4	781	5	4
	take of this for some was sold . . .	666	0	0	133	4	0
		3240	3	4	648	1	4
	To sundry things by Mr. Man pr acc[t]. . .	108	7	0	21	14	10
		3349	0	4	669	16	2
	take of Mr. Man's Tables	50	0	0	10	0	0
		3299	0	4	659	16	2

the whole drawn upon Mr. Hammon this at 510 Ducats

[Foreign Tour]

for **100£** sterling is **646£ 16** shillins str. where entered in cash book **300**

346 10

[*Note.*—Lady Grisel bases her calculations here on the ducat = 3/11, while in detailed calculations it has been taken as worth 4/; hence the discrepancy.]

					[Sterling]		
Portice, 1732		Duc.	Car.	Gr.	£	s.	d.
July 20	2 pr. silver clasps	0	1	5	0	0	7
	a pr. velvet shoes	2	0	0	0	8	0
	2 pr. silk gray stokins	3	2	0	0	12	10
	To Carmany for singing . 13 5 0				2	14	0
	hire of spinet .2 2 0				0	8	10
	Chases to Masters 3 6 0				0	14	5
	copiing music .0 4 0				0	1	7
	2 floors .	1	6	0	0	6	5
	To Doctor Piagiddel Potzzos .	4	5	0	0	18	0
	To Nicols for blooding	1	4	0	0	5	7
	For turning broun waste-coat . . .	0	6	0	0	2	5
	For 2 can velvet 6⅛ palm 2 cloks .	16	5	7½	3	6	4
	1½ can Armagin to line cloks . . .	3	3	7½	0	13	6
	making and ruban to cloks . . .	1	3	0	0	5	2
	To the Doctor .	2	7	0	0	10	10
	To Biries at the bridge	0	2	0	0	0	10
	For 5½ can Dyaper 8 C 12 servits	4	4	0	0	17	7
	18 long towills 25 gr. pr can	4	5	0	0	18	0
	1½ can 3 hagabag napkins	0	8	9½	0	3	8
	4 can servants and pantry	1	2	0	0	4	10
	2 can kitchen cloaths .	0	3	4	0	1	4
	threed 9 r r oune .	0	4	0	0	1	7

[Foreign Tour]

	Duc.	Car.	Gr.	£	s.	d.
				[Sterling]		
For 4 baths Ishi water 12 barrals each bath 15 gr. pr. barrel	7	2	0	1	8	10
caring it 4 days 3 carlins each . . .	1	2	0	0	4	10
a tub 9 days	0	9	0	0	3	7
To caposins	1	0	0	0	4	0
a can flanen	2	10	0	0	4	5
a pr velvet shoes 2^d^ plain 8 car	2	8	0	0	11	2
ar gloves 6 C. 2 pr. mittons 7 C. .	1	3	0	0	5	2
a pr. jumps and slives .	6	0	0	1	4	0
1 can silk for hoop	2	1	0	0	8	5
2 necleses 8 C. tape 2 C.	1	0	0	0	4	0
Naples Decr 1732						
a knite silk wastcoat	3	0	0	0	12	0
For 16½ Cann olive Damask to be sent home .	49	5	0	9	18	0
For rolling up silks .	0	2	0	0	0	9
To my D. . . .	2	0	0	0	8	0
For chases to Masters to Portice . . .	1	20	0	0	4	9
For 4 Moneths tuning spinets . . .	2	4	0	0	9	7
For tuning spinets to ysday .	0	6	0	0	2	5
For copiing music	1	7	0	0	6	9
For euting hair G	1	0	0	0	4	0
For 6 Can shagreen my D.	9	0	0	1	16	0
velvet for Nightgoun	7	0	0	[illegible]	[illegible]	[illegible]
velvet shag 3½ c linin	17	0	0			
gold loops for Ditt	4	0	0		[illegible]	
a wige	4	5	0			
makeing goun, etc.	1	6	0			
For a pair of shoes	0	8	0			
Cambrick weepers	1	6	0			
a black sword and gloves	1	8	0			

[Foreign Tour] [Sterling]

	Duc.	Car.	Gr.	£	s.	d.
15½ and a half black cloath . . .	19	4	0	3	17	[illegible]
3 can armazine	6	6	0	1	6	
buttons . . .	2	4		0	9	
making the sute . .	4	5		0	18	
making velvet sute	5	0	0	1	0	0
armazin .	[illegible]	[illegible]	[illegible] ½	0	[illegible]	[illegible]
molds to velvet buttons						
making goun pocks etc.			½			
18 palm cloath a full sute	2			4	1	
2 can 5 palm armazin	5	7	7	1	2	10
Damity for body lin .	0	5	0	0	2	0
making the sute and buttons . . .	4	5	0	0	18	0
twist for holls this should not be . . .	0	5	0	0	2	0
2 pr. gray slipers . .	1	6	0	0	6	5
	124	7	0	24	18	10
For my knit wastcoat this is a green one to my D. .	4	0	0	0	16	0
makeing 2 seks	4	0	0	0	16	0
a new hoop made	3	0	0	0	12	0
cover old hoop .	0	5	0	0	2	0
6 can moyhair rigote	14	4	0	2	17	7
a black fan .	0	3	0	0	1	2
a crap hood	0	3	0	0	1	2
covering my jumps	[illegible]	[illegible]	[illegible] ½	0	[illegible]	[illegible]
1 can black damask					1	
1 can armaz to line it					4	
making wastcoat					2	

Naples 1732, O.S. Decr. 27

For a velvet Muff Grisic	3	3	3	0	13	3
a p^r silk mittons .	1	2	0	0	4	10
7½ can broun velvet	30	0	0	6	0	0
making 2 Robs. .	4	0	0	0	16	0

[Foreign Tour]

		Duc.	Car.	Gr.	[Sterling] £	s.	d.
	To 6 canes Poaso Dumanz for my black seck . . .	10	0	0	2	0	0
7 Jany. N.S.	For 12 can velvet to the Boys .	48	0	0	9	12	0
	To Carmany playing Master, etc. .	10	2	0	2	0	10
	For Mushets goun	3	4	0	0	13	2
	Making . . .	1	0	0	0	4	0
	apron to her .	2	5	0	0	10	0
	Making and cloath to James .	3	5	0	0	14	0
	Lowrenchiens cloath	3	0	0	0	12	0
	John cudberts cloaths .	4	5	0		18	0
	Drinkmoney Cagnonies	8	4	0	1	13	7
20	To Mrs. Cagnonies a pies cambrick .	16	0	0	1	4	0
	For a trunk with bras Nails .	5	0	0	1	0	0
	For a book of Minuits .	1	0	0	0	4	0
	For a red trunk with nails .	7	0		1	12	0
	For blooding by Nichels	1	0		0	4	0
	vomits	0	2	0	0	0	10
	recept plaster 2 7 in gredians 1-6 . .	4	3		0	17	2
	Scots pills from England	5	1		[illegible]	[illegible]	[illegible]
	Gravel cups to cure it .	2	0				
Feb.	For beding to the Maids	7	0				
	Shiets and pillabers	2	5			1	
	Brazier $8\frac{1}{4}$ wth 22 gr. .	1	8				
	Stand and spaleta for it	1	7	0			1
	pen knif . . .	0	3				
	2 clogbag trunks .	9	1	4		1	
	belt for lead bag .	0	4	0			
	bars to trunks by Gartano	0	4	0			
	wax cloth for trunks .	1	2	0			1
	paper 27 g. .	0	2	7			

[Foreign Tour]					[Sterling]		
		Duc.	Car.	Gr.	£	s.	d.
	2 Lamps from Lighorn . . .	16	3	5	3	5	4
Feb.	For 6 snuff boxes	15	0	0	3	0	0
	cristall to my watch .	0	5	0	0	2	0
	2 fine snuff boxes Gr.	17	0	0	3	8	0
	to the Banificato .	0	8	0	0	3	2
	Dona Luisas blew Damask	3	1	0	0	12	5
	Musick paper	0	8	0	0	3	2
	copiing musick	1	8	0	0	7	2
	11 sword belts	3	3	0	0	13	2
	26 fans . . .	13	0	0	2	12	0
	18 fans . . .	2	0	0	0	8	0
	2 caps to the boys	2	2	0	0	8	10
	To John Cuthberts 4 spoons .	9	0	0	1	16	0
	more of wages	37	8	0	7	11	2
	more 6 guinys	16	2	0	3	4	10
	more	2	7	0	0	10	10
	To James of wages over his fans . .	4	1	7½	0	16	8
	more by John after he was gone .	2	0	0	0	8	0
	more by John	3	0	0	0	12	0
	For a wige . . .	4	5	0	0	18	0
	2½ p. green shagreen	0	5	0	0	2	0
	2 wige combs .	0	1	0	0	0	5
	patches 12 gr.	0	1	2	0	0	6
	padisoy for clock .	3	7	3	0	15	0
	¼ spomalincena for hood	0	8	0	0	3	
March	For 6 Torteshel combs	4	6	0	0	18	5
	For a spinet	1	4	0	0	5	2
	For spomalincina sent home 5 can and 4 palm I take the half and L. Bin the other and is .	8	8	0	1	15	2

[Foreign Tour]

10 pauls a croun, 16 byocks a paul.

Rome 1733		Crs.	Pls.	By.	£	s.	d.
29 March	For 2 wax Pops	0	8	0	0	4	2
to	For prints . .	6	2	0	1	12	6
22 April	For 4 copper Medles	4	0	0	1	1	0
	For 2 Corinthen brass pops . . .	2	0	0	0	10	6
	For 2 gold crouns and a silver croun	4	3	5	2	2	10
	For a discription of Rome .	1	6	0	0	8	4
	For 2 marbel weights for paper .	0	4	0	0	2	1
Frolenc 25 April	For 2 volums of the gallary of the great Duke .	25	2	0	6	11	4
	10 vol. Italian books	6	4	4	1	13	9
	2 alabaster figurs	1	0	0	0	5	3
	For a putter tee pot	0	6	4	0	3	3
	For Barminis Mistres off a Statue .	0	0	4	0	0	2½
	To Mrs. Colmans coachman . . .	0	5	0	0	2	7
	For a wooden box with a lock . . .	1	2	0	0	6	3
	For 2 Lyons of Marbel .	1	0	0	0	5	3
	For my gandchild Hellens Pictor	8	0	0	2	2	0
	For 3 Pictor of Mr. Baillie, my Daughter Grisie, and my grandchild Gris by Mr. Martine	36	0	0	9	9	0
	frames and glases and box to ditt	16	1	0	4	4	6
	For making my Dears wastcoat .	4	0	0	1	1	0
	For lutstring at 36 pauls pr ℔. . . .	16	0	0	4	4	0

[Foreign Tour] [Sterling]

	Crs.	Pls.	By.	£	s.	d.
Dressing hair and wires	1	9	6	0	10	3
For my lutstring .	16	0	0	4	4	0

1733 Bolonia
May 15 A Sequin 21 paul, 2 pauls a livre, 10 bycocks is a paul, and 12 Dinis a byock.

		L.	B.				
	4 pr filosel stokins	21	0	0	1	1	0
	For seeing palaces	6	0	0	0	6	0
	To the Copsin Convent	2	10	0	0	2	6
	For cariing spinet to St Donis . . .	1	0	0	0	1	0
	To Prists . . .	1	0	0	0	1	0
Bolonia,	For a pair jack boots .	22	0	0	1	2	0
1733, May	For wire and dressing hair . . .	1	10	0	0	1	6
	For a whip to John	2	10	0	0	2	6
	For tobaco powder	5	0	0	0	5	0
	For the box in the opera house . . .	85	0	0	4	5	0
	cushen in the box	10	14	0	0	10	8
	cloath to ly over the box	8	6	0	0	8	4
	18 Tickets to the opera	30	10	0	1	10	6
	2 opera book	2	0	0	0	2	0
	For caring pictors	1	5	0	0	1	3
	a book of what is to be seen here	1	0	0	0	1	0
	mending my watch	3	10	0	0	3	6
	letters 6£. 10s.	6	10	0	0	6	6
	For a pictor of the Autom	40	0	0	2	0	0
	For a wax cloth curtin to Chease . . .	4	0	0	0	4	0
	puting it up	2	6	0	0	2	4

1733
Venice A vinecian sequin is 22 Lieris, a Florence sequin 21£.

[Foreign Tour]					[Sterling]		
11 June	For a book of the curi-	L.	B.		£	s.	d.
	ositys here	2	0	0	0	1	0
	Baucaches history	36	0	0	0	18	0
	A Map of Venice .	31	0	0	0	15	6
	a Map of Germany	3	0	0	0	1	6
	the lives of the Painters	12	0	0	0	6	0
	Plans of houses .	37	10	0	0	18	9
	For 2 lb. tryackle with boxes . . .	13	0	0	0	6	6
	hipocacuana	6	0	0	0	3	0
	Sir Robert Brouns Nurs	22	0	0	0	11	0
	Sir Robert Brouns Servants .	6	0	0	0	3	0
	General Shulenbergs servants .	4	0	0	0	2	0
	Seeing a Newranberge show of Christs birth and passion .	1	10	0	0	0	9
	Sir Rob[t] Brouns garner	2	0	0	0	1	0
	a barber . .	1	0	0	0	0	6
	at a gundaliers weding to fidls . . .	2	0	0	0	1	0
	For a wastcoat to Jacome . . .	76	5	0	1	18	2
	For Mush . . .	15	0	0	0	7	6
	tobaco pip case	5	0	0	0	2	6
	a spung 1£ 5s esher 1£, steel and flint 6s .	2	11	0	0	1	6
	3 whisks .	0	16	0	0	0	5
	3 pr spectickles .	2	0	0	0	1	0
	stuffine to cushen	2	0	0	0	1	0
	For 9 ½ brack camblet 8½ lirie . . .	8	10	0	0	4	6
	12 bratch shogreen 5£ .	60	0	0	1	10	0
	make cantush and seck etc. . . .	16	0	0	0	8	0
	5 brach a la mod for sandella . .	45	0	0	1	2	6

[Foreign Tour]					[Sterling]		
		L.	B.		£	s.	d.
	black lace for mittons .	2	5	0	0	1	2
	masks . . .	3	0	0	0	1	6
	a black cap .	25	0	0	0	12	6
	For the half of the Apoticarys bill .	11	10	0	0	5	11
1733 Frankfoord							
	For 2 pair bavers stokins .	Fl. 6	K. 0	0	0	14	0
	For 5 Doun pillows	13	0	0	1	10	4
	For 30 of their ells for pillabers . . .	13	0	0	1	10	4
	For 45½ lb. hamb 5½ sture . . .	6	1	0	0	14	0
		44	48	0			

this at 4 flarans 15 kamtins to ane unger and ane unger 10 sh. strline is £5, 5 shillins sterling.

Aix la Chaple, 10 July 1733, N.S.		Livers.					
	For a pr. of shoes to me	3	10	0	0	4	1
Spa	glovs at 15 st. Doge Skin	3	0	0	0	3	6
	baver skin gloves 6 pair	9	9	0	0	11	0
	Baver at 23 sk. peticoat and clock	50	17	2	2	19	3
	Castor clock at 11 12 .	25	3	2	1	9	4
	For 6 ell castor for frok and wastcoat	69	15	0	4	1	4
Sepm	To Mr. Hays subscription	37	10	0	2	3	9
	the Judge at Dimburgh	30	0	0	1	15	0
	13 drawings of the Fountons, etc.	10	0	0	0	11	8
	3 pincils to my boys .	1	10	0	0	1	9
	a wanscote chist wt a lock	6	10	0	0	2	4
	wax frute . .	8	0				
	a play to little Grisie .	2	0				
	2 Kain strings . .	2	0				

[Foreign Tour] [Sterling]

		Livers.			£	s.	d.
	capashiens in convent	22	10	0	1	6	3
	carvie box .	1	0	0	0	1	2
	2 Peutter salts .	1	0	0	0	1	2
	a tortoy shell snuff box Gr. . .	7	0	0	0	8	2
	For Japan Dressing boxes	28	12	2	1	13	4
	a quadreel box . .	15	3	0	0	17	8
	5 Ivory boxes and 2 dyels	42	10	0	2	9	7
	6 kains and a head to one	22	0	0	1	5	8
	a comb trea	2	0	0	0	2	4
	5 brushes	2	10	0	0	3	1
	To the wemen at Geron State . .	18	18	0	1	2	0
	the wemen at the Pohone	11	7	2	0	14	3
	For Lodging at the Loup for 11 sk. pr. night from 10 July to 31 Aug. .	291	10		17	0	1
	at 8 sk. to 22 Sept.	88	0		5	2	8
	Anna Mary doughter	18	15	0	1	1	10
	the maid . . .	2	10		0	3	1
Spa Sep. 22	For mending cheases and sadles .	114	5	0	6	13	3
	a cheas for 4 persons to go to Geronstat at 3 sk. pr day in the season and 2½ sk. after it	96	10	0	5	12	7
	To a cook 72 days	36	0	0	2	2	0
	a sute cloathes to James	78	10	0	4	11	7
	James of wages half a guiny .	9	7	2	0	10	6
	John Cudbertson wages, 2 guinys .	37	10	0	2	2	0
	For letters .	38	3	0	2	4	2
	For washing 5 sow shirt and cravat and hand-kerchief 4 sows shifts						

[Foreign Tour]					[Sterling]		
	and a skillin the Doz.	Livers.			£	s.	d.
	on all other pices .	55	8	0	3	4	7
	a cours sheat for the trunk . . .	2	10	0	0	3	1
Leige							
Sep. 23	For 12 ells lace 6½ sk. 10 ell 13 sk., 10 ell 19 sk.	179	0	0	10	8	10
	2 ells lace .	33	18	0	1	19	6
	19 pr gloves Lady Harvie[1]	14	5	0	0	16	7
	3 pr mens gloves to give away . . .	3	15	0	0	4	4
	a purs Donohow .	1	10	0	0	1	9
Brusles 25	For bring brass trumpet from Ipers	1	10	0	0	1	9
	a surgeon to Grisies arm	4	0	0	0	4	8
	Seeing Arch Dutches Palice etc. . . .	4	10	0	0	5	3
	Lodging 3 nights and eating 6 of us						
	muslin	6	4	0	0	7	3

Paris,[2] friday, 20 October 1733. 24 livers a Lewidor or guiny.

For 2½ ell cloath	55	0	0	2	8	1
7½ ell silk lining .	37	10	0	[illegible]	[illegible] 1	1 [illegible]
a pr. stokins to the cloaths	15	0	0		1	
a pr. stokins or sheverin	18	0	0		1	
a pr. baver stokins	9	0	0			1
a pr. worset stokins	10	5	0			
a pr. thick traveling stokins .	3	0	0	0	2	7
a Hatt . . .	17	0	0	0	14	10
5 duz butons to cloath	5	0	0	0	4	4
plying etc. to ditt	5	0	0	0	4	4

---

[1] See p. 302.

[2] Paris accounts given in full.

[Foreign Tour] [Sterling]

	Livers.			£	s.	d.
making ditt .	10	0	0	0	8	8
2 wigs a ty one and a bob 3 Lew. . . .	72	0	0	8	8	0
taylors man	1	0	0	0	0	10½
baver gloves at 35 sturs	13	10	0	0	11	6
	271	5	0			

							£	s.	d.
For ane Alamad hood to me	5	9	0				0	4	9
a duzon combs 9£, 3 of tortoyshel 12£	21	0	0				0	18	4
making my vinice silk Rob	8	0	0				0	7	0
a sheneel Palatine	6	0	0				0	5	3
6 ells black lace	30	0	0				1	6	3
8 ells narow black lace	12	0	0				0	10	6
puder puff 10 st. wires 10 s.	1	0	0				0	0	10½
black gass hood, etc. .	9	0	0				0	7	10
thick travelling stockins	3	0	0				0	2	7
Baver skin gloves at 35 st	20	0	0				0	17	6
				115	9	0			

Paris

				£	s.	d.
For a gass head	4	0	0	0	3	6
For caps quilted for dressing 4 of them	5	15	0	0	5	0

[Foreign Tour] [Sterling]

	Livers.			£	s.	d.
For wires 10 st. patches 1£ puff 10s.	2	0	0	0	1	9
to a tire woman for dressing	3	0	0	0	2	7
13 ell floord silk goun and coat 26st.	338	0	0	14	15	9
6 breads white satin with a deep floord border for a Jupon	132	0	0	5	15	6
Neclaces slavages and earrings .	30	0	0	1	6	3
Alamode hood	5	0	0	0	4	4
Sheneel Tipit	4	10	0	0	3	9
a duzon of combs .	9	0	0	0	7	11
a flowrd and silver tipet	5	0	0	0	4	4
a black ladd Hood .	90	0	0	3	18	9
white rubans	1	4	0	0	1	0
Mantua maker	16	0	0	0	14	0
a sute Muslins	12	0	0	0	10	6
fringe at 7 st 8 ells .	2	15	0	0	2	4
Muslins for fashus .	6	6	9	0	5	6
making fashus and washing them .	1	13	0	0	1	5
2 pr shoes .	12	0	0	0	10	6
4 pr Imbrodered shoes	20	0	0	0	17	6

[Foreign Tour]										[Sterling]	
					Livers.				£	s.	d.
	Antoylage head .	13	0	0					0	11	5
	3 ells aunage, 3£ 10s.	10	10	0					0	9	2
	2 ells aunage 5£ . .	10	0	0					0		9
	palatins	10	0	0					0	8	9
	thick traveling stokins	3	0	0					0	2	7
	Baver gloves 35 st. the pr.	20	0	0					0	17	6
	Antoylage sute	37	0	0					1	12	2
					803	13	9				
					1190	7	9				
Paris Oct. 11 1733	To the person of Lord Walgraves Chaple .		6						0	5	3
	Snr Bellonys Bill from Buro at Rome .		12	0					0	10	6
	Description of Paris		15	0						13	1
	3 cookry Books		6	15					0	5	11
	a book of beasts		3	10						3	0
	4 unbound books of		6	10					0	5	8
	4 places in the opera house .		32	0					0	18	0
	seeing observator, palices, and churches .		18	0					0	15	9
	Madam la Duches and Ms. Lessis otels etc. . .		8	0					0	7	0

	[Foreign Tour]	Livers.		£	s.	d.
	Cardinal Richlieu's Monument	4 0		0	3	6
	Seing looking glass work . .	4 10		0	3	11
			116 5 0			
	For a lisene for a coach to the country .	6 0		0	5	3
errour 15	An order to see versyles					
	Diner at Mudin	8 6		0	7	8
	Lodging and eating a night at versyle	43 12		1	18	1
	Diner at Marley	7 8		0	6	6
	Lodging a night and eating at St. Jarmens	24 0		1	1	0
	Diner at .	9 18		0	8	7
	black pudins at St. Jarmans .	2 12		0	2	3
	a botle ratafia 3£ drams 12 st .	3 12		0	3	2
	Seeing Lamule .	3 0		0	2	[illegible]
	The Dary there	1 4			1	
	St. Clou etc. .	4 16			4	
	Menagery	3 0			2	
	Treanon .	3 0			2	
	Marly seeing things	4 4			3	
	the water machine near Marley	0		0	2	
	Seeing Mason	3 0		0	2	7
17	crossing the river Sean	1 10		0	1	3
	James the footman or Jacome	2 0		0	1	9
			134 2 0			

[Sterling

[Foreign Tour]

1733		Livers.				[Sterling] £	s.	d.
Paris	To Caparan teeth drawer	96	0			4	4	0
	tooth powder .	1	15			0	1	6
	teeth water .	6	0			0	5	3
	For 12 botles Lau de Carin	10	0			0	8	9
	hungary water .	6	0			0	5	3
		——119	15	0				
	For a toothpice case .	10	0			0	8	9
	4 knives 14£ a pen-knif £1	15	0			0	1	1
	2 razors	6	0			0	3	5
	a St. Clou shoe snuffbox	24	0				1	0
	another St. Clou box .	6	0			0	5	3
	2 doz. St. Clou hefts for knives	2'				1	1	0
	5 salt botles .		0			0	4	4
	2 pr. siszers .	4				0	3	6
	hinges to 2 boxes of Ivory	6	0			0	5	3
		——100	0	0				
	For ane Eparn french silver .	205	0			8	19	4
	a pr ditt Candlesticks .	22	0			0	19	3
	2 pr ditt candlesticks .	48	0			2	2	0
	2 salts of ditt	12	0			0	10	6
	a p^r. snuffers and pan	10	0			0	8	9
	2 snuff pans	12	10			0	10	11
	2 frute plates of ditt	26	0			1	2	9
		——335	10	0				

[Foreign Tour]

		Livers.			[Sterling] £	s.	d.
	For 14 ells floord silk Mally Mitchell £16, 10st.	231	0		10	2	1
	making the sute	12	0		0	10	6
	a geneel tipet Mrs. Mitchell	5	0		0	4	4
	a tipet to Miss Johnston .	12	0		0	10	6
	a handkercheff Lady Louth .	12	0		0	10	6
	2 p^r rufles to my boys T and G	34	0		1	9	9
	2 knoted tipets to give away	6	0		0	5	3
	an imbroyderd handkerchieff	6	0		0	5	3
	a block to dress upon .	2	0		0	1	9
				320 0 0			
1733 Paris. Oct. 15	To one Mr. Menzies	8	0		0	7	0
	reading new prints	1	0		0	0	10½
	Mr. Knights coachman .	3	0		0	2	7
	Mrs. Horners coachman .	3	0		0	2	7
				15			
	For the prints of versyles	20	0		0	17	6
	pocket books from nuns	31	0		1	7	[illegible]
	nidle books from nuns Ms Howard	6	0		0	5	3
	blew marking threed 7½ small hanks . .	2	5		0	1	11
				59 5 0			

[Foreign Tour]

	Livers.					[Sterling] £	s.	d.
For the coach and 2 horses and our own 2 horse 3 day to Marsils etc. .	12	0				0	10	6
Jacome the footman drink .	2	0				0	1	9
			14	0	0			
For a coach and 2 horses at 10 Livers pr day	230	0				10	1	3
to the coachman	12	0				0	10	6
Lewis Mr. Mans servant	3	0				0	2	7
			245	0	0			
Tewsday, 27 For the otel for 3 weeks and 3 days servants in Lodging			12	0	0	0	10	6
To John Cudbert of wages .	24	0				1	1	0
ditt 3¼ Lewider	90	0				3	18	9
ditt 6£ 9£	15	0				0	13	1
			129	0	0			
Jacomo	43	0				1	17	8
a lacd hat 7£ lace 15 .	22	0				0	18	3
footman Martins place .	9	0				0	7	10
			530	0	0			
For washing			20	0	0	0	17	6
132-16 Stg.[1]			2884	4	9	126	3	8

[1] This is Lady Grisell's jotting as to the value of the Paris expenditure, but if 24 livres=£1, 1s. as she states elsewhere, it is difficult to see how she arrives at her result.

Memorandums for Earl Hadinton and Mr. Baillie in their Travelling.[1] Oxford, March 10th, 1740.

Inns in France

Dijon	St. Loois.
Lyons . . .	Au Parc.
Nismes . . .	a L'Orange.
Montpellier . . .	Cheval blanc.
Avignon . . .	Au Pelican.
Aix	Au Bras d'Or.
Marseills . . .	Aux treze Cantons.
Valence . . .	A la Post.
Monteumant	A la Post.
Toulon . . .	Notre dame de Petie
Narbon . . .	A la d'Orade.
Beziers . . .	A la Croix blanche.
Carcassone .	Au Lion d'Or.
Castlevaudon	Au Lion d'Or.
Toulouze . . .	Au bon Pasteur.
Montauban . . .	Au Tapis Verde.
Bourdeaux . . .	Chez Madame Bennet.
Xaintes . . .	L'Ecu de France.
Nants . . .	Vis a vis les Carmes.
Angers . . .	L'Ours.
Samur . . .	Trois Maures.
Tours . . .	A la Galere.
Orleans . . .	Notre dame de Chaise.
Estampes . . .	A la Post.

Inns in Italy

Turin	La Bonne Femme.
Milan	Le Faucon, Al Puozza o' Tre Ré.
Genoua . . .	La Croix blanche ou Santa Martha.
Leghorne . . .	Lion blanc ou Croie d'Oro.

[1] These 'Memorandums' are contained in a note-book of 120 pages, 8″×6″, and are not in Lady Grisell's handwriting, though evidently of her composition.

Pisa	Ceremonies.
Florence . . .	Collins's, an English house, but a French house in Via Magia to be preferd.
Sienna . . .	Tre Ré.
Rome . . .	Monocos al Trinita di Monte, best apartments 20 crouns a month.
Naples . . .	Il Cappello Rosso.
Bologna . . .	Al Pellerino.
Ferrara . . .	Lione Bianco.
Venice . . .	Chez Monsieur d'Henry sopra ill Grande Canale extream good.
Padona . . .	Re e Regina d'Inghilterra.
Vicenza . . .	Le due Rote.
Verona . . .	Le due Torre.
Modena . . .	St. Georgio.
Reggio . . .	Giglio Coronato.
Parma . . .	Alla Posta.
Piacenza . . .	La Croce Bianca.
Luca	Il Corallo.
Mantua . . .	Lione d'Oro.

Inns in Germany

Wesel . . .	Le Baisin Bleu.
Dusseldorp . . .	Hoff van Holland
Cologn . . .	Hoff van Holland.
Bonn	Der Stern.
Coblentz . . .	Lillie.
Mayentz . . .	Gulden Crannerin.
Frankfort . . .	Gulden Engel.
Wurtzburg . . .	Gulden Swaan.
Donawert . . .	Gulden Sunne.
Nuremburg	Gulden Haan.
Ausburg . . .	Le Raisin d'or.
Munick . . .	The Daler.
Inspruck . . .	Gulden Rosen.
Trent	Gulden Rosen.

Directions for Holland

In general avoid lodgeing at any English or Dutch house, they being the most imposing, the French the best. A rule never to be departed from throw all Holland is constantly to make an agreement first for every thing you get, or in imploying anybody if but for a message, or you will be greatly imposed upon and pay duble. If you use them with sevilety and show them you will not be bubbled they will use you well, but in no way will bear rugh treatment, and are ever ready to impose upon any they see ignerant and careless.

At Rotterdam

Avoid the English house the most impertinently imposing of any we met with. If Mr. Baillie the banker be alive send for him, or for Mr. Knaghten a banker, both Scots men, either of them will be usefull to you, when they know who you are.

At the Hague

Send for Monsieur Piere Daniel Tonyn sur le Corte Vyverberg he is brother to Capn. Tonyn, he will assist you in anything. Lodge at Mr. Adams at the Golden Star and Lyon in the Korte Houtstraet near the plain. There is an ordinary which it is very right to dyn at when you do not stay long in a place, to see the manners and ways of different people, but a disagreeable thing to be constantly in a croud of straingers. Here you must go and wait upon the King of Britains Minister if there is one, and so you must do where ever you go where the King has a Minister. If he returns not your visit go no more.

At Amsterdam

Send for Mr. James Wedderburn, Merchant, a relation of yours, he will assist you in any thing, he lives over de Illustre School op de flucale Burghwall. Lodge at the Bible and Orange in the Warmer Straet or Ville de Lions. Hear the fine organ in the great church.

At Leyden lodge at the Castle of Antwerp on the Kopenburgh. The Phisic Gardens and other gardens there are worth seeing.

At Delft see the Prince of Oranges Tomb.

At Harlem see the Bleech field, a fine sight when covered with cloth.

At Utrecht lodge at the Casteel van Antwerp op de ganse Markt. If the Prince and Princess of Orange be at Insedyck, a house of theirs near Utrecht, or at their house in the wood near the Hague, or any where near, you must go wait upon them, and get some body to go with you to introduce you.

A Rout for seeing North Holland

Hire voitures at Amsterdam by the day, make it in your bargen that the coachman shall maintain himself and horses, otherways you will be much imposed upon in that article, if you can likeways agree with him that he shall pay all the passage and toll money, it will be better, but that they will not like to do.

Let the voiture cross the river in the morning befor you are ready, otherwise you will be detaind, you take coach just at the place where you land on the other side of the river, the first toun you come to is Munickendam, from that you come through another toun cald Edam, but in neither of those places is there any worth seeing, then go to Hoorn where you may dine at the Dool.[1] Befor you come to Munickendam you pass a village cald Brook, which is remarkable for being built without any order or regular streets, the houses all detacht from one another; it is very neat and the inhabitants reckond vastly rich. after seeing Hoorn you go that night to Enchussen, the best house is the Toorn upon the shore, see the Stadhouse there. If you stay out but two days go from Enckuyhen

[1] In most towns in Holland there were 'doelen' or shooting galleries, where archery was or had been practised. These either developed into hotels or gave the name to many hotels which still exist. The old 'Dool' at Alkmaar still survives, in the courtyard of which people may be seen even to this day practising archery. The word 'doel' means 'mark' or 'aim.'

to Alckmaer which is the prittiest toun you will see, go airly and you can be back at Amsterdam at night, remember to hear the organ in the great church of Alckmaer, the finest in the world. Lodge at the Dool.[1] Between Alckmaer and Amsterdam you come through a very fine country which formerly was three great lakes and stile retain the names of the Bumerent, the Beemster, and the Scermer, if you stay out three days go from Enchuysen to Medenblyck, the best house the Valck, you may be early in the afternoon at Alckmaer and next day return to Amsterdam by Harlem.

Some Account of the Difference of Money

Guineas are a ready coin all over Holland and Flanders if you can carry them without discovery, and is better then a bill when the Exchange is 36 Eskillings for a guinea, the Eskillings in Holland are not so good as in Flanders, those with a star are the best, those cald Mal Eskillings pass for a peny or half peny less, they will take non of the Dutch Eskillings for what they pass in Holland in Flanders, so get rid of them. The Guilders which are 1 shillin and 8 pence of our money are a good coin and taken in Flanders for the full value. At Leige and Spa and all the Bishop of Leige's Country an Eskilling gose for 10 pence, so that every Guinea passes for £1, 10 10, reckoning 37 Eskillings to the guinea.[2]

No money gose in France but the new French Louis, but they are seazable at entring into the country if they find above 5 Louis for each person, but as you loose much by bills of exchange you must hide what you have and show only a little. In a Louis there is 24 livers, in a liver 20 sols, there is 3 liver pieces which is cald Ecus blanc and 6 liver pieces which is cald Ecus grand.

Spanish or French Pistols[3] go best in Italy any other

---

[1] See note, p. 387.

[2] This statement of Lady Grisell hardly coincides with her accounts, where the schelling is valued at a little over 6d., which would appear to be more correct.

[3] About 17s. 7½d.

money loosing much, so change your French money for Spanish or French Pistols befor you go into Italy, they go all over it, and so dos Florentine, Genoese and Venetian Sequins,[1] which last are the best money, if you can get them at the same price they are allways best but do not take them in Lombardy. A Sequine is about the value of half a guinea, what is cald a Roman croun, tho I never saw the coin, is 10 Pauls, there is 20 Pauls in a Sequin, in a Venetian Sequin I think there is 21 or 22 Pauls, a Testoon is 3 Pauls.

The silver money in the Kingdome of Naples is different from that all over Italy. In a Sequin there is Naples ducats, in a ducat 10 Carlins, and a coin cald a terri which is two Carlins.

In Germany Hungars is the money most curent, a Hungar is a gold coin in which is 4 Florins and some times 10 or 12 Karrentari, 60 Karrentari make a Florin, 12 Karrentari make a Roman Paul, Spanish Pistols are also good money here and are worth 7½ Florins. In going out of the different dominions in Germany which come very quek, some times twice in a day, you must take care to get rid of your silver money, for what passes in one territory will not pass for the same in another, and they are so intricat and different little coins I can give no account of them.

In every toun where you stay a day or more you may hier a servant that knows the place and can conduct you every where, there is always plenty to be had, but you must get your Land Lord to recomend and answere for their honesty, since there are many rogues amongst them, their constant pay is a Testoon [2] a day, or the value of it alike all over Italy.

For seeing churches and palaces and most other places give a Testoon, if you see any Sovereign's house you must give two Testoons, if you have audience of any Sovereign, the guards and servants expect some thing to drink, half a Pistol amongst them all is sufficient. At Rome a Croun

---

[1] 10s. 5d. [2] 1s. 6d.

is enough to the Pope's. At the great seasons of the year if you are there they come again, as likewise the servants of all the Italian houses you go to, who also constantly come the day after you have been at their house the first time for some thing, two Testoons is enough to give them and the first time only, and again at Christianmass and Easter. If you walk often at Villas you need not give every time. A Testoon now and then is sufficient.

At Rome you must have an antiquary to conduct and show you the antiquatys and raretys who will always atend you when you send to him when you go to see any thing. 5 Pistols is enough to give him for all when you go away.

Through your whole journey you will be often stopt at coming into every different dominion to serch your trunks for merchandise as they call it. Telling them they may look if they please, at the same time assuring them you have non, and giving them a little money, will free you from any trouble, sometimes a Paul in France, one, two or three livers accoridng as you have things about you to be affrayd of a strict serch.

At every place you stay at, any acquaintens you meet, or in some things your Land Lord will inform you of the general price of things, such as the hier of your coach, how much a head for eating. All over France the general price is 25 [1] sols a head for diner, and 30 [2] sols for super and bed. But then you must make your agreement or they will make you pay a great dale more and you will not be better served. In Italy you only say when you come into your Inn you eat a Pasto and there is a fixt price all over Italy for diner and super. I think it is 2½ [3] Pauls at diner and 3 [4] pauls at super.

Going in to Italy over the Alps

We were not at Leghorn nor Genoua so can give you no derections about them. If you go to Genoua Mr. Jackson the King's Consul there will be of great use to you, he is an honest, civil, good naturd man.

---

[1] 1s. 1d. [2] 1s. 7½d. [3] 1s. 3½d. [4] 1s. 6¾d.

You are caryd over Mount Senis in chairs by men, for which you give a Pistol a piece, and your chaises and bagage by mulls for which you must make the best bargen you can, there will be fifty people tearing you to pieces to be employd.

Turin

The first toun you come to worth notice here you may see all in two or three days. Some houses of the King's a little way out of town worth seeing, a noble prospect from them. If there is a British Minister there go to him.

Milan

Here you may stop three or four days. There is many things worth seeing, the great Church St. Paolo and others, the Hospital, the Pest house, the house where the Ecco repeats above fifty times [1] etc., the Boromean Islands near Milan, which are fine, if you go will take up 3 days to go and return. In the way to Milan see the Chartereax at Pavia.

At Piacenza stop a day to see the Dukes Palace and the Theater.

At Parma—a day to see the galery of pictures and the famous Theater.

At Regio there is nothing, but within two mills out of the road there is a new house of the Prince of Modena's in the French tast worth seeing, to see how inferior it is to the Italian Palaces, etc.

At Modena—a day or two to see the Duke's Palace, etc.

Bologna

This will take up a week. Inquire for Mr. Magnoni a banker in our name. He will be of great use to you when he knows who you are, and is an honest man, ask also for Sigre. Barnachi [2] the famous singer and Sigre. Sandoni [3] the husband of the Cuzone, they will be pleasd to be of service to any of our family. See the Institute—the Churches—Palazo Sanpieri, Palazo Tavi—Pal. Bonfiglioli

[1] This is the 'Ecco' Lady Grisell paid 3s. 5d. 'for seeing.'

[2] See p. xlix. [3] See p. xlix.

—Pal. Zambeccari—Pal. Magnani—Pal Monti. They are best stored with paintings. The Toun house cald Palazo Publico. Without the toun the Convents of St. Michall in Bosco, the Certosa and Capuchins. There is here the famous Signora Laura Bassa, a learned lady who is made a doctor; she is very affable good company and makes straingers wellcome that come to see her; Mr. Magnoni will introduce you to her.

At Loretta half a day is enough where there is only the Santa Cassa and the riches in it to be seen.

Betwixt Loretta and Rome you must see the famous cascade at Terni, which is but 2 or 3 leagues going and coming out of your road.

At Rome

Here so many things are to be seen that it will take you up some months and you must have an antiquary to conduct and show you every thing. The only one I know is Sigre. Marco Parker al Caffe Inglese in Piazza di Spagnia. He is an English man and cousen to Mr. Parker the Beedle at Oxford.

At Naples

Here you need no derections, only inquire for the Marquis Rinuccini, Mr. Consul Allen and Mr. Hammond, who are so good friends of ours they will conduct and derect you in every thing. I only desire you woud wait upon Mademoiselle Louise Cagnony and her sister where ever they are and they will make you acquainted with any other of our friends. See Portici, where we lived, and Soriento, where we past some time very agreeably.

A list of posts from Naples to England by way of Germany which we came ourselves and what is worth seeing in the different places we came to.

Naples to Rome	posts to pay
Naples to Aversa, Post Royall	$1\frac{1}{2}$
To Capua	1
To Francolino	1

posts to pay

To St. Agata 1

To Carigliano where there is a river to pass, pay 3 carlini for each Chaise. 1

To Mola 1

Here you show your pass which you get at Naples and pay some thing to avoid having your trunks opend. 2 carlins.

To Itri 1

To Fondi 1

To Terracina where ends the Neapolitan State and there is a chain where you pay one Carlino per Chaize 1

To Capaccie 1

To Piperno . . . .

To Casa Nuova . . . .

To Sermoneta . . . .

To Cisterno . . . .

To Veletri . . . .

To Marino . . . .

Here they will insist upon puting 3 horses to each shaise which they cannot oblige you to, having no order.

To Torre di Mezza via 1

To Rome 1

in all 18½

At going into any great toun you pay only common post, at seting out from a great toun you pay Post Royal, which is a post and a half for only one post of way. Coming into Rome they drive you directly to the Customehouse to have your bagadge serched. Give a Festoon, and if they do not suspect you have counterband goods, they will be very sivil and just open your trunks and look into them, but if you have any thing seasable you loose it if they find it. Put your Bibles or prayer book in your pocket or hide them in the sate of the chaise which is seldome serched, or they will certainly take them from you, or any English books they think heretical.

In the Neapolitean State you pay 11 Carlini per chaise every post and 3 Carlini to each postilion.

In the Roman State you pay 8 Pauls for your horses every post for each chaise, 2 Pauls to each postilion and 3 pauls for a single horse.

Rome to Florence

Rome to La Storta, post Royal		$1\frac{1}{2}$
Passing the gate 1 paul per chaise.		
To Baccano		1
To Monte Rossi		1
To Ronciglione		1
To the Mountain of Viturbo	$\frac{3}{4}$ post	6 pauls each
To Viturbo	$\frac{3}{4}$ post	per chaise
To Monte Fiascone		1
To Belsena do not ly here		1
To St. Laurenzo	$\frac{3}{4}$ of a post	6 pauls each
To Acqua Pendente	$\frac{3}{4}$ of a post	per chaise
To Centino		1
To Re di Coffano a good place to ly at		$1\frac{1}{2}$
To Ricorso		1
To La Scala		1
To Torriero		1
To Bon Convento		1
To Montarone		1
To Sienna		1

Here see the dome and church, they are fine pices of Gothick Archetecture, the Chapel Chigi is very rich, the floor of the church deserves particular notice, it is the finest in Europe and make them take the boards of the pavement. Off the church see the Library painted in Fresco after the desins of Raphael, oposit to the Church see an hospital erected by a shoe maker, see the Market place. Sennesino[1] that was so long in England has a house

[1] Francesco Bernardi detto Senesino, one of the most famous sopranists of the century, born about 1680 at Siena, received his musical education from Bernacchi, and was brought to England by Handel. 'In 1739 Senesino was living in Florence, and sang a duet with the Archduchess Maria Theresa there. He died about 1750.'—Grove's *Dictionary of Music and Musicians*.

here and will be glad to see you if he is at home. Lodge at the 3 kings.

Sienna to Castiglioncello	1
To Pogibonsi	1
To Le Tavernelle	1
To St. Cassiano	1
To Florence	1

A French house in the Via Magia is the best to lodge at, where we were well used, Collins's, an English house there, is generally full and not the most reasonable. All English houses or any English body you employ abroad for any thing are generally the first and readyest to impose upon you, therefor to be avoided, or at least be much upon your guard.

If Mr. Mann is stile Resident here he will conduct and take care of you in every thing. In case he is not I set down what follows. See the galary, which imploys you several days, ask for the Copys in Brass of the 4 famouse status that are in the Tribuna, where there is inumerable fine and curious things, as there is in every part and room in that galery. The great Church, which is larger every way then St. Pauls in London; behind the great alter in the dome is an unfinisht statue of a dead Saviour by Michal Angelo. See Giotto's Tower from whence there is a fine prospect of the Citty and Country. Observe the gates of the Baptistry, particularly that facing the church. It is the finest piece of work of that kind perhaps in the world. The little chappel under St. Lorenzo where the bodys of the great Dukes are reposited is the design of Michal Angelo and several of the statues in it are by his own hand. The Library of St. Lorenzo, the entrence into it with the stairs are from the design of M. Angelo. The Cloysters of the Annunciata are painted by Andrea del Sarto and his scholars. The best are a Saint bringing to life a dround boy, which is the first on your right hand as you enter, and a Maddonna with Joseph leaning on a sack oposit to the entry.

In the Church of the Carmes is a handsome Chappel belonging to the Corsini Family.

The Poggio Imperiale about a mile from toun is a country seat of the Great Dukes, the apartments adorn'd with valuable paintings and other fine furnitur.

Pratolino six mills from Florence another seat of the Dukes. The great colossall statue in the garden, the water works, the grotto, the Theatre in the house, all worth seeing: when you are here ride the ring.

Boboli the Dukes garden is very fine, desire to see the Menagery there, where George will be delighted with great variety of all kinds of strange burds and beasts, if you have any brass money in your pockets it will be very good food for the Ostrich, in the uper part of the garden where the Citronades grow there is a good statue of Adam and Eve by Michel Angelo. You will have good luck if you escape being wet when the water works plays, they are very pritty.

The Capins a little way out of toun, beautiful road to it, cows are keept there, fine chise, butter and cream, people go there to breakfast, and there is several rooms and arbers for company to sit in.

The Palaces best worth seeing are Pitti, Ricardi, Strozzi, Iarini where there is a fine colection of paintings.

There is statues and paintings to be seen in the old palace belonging to the Duke, you must send over night to have leave to see the Wardrobe. The Dukes coaches are worth seeing.

The apartment of the Electrise is well worth seeing.

There are good statues in the streets as a Herculus and Centaur by John de Bologne, a Rape of the Sabins by the same, a man suporting his dead friend antique. Take notice of the beautys of the Ponte Santa Trinita.

Florence to Bologna	posts
Florence to Uccellatojio, Post Royal . . .	1

Near Uccelatojio is a house of the Dukes cald Pratolino, where are many fine water works, you pay some thing more to the Postilions to bring horses from

	posts
the next post to cary you on when you have don seing the house.	
To Ponte Assieme	

Here if you have much baggage they can oblige you to put 3 horses to each Chaise or take your baggage off and cary it on horses, the will endeavour to make you do both. We took 3 horses for the two bad posts only and did not take off our baggage.

To Giogo	1½
To Fiorenzolo a good place to ly at	1½
To Tilligare	1
To Sojano	1
The Pope's Dominions	
To Pianore	1½
To Bologna	1½
	10½

Lodge at the Pellegrino and see page 17 for what is to be seen.

Bologna to Venice

Bologna to St. Giorgio, Post Royal	1½
To St. Carlo a river to pass pay 1 paul per Chaise	1½
To Forrara	2

Here in the churches are good paintings but few by men of note. See the Senola della Madona Della Circoncisione. Cardinal Rufo, Bishop of the place, has a fine collection of paintings. Lodge at St. Marco.

Ferrara to Francolino	
	6

At Francolino we took water to Venice. We hierd two piotte (having 3 chaises in company), for which we payd at the rate of a hunger to each man that rowed. You may go by land but it is excessive bad road and dear. You will be two days going and must take provisions in the boat with you. We coud neither get beds nor any thing to eat the night stopt by the way.

At Venice

Lodge at Monsieur D'Henrys on the great Canall where we were well used and cheap. See the Church and Procuratories of St. Mark. The smal church dedicated to St. Geminiano, which stands at one end of the Place of St. Marks, was built by Sansovino. Mr. Law [1] that made such a figur in France in the Messasipie year your country man is buried there. If Mr. Consul Broun be alive who is a worthy honest Scots man send to him and he will do every thing for you when he knows who you are. Your hierd servant will cary you to all the churches worth seeing. In the Church and Convent of St. Giorgio Maggiore are fine paintings by Titian, Tintoret and other masters of the Venetian school, in the refectory is the famous Marriage of Cana by Paul Veronese. There is good paintings in the schools of St. Rocco and St. Marco. The Palaces best worth seeing are Grinani—Maniani—Grassi—Delphino—Pisani—Barberigo. The Doge's Palace and the Courts of Justice are adornd with fine paintings of Titian, Tintoret, Paul Veronese, Bassan, etc. Observe in going into the Palace the statues of Adam and Eve much esteemd. The Arsenal is well worth seeing and the Treasury and Towr of St. Mark. The Library of St. Mark contains several fine busts, statues and other remains of antiquaty, the roof is finely painted. The Realto, a bridge over the great Canal, is very fine and many fine buildings by Paladio. Eat Serbetti at a house near St. Marks famous for making every thing in Ice the best of any place, it is like a Coffie house.

Venice to Padua

We went by water doun the Brent, hierd a Bercello which is a large boat, for which we payd 48 pauls ; it conveniently holds a great many with chaises and baggage, and is a most agreeable way of going, great numbers of fine houses being all along that river.

[1] The well-known John Law, born in Edinburgh 1681, died in Venice in poverty in 1729.

At Padua

Lodge at the post house, see the Church of St. Guistina, it is one of the finest in the world, was built after a plan of Palladio's, the Convent behind the Church is very pritty, the Libary and Cellers are commonly seen by straingers. The Church of St. Antonio di Padua. The Chappel del Santo. The Bas relief that adorns it is the history of his life and miracls, very fine; the Scuola di St. Antonio is well painted by Titian. See the toun house in which is the Monument of Titus Livius the Roman Historian; see the Garden of Simples and Papafava. It is a large toun once well inhabited and fine Colleges for studying and many students but now quite ruinous and no body there.

Padua to Vicenza

	Posts	
Padua to Slesega . .	1	Here you pay 16½ pauls per chaise each post.
To Vicenza . .	1	

Vicenza, lodge at the post house. The tounhouse is a noble pice of Archetecture. Many of the Palaces within the toun were built by Palladio or Sansovano and are esteemd the best in Italy. The Olimpick Theatre is a noble work of Palladio's. The Triumphal Arch as you go out of toun, the house of Marquis Capra a little way out of toun is well worth seeing, it is cald the Rotunda.

Vicenza to Verona

	Posts
Vicenza to Montebello	1
To Caldier	1½
To Verona	1

Lodge at the due Torre. See the Amphetheatre, it coud contain 23,000 spectators—the Arsenal—the Dome—Il Giardino Gusto—the Church of St. George—the Academia Philarmonica.

From Padua quite through the Venetian State there can be no regulation for the price of post horses, they will have what they please, there being no limited order. We some times payd 18½, 16½ and 15 pauls per chaise, and in proportion for a single horse. It being thought dear makes most people go by Voiturino's, but it is a mistake. We endeavourd to agree with those people from Venice to Trent, but found afterwards their demands was realy more then it cost us post: they woud have taken double time with all the inconveniences of rising, etc., that atend traveling that way.

Verona to Trent

	Posts
Verona to Volarni	1½
A river to pass pay 2 pauls per chaise.	
To Peri	[illegible]
A difficult passage where they take out the horses and dragg the chaises up by men about 200 yards. We payd for 3 chaises 22 pauls.	
To Kala	1
To Roveredo	1
To Trent	2

From Verona hither we payd 15 pauls a chaise per post. See the church where the Counsell was held in which is a very fine organ, hear it play, it is extream curious. See St. Peters, where is keept the body of St. Simion, a child murderd by the Jews. Lodge at the Golden Rosan.

Here you must put an avan train to your chaise, for which you pay from 22 to 25 florins a pice. You may find them ready made, but further on you must wait the making; you cannot travel without these fore carriages, they not being used to drive as in Italy. Care must be taken to fit the axletrees of your chaise to your anan trains that they may both run in the same tract. Have the fore wheels higher then they commonly are if you can get them. The people there are used to fit them as they shoud be. Here the mony changes to Hungars, Florins and Karrentari, see page 11.

Trent to Inspruck

Trent to St. Michale the first post in the Imperial dominions after which no more Italian spock nothing but Germans 1
To Equa 1

Those two posts you pay one Florin per horse and 3 horses to each chaise.

	Posts	
To Bradnol	$\frac{3}{4}$	here you pay 45 Karrentari for each 3 quarters of a post.
To Bolsano	$\frac{3}{4}$	
To Tentschen	$\frac{3}{4}$	
To Colman	$\frac{3}{4}$	
To Brixen a good place to ly at .	1	
To Mittewald	$\frac{3}{4}$	45 Karrentari each.
To Sterzingen	$\frac{3}{4}$	
To Brenner	$\frac{3}{4}$	
To Stainack	$\frac{3}{4}$	
To Scamberg	$\frac{3}{4}$	
To Inspruck	$\frac{3}{4}$	

At each whole post you pay one Florin per horse and put 3 horses to a chaise. At the 3 quarters of a post you pay 45 Karrentare, which is three fourth parts of a Florin, and at every post you pay 24 Karrentari to the Postillions. Lodge at the Golden Rosen, see the Franciscans Church, a pent house belonging to the toun house, and the Emperours Garden. The pent house is coverd with gold plate.

Inspruck to Munick

Posts

Inspruck to Seafield 2
you hier an additional horse at the half way house and not at Inspruck which they will endeavour to make you do.

To Mittewald 1
To Waller—see a very odd place . . . . . $1\frac{1}{2}$
To St. Bennedict Buren . . . . $1\frac{1}{2}$

	Posts
To Wolfertshousen	2
To Munick	2
	8

Lodge at the Daler and not at the Soliel d'Or; it is an imposing house. See the Elector of Bavaria's 3 houses, that in the toun, Slysham about 4 mills out of toun, and as you go on your way to Auxburg see Nymfenberg, it is in the post road. The Jesuits Church is fine; the whol toun very pritty. The Elector has many fine houses and all well furnished, but without taking up too much time you can see no more but these three, they being at a distance from the toun. Beware here of any bodys coming to you on pretence of showing you the place. We were imposed upon by one who pretended to be a gentleman orderd by the Elector to atend staingers and was the only bite we met with in out whole journey. One cannot be enough upon ones guard; there being folks in all places upon the watch for straingers, to pick their pockets in any way they can best. Your hierd servant or your Land Lord will inform you of every thing to be seen and get a coach for you.

Munick to Auxburg	Posts
Munick to Pruch	1½
Pruch to digenpank	1½
To Auxburg	1½

Lodge at the Raisin d'Or, see the secret gates of the toun and toun house. They work plate finely here. It is worth going to the great Silver Smiths shope to see it.

Auxburg to Frankfort

	Posts
Auxburg to Meeintenham	1½
To Donnawert	1½
To Winding	1½
To Ading	1
To Dinkenpil	1½
To Kreilsheim	1

	Posts
To Blauslelden	$1\frac{1}{2}$
To Mergentheim, this belongs to the Prince of Anspach —Lutherans . .	$1\frac{1}{2}$
To Bischofsen, belongs to the Prince of Holsten—Catholicks	
To Mittenberg, belongs to the Elector of Mayence—Catholicks	2
To Aschafsenberg El. of Mayence	2
To Dettingen	1
To Hannaw see the Prince's house here	1
To Frankfort, lodge at the Bone Noir on the Parrade. See the Cathedrall and Protestent Churches	1

Frankfort to Collogne. See page 44

We went by water doun the Rhine in two days and a half. We hierd two boats, one for ourselves close coverd like a Pleasur Barge upon the Tames, in which we lay all night upon good straw and Pillows for our heads, and never went on shore. An open boat for the servants and chaises. We payd 75 Florins for all, Taxes included, of which there are many at every toun you pass by. It was in the sumer and no danger of catching cold. We caryd our provitions, had tea water boyld and every thing dresst in the Boat with the servants which was tyd to ours. The water men or servants went on shore at any toun we came to and got us what ever we wanted.

At Collogne lodge at the St. Esprit, see the toun and churches here or at Frankfort, get rid of your avan trains, which you may now go without, and will be of no use to you in Flanders, sell them for what you can get tho less then you payd. We left 3 at Spa thinking they offerd us too little for them at Frankfort; they are yet unsold. At the entrence into Germany they are wanted and necessary for people going in, and by chance you may sell them for what you gave, but take any thing reither then leave them to be sold at a better price which they will perswade you to do and you never hear more of them.

see page 45

Collogne to Aix la Chappelle

	Posts
Collogne to Bergen	1½
To Juliers	1
To Aix la Chappelle	1½

Lodge at Florentins near the Spring, see the Cathedrall —Toun house—Baths—Ramparts—where they drink the waters, etc.

Aix la Chappelle to Spa

There is no post, we hierd 3 horses to each chaise and payd 12 Eskillins per horse. The whole toun is lodging houses, you pay an Eskillin a night for each room, eat at the Ordinary. Mr. Hay a Scotsman is a Banker there, he knows us well and will be of service to you, he also lets lodgeings. See all the fountains round the toun. The Capuchins garden where all the Company walk.

Spa to Leige

We hierd 2 horses to each chaise, payd 12 eskillins per horse, dyn at Chaude Fontaine half way, see the Baths and the mashine for rasing the water which is a little like the great one at Marli.

At Leige lodge au Mouton Blanc, see the great Church. The English Jesuits Convent, ask for Father Phillips who is a Cannon of Leige, he will be glad to show you sevility, you saw him at Oxford.

From Frankfort to Collogne by land

	Posts
Frankfort to Kuningstein	1½
To Weirgas	1½
To Limperg	1
To Walmroth	1
To Frayling	1
To Gutroth	1
To Weyerbus	1½
To Warth	1
To Spieg	1

	Posts
To Collogne	2

From Collogne to Utrecht if you prefer going by Holland to tother road

Collogne to Nuyse	2
To Hofstadt bad lodgeing	2
To Santen	2
To Cleeves	2

To Nimeguen about 20 mills, lodge at White Swan.

To Utrecht about 35 mills, lodge au Chateau d'Anvers.

Frome Venice to Utrecht by this Route is computed about 940 English mills.

From Leige to Brussells to follow the Route from Page 44.

From Leige to St. Turon 3 horses to each Chaise if two persons are in it, at 12 Eskillins for 3 posts which it is reckond, it is at the rate of 4 Eskillins per post each horse, at each barrier you pay 4 sols per chaise. Postillions at the rate of one Eskillin per post.

	Posts
To Tirelemon 3 Eskillins per post each Chaise .	2
To Loven	2
To Brussells	3
	10

Lodge at the Emperour. See the Cour—the Arch-Dutches's Palace and the Toun.

Brussells to Paris

Brussells to Tubise	$2\frac{1}{2}$
To Brenlecourt	$1\frac{1}{2}$
To Chateau	$1\frac{1}{2}$
To Corignion by way of Mons which is half a league about	2
To Chivrein	$1\frac{1}{2}$

Here you are sercht. At 50 yards from Chivrein you are sercht again, at entering into France, at entering Valencienne again. We had little trouble by imediatly giving a little money, and without hesitation telling them at the same time we gave the money that they might serch if they pleasd for we had nothing counterband nor any Merchandise which is the question they ask.

From Brussells to Valencienne you pay 3 Eskillins per horse each post. If two people are in the Chaise you pay for 3 horses tho you get but two and so it is generaly all over France.

	Posts
Chivrien to Valencienne	2½

Lodge at Grand St. Martin. At every Bureau, which is the same as our Custome house officers, they inquire if you have old money, which is prohibited. If you have any you must take care to hide it well, for some times they serch very narowly, and if they find it you loose it, but a little money given in time generaly prevents it.

	Posts
To Bushein	2½
To Cambray	1½

Here they serch slightly. Lodge at the post. See the house Lord Marchmont lived in. He is stile rememberd in this place with honour and affection, which you will find if you go to the English Nunery, and but name him and say you are related to him or indeed any where ells in the whole toun.

	Posts
To Metz en Conture	2
To Peronne here you are serched again but no more till you get to Paris	2
To Marche le pot	1½
To Fouches	1
To Roy	1
To Couche Le pot	1
To Cuvilly	1
To Gournay a good place to ly at	1
To Bois de Lihu	1
To Point St. Maixence	1½
To Chantilly	1

From Pont St. Maixence you go through the Duke of Bourbon's fine Park and Gardens. When you come to Chantilly lodge at the post house and stay a day to see the house and Gardens, the finest thing to be seen in France.

Chantilli to Lusarche	1
To Ecouen	$1\frac{1}{2}$
To St. Denis where you see the Treasury of the Kings of France who are cround and burried there	1
To Paris post Royal you pay	2

Here you get a little printed book of all the posts in France which derects you very exactly.

Paris

Here we had privet lodgeings at the Hotel d'Ambour, Rue de Tour, Fauxbourg St. Germain, payd 300 livers a munth for all the first floor, containing 6 handsome well furnished rooms, 3 rooms on the floor over it, a Hall for servants and other conveniences.

A Tour we made to see some of the Kings houses
about Paris, October 1733

We set out with our own coaches, with only a pair of horses. First to La Mutte, a hunting Seat of the Kings, the house not fine, the gardens pritty. From that through the Bois de Bologne to St. Cloud, a Seat of the Duke of Orleans's, the Park and Gardens 6 Leagues round. From that about a League to Mudon, a house of the Kings finly situated. Thence to Versaills about 4 a clock and saw part of the house that evening. Lodged at the Cadran Blue. Next morning saw the rest of the house and gardens, which woud take up more then a day. Saw the Menagery where there is a smal house. Went through the Park of Versaillies to Trianon, a very pritty house of the Kings built of marble and fine gardens. From that to Marli, an exceeding fine place. The house has 4 apartments, no body gose there when the King gose but whome he names. There is on each side of the house 6 pavillions in the garden sourounded by trees, 2 familys can lodge in each. Tho this place lys high yet it apears very low, being surounded by high mountains, except towards the garden. There is no water but what is supplyd by a vast machine half a league below the house, which may be said to throw the river Sein up a vast hill, which is there received in reservoirs to throw it back again into the Garden, where water abounds in all shapes. From Marli see the Machine, which is composed of 14 vast wheels. From that to St. Germans, a very fine place where King James and his Queen died. It is quite ruinous, but capable of being made the finest place the King has. The Castle is now inhabited by Irish people of fashion adherents to that King. The Tarrass is very fine. Here we lay the second night at the Prince de Galles, and got to Paris next day by diner.

To be seen more in and about Paris

Le Cabinet de Monsieur Le Duc d'Orleans au Palais Royal, where there is the finest colection of picturs in France, or almost any where ells. That of the Holy Family by Raphael valued at 5000 pound.

La Gallerie du Luxembourg, where there is fine paintings of Rubens.

Lese Invalides.

L'Hotel du Mayne, Rue de Bourbon.

Le Palais de Madame La Duchess de Bourbon, proch les Invalides.

L'Hotel d'Antin, Rue neuve St. Augustin.

L'Hotel d'Evreux, Fauxbourg St. Honore.

L'Hotel de Toulouze, proch la Place des Victoir.

La Bibliothique du Roy—Rue de Richelieu.

L'Observatoire.

Seaux. The Duke of Maynes house, 4 leagues from Paris.

Vincennere, 1 league from Paris.

Bagnolet the Duke of Orleans's, 1 league.

St. Maur the Duke of Bourbon's, 2 leagues.

St. Ouen, 1 league.

Petitbourg, 6 Leagues.

Fountainebleau, 14 leagues.

Choisy, 4 leagues.
Issy, the Princess of Conti's.
The Tuilleries.
The Louvre.
The Gallery of Fortifications.
Notre Dame.
The Chappell of Val de Grace.
The Chartreux Convent, where are paintings esteemd good don by Le Sieurs.
The Chappelle of Carmalet Nuns, where is a pictur by Guido for which Lord Burlington offerd 3000 pound, and a Magdalen by Le Brune.
The Sorborne, where is Cardinal Richlieus Monument, extream fine.
The Church of St. Sulpice.
Place Vandome.
Place Victoire.

Paris to Callais

	Posts
Paris to St. Dennis, post Royall	2
To Ecouen	1
To Lasarche	1½
To Chantilly	1
To Lingueville	1½
To Clermont, a good place to ly at	1
To St. Just	1½
To Wavigny	1
To Bretcul	1
To Flors	1½
To Habecour	1
To Amiens	1
To Picquigny	1½
To Flexcourt	1
To Haut Cloches	1
To Abbeville a good place to ly at	1½
To Nouvion	1½
To Bernay	1
To Nampon	1

	Posts
To Montreal	1½
To Frane	1½
To Neuchatel	1
To Boulogne	1½

A good place to ly at, inquire for Mr. Smith, a wine Merchant, a Scots man; we had wine from him; he is very sivil and servisable to all his country folks.

From Boulogne to Marquise	1½
To Haut Buisson	1
To Callais	1
	30½

Here if you do not think it worth while to bring your Chaises home and they are but unwildy and troublesome in our country, sell them for what you can get. Some times it happens people just come there wanting to go to Paris or Italy will give you there value and be glad to get them. If that dos not happen, the people there who make it their business to buy chaises to sell again, will give you very little for them, but take it reither then leave them there to be sold. It will perhaps cost duble there price for the hier of there standing and not to be sold at last, as we found by two we left there.[1]

From Callais to Dover we hierd a little shipe, on of Mr. Minets, 3 guineas is the common hier for the whol shipe, if others are going you may get passage cheaper, either in those boats or in the Kings packet boats that go constantly. Ly at Dover at the Shipe. Your trunks and baggadge.

[1] 'They ask me here [Calais, 27 July 1739] extravagant prices for chaises, of which there are great choice, both French and Italian: I have at last bought one for fourteen guineas of a man whom Mr. Hall recommended me.'—*Lady Mary Wortley Montagu's Letters.*

APPENDIX I

I.—State showing various articles mentioned in the accounts, and their prices between the years 1693 and 1718. The money, weighs and quantities appearing in the Accounts are here reduced to money sterling, weight Avoirdupois and quantity Imperial Liquid Measure.

		Scotland. £ s. d.	London. £ s. d.	Present Day. £ s. d.
Almonds	p. lb.	0 0 11·6	.	0 1 6 to 0 2 9
Almond Biscuits	do.	0 1 5·4		
Aloe Berries . .	no price given	...		
Anchovies .	do.		...	
Apples	p. barrel	1 10 0	...	
Apples	per dozen	0 0 9	0 0 2	
Apples from Bemerside and Bassendean	per doz.	0 0 3		
Apples (French)	per doz.	0 1 0		..
Barley .	p. lb.	0 0 1·4	0 0 3	0 0 1½
Barley (pearl)	,,	0 0 3·6	...	0 0 2
Bee skep	.	0 1 0	...	...
Bees wax .	p. lb.	0 1 1	...	0 1 10
Blue (washing), dearer after Union . . .	p. oz.	0 0 6·5 to 0 0 10·2	.	' 0 0¾
Butter (cheaper after Union)	p. lb.	0 0 2·7 to 0 0 4·3	.	0 1
Butter from England .	p. barrel	1 8 0	...	...
Camomile	no price	...	...	...
Candles (rag wick, 6, 8, 12, and 20 to the lb.) .	p. lb.	0 0 2·9	...	
Candles (cotton wick, 6 to the lb.) .	p. lb.	0 0 4·3	...	
Candles (Irish), .	p. lb.	0 0 3·8	...	0 0 4 to 0 0 8
Candles (Mould, 6 and 10 to the lb.)	p. lb.	...	0 0 6 to 0 0 7	
Candles (wax for lighting tobacco)	p. lb.	...	0 2 6	

		Scotland. £ s. d.	London. £ s. d.	Present Day. £ s. d.
Capers .	p. lb.	0 1 1	...	...
Carmel .	p. lb.	0 8 5·8	...	...
Caraway seeds	no price given	...	...	...
Chalk,	do.	...	...	...
Cheese (Best)	p. lb.	0 0 2·2 to 0 0 3·6	0 0 3	0 0 10
,, (coarse)	p. lb.	0 0 1·6	...	...
,, (Cheshire)	p. lb.	...	0 0 3½	0 0 10
,, (Tweeddale)	no price given	...	...	...
Cherries to brandy		...	0 8 0	...
Do. to preserve .	p. 600	0 0 3	...	...
Chestnuts .	no price given	...	...	...
Chocolate .	p. lb.	0 2 2·1 to 0 2 11	..	0 1 10
Cinnamon	p. lb.	0 9 8·3	0 10 0	0 2 8
Cinnamon water .	p. pint.	0 0 8·7	0 4 0 p. bottle	
Citron peel .	p. lb.	0 1 11·1	0 3 0	0 0 8
Cloves	p. lb.	0 9 8·3	0 11 0	0 1 10
Coffee Beans (unburned)	p. lb.	0 2 6·5 to 0 3 3·2	...	0 1 8
Do. (roasted)	p. lb.	...	0 12 0	0 1 10
Coffee powder	p. lb.	...	0 6 0	0 1 4 to 0 1 10
Corks .	p. gross	0 1 0 to 0 1 4	...	0 1 0 to 0 3 0
Corn flower .	no price given	...	...	...
Cucumbers,	p. pint	0 6 0	...	...
Currants, ...	p. lb.	0 0 6·5	0 0 5½	0 0 3½ to 0 0 5
Figs	p. lb.	0 1 9·7	...	...
Fish—				
Barrel containing 30 salt cods .		1 0 0	...	...
Herrings p. barrel, exclusive of carriage		0 15 0 to 1 7 6	...	...
Herrings (Glasgow) .	p. barrel	1 6 8	...	...
,, (Lewis) . .	,,	1 1 8	...	...
,, (Hempstead, .	,,	0 16 8	...	...
,, (Dunbar) .	,,	0 17 8½	...	...
,, fresh to salt for servants .	p. 1000	0 6 8	...	...
Killine (dried) . . .	each	0 0 8	...	...
Ling		0 1 0	0 0 11	0 0 4 p. lb.

		Scotland. £	s.	d.	London. £	s.	d.	Present Day. £	s.	d.
Fish—*contd.*									...	
Oysters . .	. p. barrel	0	2	0		...			...	
Oysters (pickled)	. p. barrel		...		0	2	0		...	
Salmon for a year .	. . . .	1	7	0		...			...	
Sturgeon	p. little barrel		...		0	8	0		...	
Trout .	price not given		...			...			...	
Flambeaux	. . each	0	1	2		...			...	
			to							
		0	1	4						
Ginger .	. p. lb.	0	0	5·8		...		0	1	4
Ginger bread .	no price given		...			...			...	
Ginger confected	p. pot	0	1	10		...		0	2	0
Gooseberries to bottle	p. pint		...		0	0	1		...	
Hartshorn jelly	. . . .	0	1	6		...			...	
Honey	. p. quart	0	0	8		...			...	
Indigo	p. oz.	0	0	8·7		...			...	
Lemons	each	0	0	2½		...		0	0	1
			to						to	
		0	0	7				0	0	1½
Lemons, syrup of	no price given		...			...			...	
Loaves	each	0	0	7		...		0	0	5
			to							
		0	0	8						
Mace	p. oz.	0	1	2		...		0		
			to							
		0	1	4						
Milk Ewe .	p. pint	0	0	0·2		...			...	
Mugwort water .	. . . . .	0	0	5		...			...	
Mustard .	p. lb.	0	0	5·8		...		0	1	
Myrrh	. .	0	0	4		...			...	
Nutmeg . .	p. oz.	0	0	4·4	0	0	8¼	0	0	2
			to							
		0	0	7·2						
Nuts Pistachio	p. lb.		...		0	2	0	0	3	6
,, Spanish	p. pint	0	0	2·7		...			...	
Oil salad	p. pint	0	1	4		...		0	1	2
			to							
		0	1	8						
Olives	.	0	6	4		...			...	
Oranges .	each	0	0	0¾		...		0	0	0½
			to						to	
		0	0	4				0	0	2
Orange peel .	p. lb.	0	1	11·2	0	3	0	0	0	6
Pepper	p. lb.	0	1	4·3		...		0		
			to							
		0	1	8·3						

		Scotland. £ s. d.	London. £ s. d.	Present Day. £ s. d.
Pickles .	no price given	...	...	...
Pipes, tobacco	p. doz.	0 0 2½ to 0 0 3	...	...
Plumbs, musk	no price given	...	...	...
Potash .	p. lb.	0 0 4·5	...	0 0 6½
Prunes .	p. lb.	0 0 4·3	...	0 0 7
Prunelles, box of	1¼ lb.	...	0 2 0	
Quicknin		0 0 1	...	...
Raisins	p. lb.	0 0 3·8 to 0 0 5·8	0 0 4	0 0 4
Ratafia	no price given	...	...	
Rhubarb	p. oz.	0 2 2·1	0 1 6 to 0 3 10	...
Rice	p. lb.	0 2 2 to 0 4 4	...	0 0 2 to 0 0 4½
Rolls	p. doz.	0 0 4½	...	0 0 6
Saffron		...	0 4 2	...
Sago .	p. lb.	...	0 3 0	0 0 2¾
Salt .	p. peck	0 4 4	...	...
Saltpetre .	no price given	...	...	...
Seed for birds .	p. lb.	0 0 2·9	...	0 0 2½
Shortbread	no price given	...	...	...
Snuff .	p. lb.	...	0 4 0	0 5 6
Snuff tobacco	p. lb.	0 0 7·2	...	...
Soap (Newcastle) .	p. firkin	0 18 5 to 1 2 0	...	0 12 6
Soap .	do.	0 12 0 to 0 16 6	0 12 9	
Spermaceti	no price given	...	...	...
Spice .	p. lb.	0 1 1	...	0 1 4
Spirits of Wine .	p. pint	0 0 8 to 0 0 11	...	0 0 4
Starch .	p. stone	0 2 6½ to 0 3 4½	...	...
Sugar, candibord .	p. lb.	0 0 9¾ to 0 1 1	0 1 1½	0 0 4
,, coarse		0 0 3·6 to 0 0 8	0 0 8	
,, kitchen		0 0 6½	0 0 4	0 0 1¾

		Scotland. £ s. d.	London. £ s. d.	Present Day. £ s. d.
Sugar, powdered		0 0 4·3	0 0 6	0 0 3
Syrup, balsamic		...	0 12 0	
Tartar, red	p. lb.	0 0 7·2	...	
Tea, Bohea	p. lb.	0 16 0 to 1 9 1	0 16 0 to 1 1 0	0 1 6 to 0 3 0
,, Green	p. lb.	0 14 7	...	
,, Hyson .	p. lb.	...	1 12 0	
,, Pekoe	p. lb.	...	1 4 0	
Chocolate	p. lb.	0 7 4·8	...	
Tobacco	p. lb.	0 1 5·4	0 2 0	0 9 4
Wafers		[illegible]	...	...
Varnish	no price given	...	...	...
Vinegar	. p. pint	0 0 4	...	0 0 3

(The Present Day price "0 1 6 to 0 3 0" is bracketed for all teas, Bohea to Pekoe.)

II.—List of Wines, Ales and Spirits, and their prices, between 1693 and 1718.

		Scotland. £ s. d.	London. £ s. d.
Ale, English .	p. pint	0 0 1	
Ale from H. Y.[1]	p. pint	0 0 0⅔	
Aquavitae . .	p. pint	0 0 6⅔	...
Arrac . .	p. doz.	5 4 0	2 2 0
Beer—			
Small beer from Abbey Hill[1]	p. pint	0 0 0⅓	
Brandy	p. pint	0 0 8 to 0 1 8	.
Burgundy	p. flask	0 7 6	0 4 0 to 0 4 6 p. bottle
Canary	p. gal.	0 6 8 to 0 7 9	.
Champagne	p. bottle	...	0 4 0 to 0 7 0
Claret	p. doz.	0 13 5	1 13 2
. . . . .	p. hogshead	5 0 0 to 25 0 0	27 0 0 to 47 0 0

[1] Perhaps Harry Younger's Abbey Hill Brewery. Beer is also got from Dunfermline, Dundee, and Leith.

		Scotland. £ s. d.	London. £ s. d.
Emetic wine		0 7 0	...
Florence wine	p. doz.	0 15 0	...
French wine	p. hogshead	11 0 0 to 14 5 0	
Fruntimack, Frontignan	p. pint	0 1 9	...
Gineva, bought in England along with rhubard		...	...
Green wine	p. gal.	0 7 1	...
Hermitage	p. bottle	...	0 4 0 to 0 6 0
Madeira	no price given	...	...
Malaga	p. doz.	1 1 1	...
Mum	p. pint	0 0 6⅔	
Pontack from Bordeaux	p. hhs.	...	34 16 7
Port	p. doz.	...	0 18 0
Sack	p. gal.	0 6 1	
Sherry	p. pint	0 0 11	
Sherry sack	p. hhs.	16 13 4	
White wine for physic	p. pint	0 1 4	...

III.—Prices of Cattle, Sheep, Poultry, etc., between 1693 and 1718.

Cattle.	Milk cows	£3 2 6	
	Holland cow	1 8 4	
	Cows for killing	1 12 0	to £2 7 0
	Calfs	0 3 6	to 0 10 0
	Skin and tallow of a cow, worth	0 6 8	

Beef, back, say, and rump, 5s.; ½ leg of beef, 7s.; in England, 3d. p. lb.; Veal, leg of, 2s. 1d.; leg of veal from Berwick, 5s.

Sheep. Rams, 15s. 6d.; Ewes, 5s. to 10s. each; Sheep for servants, about 5s. each; Lambs, 1s. 8d. to 4s. each; skin of a sheep, worth about 1s. 4d.; killing sheep, 6d.; Mutton, leg of, 5s.; in England, 3½d. p. lb.

Pigs. Pigs, £1 to £1, 5s. each; hams in Scotland, 7s. each; in England, hams (Westphalian), 6d. to 11d. p. lb.; other hams, 1s. 2d. p. lb.

Birds. Hens, 5d., capons, 8d. each; chickens, 2⅔ each; turkeys, 1s. 4d. to 3s. 1d. each; geese, 10d. each; goslings, 6d. each; carrying same from Border, 1d. each; grey plovers, 6d. p. pair; green plovers, 5d. p. pair; wild ducks, 4d. to 6d. each; small teal, 4d. each.

IV.—Prices of Fuel between 1693 and 1718.

		Scotland. £	s.	d.	London £	s.	d.
Coal							
Carberry	p. cart	0	4	8			
Carlops	p. load	0	[illegible]	0			
Woolmit	p. dale	0		0			
Clackmannan, put down in the close	p. dale	0		6			
Alloa	p. ton	0		8			
Carting same from Leith	p. ton	0		2			
Etal (Northumberland)—							
Small coal	p. load	0	0	3			
Great coal	p. load	0	0	6		..	
Cost of carrying same	p. load	0	0	9		...	
Scots coal	p. ton		...		1 14 to 1 16		0 to 0
Coal	p. ton		...		1 8 to 2 0		6 to 0
Peat	p. stack	0	3	4		..	
Charcoal	p. bushel		...		0	4	6
Billets of wood	p. 100		...		0	1	4
Roots and brushwood used in England . .			...			...	

Note.—There is nothing in the accounts to show what weight is represented by the words 'dale,' 'cart,' and 'load.' A dale, however, seems to be used as synonymous with a ton, and as we see from the Accounts (1703) that it took two carts to carry a dale, a cart probably represents a $\frac{1}{2}$ ton. A load nowadays means 3 cwt., and it probably meant the same then.

In London the Accounts show that a cart carried nearly a ton ($\frac{5}{6}$).

APPENDIX II

STATEMENT showing money wages per annum of servants, etc.

	Scotland Prior to 1714.	Scotland In 1740.	London 1718.	Continent. 1732.	
	£ s. d.	£ s. d.	£ s. d.	£ s. d.	
Master Household	5 0 0	...	...	...	...
Butler	3 0 0	14 0 0	...	...	...
Footman	1 13 4 to 2 10 0	5 0 0	4 0 0 to 6 0 0	...	...
Coachman	3 0 0 to 4 0 0	8 0 0	[1]3 0 0	...	...
Groom	1 10 0 to 2 0 0	2 10 0	...	...	...
Postillion	...	2 0 0	...	...	...
Carter	...	4 0 0	...	...	...
Valet	3 0 0		5 0 0	...	...
Barnman	2 3 4	...	...	...	...
Gardener	4 0 0 with house 5 0 0 without	14 0 0	...	...	...
Housekeeper	4 0 0 to 5 0 0	5 0 0	...	...	...
Ladysmaid	3 6 8	5 0 0	5 0 0		...
Cook	1 13 4 to 3 0 0	8 0 0	6 0 0 to 8 0 0	10 10 0 16 16 0	Spa Naples
Under Cook	1 12 0 to 2 0 0	3 0 0		3 12 0	Naples
Kitchen Maid	1 3 4 to 2 10 0	2 0 0	...	...	...
Chambermaid	1 13 4 to 2 10 0	2 0 0	4 0 0 to 5 0 0	3 12 0	Naple

[1] This was the Baillies' Scots coachman, so £3 cannot be fairly regarded as the English wage.

	Scotland Prior to 1714.	Scotland In 1740.	London 1718.	Continent. 1732.	
	£ s. d.	£ s. d.	£ s. d.	£ s. d.	
Laundrymaid .	1 14 0 to 1 17 4	2 0 0	...	...	...
French Maid . .	...	...	3 0 0	...	...
Nurse . . .	3 6 8	...	...	...	...
Woman to wait on Children .	5 0 0	...	...	...	...
Dairy Maid . .	...	2 0	...	...	...
Fowl and swine girl	1 4 0	...	...	...	...
Woman to wash and spin . . .	1 14 0	...	...	...	...
Woman haymaking, without food .	0 0 $3\frac{3}{4}$ p. day	...	...	...	...
Field labourer, Do.	0 0 5 p. day	...	...	...	...
Thresher, Do.	0 0 $11\frac{3}{4}$ p. day	...	...	...	...
Herd, without meat	...	5 0 0	...	...	...
Officer, Do.	...	7 5 0	...	...	...

Tradesmen in Scotland prior to 1714: Tailor, 4d. p. day and food; mason, 1s. p. day; wright, 10d. p. day; thatcher, 1s. p. day. Drystone dykes cost 1s. p. rood, and turf dykes 8d. p. rood.[1]

[1] See note, p. lxiii.

APPENDIX III

NOTE of FEES paid in connection with Education in Edinburgh except where otherwise marked.

		Stg. £ s. d.
Miss May Menzies Governess	p. annum	8 6 8
Arithmetic	a quarter	1 0 0
Book-keeping	a course	3 2 0
Cooking lessons	a course	1 6 0
Dancing—		
A course to perfect Lady Grisell (Edinburgh)		8 0 0
Children	p. month	1 3 8 to 1 9 4
In London	p. month	3 4 6
Fiddler for same	p. month	0 10 9
Flute[1] lessons	p. quarter	1 10 0 to 2 1 9
French (London). To the French Mistress	p. month	0 10 0
French (London). To the French Master	p. month	1 1 6
Geography	p. quarter	0 1 6
Harp lessons (London)	the first month	3 0
Italian Lessons (Naples)	p. month	13 7
Painting lessons	p. month	1 0 0
Playing (spinet and virginel)	p. quarter	1 9 7 to 1 12 3
Tuning do.	p. quarter	0 4 10
Playing lessons, spinet (Naples)	p. month	0 18 0
Reading	p. quarter	0 4 10
To perfecting reading		1 10 0
Reading School	p. quarter	0 2 5 to 0 5 5
Singing	p. month	0 12 4 to 1 0 0
Singing (Naples)	p. month	0 18 0
Theory of Music. Thorough Bass	p. quarter	2 2 0
Viol lessons	p. month	1 0 0
Writing Lessons	p. month	0 4 10

[1] Two flutes are bought, one for 10s. stg. and the other for £1, 5s. stg. Prices of spinets and virginels are not given.

APPENDIX IV

TABLES OF SCOTS AND ENGLISH MONEY AND MEASURES[1]

I.—Money

12 Scots pennies	= 1 Scots shilling	= 1 penny stg.
20 Scots shillings	= 1 Scots pound	= 1s. 8d. stg.
A guinea	between £1, 1s. and £1, 3s. 6d.	
A jacobus	– about £1, 6s.	
A mark	– 13s. 4d. Scots	= 1s. $1\frac{1}{3}$d. stg.
A rex dollar	– 7s. 3d.	
A dollar	– 4s. $2\frac{1}{2}$d.	

II.—Measures of Extension

Scots Lineal Measure.

1 Scots inch	= 1	=	1·001616	imp. inches.
8·88 Scots inches	= 1 link	=	8·89435	,, ,,
1·35 Scots links	= 1 Scots foot	=	12·0194	,, ,,
$3\frac{1}{12}$ Scots feet	– 1 ell	=	37·0598	,, ,,
6 ells	– 1 fall	=	222·3588	,, ,,
4 falls	– 1 chain	–	889·4352	,, ,,
10 chains	– 1 furlong	–	8894·352	,, ,,
8 furlongs	– 1 mile	–	71154·816	,, ,,
		or	1976·522	imp. yds.

Imperial Lineal Measure.

7·92	imp.	inches	= 1	imp.	link.
1·515	,,	links	= 1	,,	foot.
3	,,	feet	= 1		yard.
$5\frac{1}{2}$	,,	yards	= 1	,,	pole.
4	,,	poles	= 1	,,	chain.
10	,,	chains	= 1	,,	furlong.
8	,,	furlongs	= 1	,,	mile, or 1760 yards.

III.—Measures of Weight

(1) *Scots Troyes or Dutch Weight raised from the Standard Lanark Stone.*

16 drops	= 1 ounce	=	475·56	imp. troy grains.
16 ounces	= 1 lb.	=	7608·95	,, ,,
16 lbs.	= 1 Lanark stone	=	121743·195	,, ,,

[1] The following measures are taken from the tables, etc. published in 1827 by the authority of the Magistrates and Justices of the City and County of Edinburgh.

(2) *Imperial Troy Weight.*

24 grains	= 1 pennyweight	= 24	imp. Troy grains.
20 pennyweights	= 1 ounce	= 480	,, ,,
12 ounces	= 1 lb.	= 5760	,, ,,

(3) *Scots Tron Weight raised from the Edinburgh Tron Pound.*

16 drops	= 1 ounce	= 601·417	imp. Troy grains.
16 ounces	= 1 lb.	= 9622·67	,, ,,
16 lbs.	= 1 stone	= 153962·72	,, ,,

(4) *Imperial Avoirdupois Weight.*

16 drams	= 1 ounce	= 437·5	imp. Troy grains.
16 ounces	= 1 lb.	= 7000	,, ,,
14 lbs.	= 1 stone	= 98000	,, ,,
1 dale	= 1 ton.		

1 Scots Troy pound = 1 lb. 1 oz. 6·3 dr. imperial avoirdupois.
1 Edinburgh Tron pound = 1 lb. 6 oz. ,, ,,

Assuming that Lady Grisell in her Accounts used the Edinburgh Tron Weight, it is necessary in order to compare the prices then and now to multiply the quantity or divide the price by $\frac{22}{16} = \frac{11}{8}$.

IV.—Measures of Capacity

(1) *Scots Liquid Measure.*

4 gills	= 1 mutchkin	= 26·0508	imp. cubic inches.
2 mutchkins	= 1 chopin	= 52·1017	,, ,,
2 chopins	= 1 pint	= 104·2034	,, ,,
8 pints	= 1 gallon	= 833·6272	,,

(2) *Scots Dry Measure for Barley and Oats.*

4 lippies	= 1 peck	= 807·576	imp. cubic inches.
4 pecks	= 1 firlot	= 3230·305	,, ,,
4 firlots	= 1 boll	= 12921·222	,, ,,
16 bolls	= 1 chalder	= 206739·546	,, ,,

A forpet, forper, or fourtpert = according to Jameson $\frac{1}{4}$ of a peck, or $\frac{1}{16}$ of a firlot; according to Lady Grisell it equalled $\frac{1}{16}$ of a firlot.

6 firlots	= A Lothian boll.	
1 boll oats	= 10 stones weight.	
2 bolls oats	= 1 load	= 20 stone = $2\frac{1}{2}$ cwt.
A chalder	= 1 ton	= 160 stones.
1 cwt.	= 8 stones.	

(3) *Imperial Liquid or Dry Measure.*

4 gill	= 1 pint	= 34·659	imp. cubic inches.
2 pints	= 1 quart	= 69·318	,, ,,
4 quarts	1 gallon	= 277·274	,, ,,
2 gallons	= 1 peck	= 554·548	,, ,,
4 pecks	1 bushel	= 2218·191	,, ,,
8 bushels	= 1 quarter	= 17745·526	,, ,,

1 Scots pint = 3 imperial pints.
1 Scots peck = $1\frac{3}{8}$ imperial pecks.

TABLES OF FOREIGN MONEY

Rotterdam, Leyden, Utrecht, Gildermause (?), Buss (?), and Lumpt

8 doits or duyten	= 1 stur (stuyver ?).	1 doit or duyt	= $\frac{11}{80}$d. stg.
20 stur	= 1 guilder.	1 stur	= $1\frac{1}{10}$d. stg.
		1 guilder	= 1s. 10d. stg.

Maastricht

6 doits or duyten	= 1 mark.	1 doit or duyt'	= ·11d. stg.
10 marks	= 1 skillin or schelling.	1 mark	= ·68d. ,,
37 skillins	= a guinea.	1 skilling or schelling	= 6·8d. ,,

Aix la Chapelle

6 doits	= 1 mark.	1 doit	= ·12d. stg.
9 marks	= 1 skilling.	1 mark	= ·74d. ,,
8 skillings	= 1 crown.	1 skilling	= 6·75d. ,,
		1 crown	= 4s. 6d. ,,

Spa

4 liers	= 1 sou.	1 lier	= ·17d. stg.
10 sous	= 1 skilling.	1 sou	= ·67d. ,,
		1 skilling	= 6·75d. ,,

French Money

20 sous	= 1 livre.	1 sou	= ·67d. stg. to ·7d. stg.
3 livres	= 1 ecu blanc.	1 livre	= from 1s. 1½d. to 1s. 2d.
6 livres	= 1 ecu grand.		
24 livres	= 1 louis.		

Lorraine

20 sous	= 1 livre.	1 sou	= ·39d. stg.
32 livres	= 1 louisdor = a guinea.	1 livre	= 7·8d. ,,

Burgundy and Paris

20 sous	= 1 livre.	1 sou	= ·52d.
24 livres	= 1 louisdor = 1 guinea.	1 livre	= 10½d. stg.

Turin

20 sous = 1 livre.	1 sou = ·65d. stg.
9½ livres = 1 sequin = 26 carlins.	1 livre = 1s. 1·1d. stg.
10 carlins = 1 ducat.	1 carlin = 4·8d.
	1 ducat = nearly 4s.
	1 sequin – ,, 10s. 5d.

Millan

20 sous = 1 livre.	1 sous = ·45d. stg.
14 livres = 1 sequin.	1 livre = 9d. stg.
	1 sequin = 10s. 5d.

Plasentia, Parma, Reggio, Modena, Loreto, Rome

10 biocks (baiocchi) = 1 julio or paul (paolo).	1 biock – ·62d. stg.
10 julios or pauls = 1 Roman crown or scudo.	1 julio or paul = 6¼d. ,,
20 julios or pauls = 2 crowns = 1 sequin.	1 Roman crown = 5s. 2½d. ,,
3 julios or pauls = 1 testoon.	1 sequin – 10s. 5d. ,,

Bologna

12 demis = 1 biock.	1 demi = ·05d.
20 biocks = 1 livre = 2 julios or pauls.	1 biock = ·6d.
10½ livres = 1 sequin.	1 livre = 1s.

Naples

10 grains = 1 carlin.	1 grain = ·48d. stg.
2 carlins = 1 terri.	1 carlin = 4·8d. ,,
10 carlins = 1 ducat.	1 ducat = nearly 4s. ,,

Venice

20 soldi = 1 lira.	1 soldo = ·3d. stg.
21 liras = 1 Florentine sequin.	1 lira = nearly 6d. ,,
22 liras = 1 Venetian sequin.	1 sequin = 10s. 5d ,,

Frankfort

60 karrentari – 1 florin.	1 karrentari = ·47d. stg.
4 florins 15 karrentari = 1 hungar.	1 florin – 2s. 4d. ·2 ,,
7½ florins = 1 Spanish pistole.	1 hungar = 10s. ,,
	1 Spanish pistole = 17s. 7·5 ,,

From Liége to Calais

20 ous = 1 livre.	1 sous = ·55d. stg.
	1 livre = 11d. ,,

NOTES as to SALARIES and WAGES in 1707 and now

	Paid by City. £	s.	d.	Queen Anne's Grant. £	s.	d.	Class Fees. £	s.	d.	1707. £	s.	d.	Present Time. £	s.	d.	Increase.
Judges										500	0	0	3,600	0	0	7·2
Church.[1] (1) Best Charges . .										138	17	9$\frac{2}{3}$	1,000	0	0	7·2
(2) Average Stipend .										50	0	0	300	0	0	6
Education.[2]																
Edinburgh University.																
Principal . .	111	2	2	.			...			111	2	2	1,600	0		
Divinity . .	88	17	9	...			30	0	0	110	17	9	570	0	0	
Hebrew . . .	50	0	0	35	14	3	no fees.			85	14	3	800	0	0	.
Church History	100	0	0	.			30	0	0	130	0	0	440	0	0	.
Public Law .	150	0	0	...						150	0	0	600	0	0	.
Mathematics .	50	0	0	35	14	3	30	0	0	115	14	3	1,100	0	0	.
Greek . . .	22	4	5	35	14	3	50	0	0	107	18	8	1,100	0	0	.
Logic and Metaphysics . .	22	4	5	35	14	3	50	0	0	107	18	8	900	0	0	.
Natural Philosophy . . .	22	4	5	35	14	3	50	0	0	107	18	8	1,100	0	0	.
Moral Philosophy . . .	22	4	5	35	14	3	50	0	0	107	18	8	900	0	0	...
Humanity . .	24	9	5	35	14	3	50	0	0	110	3	8	1,100	0	0	.
Librarian . .	36	13	4	.			20	0	0	56	13	4	400	0	0	.
										1302	0	1	10,610	0	0	8·1
Tradesmen,[3] *etc.*																
Masons . . . . . p. day										0	1	0	0	7	1	7
Joiners . . . . . p. day										0	0	10	0	7	6	9
Tailors . . . . p. day										0	0	8	0	6	0	9
Dykers . p. rood of 6 yds. 6 inch.										0	1	0	0	6	0	6
Field labourer . . . . p. day										0	0	5	0	4	2	10

1. *The Church.*—The stipends of the ministers of the Edinburgh churches were raised in 1694 to 2500 merks Scots, or £138, 17s. 9$\frac{2}{3}$d. stg. They were reduced in 1708 to 2000 merks, but were raised again to the old figure in 1712 for three of their number (*City of Edinburgh Records*). As to the average stipend of the Ministers, Mr. Steel, the minister of Sorn in Ayrshire, speaking in 1749, stated that at that time it did not exceed £52. This figure was apparently an underestimate, for it appears from the statistics collected by the Committee, who reported upon the stipends to the General Assembly in the following year, that the average stipend at that time must have been nearer £65. As there must have been some increase during the forty years that had elapsed since the Union, it cannot be far wrong to take £50 as the average stipend in 1707. In regard to the average stipend of to-day, Mr. Simpson, minister of Bonhill, estimates it for landward parishes at about £260. Mr. P. C. Robertson, however, the Interim Auditor of the Church of Scotland, considers that if the city churches, with their largely augmented stipends, be included, the average is nearer £300.

2. *Education.*—The figures entered as paid by the city are taken from the City Accounts; the figures entered as paid from Queen Anne's grant are taken from Sir Alexander Grant's *History of the University;* the figures entered as derived from fees in the classes of Greek, Logic and Metaphysics, Natural Philosophy, Moral Philosophy and Humanity, are based on the fact that when the Professor of Moral Philosophy in 1708 was forbidden to charge class fees, he received an additional salary of £50 in lieu thereof. It is therefore probable that £50 also represents the value of the fees in these other classes which formed part of the same course of study. The sums entered as class fees for Divinity, Church History, and Mathematics are merely estimates. The fees drawn by the Librarian were for issuing diplomas, and the figure entered is an estimate founded on the number of graduates, and the fees he was allowed to charge. In judging of the salaries of the Principal and of the Professor of Divinity, it has to be remembered that these gentlemen also held as ministers city charges, which brought each of them in an additional sum of £122, 4s. 5d. Graham in his *Social Life of Scotland* states that the salaries of Professors in Scotland during the first quarter of the eighteenth century averaged from £25 to £30, exclusive of class fees. As will be seen from the above state, the salaries of the regular professors in Edinburgh averaged considerably more.

It is more difficult to ascertain what rise has taken place in the remuneration of the parish 'Dominie.' According to statute he was entitled in 1707 to a salary from the heritors of not less than £5, 18s. 3d., and not more than £11, 2s. 6d. In a Memorial drawn up in 1782 for the Parochial School Masters in Scotland, it is stated that this remuneration, 'though not great, was yet well suited to the times, the funds, and distinction of rank at the period. The emoluments of their office placed them above day labourers, and the poorer class of mechanics and farmers; nay, raised them to an equality with the more opulent farmers, respectable tradesmen and citizens; among whom their employment, their manners, and prospects in life procured them a degree of respect very advantageous to their profession.' Still in spite of this opinion, and of our knowledge that they enjoyed in addition certain perquisites, their pay seems to have been relatively poor. On the other hand an examination of the fees paid by Lady Grisell for the education of her daughters as shown in Appendix III., would indicate that private tuition was relatively well paid, and taken all over, it may be assumed that the increase in their professional incomes lies between six and ten.

3. *Tradesmen, etc.*—In comparing the wages paid to tradesmen then and now, it is necessary to bear in mind that whereas they worked at least 10 hours a day in 1707, they only work at most 9 hours nowadays. This has been taken into account in the foregoing state. The amounts entered as presently paid are based on the wage per hour paid to the tradesman, not the sum per hour charged by his master against the customer.

It will be observed that in the foregoing state no notice has been taken of the earnings of Solicitors, Doctors, and Surgeons, nor of the pay of the Army. In regard to the first three of these, it has been found impossible to arrive at any true method of comparison, the work performed by them then and now being so different. The few items capable of comparison, such as drawing bonds for money, bleeding, syringing the ears, etc., indicate that a man in the position of George Baillie would have had to pay eight times more now than he did then.

(Syringing the ears, 5s. then, £2, 2s. now; bleeding, 9s. 8d. then, £4, 4s. now.)

As to the pay of the army, it was relatively so high that it stands alone, and must be judged by itself. The generous treatment meted out to soldiers does not appear to have arisen from any attempt to place the Scottish army on the same footing as the English army, alongside of which it was called upon to fight, for we find the same high rate of pay ruling in Scotland during the reigns of Charles II. and James VII. before the beginning of the great Continental war. It arose more probably from the desire to ensure the loyalty of the army, and it no doubt accounts for the fact that so many gentlemen were to be found serving as non-commissioned officers and privates, and that desertion was at that time practically unknown. The following state, for which the editor is indebted to Mr. Andrew Ross, Ross Herald, shows how small has been the increase in the pay of the army during the last two hundred years, and indicates that in spite of its pay being occasionally a year or two in arrears, the army was either largely overpaid then, or miserably underpaid now. In looking at the figures it must be borne in mind that colonels, lieutenant-colonels, and majors had companies, and drew captain's pay in addition to their pay as field officers.

	Colonel.	Lt.-Colonel	Major.	Captain.	Lieutenant.	Ensign.	Sergeant.	Corporal.	Drummer.	Private.
					Foot Guards. Per diem.					
	s. d.	*s. d.*	*s. d.*	*s. d.*	*s. d.*	*s. d.*	*s. d.*	*s. d.*	*s. d.*	*s. d.*
1. 1677 . .	12 0	7 0	5 0	8 0	4 0	3 0	1 6	1 0	1 0	0 6
2. 1702 . .	12 0	7 0	5 0	8 0	4 0	3 0	1 6	1 0	1 0	0 7
3. 1707 (England)	20 0	12 0	8 0	14 0	7 0	5 0	1 6	1 0	1 0	0 10
4. 1911 . .	18 0	18 0	13 7 to 16 0	11 7	6 6 to 7 6	5 3	2 6	1 9	1 2	1 1
					Marching Regiments. Per diem.					
	s. d.	*s. d.*	*s. d.*	*s. d.*	*s. d.*	*s. d.*	*s. d.*	*s. d.*	*s. d.*	*s. d.*
1. 1685 . .	12 0	7 0	5 0	8 0	4 0	3 0	1 6	1 0	1 0	0 5
2. 1702 . .	12 0	7 0	5 0	8 0	4 0	3 0	1 6	1 0	1 0	0 6
3. 1707 (England)	12 0	7 0	5 0	8 0	4 0	3 0	1 6	1 0	1 0	0 8
4. 1911 . .	18 0	18 0	13 7 to 16 0	11 7	6 6 to 7 6	5 3	2 4	1 8	1 1	1 0

NOTE.—There was no line regiment on the 1677 Establishment, and the pay of the Foot Guards was the same in 1685 as in 1677.

APPEND[IX]

Year.	I. House-keeping Accounts (Food, drink, firing, lighting, washing, and all expenses in connection therewith.)	II. Sundry Disbursements, including taxes, feu-duties, etc.	III. Servants' Wages.	IV. Servants' Clothes.	V. Clothes for Family.	VI. Furniture and Furnishings.	VII. Expenses of Horses, etc.	VIII. Doctors and Surgeons
	£ s. d.	£ s. d.	£ s. d.	£ s. d.	£ s. d.	£ s. d.	£ s. d.	£ s. d.
1693, 1694, and 1695	175 0 0	257 9 4	[7] 29 17 2	..	89 15 0	109 4 6	62 0 0	52 3 10
Average for these years	58 6 8	85 16 5	9 19 1	..	29 18 4	36 8 2	20 13 4	17 7 11
1696	79 15 0	46 5 0	16 0 0	..	50 13 2	50 1 4	8 15 8	16 9 0
[1] 1697	149 3 0	70 9 8	14 9 4	31 11 8	48 15 10	31 9 6	..	..
1698	78 1 8	8 19 4	4 10 0	..	27 15 6	1 15 3	..	..
[2] 1699	165 8 2	246 15 8	29 2 0	..	..	29 18 2	19 17 9	7 0 2
1700	242 10 4	[3] 234 15 6	21 18 0	9 0 0	..	14 12 2	10 1 8	23 18 6
1701	250 13 7	82 17 10	19 11 2	13 5 5	44 9 3	42 4 9	41 2 1	7 6 0
1702	235 5 5	59 3 8	18 0 4	16 8 10	60 15 2	66 14 8	30 19 0	5 6 4
1703	237 14 3	104 1 7	19 3 6	10 5 3	65 1 8	67 5 0	27 16 0	21 12 5
1704	212 7 6	103 4 2	15 8 7	5 8 6	49 7 2	90 14 10	42 0 0	2 9 9
1705	214 0 4	110 4 9	29 8 0	11 14 1	53 15 5	71 7 3	50 3 9	3 4 0
1706	213 10 4	81 9 6	24 8 3	8 10 0	86 5 5	68 11 8	45 7 9	6 7 2
1707	197 10 0	101 1 1	45 5 6	4 3 7	97 12 5	57 18 1	33 7 6	52 0 5
[9] 1708	78 5 10	164 2 3	29 3 6	17 3 10	37 18 3	18 10 1	37 13 0	1 3 11
1709	178 13 6	123 6 5	[10] 58 6 0	6 8 10	20 18 7	63 3 11	45 17 2	17 19 9
1710	318 3 1	196 9 2	54 4 7	16 1 1	315 1 9	15 0 0	51 10 4	11 16 9
1711	231 6 9	248 11 11	41 6 7	6 2 7	63 0 9	35 0 3	73 10 11	1 1 6
1712	206 9 9	173 16 7	51 4 6	13 0 0	74 13 8	36 0 4	34 4 4	4 9 0
1713	133 10 2	144 18 9	23 16 10	1 11 7	57 15 3	30 2 3	61 15 6	3 14 6
[12] 1714	256 13 7	184 10 8	43 13 7	1 19 0	40 17 5	66 8 7	54 8 4	7 10 7
1715	441 4 10	183 10 6	48 16 2	28 16 2	346 15 4	559 0 4	[14] 129 9 2	2 14 0
1716	505 3 8	189 5 11	40 12 8	8 15 4	351 15 8	10 15 11	82 5 6	15 17 6
1717	539 8 3	[15] 706 7 7	96 6 7	23 9 11	702 15 10	20 18 0	77 15 0	7 19 9
1718	618 19 0	237 14 8	18 18 2	34 8 7	[17] 513 9 8	62 5 7	83 4 0	17 13 0
Average for years 1693 to 1714 inclusive, being years family resident in Scotland	175 0 0	[18] 121 0 0	£35 0 0		62 0 0	44 0 0	35 0 0	12 0 0

[1] Old Mrs. Baillie died this year, and the Baillies flitted to a house belonging to Bailie Hamilton.

[2] Lady Grisell has an entry to the effect that her book 'was not rectified, and it was to great truble to writt them all out.' This probably accounts for the want of detail in that and the two preceding years.

[3] This figure includes the family clothes, but no details are given to enable a separation to be made.

[4] Flits to Lord Colinton's house, probably in Foulis Close.

[5] Expenses of going to London on 1st April, staying there and returning by 15th May.

[6] Includes Bonds for borrowed money.

[7] This and the two entries immediately below include servants' clothing.

[8] This should be £160, 13s., but Lady Grisell enters it as shown here.

[9] Lady Grisell and her husband seem to have been in London for several months at the beginning of the year.

[10] Includes a payment of £27, 15s. 6d. to Miss Menzies, 'over and above her fie for her care of the bairens when they had the fever.'

DIX V

IX. Business Charges.	X. Rent.	XI. Estate Expenses. Building and repairing mansion houses, tenants' houses, dykes, etc.	XII. Pocket Money.	XIII. Expenses in connection with political journeys to London.	Total.	Probable Income.	YEAR.
£ s. d.	£ s. d.	£ s. d.	£ s. d.	£ s. d.	£ s. d.	£ s. d.	
81 7 10	50 0 0	..	54 10 4	329 7 10	1290 15 10	..	1693, 1694, and 1695
27 2 7	16 13 4	..	18 3 5	109 15 11	430 5 3	550 0 0	Average for these years
8 9 8	16 13 4	46 7 8	26 16 8	84 0 0	450 6 8	Do.	1696
20 7 1	38 6 0	6 18 4	20 1 8	..	431 12 1	Do.	1697
13 6 4	38 17 7	5 11 1	4 13 4	..	183 10 3	650 0 0	1698
..	38 6 1	20 16 6	..	..	557 4 6	Do.	1699
..	[4]30 11 1	11 6 8	..	..	598 13 11	Do.	1700
1 13 0	33 6 8	70 19 8	14 3 0	.	618 12 5	Do.	1701
13 6 6	30 10 0	..	28 11 4	[5]96 1 4	661 2 7	Do.	1702
..	33 6 8	13 12 8	22 12 0	.	622 11 0	Do.	1703
16 10 1	33 6 8	181 11 0	9 10 8	.	761 19 0	Do.	1704
[6]31 1 8	33 6	51 10 0	40 9 0	.	700 4 11	Do.	1705
[6]0 4 10	33 6	31 6 9	26 0 0	..	625 8 4	Do,	1706
[6]11 10 9	33 6	36 11 5	9 17 4	[8]133 19 2	814 3 11	Do.	1707
1 6 0	33 6 8	149 13 1	6 1 ·7	.	574 8 0	1350 0 0	1708
24 0 1	..	130 13 8	15 0 0	.	684 7 11	Do.	1709
7 17 3	..	66 19 3	7 17 0		[11]1061 0 3	1770 0 0	1710
1 1 4		71 5 0	5 0 6		777 8 1	Do.	1711
5 16 9		117 11 10	14 14 9		732 1 6	Do.	1712
4 0 0		47 0 0	11 12 0		519 16 10	Do.	1713
5 4 11	..	68 15 3	3 15 0		733 16 11	Do.	1714
1 6 6	[13]98 0	17 17 0	15 8 10		1872 18 10	Do.	1715
0 3 0	45 0	2 14 0	39 5 0		1291 14 2	Do.	1716
5 7 6	45 0	135 4 6	38 9 4		[16]2399 2 5	Do.	1717
0 5 0	45 0 8	7 4 0	55 17 0		1717 8 8	2830 0 0	1718
12 0 0	30 0 0	60 0 0	15 0 0	29 0 0	630 0 0	..	..

11 This is the year their daughter Grisell was married to Mr. Murray, and the expenses directly attributable o this event amount to nearly £280.

12 In the autumn the family go to London.

13 Furnished lodgings at £14 p. month.

14 This includes £45 paid to a carriage builder 'to account,' and was no doubt part of the price of a new arriage. Two horses and a coachman are hired at £25 a quarter.

15 This includes three years' cess, etc., for Scottish Estates.

16 This year their daughter Rachel is married to Lord Binning, and the expenses directly attributable to his amount to about £300, besides the expenses of the journey to and from Edinburgh, where the marriage ook place.

17 This includes £113, 3s. 6d. for 'My Rachels cloaths to her child.'

18 This sum includes Cess and Poll Tax and Poor money, averaging about £36 p. ann.

[illegible] BAILLIE, [illegible] son o' [illegible]ilie of St. John's Kirk, Merchant in Edinburgh, purchased [illegible] of Jerviswood in 1636 and Me[illegible] in [illegible]643; *m.* [illegible] Johnston, daughter of James Johnston, Merchant Burgess of Edinburgh, *d.* about 16[illegible].

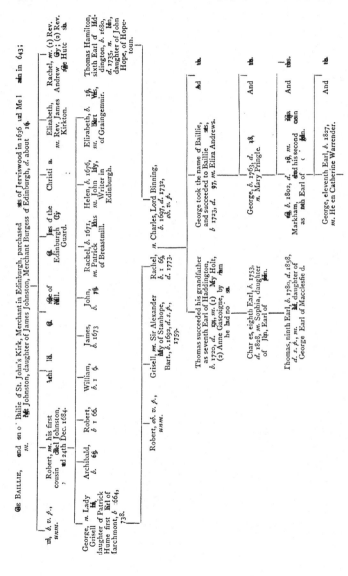

[illegible], *b. v. p.*, *unm.*

Robert, *m.* his first cousin [illegible] Johnston, [illegible] 24th Dec. 1684.

[illegible]

[illegible]

[illegible] of [illegible].

[illegible] of the Edinburgh [illegible] Guard.

Christi[illegible].

Elizabeth, *m.* Rev. James Kirkton.

Rachel, *m.* (1) Rev. Andrew [illegible]; (2) Rev. [illegible] Hutc[illegible].

George, *m.* Lady Grisell [illegible], daughter of Patrick Hume first Earl of [M]archmont, *b.* [1]664, [1]738.

Archibald, *b.* [illegible].

Robert, *b.* 1[illegible]66.

William, *b.* 1[illegible].

James, *b.* 1673.

John, *b.* [illegible].

Rachel, *b.* 1671, *m.* Patrick [illegible] of Breastmill.

Helen, *b.* 1676, *m.* John [illegible], Writer in Edinburgh.

Elizabeth, *b.* 1[illegible], *m.* [illegible] of Graingemuir.

Thomas Hamilton, sixth Earl of Haddington, *b.* 1680, *d.* 1735, *m.* [illegible], daughter of John Hope, of Hopetoun.

Robert, *ob. v. p.*, *unm.*

Grisell, *m.* Sir Alexander [illegible] of Stanhope, Bart., *b.* 1692, *d. s. p.*, 1759.

Rachel, *b.* 1[illegible], *d.* 1773. *m.* Charles, Lord Binning, *b.* 1697, *d.* 1732, *ob. v. p.*

Thomas succeeded his grandfather as seventh Earl of Haddington, *b.* 1720, *d.* [illegible], *m.* (1) [illegible] Holt, (2) Anne Gascoigne, by [illegible] he had no [illegible].

George took the name of Baillie, and succeeded to Baillie [illegible], *b.* 1723, *d.* [illegible], *m.* Eliza Andrews.

And [illegible].

Char[l]es, eighth Earl, *b.* 1753, *d.* 1828, *m.* Sophia, daughter of J[illegible], Earl of [illegible].

George, *b.* 1763, *d.* [illegible], *m.* Mary Pringle.

And [illegible].

Thomas, ninth Earl, *b.* 1780, *d.* 1858, *d. s. p.*, *m.* [illegible], daughter of George Earl of Macclesfie[l]d.

[illegible], *b.* 1802, *d.* [illegible], *m.* [illegible] Markham, [illegible] his second [c]ousin as [illegible] Earl of [illegible].

And [illegible].

George, eleventh Earl, *b.* 1827, *m.* He[l]en Catherine Warrender.

And [illegible].

GLOSSARY

Alamode, *a silk material, à la mode, in the seventeenth century.*
Antoylage, entoilage, *linen or other material to which lace is sewed.*
Armogeen, *a stout silk almost invariably black.*
Attles, *a silk stuff wrought with threads of gold and silver imported from India.*

Bast, *matting made of the inner bark of the lime.*
Batthel or bathel, *beadle.*
Bear, *barley.*
Bongrace, *a sort of front standing erect round the face attached to the hood.*
Bragad, *brocade.*
Buffing, *buffines* (?), *a kind of coarse material.*
Bufft, *covered with buffines.*
Bustin, bustian (?), *same as fustian, a coarse twilled cotton cloth.*
Busum, *besom, broom.*

Calamanka, calimanco, *a woollen material made plain and glazed in finishing.*
Camlet, camblet, *a cloth made of wool, silk, or hair, or all three.*
Capillaire. See note, p. 321.
Chutches, cuches, *donkeys.*
Clogbag, *saddle bag.*
Cods, *pillows.*
Codwars, *pillowslips.*
Cog, *pail.*
Cruk, crook, *an iron hook suspended in kitchen chimney on which pots were hung.*

Dail, *a load, a ton.*
Dails, *wooden boards.*
Damaty, dimity, *a fine sort of fustian.*
Dicks, *dykes, stone walls.*
Divits, *divots, turfs cut into squares.*
Dornick, dornock, *chequered table linen.*
Drogat, drugget, *a sort of woollen stuff.*

Fairins, *a gift of money for spending at a fair or a gift bought at a fair.*
Furd, *made of fur.*

Galown, galloon, *a hard braid of silk or wool used for edging.*
Gass or gaz, *gauze.*

Hagabag, *coarse table linen.*
Harden, *a common linen or the coarsest quality of hemp or flax.*
Hatted kit, *a preparation of milk, etc., with a creamy top.* See note, p. 290.

Jacolit, *chocolate.*
Jumps, jimps, *a kind of easy stays open in front, worn by nurses.*

Kains, *canes.*
Kevelmell, *a heavy mell or hammer.*

Lame, *earthenware.*

Lutestring, lustring, *a bright silk much used, said to have been introduced into this country by the French refugees after the Revocation of the Edict of Nantes in* 1685.

Manto, *manteau.*
Maskarad, *masquerade.*
Milsy, *a milk strainer.*
Mohair, *cloth made of mohair; the fine silken hair of the Angora goat.*

Panscratch, *the thick scale that forms on the bottom of a salt pan.*
Pertian, persian, *a thin plain silk, much used for linings.*
Pice, pièce, *a hogshead.*
Pillabers, pillowberes, *pillowslips.*
Pittipan, pettypan, *a white iron mold used for pastry.*
Podisoy, paduasoy, *a strong silk, usually black.*
Pother, *pewter.*

Queches, quaich, *a small and shallow drinking cup.*

Rimin dish, *perhaps the rimmer or vat in which curd is set to harden for cheese.*

Salmagundy, salmagunde, *a dish of minced meat with eggs, anchovies, vinegar, pepper, etc.*
Scout, schuit, *a public boat drawn by horse through the canals.*
Sesnet, *sarcenet.*
Shad, *flat.*
Shagreen, *a sort of baize.*
Sheneal, chenille, *striped taffata.*
Shill, *shovel.*
Skep, *basket hive.*
Snakes, *snecks, fastenings.*
Sods, *a sort of saddle used by the poorer classes made of cloth stuffed.*
Stenting, *stretching.*
Stinging, *thatching.*
Stoup, *flagon.*
Strakins, *linen cloth made of coarse flax.*

Tabie, tabby, *a kind of silk watered or waved.*
Tafita, taffeta, *a sort of thick silk.*
Thack, *thatch.*
Thicking, *thatching.*
Tolliduse, taille-douce. See note, p. 39.
Tourdelie, tour de lit, *the valance of a bed.*
Tows, *ropes.*
Trivet, *a movable iron frame for supporting kettles, etc.*
Tusk, *a fish as big as a ling, much esteemed for its delicacy.*

Wort shill, *a shovel for wort for brewing.*

Yettin, *cast-iron.*
Yrone, *iron.*

INDEX

Printed by T. and A. CONSTABLE, Printers to His Majesty
at the Edinburgh University Press

REPORT OF THE TWENTY-FOURTH ANNUAL MEETING OF THE SCOTTISH HISTORY SOCIETY

The Twenty-fourth Annual Meeting of the Society was held in Dowell's Rooms, Edinburgh, on the 26th November 1910,—Mr. W. B. Blaikie in the chair.

The Secretary read the Report of the Council as follows:—

During the past year ten members have died, and ten have resigned membership.

Dr. John Dowden, Bishop of Edinburgh, Chairman of Council, was so intimately associated with the daily work of the Society, and its officials and other workers had so learned to lean on his help and encouragement, that his death is felt as the greatest of the great losses which the Society has sustained in recent years. His work on the Lindores and Inchaffray volumes, invaluable as it is, represents only a small fraction of the Society's debt to him.

After filling the vacancies, twenty-four candidates for membership remain on the list.

Except Craig's *De Unione*, announced in the last Report as about to appear, no volume has been issued since the last General Meeting. *Wariston's Diary* and *Miscellaneous Narratives relating to the* '45 will it is hoped be sent out early in 1911, and the other volumes promised for 1909-1910, viz. *Lady Grisell Baillie's Household Books*, and *Seafield Correspondence*, are well advanced at press.

The difficulties which have so seriously delayed the issue of

The Scots in Poland will, it is now hoped, be shortly overcome, and the volume issued during the coming year.

For 1910-1911 it is intended to issue two of the three volumes following :—

1. *The Book of the Accounts of the Granitars and Chamberlains of the Archbishopric of St. Andrews* during Cardinal Beaton's tenure of the See, A.D. 1539 to 1546. Edited by R. K. Hannay.

2. *Letter-book of Bailie John Stuart, Merchant in Inverness*, 1715-1752. Edited by William Mackay.

3. *Miscellany of the Scottish History Society*, vol. 3. This will include, among other items, selections from the Wardrobe Book of Edward I. for the 33rd year of his reign (A.D. 1304-05), from the original in the British Museum, which contains a great deal of matter relating to Scotland; a batch of seventeenth-century Haddingtonshire Trials for Witchcraft, edited by Dr. Wallace James; List of Pollable Persons in St. Andrews in 1693, edited by Dr. Hay Fleming; Papers relating to the '15 and the '45 from the originals at Perth; and perhaps Mr. Archibald Constable's long promised translation of Ferrerius' *Historia Abbatum de Kynlos.*

In accordance with the resolution of last year's Meeting, a general index to the first series of the Society's publications is in preparation, and will in due time be offered to Members.

There are four vacancies in the Council to be filled up, caused by the election of Mr. Donald Crawford as Chairman of Council, and by the retirement in rotation of Sir James Balfour Paul, Lord Guthrie, and Mr. W. B. Blaikie. It is recommended that Sir J. Balfour Paul and Mr. Blaikie be re-elected, and that the other vacancies be filled by the appointment of The Hon. Hew Hamilton Dalrymple and Mr. C. S. Romanes, C.A.

The Accounts of the Hon. Treasurer, of which an abstract is appended hereto, show that the balance in the Society's favour on 10th November 1909, was £472, 1s. 1d., the income for 1909-1910, £529, 10s. 9d., the expenditure, £329, 15s. 11d., and the credit balance on 10th November 1910, £671, 15s. 11d

The Chairman, in moving the adoption of the Report, said:—It must be a matter of regret to the Society that I should occupy this place to-day, but our President, Lord Rosebery, who has so frequently given us illuminating addresses from this chair, is perforce absent in the act of making history, and has naturally little time for speaking about history. You have before you the Annual Report for the current year. The Report is short and somewhat laconic, but if you examine it you will find that it is teeming with interest. We have this year to deplore the death of him who was Chairman of Council from the time Professor Masson left us until this year. Bishop Dowden, as you probably are aware, was the life and the soul of the Council of this Society. Mr. Law told us in his last speech in 1903 how the inception of the Society was that of Lord Rosebery, who suggested its establishment in a letter to the *Scotsman* nearly twenty-five years ago, and that his suggestion was first taken up by Bishop Dowden, who became chairman of a committee that carried the preliminaries through. The interest taken by the Bishop in the Society, and the counsel and assistance he ever gave to those who were doing historical work, can never be forgotten by those who sought his aid. He edited for the Society, *The Chartulary of Lindores*, and inspired and assisted in the editing of *The Charters of the Abbey of Inchaffray*. Strange to say, like our first Secretary, Mr. Law, Bishop Dowden was not a Scotsman by birth, but like Mr. Law he became a Scotsman by adoption and association, and these two men did as much to further the study of Scottish history as any Scotsman amongst us.

The Council have elected as their Chairman Sheriff Donald Crawford, a gentleman who has given much service to the Society and who has edited one of its most interesting books.

It is the custom of the Chairman at these annual meetings to give a slight foretaste of the bill of fare which is offered to the members of the Society. I do not think that at any previous meeting the Council have been able to offer a more tempting programme than they have to-day. It is true that only one book has been issued since our last meeting (Professor Terry's *Translation of Craig's De Unione*), but there are no fewer than five volumes in type awaiting the finishing touches of the various editors. The volume of *The Scots in Poland* has been provokingly and unavoidably delayed by the difficulty of verifying descriptions and getting documents from Warsaw, but the Council hope that these difficulties will be overcome in the current year.

The issue of *The Diary of Johnston of Wariston* will complete the first series of the Scottish History Society's publications, and the Council have resolved to prepare a general index of the whole of the sixty-one volumes comprising that series. This it is hoped will be issued to members in the course of the year, and it is believed that it will be a work of the greatest use to students of history. It is possible that the Council may print a small extra edition which may be purchased by libraries and collectors who are not members of the Society, and thus extend the usefulness of the Society's work.

Of the books promised, the first that may be mentioned is *The Diary of Johnston of Wariston*, 1632-34, and again in the momentous years, 1637-39. This book is edited by Mr. George M. Paul, Deputy Keeper of the Signet, whose sympathetic work on a Diary of Archibald Johnston, issued in 1896, is well known to later members. This new instalment, referring, however, to an earlier period, is of absorbing interest, for it embraces that crucial period in which Laud's Service Book was imposed upon the people of Scotland, and the National Covenant (practically the work of Johnston himself) was prepared and signed. We have here at first hand this epoch-making event graphically told by one of the principal actors. The *Diary* is, however, more than the mere relation of events; it shows the mental working of a strange, nervous, intensely religious Puritan, full of egotism and introspection, but whose whole soul is filled with a desire to walk closely with his God, whom he consults and to whom he gives information on nearly every page of the journal. There have been few portrayals of the real Covenanter. The Covenanter of romance must disappear when we read this *Diary of Johnston of Wariston* and compare with it the work, edited by Sheriff Scott Moncrieff twenty-one years ago, *The Narrative of James Nimmo*. If the Scottish History Society had done nothing else than given these introspective memoirs, showing the inward working of the Covenanter's mind, it would have accomplished a great work.

The *Household Book of Lady Grisell Baillie* is a volume edited by Mr. R. Scott Moncrieff to be ready shortly. It gives the daily expenditure of an aristocratic family in the last decade of the seventeenth century and the beginning of the eighteenth.

The Correspondence of the first Lord Seafield, edited, from the originals at Cullen House, by Mr. James Grant of Banff, is another book of much historical value. Lord Seafield was Chancellor of Scotland at the time of the Union; it was he who uttered the historical *obiter dictum,* 'This is the end of an auld sang,' when the last Scottish Parliament accepted the Union.

Then there is a volume of *Narratives relating to the* '45 with which I am entrusted. To me at least they are all full of interest. They belong to that type of article classed as 'fragments which must not perish,' and the incentive to the collection of these is the motto engraved on the Society's insignia. Among them is a portion of a mutilated manuscript of John Murray of Broughton picked up on the field of Culloden. There is the narrative of a Captain in Lord Balmerino's Horse, an Englishman, occasionally referred to by historians, but which has never before been printed. There are several narratives written by ministers from various parts of the country giving minute local details to be found nowhere else. There is the apology of the Laird of Grant for his somewhat ambiguous conduct during the rising. There is the narrative relating to the capture of Edinburgh and the Battle of Prestonpans. Jack, its author, was a writing-master in Edinburgh, who assisted Professor M'Laurin to prepare the defences of the city, and who attempted to assist Cope's artillery at the Battle of Prestonpans. Lastly, it contains a good deal of narrative and many accounts of secret service performed by Walter Grosset, Commissioner of the Excise, who was an active agent of the Government in the '45.

The programme for the following year begins with a volume by Mr. Hannay on the *Accounts of the Granitars and Chamberlains of the Archbishopric of St. Andrews* shortly before the Reformation, a theme which has been little written of, yet there is no doubt that it was the inordinate care of the worldly goods of the great ecclesiastics that exasperated the nobility and commons, and contributed largely to the unanimity of the Reformation.

Mr. Maitland Thomson is collecting material for a *Miscellany* which comprises historical tit-bits ranging over four and a half centuries. Whether that book will be included in the next year's issues remains to be seen.

One work I have left to the last and that is the *Letter Book of Bailie John Stuart,* to be edited by Mr. William Mackay of Inverness. The Society has hitherto had only one book on commercial affairs, and this volume, giving the details of a Highland merchant's business in the early eighteenth century, will be of much historical value. John Stuart, a bailie of Inverness, who was of the family of Kinchardine in Strathspey, and was related to several other Highland families, was a merchant in Inverness from about the year 1700 till 1752. During that period he carried on an extensive trade, in all kinds of commodities, with Highland chiefs and Government garrisons in the Highlands, as well as with Edinburgh, London, and various parts of the Continental seaboard from Norway and Sweden to Venice. Hugh Miller states in his *Scotch Merchant of the Eighteenth Century* that coal had not found its way into the Cromarty Firth before 1750, but we find Bailie Stuart bringing coals from Newcastle thirty years before this, probably even earlier. He owned about a dozen ships, some of which were built at Inverness; the oak timber for these was brought from Darnaway and Loch Ness side, and part of the iron and timber frame-work came ready made from Dantzig. Stuart was factor on the Inverness-shire estates of the Earl of Moray. His business transactions and ventures, his successes and misfortunes, are recorded in his letters, which give a vivid picture of the conditions under which trade was carried on in the capital of the Highlands during the first half of the eighteenth century. Among the Bailie's partners in business was William Duff of Braco, afterwards the first Earl of Fife; and his numerous customers and correspondents comprised the Duke of Gordon, the Earls of Moray, Seaforth, Cromartie, Sutherland, and Caithness, Lord Lovat, Lord Reay, Lord President Forbes, The Mackintosh, Lochiel, Mackintosh of Borlum, Glengarry, Stewart of Appin, the Laird of Grant, Sir Alexander Macdonald of Sleat, MacLeod of MacLeod, General Wade, Captain Burt, and the Bailie's cousin, the famous Colonel

John Roy Stuart, the Jacobite soldier and poet. One of Stuart's descendants made his mark in British history, for his grandson was that Sir John Stuart who beat the French at the battle of Maida in 1806, the first British general who defeated Napoleon's veterans on European soil. With this programme before you I think you will agree that the Council is not neglecting the interests of the Scottish History Society.

The motion was seconded by Sir James Balfour Paul, and unanimously agreed to.

ABSTRACT OF THE HON. TREASURER'S ACCOUNTS.

For the Year ending 10*th November* 1910.

I. Charge.

I. Balance from previous year—						
(1) In Bank on Deposit Receipt,	£400	0	0			
(2) In Bank on Current Account,	72	1	1			
				£472	1	1
II. Subscriptions, viz.						
(1) 400 Subscriptions for 1909-1910, .	£420	0	0			
8 in arrear for 1908-1909,	8	8	0			
7 in advance for 1910-1911,	7	7	0			
	£435	15	0			
Less 25 in arrear and 3 in advance for 1909-1910,	29	8	0			
				406	7	0
(2) 89 Libraries, ...	£93	9	0			
1 in arrear for 1908-1909 and 4 in advance for 1910-1911, ...	5	5	0			
	£98	14	0			
Less 1 in arrear for 1909-1910, ...	1	1	0			
				97	13	0
III. Copies of previous issues sold to New Members,				10	17	0
IV. Interest on Deposit Receipts, ...				14	13	9
Sum of Charge,				£1001	11	10

II. Discharge.

I. Incidental Expenses—

(1) Printing Cards, Circulars, and Reports, . . .	£6	7	9			
(2) Stationery, and Receipt Book, ...	1	17	9			
(3) Making-up and delivering Publications, . . .	12	15	5			
(4) Postages of Secretaries and Treasurer, ...	4	3	0			
(5) Clerical Work and Charges on Cheques, ...	2	11	0			
(6) Hire of rooms for Annual Meeting and Advertising, .	1	18	0			
				£29	12	11

II. *De Unione Regnorum Britanniæ*—

Composition, Printing, and Paper 540 Copies, ...	£115	10	6			
Proofs and Corrections, .	56	13	6			
Binding Stamp, . . .	1	1	0			
Binding 540 Copies at 8d.,	18	0	0			
Photogravure Portrait of Prof. Masson, ...	6	16	6			
	£198	1	6			
Less paid to account October 1909, ...	145	6	0			
				52	15	6

III. *The Scots in Poland.* Expense to date—

Composition, ...	£72	1	0			
Corrections, ...	19	18	0			
Engraving Map, . .	5	5	0			
Carry forward,	£97	4	0	£82	8	5

Brought forward,		£97 4 0	£82 8 5
Less paid to account, October 1908,	£77 17 0		
Less paid to account, October 1909,	12 5 0		
		90 2 0	
			7 2 0
IV. *Miscellaneous Narratives relating to the '45.* Expense to date			
Composition, ...			39 12 6
V. *Household Books of Lady Grisell Baillie.* Expense to date—			
Composition, ...		£53 6 0	
Corrections, ...		10 11 0	
			63 17 0
VI. *Correspondence of James, Fourth Earl of Findlater.* Expense to date			
Composition, ...		£27 4 0	
Corrections, ...		14 3 0	
			41 7 0
VII. *Diary of Archibald Johnston, Lord Wariston.* Expense to date			
Composition, ...		£58 14 0	
Alterations, ...		32 14 6	
Transcribing, ...		72 15 0	
		£164 3 6	
Less paid to account, October 1908,	£3 18 0		
Less paid to account, October 1909,	. 64 16 6		
		68 14 6	
			95 9 0
VIII. Balance to next account—			
(1) On Deposit Receipt, .		£650 0 0	
(2) On Current Account, .		21 15 11	
			671 15 11
Sum of Discharge,			£1001 11 10

EDINBURGH, *22nd November* 1910.—Having examined the Accounts of the Hon. Treasurer of the Scottish History Society for the year ending 10th November 1910, of which the foregoing is an Abstract, we find the same to be correctly stated, and sufficiently vouched,—closing with a balance of £671, 15s. 11d. in Bank, whereof £650 is on deposit receipt and £21, 15s. 11d. is on current account.

RALPH RICHARDSON, *Auditor.*
WM. TRAQUAIR DICKSON, *Auditor.*

Scottish History Society.

THE EXECUTIVE.

1910-1911.

President.

The Earl of Rosebery, K.G., K.T., LL.D.

Chairman of Council.

Donald Crawford, K.C., Sheriff of Aberdeenshire.

Council.

Sir James Balfour Paul, C.V.O., LL.D., Lyon King of Arms.
Walter B. Blaikie.
The Hon. Hew Hamilton Dalrymple.
C. S. Romanes, C.A.
Sir G. M. Paul, D.K.S.
Ralph Richardson, W.S.
Sheriff W. G. Scott Moncrieff.
Professor P. Hume Brown, M.A., LL.D., Historiographer Royal for Scotland.
William K. Dickson, Advocate.
A. O. Curle, B.A., W.S.
D. Hay Fleming, LL.D.
Professor John Rankine, K.C., LL.D.

Corresponding Members of the Council.

Prof. C. H. Firth, LL.D., Oxford; Rev. W. D. Macray, Ducklington Rectory, Witney, Oxon.; Prof. C. Sanford Terry, Aberdeen.

Hon. Treasurer.

J. T. Clark, Crear Villa, 196 Ferry Road, Edinburgh.

Joint Hon. Secretaries.

J. Maitland Thomson, LL.D., Advocate, 3 Grosvenor Gardens, Edinburgh.

A. Francis Steuart, Advocate, 79 Great King Street, Edinburgh.

RULES

1. The object of the Society is the discovery and printing, under selected editorship, of unpublished documents illustrative of the civil, religious, and social history of Scotland. The Society will also undertake, in exceptional cases, to issue translations of printed works of a similar nature, which have not hitherto been accessible in English.

2. The number of Members of the Society shall be limited to 400.

3. The affairs of the Society shall be managed by a Council, consisting of a Chairman, Treasurer, Secretary, and twelve elected Members, five to make a quorum. Three of the twelve elected Members shall retire annually by ballot, but they shall be eligible for re-election.

4. The Annual Subscription to the Society shall be One Guinea. The publications of the Society shall not be delivered to any Member whose Subscription is in arrear, and no Member shall be permitted to receive more than one copy of the Society's publications.

5. The Society will undertake the issue of its own publications, *i.e.* without the intervention of a publisher or any other paid agent.

6. The Society will issue yearly two octavo volumes of about 320 pages each.

7. An Annual General Meeting of the Society shall be held at the end of October, or at an approximate date to be determined by the Council.

8. Two stated Meetings of the Council shall be held each year, one on the last Tuesday of May, the other on the Tuesday preceding the day upon which the Annual General Meeting shall be held. The Secretary, on the request of three Members of the Council, shall call a special meeting of the Council.

9. Editors shall receive 20 copies of each volume they edit for the Society.

10. The owners of Manuscripts published by the Society will also be presented with a certain number of copies.

11. The Annual Balance-Sheet, Rules, and List of Members shall be printed.

12. No alteration shall be made in these Rules except at a General Meeting of the Society. A fortnight's notice of any alteration to be proposed shall be given to the Members of the Council.

PUBLICATIONS

OF THE

SCOTTISH HISTORY SOCIETY

For the year 1886-1887.

1. Bishop Pococke's Tours in Scotland, 1747-1760. Edited by D. W. Kemp.
2. Diary and Account Book of William Cunningham of Craigends, 1673-1680. Edited by the Rev. James Dodds, D.D.

For the year 1887-1888.

3. Grameidos libri sex: an heroic poem on the Campaign of 1689, by James Philip of Almerieclose. Translated and Edited by the Rev. A. D. Murdoch.
4. The Register of the Kirk-Session of St. Andrews. Part i. 1559-1582. Edited by D. Hay Fleming.

For the year 1888-1889.

5. Diary of the Rev. John Mill, Minister in Shetland, 1740-1803. Edited by Gilbert Goudie.
6. Narrative of Mr. James Nimmo, a Covenanter, 1654-1709. Edited by W. G. Scott-Moncrieff.
7. The Register of the Kirk-Session of St. Andrews. Part ii. 1583-1600. Edited by D. Hay Fleming.

For the year 1889-1890.

8. A List of Persons concerned in the Rebellion (1745). With a Preface by the Earl of Rosebery.

   Presented to the Society by the Earl of Rosebery.
9. Glamis Papers: The 'Book of Record,' a Diary written by Patrick, first Earl of Strathmore, and other documents (1684-89). Edited by A. H. Millar.
10. John Major's History of Greater Britain (1521). Translated and edited by Archibald Constable.

For the year 1890-1891.

11. The Records of the Commissions of the General Assemblies, 1646-47. Edited by the Rev. Professor Mitchell, D.D., and the Rev. James Christie, D.D.
12. Court-Book of the Barony of Urie, 1604-1747. Edited by the Rev. D. G. Barron.

For the year 1891-1892.

13. Memoirs of Sir John Clerk of Penicuik, Baronet. Extracted by himself from his own Journals, 1676-1755. Edited by John M. Gray.
14. Diary of Col. the Hon. John Erskine of Carnock, 1683-1687. Edited by the Rev. Walter Macleod.

For the year 1892-1893.

15. Miscellany of the Scottish History Society, First Volume—The Library of James vi., 1573-83. Edited by G. F. Warner. Documents illustrating Catholic Policy, 1596-98. T. G. Law. —Letters of Sir Thomas Hope, 1627-46. Rev. R. Paul.—Civil War Papers, 1643-50. H. F. Morland Simpson.—Lauderdale Correspondence, 1660-77. Right Rev. John Dowden, D.D.—Turnbull's Diary, 1657-1704. Rev. R. Paul.—Masterton Papers, 1660-1719. V. A. Noël Paton.—Accompt of Expenses in Edinburgh, 1715. A. H. Millar.—Rebellion Papers, 1715 and 1745. H. Paton.
16. Account Book of Sir John Foulis of Ravelston (1671-1707). Edited by the Rev. A. W. Cornelius Hallen.

For the year 1893-1894.

17. Letters and Papers illustrating the Relations between Charles ii. and Scotland in 1650. Edited by Samuel Rawson Gardiner, D.C.L., etc.
18. Scotland and the Commonwealth. Letters and Papers relating to the Military Government of Scotland, Aug. 1651-Dec. 1653. Edited by C. H. Firth, M.A.

For the year 1894-1895.

19. The Jacobite Attempt of 1719. Letters of James, second Duke of Ormonde. Edited by W. K. Dickson.

20, 21. The Lyon in Mourning, or a Collection of Speeches, Letters, Journals, etc., relative to the Affairs of Prince Charles Edward Stuart, by Bishop Forbes. 1746-1775. Edited by Henry Paton. Vols. i. and ii.

For the year 1895-1896.

22. The Lyon in Mourning. Vol. iii.

23. Itinerary of Prince Charles Edward (Supplement to the Lyon in Mourning). Compiled by W. B. Blaikie.

24. Extracts from the Presbytery Records of Inverness and Dingwall from 1638 to 1688. Edited by William Mackay.

25. Records of the Commissions of the General Assemblies (*continued*) for the years 1648 and 1649. Edited by the Rev. Professor Mitchell, D.D., and Rev. James Christie, D.D.

For the year 1896-1897.

26. Wariston's Diary and other Papers—

Johnston of Wariston's Diary, 1639. Edited by G. M. Paul. The Honours of Scotland, 1651-52. C. R. A. Howden.—The Earl of Mar's Legacies, 1722, 1726. Hon. S. Erskine.—Letters by Mrs. Grant of Laggan. J. R. N. Macphail.

Presented to the Society by Messrs. T. and A. Constable.

27. Memorials of John Murray of Broughton, 1740-1747. Edited by R. Fitzroy Bell.

28. The Compt Buik of David Wedderburne, Merchant of Dundee, 1587-1630. Edited by A. H. Millar.

For the year 1897-1898.

29, 30. The Correspondence of De Montereul and the brothers De Bellièvre, French Ambassadors in England and Scotland, 1645-1648. Edited, with Translation, by J. G. Fotheringham. 2 vols.

For the year 1898-1899.

31. Scotland and the Protectorate. Letters and Papers relating to the Military Government of Scotland, from January 1654 to June 1659. Edited by C. H. Firth, M.A.

32. Papers illustrating the History of the Scots Brigade in the Service of the United Netherlands, 1572-1782. Edited by James Ferguson. Vol. i. 1572-1697.

33, 34. Macfarlane's Genealogical Collections concerning Families in Scotland; Manuscripts in the Advocates' Library. 2 vols. Edited by J. T. Clark, Keeper of the Library.

Presented to the Society by the Trustees of the late Sir William Fraser, K.C.B.

For the year 1899-1900.

35. Papers on the Scots Brigade in Holland, 1572-1782. Edited by James Ferguson. Vol. ii. 1698-1782.

36. Journal of a Foreign Tour in 1665 and 1666, etc., by Sir John Lauder, Lord Fountainhall. Edited by Donald Crawford.

37. Papal Negotiations with Mary Queen of Scots during her Reign in Scotland. Chiefly from the Vatican Archives. Edited by the Rev. J. Hungerford Pollen, S.J.

For the year 1900-1901.

38. Papers on the Scots Brigade in Holland, 1572-1782. Edited by James Ferguson. Vol. iii.

39. The Diary of Andrew Hay of Craignethan, 1659-60. Edited by A. G. Reid, F.S.A.Scot.

For the year 1901-1902.

40. Negotiations for the Union of England and Scotland in 1651-53. Edited by C. Sanford Terry.

41. The Loyall Dissuasive. Written in 1703 by Sir Æneas Macpherson. Edited by the Rev. A. D. Murdoch.

For the year 1902-1903.

42. The Chartulary of Lindores, 1195-1479. Edited by the Right Rev. John Dowden, D.D., Bishop of Edinburgh.

43. A Letter from Mary Queen of Scots to the Duke of Guise, Jan. 1562. Reproduced in Facsimile. Edited by the Rev. J. Hungerford Pollen, S.J.

Presented to the Society by the family of the late Mr. Scott, of Halkshill.

44. Miscellany of the Scottish History Society, Second Volume—
The Scottish King's Household, 14th Century. Edited by Mary Bateson.—The Scottish Nation in the University of Orleans, 1336-1538. John Kirkpatrick, LL.D.—The French Garrison at Dunbar, 1563. Robert S. Rait.—De Antiquitate Religionis apud Scotos, 1594. Henry D. G. Law.—Apology for William Maitland of Lethington, 1610. Andrew Lang.—Letters of Bishop George Græme, 1602-38. L. G. Græme.—A Scottish Journie, 1641. C. H. Firth.—Narratives illustrating the Duke of Hamilton's Expedition to England, 1648. C. H. Firth.—Burnet-Leighton Papers, 1648-168–. H. C. Foxcroft.—Papers of Robert Erskine, Physician to Peter the Great, 1677-1720. Rev. Robert Paul.—Will of the Duchess of Albany, 1789. A. Francis Steuart.

45. Letters of John Cockburn of Ormistoun to his Gardener, 1727-1743. Edited by James Colville, D.Sc.

PUBLICATIONS

For the year 1903-1904.

46. Minute Book of the Managers of the New Mills Cloth Manufactory, 1681-1690. Edited by W. R. Scott.

47. Chronicles of the Frasers; being the Wardlaw Manuscript entitled 'Polichronicon seu Policratica Temporum, or, the true Genealogy of the Frasers.' By Master James Fraser. Edited by William Mackay.

48. The Records of the Proceedings of the Justiciary Court from 1661 to 1678. Vol. i. 1661-1669. Edited by Sheriff Scott-Moncrieff.

For the year 1904-1905.

49. The Records of the Proceedings of the Justiciary Court from 1661 to 1678. Vol. ii. 1669-1678. Edited by Sheriff Scott-Moncrieff. (Oct. 1905.)

50. Records of the Baron Court of Stitchill, 1655-1807. Edited by Clement B. Gunn, M.D., Peebles. (Oct. 1905.)

51. Macfarlane's Geographical Collections. Vol. i. Edited by Sir Arthur Mitchell, K.C.B. (April 1906.)

For the year 1905-1906.

52, 53. Macfarlane's Geographical Collections. Vols. ii. and iii. Edited by Sir Arthur Mitchell, K.C.B. (May 1907; March 1908.)

54. Statuta Ecclesiæ Scoticanæ, 1225-1559. Translated and edited by David Patrick, LL.D. (Oct. 1907.)

For the year 1906-1907.

55. The House Booke of Accomps, Ochtertyre, 1737-39. Edited by James Colville, D.Sc. (Oct. 1907.)

56. The Charters of the Abbey of Inchaffray. Edited by W. A. Lindsay, K.C., the Right Rev. Bishop Dowden, D.D., and J. Maitland Thomson, LL.D. (Feb. 1908.)

57. A Selection of the Forfeited Estates Papers preserved in H.M. General Register House and elsewhere. Edited by A. H. Millar, LL.D. (Oct. 1909.)

For the year 1907-1908.

58. Records of the Commissions of the General Assemblies (*continued*), for the years 1650-52. Edited by the Rev. James Christie, D.D. (Feb. 1909.)

59. Papers relating to the Scots in Poland. Edited by Miss Beatrice Baskerville. (*Publication delayed.*)

For the year 1908-1909.

60. Sir Thomas Craig's De Unione Regnorum Britanniæ Tractatus. Edited, with an English Translation, by C. Sanford Terry. (Nov. 1909.)

61. Johnston of Wariston's Memento Quamdiu Vivas, and Diary from 1637 to 1639. Edited by G. M. Paul, LL.D., D.K.S. (May 1911.)

Second Series.

For the year 1909-1910.

1. The Household Book of Lady Grisell Baillie, 1692-1733. Edited by R. Scott-Moncrieff, W.S. (Oct. 1911.)

2. Miscellaneous Narratives relating to the '45. Edited by W. B. Blaikie.

3. Correspondence of James, fourth Earl of Findlater and first Earl of Seafield, Lord Chancellor of Scotland. Edited by James Grant, M.A., LL.B.

For the year 1910-1911.

4. Accounts of the Chamberlains and Granitars of Cardinal David Beaton, 1539-1546. Edited by R. K. Hannay.

5. Selections from the Letter Books of John Stuart, Bailie of Inverness. Edited by William Mackay.

In preparation.

Register of the Consultations of the Ministers of Edinburgh, and some other Brethren of the Ministry since the interruption of the Assembly 1653, with other Papers of public concernment, 1653-1660. Edited by the Rev. James Christie, D.D.

A Translation of the Historia Abbatum de Kynlos of Ferrerius. By Archibald Constable, LL.D.

Miscellany of the Scottish History Society. Third Volume.

Analytical Catalogue of the Wodrow Collection of Manuscripts in the Advocates' Library. Edited by J. T. Clark.

Charters and Documents relating to the Grey Friars and the Cistercian Nunnery of Haddington.—Register of Inchcolm Monastery. Edited by J. G. Wallace-James, M.B.

Records relating to the Scottish Armies from 1638 to 1650. Edited by C. Sanford Terry.

Papers relating to the Rebellions of 1715 and 1745, with other documents from the Municipal Archives of the City of Perth.

The Balcarres Papers. Edited by J. R. Melville.

Lightning Source UK Ltd.
Milton Keynes UK
UKOW05f1913290317
297858UK00016B/232/P

9 781331 980421